An A to Z of the Accordion

& Related Instruments

*A celebration of the accordion family
of instruments, with particular reference
to the British Isles*

by

Rob Howard

*Published by
Robaccord Publications, Stockport*

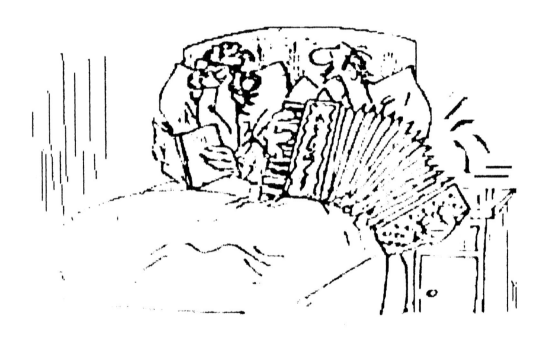

"Do I complain about you reading?"

Robaccord Publications, 42 Avondale Road, Edgeley, Stockport, Cheshire, SK3 9NY, UK. E-mail: robaccord5@hotmail.com Telephone: 0161-480 8858.

Printed and bound by Deanprint, Stockport Road, Cheadle Heath, Stockport, Cheshire.

Foreword

The accordion has been around in one form or another for well over a century and a half, and in its time has produced many characters and a fund of interesting stories. It has taken a book like this one to bring them all together, and I believe it is the only one of its kind available today.

A well-researched and unique celebration of the instrument and its players, '*An A to Z of the Accordion & Related Instruments*' will be greatly enjoyed by accordionists and enthusiasts alike.

Rob is to be congratulated upon producing a fascinating and very readable account of the accordion scene, from its origins to the present day.

Jack Emblow

Acknowledgements

This book has taken a great deal of patient and painstaking research to put together, and I am forever grateful to all those kind people who have helped in different ways – especially those who contributed the superb feature articles on specialist topics.

The author is indebted to the following, without whose contributions this *A to Z* would never have seen the light of day. These include Pearl Adriano, Ken Astin, Andy Banks, Hugh Barwell, David Batty, Dave Berry, Gary Blair, Sylvia Bishop, Anna Bodell, Larysa Bodell, Ray Bodell, Gina Brannelli, Renaldo Capaldi, Johnny Coleclough, Tony Compton, Sue Coppard, Al Crompton, Barry Crossland, Gerald Crossman, Adrian Dante, Pamela Deakin, Alice Dells, Tom Duncan, Jim Easton, Jack Emblow, Ken Farran, the late Malcolm Gee, Gordon Glenn, John Higham, Ron Hodgson, Marj, Jane & Helen Howard, Brian Hulme, Eddie Iddon, Brian Jenkins, John Jones, David Kemp, Les Leveson, Angela Lukins, the late Charles Magnante, Dave Mallinson, Pat Mancini, Jennifer Maxwell, Jerry Mayes, Peter McCoy, John Nixon, Eamonn O'Neal, David Phillips, Ingrid Prince, Anthony Rea, Philomena Rea, the late Graham Romani, Robert Rolston, Loretta Rolston, Tommy Scruton, Jimmy Shand Jr, Eric Smith, Heather Smith, Karen Street, John Sworack, George Syrett, Douglas Tate, Trevani, Dr Sandy Tulloch, Alan Venn, Charlie Watkins, Peter Whiteley, Rosemary Wright, Tony Wynroe and Janusz Zukowski. My sincere thanks to each of them for their time and trouble.

Tony Wynroe, Chairman of Stockport Accordion Club, deserves special thanks for his unstinting time and expertise with computerised images in producing many of the photographs.

There are some articles included that have been specially written, and I am especially grateful to Club Accord's Andy Banks for his excellent résumé of the *Shand Morino*, to Johnny Coleclough for his article *Performing in Public* – a subject he has specialised in for much of his life, to Charlie Watkins – Britain's No 1 *amplification* expert for his illuminating summary of that topic, and to Peter Whiteley for presenting a clear definition of *MIDI*. There are also excellent articles that have previously appeared elsewhere, written by people such as Tony Compton, Gerald Crossman, Adrian Dante, Ken Farran, the late Percy Holland, the late Charles Magnante, John Nixon, Joseph Scott, Douglas Tate, Trevani and Rosemary Wright. My sincere thanks go to all concerned for permission to include their material for the benefit of present and future generations of accordion players and enthusiasts.

My thanks also must go to Adrian Dante (*World Accordion Review*), David Keen (*Accordion World*), Loretta Rolston (*Accordion Times & News*), Heather Smith and Tom Duncan (*Accordion Profile*), Charlie Watkins (*Accordion Today*) for their assistance in facilitating the production of this book. Gary Blair, Heather Smith and Tom Duncan are thanked for their bountiful supply of photographs, and also for their encouraging comments. Ken Astin, Heather Smith and Janusz Zukowski are similarly thanked for their generous loans of old *Accordion Times* and *Accordion Review* magazines. Sylvia Bishop – the widow of Chiz Bishop – loaned me the great man's scrapbooks, and was incredibly helpful in discussing accordion matters from previous eras. Pearl Adriano (who now uses her married name Adriano in preference to Fawcett) was similarly exceptionally helpful in researching and providing data plus photographs in connection with the British Association of Accordionists.

One criticism that is likely to be made of this book is that some famous names are missing. My answer is that it has proved impossible to include all the accordionists who have become well known – there are just too many – and I have opted to write about a cross section of people who represent different genres and eras. It has also proved virtually impossible to contact everyone whose name appears or who might have been included – there are not enough hours in the day.

Special thanks go to Jack Emblow for his kind words of encouragement in the Foreword. It is an honour to have such a distinguished musician's endorsement.

The onerous task of proof reading the script fell on my wife Marj and daughter Jane, the 'Dynamic Duo'. They are the best team a man could wish for. *Saluté!*

St Vincent de Paul RC High School Accordion Band, 1986

Introduction

Until the publication of *An A to Z of the Accordion & Related Instruments*, there has never previously been a work of reference written about the British accordion scene. The accordion movement in this country is really quite diverse and its history is rich with interesting characters, and the task of research and writing it all down coherently was at first daunting. Nonetheless, I have 'taken the bull by the horns' and attempted to present a broad general survey of the accordion in its various forms, its development over the years, and a representative sample of players and personalities past and present. The book is largely concerned with solo accordionists rather than bands and orchestras, and this is entirely due to considerations of space and size of the topic. Although the majority of entries refer to Great Britain, a number of overseas players have been included due to their connections with this country. A glance through the pages of this book will show that the content also includes many articles of practical use to the accordion player – especially those who are newcomers to the instrument and would like to broaden their knowledge of its capabilities.

This unique book, *An A to Z of the Accordion & Related Instruments*, has taken six months to write, but has actually been in preparation over the course of many years – ever since I first became interested in, and a part of, the wonderful and fascinating world of the accordion. This process began back way back in 1968 when I was a student at Christ's College in Liverpool, doing teacher training. My next-door neighbour in the Hall of Residence where I lived at that time, one Alfred J. Weston, returned from a visit home with his piano accordion. Alf would each day go to his room *"for a blast"*, and I would listen with growing interest to his renditions of *Roddy McCorley, Maggie May, In The Mood*, etc. Eventually I acquired my own accordion – a pre–war Hohner Tango IV – and started to teach myself. When Alf told me that he did not think I had any chance of learning to play – especially by teaching myself – I decided there and then to prove him wrong. By the time I left college in 1970, I had attained a basic idea of how to play.

Over the next few years I had lessons on and off at the Manchester School of Music, first from Kevin Munster and later from Ken Farran. A change of schools forced on me by a major reorganisation of Catholic secondary education in Manchester in 1977 resulted in me joining the staff of St Pius High School, an inner city comprehensive that served a large Irish community. Soon after starting there I was approached by three boys – John O'Grady, Gerard Mannion and Billy Jordan – who all played accordion and had heard that I could play. They asked me if I would teach them, and before long we were playing a repertoire of mainly Irish music as a band. Thus was born the *St Pius RC High School Accordion Band*, which eventually grew in size to 25 members, including a drummer. We also featured one outstanding solo accordionist, Peter Durcan, whose fantastic technique on Irish music was already formed by the time he was thirteen years old. The headmaster, Mr Kevin Madden, came up with the idea of sending the accordion band out, together with the school brass band (led by music teacher, Mike Walsh, then later, Damian Collins), performing concerts in each of the seven local junior schools as a marketing exercise. These concerts were the real start of my education as an accordion entertainer. Putting on a fast–moving show to entertain large numbers of young children, most of whom had a fairly short attention–span, made me learn to think on my feet – literally! The series of concerts was, however, a great success everywhere we went and became an annual event in the school calendar for the next few years.

When St.Pius reorganised yet again and changed its name and identity to St.Vincent de Paul RC High School in 1985, the accordion band continued to play regular concerts, and I then formed an Irish dancing team that became a part of our 'touring concert party'. We had an all–girls dancing team, and I was their solo accompanist for the reels, jigs, hornpipes and set dances that formed their repertoire. On many of our band's performances we also featured the exceptional talents of Dezi Donnelly, World & All-Ireland Fiddle Champion by the time he was thirteen. Des Donnelly was then a pupil at St Vincent de Paul, and has since gone on to win the BBC Young Tradition Award on the way to a successful career in the worlds of Irish and folk music. Happy days! Mrs Rita Johnson, the Head of St Vincent de Paul, gave enthusiastic and unstinting support to all of our activities, and these years were indeed the best of times in my career.

Although I was playing regularly with my school band, and also performing in my local folk club, I was still blissfully unaware that there was any such thing as an accordion movement in existence in this country. All that changed forever when, in early 1979, my teacher, Ken Farran, casually mentioned that the NAO North West Accordion Championships were soon to take place at the Champness Hall in Rochdale. Although I had played the accordion for about ten years and had played many times in concerts at schools where I had taught, I had absolutely no idea that there was any such thing as competitive festivals. Like a lot of players who begin by themselves, I tended to think that I was probably the only person in the country playing the accordion! I was also largely ignorant about most of the great players of the past and present times, or about anything to do with the accordion's history or development.

I went to the Champness Hall on a cold Saturday afternoon in February 1979, filled with curiosity, but with no preconceptions. What I saw that day changed my life! I had only previously thought of the accordion in terms of folk dance tunes and songs, and was greatly impressed by the range and quality of the playing from the competitors of all ages. In particular the performance of a young teenager by name of Simon Gledhill caught my attention, especially when he played an arrangement of a suite of tunes from the James Bond movies. That was it – I was hooked! After that, all I wanted to do was to know more about the accordion and to play as much music as possible, and with as great a variety as I could find. Simon

Gledhill, incidentally, has since become an internationally renowned Wurlitzer theatre organ star.

During the 1980s I played in ceilidh bands, and also as an accompanist for Irish dancing. I began this decade as a member of a folk group that rejoiced in the name of the *Nicaraguan Over Eighties Nudist Leapfrog Troupe*, playing every Friday night as residents at a folk club in Wythenshawe. This was followed by a period as an accompanist playing for a Polish dance team known as Young Polonaise, the highlights of which were guest appearances at the 1981 Fylde Folk Festival and in a concert at Wembley Conference Centre. I had unwittingly become a global traveller, becoming involved in Irish, Polish and Nicaraguan music (okay, the last one is definitely stretching the truth, but it sounds good if said quickly enough!).

In 1983 I joined the recently formed Weaver Valley Accordion Band, teaming up once again with Ken Farran. One memorable performance with the WVAB was at a country fair somewhere in Cheshire when we alternated with the Bootle Concertina Band, a 42 strong band of Liverpool–based Orangemen. I learned from them that there was also in existence the rival Bootle & District Concertina Band with no less than 46 players – another group of Orangemen, and all from the Liverpool area.

1987 saw the revival of the Clifford Wood Accordion Orchestra, which eventually reinvented itself as the Stockport Accordion Club Band & Orchestra. The CWAO developed rapidly, and my wife Marj and I became members at the band's inception. The following year Cliff Wood entered the CWAO in the UK Championships (achieving 3rd place in the Entertainment Section), and also assumed responsibility for organising the 1988 NAO North West Championships at Stockport Town Hall. Becoming a member of the NAO and helping to organise the first of a series of very successful local festivals initiated me fully into the competitive accordion scene.

Clifford Wood, working on the basis that, as a teacher, I must be at least semi–literate, appointed me newsletter editor for CWAO/SAC. Soon after this I became Concert Secretary (organiser & compère) for the Club's guest nights. This was a development that pleased me enormously. For a long time I had met and listened to people talking about great players such as Toralf Tollefsen, Martin Lukins, Charles Camilleri, and their like. The sad part was that the comments were always strictly in the past tense, and it was as if something precious had been lost from their lives. I decided that it was time our area staged some accordion concerts, to at least try to bring back the good times, as it were. This was the start of Stockport Accordion Club as a highly successful concert venue, and has since led me into direct contact with many fine players from this country and abroad.

In recent years, my playing has been varied and a source of great pleasure. Since 1992 I have played regularly with local ceilidh band *Fiddlesticks* (along with Alan Forster – fiddle, Len Hirst – bass guitar/keyboard, Stewart Ramsden – bass guitar and John Hyland, caller/banjo/guitar). I have also played many times as part of the *Baron Wolfgang Bavarian Band*, appearing in Bierkellers around the country. This was an unmissable experience. Baron Wolfgang, now sadly no longer with us, was a real character who taught me a lot about entertaining and about show business. Baron Wolfgang, real name Stan Walker, had led a colourful life, and his experiences included service in the Royal Navy aboard the battle cruiser HMS Prince of Wales – taking part in the action that sank the German battleship Bismarck in 1941, and surviving his ship's sinking by the Japanese the following year. He had also at various times been a vocalist with the Geraldo orchestra, played bass with Jimmy Shand, and been a professional boxer, wrestler, and Rugby League player with Salford and Swinton. I soon discovered that to play in the Baron's band, you had to be adaptable and quick thinking. He never had a set programme, never used sheet music, and was likely to suddenly introduce a new song into a medley that he had *"written just the other day"*. He also had the habit of finishing a song, then announcing to the audience that *"Our accordionist will now play a couple of polkas"*, or something similar. That, by the way, would be the first I knew about this! Yes, you had to be able to improvise in a gig with the Baron.

More recently I have been playing as a duo with John Jones, doing French themed nights, and playing occasional gigs in Stockport Air Raid Shelters where we sing and play all the old wartime songs at the end of organised tours. These mainly take place around Christmas, commemorating the Manchester Blitz, which began on December 22nd 1940. The Air Raid Shelters, by the way, are a fascinating place to explore, and really do take the visitor back in time to those dark times of 1940/41.

Writing newsletters and club reports for the accordion magazines, plus the organising of what we call 'Club Night' concerts, has led me personally further and deeper into the accordion world. A consequence of this is that, over the years, people far and wide have contacted me asking about all kinds of accordion–related matters – everything from *"Where can I find a teacher for the Anglo concertina?"* to *"I play in a rock band, and we need an accordion player for our next recording session. Can you help?"* Trying to assist people with their enquiries and realising that there are very few sources of information available has led to the production of this book.

Over the years I have had piano and guitar lessons, but my real interest and passion (some would even call it an addiction) is the piano accordion. *An A to Z of the Accordion & Related Instruments* has most certainly not been written for financial gain. If I had wanted to make money I would have tried to emulate JK Rowling and write a Harry Potter type novel, with children in mind, or write a seamy Jeffrey Archer–type story for adults, testing the old adage that *"sex sells"*. It is more the case that I have spent so long haunted by stuff about accordions and the people who play them that I have decided to try to exorcise some ghosts that exist within me.

I hope you enjoy exploring the pages of this book, and that it provides an illuminating picture of the British accordion scene past and present, and at least provides a few answers to the questions people ask about this most fascinating and under–valued family of instruments. Now, read on…

An A to Z of the Accordion
& Related Instruments

Accordion Oscar Wilde once famously declared that: *"A gentleman is someone who can play the accordion, but doesn't."* Whatever one may think of the controversial 19th Century playwright's definition of a gentleman, he can perhaps be excused by the fact that in the Victorian age accordions were very primitive in comparison to the sophisticated instruments around in today's world. Maybe he lived next door to someone who had just begun to learn, and practised relentlessly at all hours of the day and night – a sort of 19th Century *'neighbour from Hell'*!!?? We just don't know.

The accordion family has, of course, grown considerably from its origins in Germany and Austria in the early 19th Century, and the free reed category of instruments now includes: the piano accordion, the Continental chromatic, the diatonic accordion, the melodeon, the concertina, the helixon, the bandoneon, and the harmonica, plus numerous variations and hybrids of these. Each of these instruments is defined somewhere in the following pages, and it is a pity Oscar Wilde is not around today to see and hear some of the members of the accordion family in action. He would surely be made to think again.

Seamus Shannon, one of Ireland's best present day accordionists, once declared that *"Anyone who plays the accordion is my friend, whether they realise it or not"*. That must be the best response to Oscar Wilde that anyone could possibly make.

Accordion Champions of Great Britain/United Kingdom – 1935 to 2003 In 1935, the leading accordion teachers working in league with M. Hohner Ltd and the music magazine *Rhythm* formed a committee and together staged the first national competition, known as the *All-Britain Accordion Championships* at the Central Hall, Westminster.

The outbreak of war in September 1939 led to the championships for that year being cancelled, and it was not until hostilities ended six years later in 1945 that there would be a revival. When the revival came, however, there emerged two separate administrative governing bodies, both claiming to be national organisations, and with rival championships and title claimants – a schism within the accordion movement.

Desmond A. Hart, who had been one of the leading organisers of the 1937 and 1938 All-Britain festivals in London, collaborated with accordionist and teacher Adrian Dante to form the British Association of Accordionists in 1946. The BAA held its first national championships in 1947, at St Pancras Town Hall. The BAA became affiliated to the newly formed CIA (Confédération Internationale de l'Accordéon), but soon withdrew to join the rival CMA (Confédération Mondiale des Accordéonistes). The CIA organised the Coupe Mondiale (World Championships), from 1948, whilst the CMA's

Trophée Mondiale (World Championships) commenced in 1951. The BAA Open British Champion and runner-up became eligible to compete in the Trophée Mondiale. The BAA's list of Open British Champions contains many distinguished names, and a (partially complete) list is provided here for posterity.

In 1948 a group of accordion teachers and other interested parties, most of whom had been involved in the pre-war championships, met together under the chairmanship of Dr Otto H. Meyer (the head of M.Hohner Ltd's UK operation), and plans were drawn up for the formation of the National Accordion Organisation of Great Britain, together with the revival of the original national championships. The following year, 1949, the NAO came into being and the All-Britain Championships were re-instated, again at the Central Hall, Westminster. Upon its inception, the NAO became a member of the CIA, providing representatives for Great Britain in the Coupe Mondiale (World Championships).

In 1988 the NAO All-Britain Championships were renamed the UK Championships, reflecting the growing involvement of competitors from Northern Ireland, especially in the band and orchestral sections.

Looking at the lists of NAO solo champions, there are some notable facts and statistics. The very first All-Britain Champion, Peter Valerio, was only ten years of age at the time. The first family members to win national titles are Bill Smith and his son Liam, Advanced Champions in 1964 and 1995 respectively. Graham Williams, the 1963 Virtuoso Champion, an Australian living in England, became the first overseas player to win a British title. Raymond Bodell has the distinction of being the only person to date to win all four major NAO solo titles, i.e. Virtuoso, Advanced, Bell Trophy and Junior. In the 1970s, Mario Conway won the Virtuoso Championship no less than five consecutive times, dominating the middle years of that decade. The *'Champion of Champions'*, however, is the late, great Charles 'Chiz' Bishop – the man whose long-term dominance of NAO major national solo events at *Accordion Day* was extraordinary. The championship winning feats of Chiz Bishop seem unlikely ever to be beaten: Advanced Solo Champion in 1937 at ten years of age, then a fourteen year hiatus followed by two more Advanced titles and an incredible seven All-Britain Virtuoso titles, spanning a period of 25 years.

Listed below are the winners of the NAO *Advanced Solo Championship* (at various times over the years also referred to as the *Amateur* and the *Senior*), and the *Virtuoso Championship* (instituted in 1950 to allow the participation of professional accordionists). Unfortunately, lack of space prevents the vast numbers of other solo, duet, group, band and orchestra section winners being similarly published – they would collectively take up an entire book of their own!

NAO All-Britain/UK Accordion Champions'
Roll of Honour

Year	Advanced (*aka* Senior or Amateur)	Virtuoso
1935	Peter Valerio (Portsmouth)	
1936	Alice Swindells (Macclesfield)	
1937	Chiz Bishop (Portsmouth)	
1938	Sonny Drinkwater (Brixton)	
1949	Jean Bacon (Lancaster)	
1950	Fred Parnell (Nottingham)	Fred Parnell
1951	Chiz Bishop	Chiz Bishop
1952	Chiz Bishop	Chiz Bishop
1953	Pamela Deakin (Birmingham)	Chiz Bishop
1954	Pamela Deakin	Sylvia Lee (London)
1955	*No competition held*	*No competition held*
1956	David Darvill (Southampton)	Pamela Deakin
1957	Sylvia Wilson (Glasgow)	Sylvia Wilson
1958	Sylvia Wilson	Phyllis Gillingham (Twickenham)
1959	Barbara Sheen-Watson (London)	Chiz Bishop
1960	Barbara Sheen-Watson	Chiz Bishop
1961	Jean Cox (London)	Chiz Bishop
1962	Carole Chesterton (Burton-on-Trent)	Chiz Bishop
1963	Olive Sargent (Surbiton)	Graham Williams (Kettering)
1964	Bill Smith (Kinross)	Pamela Rishton (Kettering)
1965	Keith Jones (Nottingham)	Olive Sargent
1966	Janusz Zukowski (Bury)	Olive Sargent
1967	Christopher Richardson (Leeds)	Pamela Dickie (Kettering)
1968	Barbara Szyszka (Coventry)	Janusz Zukowski
1969	Constanzo Moreno	Janusz Zukowski
1970	Brian Bayliss	Barbara Szyszka
1971	David Lukins (Uxbridge)	John Gould (Birmingham)
1972	Paul Clements	Mario Conway (Cardiff)

Year	Advanced (*aka* Senior or Amateur)	Virtuoso
1973	Neil Rowan	Mario Conway
1974	Martin Kinrade	Mario Conway
1975	Rajinder Singh Suthar	Mario Conway
1976	Alan Driver	Mario Conway
1977	Kay Harper	Rajinder Singh Suthar
1978	Raymond Bodell (Stanmore)	Rajindar Singh Suthar
1979	Karen Street (Burton-on-Trent)	Neil Rowan
1980	Gary McLoughlin	Edward Hession
1981	Jane English	Edward Hession
1982	Ingrid Prince (Birmingham)	Karen Street
1983	Shona Maitland	Karen Street
1984	Donald Shaw	James Crabb
1985	Amanda Tyson	James Crabb
1986	James Grant	Raymond Bodell
1987	Nicola Reid	Amanda Tyson
1988	Michael Paton	Tracey Goldsmith
1989	David Preston	Amanda Tyson
1990	Craig Drysdale	Nicola Reid
1991	Elspeth Chapman	*No competition held*
1992	Julie North	*No competition held*
1993	Anna-Marie Tkacz	Julie North
1994	Martin Game	Anna-Marie Tkacz
1995	Liam Smith (Kinross)	*No competition held*
1996	Barry Howieson	Liam Smith
1997	Lyndsey-Ann Allan	*No competition held*
1998	Beverley Loates	Lyndsey-Ann Allan
1999	Neil Brunton	James Grant
2000	Marie Leonard	Lyndsey-Ann Allan
2001	Sarah Diggens	Robert Cherry
2002	William Langton (Blackpool)	Robert Cherry
2003	Caroline Hodgkinson	Larysa Bodell (Stanmore)

The NAO All-Britain & UK Under 17 Championship
The Arthur Bell Memorial Shield (a.k.a The Bell Trophy)

Year	Winner	Year	Winner
1964	Gordon Halliday	1984	Amanda Tyson
1965	Kathleen Fithyan	1985	Neil Varley
1966	Peter Balneaves	1986	Gordon Stewart
1967	Anthony Crossman	1987	David Preston
1968	Andrew Ball	1988	Morag McFarlane
1969	Patrick Russell	1989	Gordon Haddow
1970	Brian Askew	1990	Russell Torrie
1971	Wendy Tucker	1991	Stuart Holmes
1972	Alan Driver	1992	David Farmer
1973	Karen Barwell	1993	Lindsay Torrie
1974	Stewart Wilson	1994	Liam Smith
1975	Susan Thwaytes	1995	Lyndsay-Ann Allan
1976	Kay Harper	1996	Victoria Molnar
1977	Raymond Bodell	1997	David Ritchie
1978	Gary Blair	1998	Kara Bowman
1979	Colin McKee	1999	Johnny-Lee Leslie
1980	Anne Joyce	2000	Johnny-Lee Leslie
1981	Ian Slater	2001	Stefan Bodell
1982	Shona Maitland	2002	Larysa Bodell
1983	Tracey Goldsmith	2003	Lara Brincat

The NAO All-Britain & UK Junior Championship

Year	Winner	Year	Winner
1957	Jean Taylor	1981	Roy Hendrie
1958	Mary Passmore	1982	Ian Slater
1959	Pamela Rishton	1983	James Crabb
1960	Keith Nicholls	1984	Michael Paton
1961	Verona Chambers	1985	Tony Cucchiara

Year	Winner	Year	Winner
1962	Judith Murray	1986	David Preston
1963	Janusz Zukowski	1987	Morag McFarlane
1964	Claire Newman	1988	Angeline McCloy
1965	Christopher Richardson	1989	Mark Bousie
1966	Barbara Szyszka	1990	Liam Smith
1967	Rosemary Wright	1991	Alan Small
1968	David Innis	1992	Anna-Marie Tkacz
1969	Wendy Tucker	1993	Ian Watson
1970	Helen Hewelt	1994	Victoria Molnar
1971	Karen Barwell	1995	Laura-Lee Leslie
1972	Neil Rowan	1996	Sarah Diggens
1973	Susan Thwaites	1997	Johnny-Lee Leslie
1974	John Tranter	1998	Johnny-Lee Leslie
1975	Iain Duff	1999	Stefan Bodell
1976	Raymond Bodell	2000	Sarah Curry
1977	Nelson McMillan	2001	Vanessa Williams
1978	Edward Hession	2002	No competition held
1979	Iain Horsburgh	2003	Jennifer Maxwell
1980	Ian Slater		

British Association of Accordionists – Championship *Roll of Honour*

In 1947, the newly formed BAA established its own national championships – two years before the formation of the NAO. Listed below are tables showing the winners and second place solo awards (known as the Silver Medal), plus the Commonwealth Champions (a competition held during the national championships), and a table presenting the BAA Junior Champions over the same period, until 1963. Records covering the years 1964 to 1972, when the BAA was dissolved, are not available.

Year	Open British Champion	2nd place - Silver Medal	British Commonwealth Accordionist-of-the-Year Challenge Cup
1947	Frank Clarke		
1948	John Salussolia		
1949	John Salussolia		
1950	Martin Lukins		
1951	Martin Lukins	Derek Deutz	
1952	Martin Lukins	Pamela Deakin	
1953	Ronald Powell	Myrna Lambden	
1954	Gordon Campbell	S.G. Smith	
1955	S.G. Smith	Donald Harris	
1956	Donald Harris	John Leslie	Patricia Sally
1957	Joan Berner	Janet Quinion	Patricia Sally
1959	Pearl Fawcett	Pearl Fawcett	
1960	Barry Crossland	Joseph Tobin	Pearl Fawcett
1962	Heather Smith	Sonia Zaremba	Pearl Fawcett
1963	Anthony Lowe	Alastair Gillespie	Pearl Fawcett

The B.A.A. Great Britain Junior (Under 16) Solo Championship

Year	BAA Junior Champion of Great Britain
1947 (November)	No section
1948 (November)	Gwenda Wilkin
1949	Alistair McAllister
1950	David Huxtable
1951	George Reilly
1952	Alf Powell
1953 (special Coronation Festival)	Myrna Lambden
1953	Gordon Campbell

Year	BAA Junior Champion of Great Britain
1954	Pearl Fawcett
1955	Pearl Fawcett
1956	Pearl Fawcett
1957 (took place January 1958)	Pearl Fawcett
1958	No Festival
1959	Heather Smith
1960	Sonia Zaremba
1962	Raymond Newton
1961	No Festival
1963	Brian Kerr

Accordion Clubs Since the early 1930s, there have been accordion clubs in Great Britain, plus many accordion bands/orchestras that often also function as clubs. Membership of a club is a great way to improve your knowledge of music and accordions, to hear and meet the best players, and to make new friends and contacts. For contact details and news of their activities, it is best to subscribe to one of the specialist accordion magazines – see the section **Magazines**.

Accordion Clubs – *Thinking of Running a Club?* *Forming and running an accordion club is a challenging task, but also a very rewarding one. Listed below are some ideas to help you get organised and make a start. The suggestions are based on my personal experience from many years acting as Concert Secretary at Stockport Accordion Club, and also the good practice observed in other clubs. SAC was originally formed to give local accordionists the opportunity to meet and play together. Over the years it has grown tremendously, and now consists of two bands of varying ability that meet to practice weekly and compete in national competitions. We also host regular 'club nights' where we showcase a guest artiste and give anyone who wants to a chance to play in front of an audience. It should be noted that SAC meets at the Cheadle Heath St John Ambulance Brigade Divisional HQ, and the club does not meet on licensed premises; it is also a non-smoking venue. The absence of alcohol and tobacco, however, has not detracted from the success of our concert evenings.*
1) Use the accordion magazines to publicise what you intend to do; your local newspapers may also be willing to help, especially if you make it easy for them by writing out a short, concise article.
2) Get help as soon as possible. It is impossible to run a club by yourself –

there are too many jobs to do ranging from making refreshments to collecting money. Form a small committee, and delegate tasks. You will need a compère.

3) The accessibility of your club premises can be a big factor in your success. Stockport Accordion Club's 'home' is situated one minute away from a major motorway network, and is readily accessible also from most of Greater Manchester via main roads.

4) Be punctual with the timing of your concerts: if you have advertised you begin at 7.30 or 8pm, then stick to your timing; it is helpful for your audience also if they know approximately what time the proceedings finish.

5) Make a list of contact details for all the people who visit your club; by doing this, you can build up a regular audience by keeping visitors in touch with what you are doing, and this will also make them feel part of your club.

6) Produce a regular newsletter detailing what you are planning to do, what else goes on in your area and beyond, and add in anything else of general interest. Mail the newsletter to people on your members' list. Produce/display posters.

7) When booking guest artistes, try to vary the styles/genres of the accordionists so that there is some variety. This will prevent the unwelcome comment that *"it all sounds the same"* at your club.

8) Try to avoid booking the same acts too frequently, otherwise you are likely to suffer from what the economist John Maynard Keynes called *"the law of diminishing returns"* whereby part of your potential audience stays away because they believe that, as they have only recently seen/heard your guest, they would rather watch Emmerdale or clean the bath or whatever else comes to mind as an alternative to be entertained by a guest you have booked for their imagined pleasure. Once every two years is about right for the majority of accordion acts.

9) Make space in your concert for anyone else who would like to play, but limit all supporting spots to a maximum of two numbers. Make sure the supporting players know their place in the playing order, and are ready with instruments and music to perform. This will maintain continuity, thus preventing awkward breaks in the proceedings.

10) Consider having occasional special events. At Stockport AC we have held what we term *Musical Goods Sale Evenings*, where records, cassettes, CDs, LPs, sheet music, instruments, etc, have been put on open sale in the style of a car boot sale; we have also had musical workshop evenings led by a guest musical specialist. Another special event is the occasional *President's Evening*, where there is no guest artiste booked, and the whole evening is geared up to the contributions of club and visiting players. Each of these special events has been highly successful.

Rob Howard, Stockport Accordion Club, 2003

*'**Accordion Contest**', is the title of a humorous story written in 1950 by Chiz Bishop, and reprinted by kind permission of Mrs Sylvia Bishop.*

Accordion Contest

You're entering an Accordion Contest are you? Ha! Ha! Ha! Don't let ME discourage you – but do you *really* know what you are letting yourself in for? Don't you? Well, my friend, let me tell you:

There are several types of people one finds entering Contests, but the majority belong to one of three types, which I itemise herewith…

TYPES 1, 2 AND 3

Type One – The fellow who thinks to himself, *"You poor fish! What chance do you think you'll stand?"* This is the TIMID type.

Type Two – The bloke who thinks, *"Contests? Pooh! I'll walk away with it!"* He is the CONCEITED type.

Type Three – The chap who thinks, *"Well, I'm going to do my best, but if another fellow wins, then good luck to him!"* He is the NON-EXISTANT type!

Still, it takes all sorts to make a Contest, as the monkey said when he did something or other.

Right, then, you are now entering the Contest of the year – in fact, the Contest of your Life!

THE GREAT DAY ARRIVES

Let us take it for granted that you have done your preliminary training, practised your piece, changed your *'own choice'* at the last minute, and played at sufficient gigs, weddings and kiddies' bun-fights to afford the entrance fee. If you are a cut above the rest, you may have won a small competition organised by 'Gobbo Toothpaste' ('Gobbo' for a Good Paste in the Mouth) and now you feel the urge to do greater things. So we skip the anxious weeks and come to the date on the calendar, which you have marked with red pencil.

The Great Day dawns – cold, clammy and drizzling with rain. You find that you have a touch of the 'flu which makes you shake so much at breakfast that the family think you are practising the bellows shake.

You try to hide your trembling paws in your pockets – only to find you have no trousers on!

Okay! So what? Maybe you *ARE* a little nervous, but as every NON-contestant will tell you, you'll be all right *when your time comes*! WHEN YOUR TIME COMES! It sounds like a death sentence at that hour of the morning, doesn't it?

Well, you finish your custard and kipper, or whatever you manage to force down your constricted throat, and set out for the Contest Hall.

If you have a train journey to make, leave your accordion in the corridor where everyone will fall over it. As your victims pick themselves up, hand them your visiting card. This makes a good publicity stunt and helps to while away the time.

A word of warning here…don't carry cream cakes or jam tarts (unwrapped) in your accordion case. I did this once, and played some very sticky passages afterwards. Besides, it messes up the cakes! And the jam tarts get fluffy!

SOME OLD BUSKERS

On your way to the Contest Hall you may pass an old busker in the street. Have pity on him. Very likely, he was a child prodigy once. They all go the same way – first their names are in the headlines – a few years later they make a comeback and get a column on the inside page – still more years go by and you see a very small paragraph on the back page which reads *"Ex-child prodigy pushes ex-child prodigy under train."*

So, if you see one, take pity on him…it might be me!

        *   *   *

You arrive at the hall. Thousands of people are there, and the accordions at the Trade displays make yours look like an old bully-beef can.

The Contestants' room is a cacophony of noise. You try to find a nice corner to yourself, but succeed only in being collared by a representative from the lower Balkans who grins broadly and says some very rude things that he has obviously learned from a soldier with a misplaced sense of humour.

Already you are chewing your fingernails. STOP THIS AT ONCE!!! I remember a chap who did that, and by the time he was ready to play he was gazing despondently into space and nibbling at the frayed stump of his right wrist.

The hands of the clock creep remorselessly round and suddenly a haggard-looking man, with a French-English: English-French dictionary and straggling moustache comes to tell you that you are *"on"* in two minutes.

Get your accordion strapped on, and STOP BITING YOUR NAILS!!! You're on! You're *actually* on!!

The stage stretches away into the far distance, and that sea of faces looks remarkably like a row of cods' heads on a fishmonger's slab. IT *IS* A ROW OF CODS' HEADS! No, it isn't – it's the audience! Somebody is waving to you and saying to her neighbour, *"Look, Flo, it's our 'Arry. Good old 'Arry boy!"*

Don't wave back, it's bad form and besides, the organisers might think you want to leave. You DO want to leave? But you CAN'T! You're on…alone.

You see a shape in front of you. It looks like – no, it can't be – but it – no, it isn't – yes, it is! It's a microphone leering at you.

HIGHER AND HIGHER

Naturally, the preceding player was a giant of some seven feet high, and so the mike head is way above you. You begin laboriously climbing up the swaying structure, vaguely wondering whether you can hold on with your feet while you play.

Then the haggard young man runs across the stage and explains that the little screw on the side of the stand is to lower it.

You fumble with this screw and wish that you had a pair of pliers with you.

OOPS! The mike crashes down on your fingers and everybody giggles. Everybody, that is, except you. YOU want a drink. YOU want your Mum. You want, passionately, to be sick.

You have the mike there, your accordion at the ready, and the Test Piece is hovering around in the back of your mind.

Now, how does it go? Oh, yes…

You pull eastwards like the blazes, determined to startle the audience out of their somnolence.

You spin round and fall flat on your bellows.

You pick yourself up and undo your bellows-straps.

The crowd out front is getting restless. Somebody crackles a bag of potato crisps, and you can faintly hear another competitor in the back room playing the Test Piece faultlessly.

THE TEST PIECE! You come back to earth with a start…go on, play!

* * *

You stumble blindly from the platform after giving a terrible rendering – wrong coupler-changes at the second time bar on page two – you fluffed that simple bass run – your right hand seemed to turn into a claw on the chromatic run.

Everyone on the side of that stage is giving you sickly grins. They're gloating over you!

THE OTHERS!

You realise it's all over and go back to the Competitors' Room. People nudge each other, look at you as if you either have the plague or are the World Champion (this latter applies mainly, of course, to the 'Under Four' contestants).

Every contestant who plays after you is *superb* – perfect in phrasing – clear *staccato* bass runs – chromatic treble runs that flow smoothly from under controlled fingers.

* * *

Then it's the end of the Contest, and they are waiting for the winners to be announced.

You spot the nearest Exit and begin making your escape, when, faintly, as if from a long way off, you hear your name being spoken.

You whirl round ready to defend your honour, and quickly think up all the excuses you can.

But everybody is clapping and pointing at you!

No, not that! Derision! You cannot bear it!

And then, it dawns on you…

"Go on, 'Arry, get your pot!!!!"

You've won!

Excuse me while I faint.

Accordion Crimes is the title of a critically acclaimed novel written by E. Annie Proulx that tells the story of an accordion through the years, in the hands of different owners. *Accordion Crimes* begins in 1890 in Sicily, as an accordion maker completes what he considers to be his finest instrument, and dreams of owning a music shop in America. He and his young son sail to a rough part of New Orleans where, a short time later, the accordion maker is murdered. The man's instrument passes into other hands, and the accordion's travels across America are filled with incidents. Published in 1996 by Simon & Schuster, *Accordion Crimes* is also available on audiocassette, read by Edward Herrmann.

Accordion Day Ever since the first All-Britain Championships were held in November 1935, this annual competitive festival has been affectionately known as '*Accordion Day*,' even though for many years the event has actually begun on Friday evening and finished on Sunday afternoon!

There were four *Accordion Day* competitions held before World War Two, from 1935 to 1938, and then in 1949 the National Accordion Organisation was formed to administer the running of area festivals and the revived national finals – the All-Britain Championships a.k.a. *Accordion Day*.

From 1935 through to 1964, *Accordion Day* was held at the Central Hall, Westminster, London – apart from 1955 when there was no festival due to the NAO staging the Coupe Mondiale (World Championships) in Brighton. From 1956, *Accordion Day* has been held in the Spring rather than November.

From 1965 to 1970, Leicester was the venue for *Accordion Day* (Francis Wright was the organiser). The Edward Wood Hall (once) and the De Montfort Hall were the venues in that period.

From 1970, the NAO turned *Accordion Day* into a travelling event for almost two decades, and venues included Southampton, Birmingham, Perth, Brighton, Scarborough, Weston-Super-Mare, Morecambe, Margate, Portsmouth, Ayr, Llandudno, Eastbourne, Buxton, Skegness, Bridlington and Blackpool. Since the early 1990s, *Accordion Day* has become resident at the Spa Complex, Scarborough.

There have been numerous changes to *Accordion Day* over the years. There are many more sections nowadays, requiring more halls and adjudicators. In 1987, the rapidly growing number of competitors from Northern Ireland resulted in the All-Britain Championships evolving into the UK Championships. Up until the early 1970s, there was traditionally a full-scale evening concert involving guest stars plus winners from some of the competition sections, and in the 1950s some of these concerts were actually broadcast live by the BBC Light Programme. The concerts gave way to a Gala Dance featuring a show band, and this in turn became a Scottish ceilidh. In recent years the ceilidh has seen the dancers take to the floor to the lively music of Gary Blair, with a cabaret spot featuring a guest accordionist or band such as Keith Dickson's K.O.D.A.

The NAO's *Accordion Day* has survived, indeed flourished, since the mid-1930s, and remains as the flagship event of the British competitive accordion scene.

Accordion Enthusiast's Appointments Calendar, The Each year a beautifully produced, full colour calendar featuring twelve vintage accordions (or other free reed instruments) is available from Caroline Hunt, 4a John St, Avoch, Ross-shire 1V9 8PZ, Scotland; telephone 01528 544361. Caroline requests anyone with photographs of instruments made before 1960 to write to her.

Accordions Go Crazy is the name of an accordion-driven band of multi-instrumentalists from the 1980s/90s whose experimental and eccentric mixture of original music and 'world music' sounds resulted in a concert repertoire and recordings that defied description and label. Their leader was Mike Adcock, and the band *Accordions Go Crazy* – probably due to the international flavour of much of their music –

were ultimately better known and more successful abroad, especially in Germany, than in this country. Their line up included: Mike Adcock (piano accordion, guitar, vocals); Clive Bell (piano accordion, flute, percussion, vocals); Dean Speedwell Brodrick (piano accordion, piano, percussion, vocals); Nicola Hadley (piano accordion, percussion, vocals); Ann Day (drums, percussion); Sylvia Hallett (violin, concertina, trombone); Stuart Jones (bass guitar, trumpet, vocals).

Discography: *Overboard* (1988); *Zombie Dancer* (1989)

Accordion, History of the *The article that follows is really a short history of the accordion in Great Britain, but the chronological list of dates which follow is more of a general timeline. There have been so many developments within the accordion family of instruments that some editing has been necessary to prevent the timeline taking up most of the rest of this book!*

    Writing a history of the accordion is anything but a straightforward task as there are conflicting and contradictory views about its invention and development. The origin of the accordion and its close relatives such as the concertina, melodeon and bandoneon (often categorised in music dictionaries as the 'free reed' instruments) dates all the way back in time to somewhere around 2,700 BC when the Sheng, a mouth-blown reed instrument (the ancestor of the harmonica) was invented in China. The invention of the accordion, however, belongs to a period much closer to our own times i.e. the 1820s, though there are several conflicting accounts as to exactly where, when and by whom the first instruments were built. Furthermore, the instrument's further development through the 19th and early 20th centuries is complicated by the various claims made by the many different German and Italian manufacturers, some of whom are inclined to put their own 'spin' on how things came about. It is, however, now generally accepted that the accordion was invented in the third decade of the 19th Century, and available records show that on May 6th 1829, Cyril Damien (also spelt Cyrilius Demian) patented a design for the accordion (also called a flutina) – with treble and bass - in Vienna, Austria. Damien's instrument was diatonic (two notes per button, changing on pull or push of the bellows), but played only chords on the treble side, and was intended for accompanying singing. An accordion (a.k.a. 'flutina') that had single treble notes, and could therefore play melodies came two years later in 1831, designed in Paris by Pichenot Jeune. This was also known as a clavier melodique, and was the ancestor of the present day melodeon, and the development of the fully chromatic button accordion (each button produces one note irrespective of bellows direction) came around twenty years later in the 19th Century.

Flutina Accordions

The records also show that on June 19th 1829 in London, England, Charles Wheatstone patented the English concertina. Some historical records, however, claim that Friedrich Buschmann in Berlin invented the accordion – with treble keyboard only, in either 1822, 1825 or 1829. The American musicologist Sigmund Spaeth, writing in the *Merit Students Encyclopaedia* (1980) suggests that Buschmann made the first accordion in 1825, and that Wheatstone's concertina four years later was meant to be an improvement on the Buschmann accordion. In Chemnitz, Germany in 1835,Carl Uhleg invented a free reed instrument that is related to the concertina, and known as a Chemnitzer. The Chemnitzer never made it to Britain or Ireland, but has become popular in parts of the USA where it is used by Americans of European descent for playing ethnic music. The various efforts of Damien, Buschmann, Wheatstone and Uhleg certainly set in train a long series of developments leading up to the various free reed instruments we have in the 21st Century. The concertina business started in London in 1829 by Charles Wheatstone, by the way, is still very much in business as we enter the 21st Century!

The Age of the Concertina

The button accordion and English concertina existed side by side in Great Britain during the 19th and early 20th Centuries, but for a long time it was the concertina that was more popular, evidenced by higher instrument sales, the great popularity of the concertina in the music halls, and the widespread existence of large concertina bands. Many old photographs show concertina bands with twenty, thirty, forty plus members. National band contests were held annually at Belle Vue, Manchester, from 1905 until 1939. The concertina's popularity waned steadily after the First World War, partly due to the large number of men who were killed (thus decimating many of the concertina bands) and also changing musical trends (e.g. the advent of the wireless and the phonograph badly hit the sales of all musical instruments and sheet music in the 1920s). However, as the concertina lost favour, the introduction of the more recently developed piano accordion led to this instrument becoming the new, 'must-have' fad of the late 1920s and 1930s.

Enter the Piano Accordion

The first person to design a piano-keyed accordion is believed to be Jacques Bouton of Paris, in 1852, although in Vienna Philip de Ponts and Johann Forster about eight years later produced a piano accordion design that was actually put into limited production.

In 1863, when Paolo Soprani opened the first accordion factory in Castelfidardo, Italy, he claimed, with some justification, to have introduced to the world the piano accordion, as later generations would recognise it. From this point on, the piano accordion began to spread to many parts of Europe, where it became useful for pianists as a double-up instrument with music such as the tango. The Trossingen-based Hohner company, already established as manufacturers of harmonicas, began to produce piano accordions, and this instrument became the most popular type in Germany. However, it was not until Guido and Pietro Deiro introduced the piano accordion to American audiences in 1910/11 that this form of the accordion really became popular on the other side of the Atlantic. It was the widespread international enthusiasm for the tango in the first quarter of the 20th Century, however, that was to give the piano accordion its greatest boost.

In 1927, pianist George Scott-Wood imported a piano accordion from Italy, and introduced this then novel instrument into his dance band work in an attempt to produce more authentic sounding tangos, and this was the beginning of the piano accordion's rapid rise in popularity in Great Britain. The rise in instrument availability and sales plus general interest thereafter was phenomenal, and demand for the piano accordion in this country grew beyond anyone's expectations. By the early 1930s, piano accordions were all the rage with the general public, with accordion clubs and bands springing up all over Britain.

George Scott-Wood

1935 was really the key year in the accordion's development and popularity in Great Britain, evidenced by the organisation of the first All-Britain Championships (organised and sponsored by M. Hohner Ltd and the monthly music magazine *Rhythm*), held at the Central Hall, Westminster, and the publication of the monthly *Accordion Times & Harmonica News*. The London-based British College Accordion Playing also came into existence that year, though in 1936 the title was changed to the British College of Accordionists. These historic developments were accompanied by a continuing growth in the number of accordion clubs, compositions for accordion, and recordings made by solo players, duos and bands. The accordion scene in the 1930s in Great Britain is covered in more detail in the section called **Nostalgia: The Thirties Accordion Scene**.

The outbreak of war with Germany on September 3rd 1939 signalled the end of what had been a golden decade for the accordion in this country. All public entertainment was severely curtailed, at least for the first few months, and most accordion players – male and female – became caught up in the war effort in one way or another. The import of instruments from Germany and Italy ceased for the duration of the conflict, and when the war ended in 1945, musical tastes were changing, and the accordion's great pre-war popularity with the general public went into a gradual decline.

Post-War Developments

In the post-war years, the competitive accordion movement in Britain revived and the British Association of Accordionists was founded in 1946/47 by teacher/composer Adrian Dante and pre–war festival organiser Desmond A. Hart, setting up its own British Accordion Championships. 1949 saw the formation of the National Accordion Organisation, founded by Dr Otto H. Meyer, HJ Bridges and James Black. The NAO then revived the All-Britain Championships at the Central Hall, Westminster, to pick up where these contests had left off in 1938. The *Accordion Times* was re-launched, closely aligned with NAO activities, whilst the BAA sponsored its own magazine, *Accordion Review*. The magazines of the period, and the NAO and BAA thus pursued their respective interests and activities with little or no reference to each other.

Although the accordion post-war was less popular than in the 1930s, the instrument was still popular enough with the general public to be heard regularly on the radio, and there were even specialist programmes such as *Accordion Club* heard every week on the BBC Light Programme. Accordionists such as Martin Lukins, Delmondi, Tito Burns, Gerald Crossman, Albert Delroy and Jack Emblow were frequent broadcasters throughout the 1950s and into the 60s. Accordionists were also active in the variety theatres, and tours by stars from Europe such as Marcosignori, Yvette Horner, Kramer & Wolmer, Hans Rauch and Charles Camilleri were commonplace. The professional accordion bands such as Primo Scala, however, began to disappear by 1950, suffering the same fate of changing public taste and economic liability as the great swing orchestras and dance bands of the previous decades. Work opportunities became steadily fewer through the decline in variety shows and dancing venues, and the cost of maintaining large bands on a full-time basis proved to be too much.

The Years of Decline.

In the mid-1950s, the skiffle and rock n' roll crazes reached this country from America, and the age of the guitar had well and truly arrived. Guitars were relatively inexpensive (certainly in comparison to accordions), and it was also easy to attain a basic standard of strumming sufficient to play a lot of the skiffle and popular songs of the period. As the 1950s moved towards the end of that decade, the accordion steadily lost popularity with the general public – as did other forms of music such as big bands, and singers in the big band style – and rock n' roll artistes such as Elvis Presley, Cliff Richard, Buddy Holly, Chuck Berry, Billy Fury, Adam Faith and Helen Shapiro were all big record sellers. Fortunately, the competitive accordion movement in Britain was well organised enough through the teachers of the NAO and BAA to sustain their annual festivals, although these events were now of less interest to the media, and correspondingly less visible to the general public.

Sadly, as the 1960s rapidly became dominated by the sounds of The Beatles, Gerry & The Pacemakers, The Searchers and the rest of the Liverpool beat groups, the accordion (and many other forms of non-pop music) gradually faded from the airwaves. In 1967, when the BBC transformed the Light Programme and Home Service, etc, into Radio 1, 2, 3 and 4, all forms of live music became heard less and less often. This policy has continued to the extent that musical broadcasts (i.e. people playing instruments live on air as opposed to a DJ playing records) are nowadays a rarity on the radio. On television there is almost no live music played at all. On New Year's Day the BBC televise the annual Strauss Gala live from Vienna, and that is about it (apart from an annual summer series of the BBC sponsored Henry Wood Promenade concerts) for the next twelve months! None of the television channels nowadays seem to show much interest in screening people playing musical instruments. Broadcasts by accordionists on radio or television were casualties of the changes in programming policy, and have now been consigned to history.

On the radio, the airwaves have been so impregnated by the prevailing pop music of the day that specialist music programmes have come into their own on BBC Radio Two and some of the local BBC stations. Starved of exposure on the usual music programmes, folk music has *Folk On Two*, there is *The Organist Entertains* and there is also *The Dance Band Days*. In effect, these kinds of non-pop music have been driven into ghettoes – almost like Red Indian reservations in America, driven there under the remorseless advance of the 'white man' and his so-called 'civilization.' The accordion has fared much worse, however, with no specialist programme of its own at all. There used to be the occasional series by Jimmy Shand, then Jim McLeod; now these essentially Scottish radio shows have disappeared. There also used to be the occasional series by The Yetties, but since *Folk On Two* presenter Jim Lloyd (who once managed The Yetties, and was their unofficial sponsor) and his wife, Frances Line (the Programme Controller on Radio Two) both retired a few years ago, these have now also gone.

The steady decline in variety shows, both in theatres and on television throughout the late 1950s, 60s and 70s, was also bad news for accordionists, drastically cutting down the public's exposure to the instrument. As we move into the 21st Century, if you play the accordion in public, the chances are quite high that someone somewhere will tell you that they *"haven't seen an accordion in years."*

Revival At Last!

In the late 1970s/early 80s, the energetic activities of Malcolm Gee, a latecomer to music who only took up playing the accordion in his late thirties, led to a renewal of interest in the accordion. He founded the Birmingham-based Club Accord, published the Accordion Monthly News magazine, organised concerts and introduced the concept of the non-competitive accordion festival, and in the process brought many overseas top-class accordion stars to this country. Of all the accordion luminaries that were around in his era, Malcolm Gee did the most to stimulate interest in the average accordion enthusiast, players and non-players alike. Others have been inspired to follow this lead, and opportunities for accordionists and the retail trade have improved.

Despite all changes with regard to musical, social and media trends, the NAO festivals have continued regardless through thick and thin over the years (the BAA festivals, however, have long since disappeared) and people are still buying accordions, taking lessons and entering both examinations and competitions. In the 1980s electronic accordions became fashionable, and free bass acoustic instruments began to be studied by serious students of the accordion. Also, the last years of the century saw greater interest in 5-row button accordion systems, including the Russian 'Bayan' type of instrument.

The so-called 'Folk Revival' of the 1960s, aided and abetted by the rapid expansion of higher education in colleges and universities, led to the founding and establishment of folk clubs and festivals around the country. This naturally led to increased interest in the use of the accordion from the direction of folk song, music and dance, and also caused a revival in the fortunes of the concertina thanks to the involvement of the likes of Louis Killen, Harry Boardman, Alan Bell, Mike Harding, Tony Rose, Peggy Seeger, Roger Watson, John Kirkpatrick and Alistair Anderson. The more recent advent of 'World Music' has further led to accordion music from Cajun, Zydeco and Tex-Mex traditions being heard and added to the homegrown folk music scene in this country. The Irish traditional music scene in Britain has similarly grown and developed, and the extensive network of music lessons organised by the educational body Comhaltas Ceoiltori Eireann, have done much to promote interest in all kinds of button accordions, concertinas and the piano accordion.

Signposts for the Future.

Although the total number of people playing the piano accordion and related instruments is nowadays relatively small compared to the 1930s and 40s, the accordion scene in Britain is fortunately very well organised and there are keen areas of interest in many places. The efforts and enthusiasm of such indefatigable organisers as Bill Wilkie, Malcolm Gee, Robert & Loretta Rolston, Ron Hodgson, Francis Wright, Tom Duncan and Heather Smith has spearheaded activity and galvanised interest on a major scale.

The competitive accordion festivals continue to attract a lot of entries, and playing standards are consistently high, there are also a high proportion of children and young people vying for honours each year. Perhaps most encouraging of all is the fact that the music 'establishment' is now starting to take the accordion seriously, and more young accordionists than ever before are studying the instrument at music colleges such as Chetham's Music School in

Manchester, and The Royal Academy of Music in London. The articulate persuasion and long-term persistence of Professor Owen Murray has led the way in demonstrating the potential of the accordion within the classical world, and the future is looking good thanks to his entirely positive approach.

The accordion is seen and heard in various guises – often amongst other instruments. For example, in August 2003, Finland's Kimmo Pohjonen appeared in a World Music BBC Proms concert at the Royal Albert Hall, broadcast live on Radio 3. The publicity claimed that Pohjonen *"does for the accordion what Jimi Hendrix did for the electric guitar."* A few weeks earlier, Paul McCartney's world tour included a keyboard player, Tex Wickens, who doubled on a full size Allodi piano accordion. Millions saw the accordionist worldwide, as he stood right next to the ex-Beatle, and his playing was featured on the resulting DVD, video and CD of the tour. In recent years popular artistes such as Bruce Springsteen, Paul Simon, U2, The Waterboys and Dexy's Midnight Runners have all featured accordions. There are other bands using accordions. In the 1980s, the Irish duo Foster & Allen had a series of best selling singles and albums, and even appeared live on the BBC's *Top of the Pops* – exposing the accordion to new audiences. Times change, and so do musical trends, but the accordion has, to a certain extent, re-invented itself and adapted surprisingly well. The accordion also pops up in some unlikely places, such as in the televised opening ceremony of the Rugby World Cup in Sydney, Australia in October 2003, when accordionist James Crabb and violinist Richard Tognetti performed a lively and stirring piece of original Celtic-style music – seen and heard by a worldwide audience of millions.

The increasing numbers of people retiring early from work since the 1980s has encouraged many to seek lessons to play instruments, and the accordion has benefited from this development. In Scotland there is a network of scores of well-supported and well-run 'Box & Fiddle' clubs, and in England and Wales there are accordion clubs and festivals functioning because of the unflagging efforts of some very dedicated people. The establishment of accordion bands/orchestras for children and teenagers, arguably the most important work of all, is happening in some places – surely a trend that needs encouraging by all who wish to see the accordion survive and prosper into the future.

Britain has hosted the World Accordion Championships on four occasions to date in the post-war years, and as long as there are interested people prepared to organise and support events, the accordion movement will move forward confidently into the future.

Accordion Lineage

The Accordion – an Historical Timeline
Listed below in chronological order are some of the key dates in the history of the accordion – many with particular reference to Great Britain, and shown as follows: -

2,700 BC	The 'Sheng' (a mouth-blown forerunner of the harmonica) appeared in China.
1825 AD	In Berlin, Friedrich Buschmann invented a diatonic button-keyed accordion, originally called the *'handaoline'* by its creator.
1829	In Vienna, Cyril Damien produced his first button-keyed diatonic accordion.
1829	Charles Wheatstone invented the first English concertina, patented in London.
1831	Pichenot Jeune designed an improved version of Damien's accordion.
1831	The first tutor book for accordion, written by Pichenot, was published in Paris.
1832	The Reisner accordion tutor, a rival to the Pichenot book, appeared in Paris.
1835	In Germany, Carl Uhleg designed the first of his 'Chemnitzer' concertinas.
1836	Drollinger & Hermann produced the first accordions in Switzerland.
1846	Alexandre in Paris produced the first accordion with couplers.
1852	Jacques Bouton of Paris designed the first piano accordion.
1852	In Klingenthal, Germany, production of the Herold Akkordeon – a chromatic button accordion - began.
1857	Matthias Hohner began production of harmonicas in Trossingen, Germany.
1863	Paolo Soprani started producing accordions in Castelfidardo, Italy. This was the beginning of Castelfidardo as the world centre of accordion manufacturing. As a result, Castelfidardo has become virtually a 'Mecca' for accordionists worldwide.
1865	Cesare Pancotti founded the second Italian accordion factory in Macerata.
1870	Russian-born musician N.I. Beloborodov constructed the first fully chromatic button accordion.
1871	Composer Giuseppe Verdi suggested to the Italian Ministry of Education that the accordion be taught in the country's Conservatoires.
1872	Settimo Soprani started manufacturing accordions in Castelfidardo.

1876	Mariano Dallape invented and constructed the Stradella bass system.
1883	Russian composer P.I.Tchaikovsky introduced a musical score for the accordion in his *Suite No 2 in C major*.
1897	Paolo Soprani patented a chromatic button accordion from a design by Beraldi and Piatenesi.
1903	M. Hohner began manufacturing chromatic accordions in Trossingen.
1905	Pietro Frosini arrived in the USA.
1907	Pietro Deiro arrived in the USA, followed by his brother Guido a year later.
1910	Guido Deiro became the first to play the piano accordion on stage in the USA.
1911	Guido Deiro was the first to make a record using piano accordion.
1927	Pianist George Scott-Wood imported a piano accordion from Italy, and became Britain's first professional player.
1929	George Scott-Wood wrote the first tutor book for piano accordion to be published in Great Britain.
1935	The first All-Britain Accordion Championships (a.k.a. *'Accordion Day'*) were held in Central Hall, Westminster, London.
1935	*The British College of Accordion Playing* (renamed *The British College of Accordionists* the following year) was founded in London.
1935	The *Accordion Times & Harmonica News* was founded by James.J.Black and Dr Otto Meyer in London.
1939	The outbreak of World War II put an end to accordion imports into Britain from either Germany or Italy for the next six years.
1946	Foundation of the British Association of Accordionists, by teacher/performer Adrian Dante and journalist/contest organiser Desmond A. Hart.
1949	Foundation of the National Accordion Organisation of Great Britain.
1955	The World Championships (CIA Coupe Mondiale) were held in Brighton. The winner was Kurt Heusser (Switzerland).
1964	The British College of Accordionists was relocated to Leicester, under the direction of Mr Francis Wright.

1968	The World Accordion Championships – the Coupe Mondiale - were held at the De Montfort Hall in Leicester. Winner – Juri Vostrelov (USSR).
1972	The last BAA contest was held, billed as the Yorkshire Accordion Festival – Open Solo winner was Brian Askew. The British Association of Accordionists ceased to function thereafter.
1974	The *Accordion Times* ceased publication.
1976	Club Accord was formed by Malcolm Gee.
1981	Malcolm Gee started the *Accordion Record Club*, a mail-order service that made accordion records from around the world easily available in Britain.
1982	Francis Wright revived the *Accordion Times*.
1982	Malcolm Gee organised Britain's first non-competitive accordion festival at Pontin's Sand Bay Holiday Centre, Weston-super-Mare.
1983	Malcolm Gee upgraded the Club Accord newsletter into the *Accordion Monthly News*.
1984	The Coupe Mondiale was held again in Britain, in Folkstone. The winner was Peter Soave (USA).
1986	The first Caister Autumn Accordion Festival was held, starring Toralf Tollefsen.
1989	Madame Claudine Aucher organised the first Chartres Accordion Festival, in northern France. Jack Emblow & Tony Compton were the first guests invited from the UK.
1997	Malcolm Gee died suddenly after suffering a stroke. Robert & Loretta Rolston took over the running of the Caister Autumn Accordion Festival. The *Accordion News* was incorporated into the *Accordion Times*, hence *The Accordion Times & Monthly News*.
1997	The monthly magazine *Accordion Profile* was launched by Tom Duncan and Heather Smith.
2001	The Coupe Mondiale was held in Harrow, won by Russia's Aidar Gainullin.
2001	Bridlington and Pakefield Accordion Festivals were launched by the Rolstons and by Heather Smith respectively, followed by the first London Accordion Festival organised by Roman Viazzini. These festivals plus the Coupe Mondiale, all held between September and December, collectively represent the most sustained period of organised accordion activity ever staged in Great Britain.

Accordion Magazines The following magazines dedicated to the accordion are published in Great Britain and are all available by mail-order: -
- *Accordion Profile* – a monthly publication. Contact Heather Smith on 01482 345 959; e–mail: heather@accordions.karoo.co.uk
- *Accordion Times & Monthly News* - a monthly publication, with club reports, reviews and other info. This magazine has a history whose lineage can be traced all the way back to 1935. Contact Loretta Rolston on 01501 820 910
- *Accordion Today* – an occasional publication from the outspoken but very knowledgeable Charlie Watkins; telephone 020 8679 5575
- *Accordion World* – a glossy A5-sized bi-monthly magazine. Contact editor David Keen on 01923 236 880
- *Box & Fiddle* – an A5-sized magazine specialising in the Scottish accordion scene, with regular reports from the Accordion & Fiddle Clubs; contact Karin Ingram on 01450 850 262

Accordion Repairs and Tuning The old saying: *"A little knowledge is a dangerous thing,"* could have been coined with reference to the inside of an accordion! Repairing or tuning an accordion is a specialised job, requiring the skills of an experienced person. Anyone requiring the services of a reputable repair or tuning technician should consult any of the entries in the section

Accordion Retailers in the United Kingdom.
Another old saying: *"Prevention is better than cure,"* also firmly applies to musical instruments. A basic understanding of the inside of an accordion should, however, help prevent problems arising and lead to better care of your instrument. Thierry Benetoux, one of France's most experienced and respected tuners/repairers, has written a book, available in the English language, titled *The Inns and Outs of the Accordion,* on the subject of accordion maintenance. The purpose of the book is to help accordionists to understand more fully the inside workings of instruments and also how to avoid typical problems. There are chapters covering the internal workings of an accordion, including the bellows, reeds, reed blocks, leathers, couplers, pallets, bass buttons, right/left hand mechanisms; tuning and standard repairs are also dealt with. There are 264 pages, with hundreds of illustrations and colour photographs.

Accordion Retailers in the United Kingdom
Listed below are the UK's principal accordion retail outlets: -
- **Accordion Centre**
  Rob Beecroft, 131 Midland St, Birmingham B9 4DQ; telephone/fax 0121 753 3709.
- **Accordion Exchange & Music World (UK)**
  17 Marsh Mill Village, Thornton Cleveleys, Blackpool, Lancashire

FY5 4JZ; telephone 01253 822046; fax 01253 863289;
e-mail address – accordions.musicworld@btinternet.com
- **Accordions of Coventry**
  192 Binley Rd, Coventry CV3 1HG; telephone 02476 448933
- **Accordions of London**
  92 Loveridge Rd, Kilburn, London NW6 2DS; telephone 020 7624 9001; e-mail address – johnleslie@accordeons.freeserve.co.uk
- **Chris Algar**: concertina sales/repairs specialist;
  telephone 01782 851449
- **Allodi Accordions**
  143-145 Lee High Rd, Lewisham, London SE13 5PF; telephone & fax 020 8244 3771; website address – www.accordions.co.uk
- **Cooke's Accordions**
  AW Cooke & Son (Music) Ltd, 19 St Benedict's, Norwich, Norfolk NR2 4PE; telephone 01603 625970; fax 01603 630598
- **Geoff Holter Accordions**
  Unit 22, Whessoe Rd, Darlington DL3 OQP; telephone & fax 01325 381223; mobile 0378 335022
- **Hobgoblin Music**
  Main shop & branches – telephone Crawley 01293 515858; London 020 7323 9040; Leeds 0113 245 3311; Manchester 0161 273 1000; Wadebridge 01208 8122; Bristol 0117 929 0902; Nottingham 0115 911 9440; website address- www.hobgoblin.com; mail order telephone hotline 0845 130 9500
- **Jimmy Clinkscale Musicstation**, 81 High St, Galashiels, Scotland. Website: www.clinkscale.co.uk/; telephone 01896 750588
- **John Douglas Music**
  9 Great King St, Dumfries DG1 1BA, Scotland; telephone 01387 256479; fax 01387 249035;
  e-mail address – music@johndouglasmusic.co.uk;
  website address – www.johndouglasmusic.co.uk
- **The Accordion Shop** (a.k.a. **Electronic Accordions Ltd**)
  Verve House, London Rd, Sunningdale, near Ascot, Berkshire SL5 ODJ; telephone 01344 873717. Northern branch: 54 Drake St, Rochdale, Lancashire OL16 1NZ; telephone 01706 658283.
- **Music Corner**
  88 Mary Square, Laurieston, Falkirk FK2 9PP, Scotland; telephone 01324 627100; e-mail address – morag@musiccorner.freeserve.co.uk; website address – www.musiccorner.org.uk
- **The Music Room**
  35 Bradford Rd, Cleckheaton, near Bradford, West Yorkshire BD19 3JN, telephone 01274 879768; fax 01274 852280;
  e-mail address – info@the-music-room.com;
  website address – www.the-music-room.com
- **Rolston Accordions**
  33 Clydesdale St, Mossend, Bellshill ML4 2BS, Scotland;

telephone 01698 733787; fax 01698 734706;
e-mail address – enquiries@accordion.co .uk

- **Thrift Music**
  21 Connaught Ave, Frinton On Sea, Essex CO13 9PN;
  telephone 01255 679232; e-mail address – info@thrift-music.co.uk;
  website address – www.thrift-music.co.uk
- **Trevani**
  14 Mapledale Ave, Croydon DRO 5TB; telephone 020 8656 1450
  fax 020 8409 1461; e-mail – music@trevani.co.uk
- **Watkins Accordions** (a.k.a. **WEM**)
  'Southview,' 3 Biggin Hill, London SE19 3HT; telephone/fax 020
  8679 5575; e-mail address – WEM.Watkins@BTInternet.com
- **West Country Accordions** (a branch of the Hobgoblin folk music
  company) Polmoria House, Polmoria Walk, Wadebridge PL27 7SF;
  telephone 01208 812230; e- mail address - Post@hobgoblin.co.uk
- **Wilkie's Music House** 2/4 Canal Crescent, Perth, Scotland:
  telephone 01738 623041

Accordion Tunings – Straight or Musette?

*Those who are new to the accordion are often confused by the different reed tunings
that exist – straight, tremolo, musette and cassotto. In the article that follows, leading professional Gerald Crossman discusses some of the main considerations.*

Tremolo Tuning and the Cassotto

Accordionists cannot obtain all the tone colours that they might desire
from instruments with only four, or even five, sets of reeds in the treble, though
a very useful number are available on these. It would be necessary to have more
voices to cover all the possibilities that might be required, but it is not practical
as it would make an accordion too bulky and expensive.

When a player buys an instrument, one of the main points to be considered
is the type of music that will usually be performed on it. This leads to further questions such as: - how many sets of reeds? What combination of sets? Should any sets
be in cassotto (special resonance tone chamber)? Is the accordion to be straight,
mild (slight or fine) tremolo, or musette (strong tremolo) tuned? And so on.

True French musette tuning requires three 8' pitch sets of reeds not in
cassotto. One set is tuned sharp to the normal pitch set, and one set is tuned flat.
With proper tuning, a nice, even 'tremolo' results. The amount of tremolo
depends on the difference between the pitches.

A number of professional accordionists possess a musette-tuned accordion in addition to their usual straight-tuned or mild tremolo-tuned instrument.
The extra accordion is retained for use in special musical items only. Orchestral
players know that a strong tremolo is by no means ideal for normal orchestral
or dance band use.

Two 8' pitch sets of reeds cannot give the true musette tone, however tuned, though with one set slightly sharp they can provide a useful mild tremolo tone for general purposes, as, for example, in certain continental-style items, and in blending with violins.

Absolutely straight tone tends to be akin to a singer or string-instrumentalist performing without any vibrato whatsoever, resulting in a rather uninteresting sound in some circumstances.

An 8' set in cassotto, and one 8' set out of cassotto, with individual couplers (registers) gives a choice of single-reed tones when tuned identically. These two sets played together in unison strengthen the normal pitch straight tone. If tremolo tuned (slightly sharp open set) and played together, they will provide a tremolo with a slightly sharp bias, but of course their qualities are not equal. Tremolo tuned with individual couplers for each set allows a choice of pitch if this should prove necessary!

Accordions without cassotto but fitted with a grille blind or shutter mute have certain advantages over those with cassotto in allowing more variations of tone colour, and in matching up all sets at once. When the mute is in use, an imitation of the cassotto tone is achieved to some extent because the 'edge' of the open tone is reduced.

It should not be forgotten that the tremolo can be omitted when desired by means of the couplers, leaving just the straight-tuned sets, but this naturally diminishes the presence of the 8' pitch voice and alters the balance.

Gerald Crossman, Accordion Times, August 1962

Adamson, Deirdre. Scotland's Deirdre Adamson began playing the accordion and piano whilst very young, and was a solo entertainer, accordion champion and recording artiste by the time she reached secondary school. This explains why she seems to have been around forever! Deirdre is an extremely competent concert accordionist who has played in accordion clubs all around Great Britain including Jersey. Her playing is technically accurate, neatly phrased and expressive, and her repertoire extends beyond Scottish traditional music into the music of European and Latin American countries, with some classical stuff thrown in now and again to provide extra contrast. Deirdre has made many excellent recordings, and has arranged and composed pieces – all of which have been published by her father, Doug, under the trade name Deeay Music.

Selected discography: *Off She Goes* (1983), *Swinging Along* (1986); *Deirdre's Fancy*; *Magic Fingers* (1990); *Grand Slam*; *Encore!* (1994); *Homeward Bound* (1996); *Come Scottish Country Dancing*; *Come Ceilidh Dancing* (1997); *The Perfect Blend* (1998); *Come Old Time Ceilidh Dancing* (1999); *Deirdre Adamson Plays Mainly Scottish* (2000).

Adler, Larry.   (1914-2001) American-born Larry Adler was one of the music world's great characters, often quoted by the media on a wide variety of topics ranging from sport to politics. As a teenager, he entered the Conservatory of Music in Baltimore, but was thrown out for playing *Yes, We Have No Bananas* instead of Grieg at a recital! After this, he moved to New York where he was discovered by the singer Rudy Vallee, who gave Larry his first show business break playing at a club. From this point on, 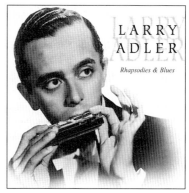 Larry Adler's great talent and adaptability enabled him to make progress in the music world, and he came into contact with the likes of George Gershwin, Charlie Chaplin, Greta Garbo, Ingrid Bergman (with whom he had an affair), Jack Benny, Salvador Dali, and the legendary gangster, Al Capone. Adler performed and recorded with Gershwin, most notably on a duet of Gershwin's *Rhapsody in Blue*, after which the composer famously commented to Adler: *"the god-damned thing sounds as though I wrote it for you."*

In the late 1930s, Larry Adler visited Europe, a highlight being the opportunity to play jazz and record with the legendary Quintet of the Hot Club of France. A 1939 recording of Gershwin's *I Got Rhythm* is especially notable for the brilliant jazz solo breaks by Adler's harmonica, Django Reinhardt's guitar and Stephane Grappelli on piano (rather than his usual violin).

During World War Two, Adler entertained Allied troops in Europe, the main highlight being a performance of *Rhapsody in Blue* in the infamous Nuremberg Stadium. This was a Jewish musician playing music by a Jewish composer in the same place where Hitler had rallied the Nazi masses only a few years before.

After the war, Adler was blacklisted during the so-called anti-communist 'witch-hunt' and summoned to appear before the Senate Un-American Activities Committee. He refused, commenting later that: *"The only way to get off that blacklist was to go before the Committee and shop your friends. There was no way I was going to do that. I'd been in trouble before. At our shows during the war, they always tried to segregate the audiences, keeping the white and black soldiers apart. I told them that I wouldn't appear unless they were mixed. This hadn't gone unnoticed."* In 1949, Adler left the USA to live in London, largely to get away from the political atmosphere, and he became permanently resident in Britain.

Even in Britain, Larry Adler could not shake off the McCarthyite zeal, and in 1953 when he wrote and played the now famous theme music for the British-made film *Genevieve*, his name was omitted at the Hollywood Oscar awards ceremony, and also from the original film credits. For the rest of his life, Adler was to be a thorn in the side of successive American administrations, especially during the Vietnam War, to which he was vehemently opposed.

In Britain, Adler became part of the music establishment, and this was made manifest when he performed *Romance for Harmonica and Orchestra*, written for him by Ralph Vaughan Williams, and premiered at the BBC Henry Wood Proms in September 1952 with the BBC Symphony Orchestra, conducted by Sir Malcolm Sargent. In later years, Adler performed *Rhapsody in Blue* at the BBC Proms to the accompaniment of a piano roll made by Gershwin himself – something that Adler described as a very strange experience.

In the 1960s Larry Adler became a Vice President of the NAO, and performed at the evening concerts at *'Accordion Day'* on more than one occasion. He championed the cause of the harmonica, and with his forthright views on life and music was always an interesting guest whenever he was interviewed on the radio or on television chat shows.

One of Adler's last musical projects was the recording *The Glory of Gershwin*, a salute to the great man of American music. Initially, Adler thought he would involve Sting and Elton John, and (to use his own words): *"When they said yes, I was away – they were all clamouring to get on board."* Eventually, the maestro featured the vocal talents of such famous modern-day singers as Peter Gabriel, Chris de Burgh, Sting, Carly Simon, Cher, Jon Bon Jovi, Kate Bush, Meatloaf, Willard White, Sinead O'Connor, Oleta Adams, Robert Palmer, Issy Van Randwyk, Elvis Costello, Lisa Stansfield, Elton John, and the trumpeter, Courtney Pine. The last number was Adler performing *Rhapsody in Blue*, backed by an orchestra conducted by George Martin, of Beatles' fame. What became Larry Adler's last album stemmed from his long-felt despondent feeling that *"too many young people today have never even heard of this guy George Gershwin. Do you know he was only 39 when he died? All the artistes treated the songs with respect. I tell you one thing, I never knew there were so many good singers around."*

Larry Adler passed away in 2001, admired and respected for his lifetime contribution to the world of music and the harmonica.

Selected discography: *The Glory of Gershwin* (1995); *Larry Adler – Rhapsodies & Blues* (1998); *The Larry Adler Collection* (2000)

Adriano, Pearl. Pearl Adriano, previously known as **Pearl Fawcett**, comes from Barnsley, and attended the Royal College of Music in Manchester where she studied the pianoforte. After graduation, she taught the piano and the accordion at the college for a while before becoming a professional musician. Pearl entered and won many accordion championships, and went to Ancona, Italy, in 1961 where she won the CMA version of the Junior World Championship. The following year, 1962, Pearl won the senior CMA World Championship, after which she became a full-time professional accordionist and pianist.

In the accordion world, she was one of the pioneers of the electronic accordion, and was active around the country doing demonstrations on behalf of

Farfisa. She was also featured every Sunday afternoon on Charlie Chester's programme on BBC Radio 2 during the 1970s and 80s, usually playing French musette with a unique mixture of acoustic musette plus additional electronic sounds. Pearl is also a highly skilled performer of classical music, and her concerts present well-known classical masterpieces using the full range of acoustic and electronic voices available on her electronic accordion. In 1984, she and Russian Bayan maestro, Yuri Kasakov, did a short tour of this country, and a souvenir LP was issued of studio recordings featuring Pearl on one side and Kasakov on the

other. Pearl has performed concerts in many countries, including the USSR, where her music has been especially appreciated.

One of Pearl's most impressive projects in recent years has been her *Ettore Fantasia*, a CD featuring solo arrangements of a cross-section of the music of the Italian-American composer/accordionist, the late Eugene Ettore. Ettore was stylistically an heir to the musical traditions of the two great Pietros, Frosini and Deiro. On this recording, Pearl excels herself, even by her own high standards, to produce a recording that really does justice to the music of this wonderful accordion composer. A triumph for Pearl, and for Ettore.

In recent times, Pearl has assumed the name Pearl Adriano, and most of her playing engagements have been abroad.

Selected discography: *Accordion Tapestry* (1982) – an LP of classical music favourites using electronic and acoustic accordion sounds; *Musette Parisienne* (1982); *Music on the Move* (1985); *Viva Frosini* (1986) – a cassette of Frosini pieces; *Ettore Fantasia* (1999); *Allegria Continentale* (2001) – a CD containing a mixture of French musette, accordion classics and classical music.

Advice for the Aspiring Accordionist.

In the following article, writing as one who has played in a wide variety of situations, including restaurants, French and Italian themed evenings, parties, musical shows, school shows, in a Bavarian band, as an accompanist for English, Irish and Polish dancing, in a folk group, and in several ceilidh bands, I make the following points in the hope that they will be of use to other accordionists: -

1) When practising, try to be correct in all aspects of your music, playing your pieces through slowly and with as much accuracy as possible. *'Practice makes perfect'* is an often-quoted phrase, but not necessarily true! However, if that hoary old saying is re-phrased to *'Perfect practice makes perfect,'* we are much closer to the truth. In other words, if you know you make mistakes, try not to rehearse them so many times over that they become a habit you can't break!

2) My experience has been that short but frequent practice sessions are

more fruitful than occasional long practices. Skill is accumulated more quickly, and retained, if you pick up your accordion frequently.

3) Pay attention to any phrase marks on your music, and if there aren't any, phrase in two or four bars. Good phrasing is vital if you are to bring out the expression in your pieces, whatever the genre – Scottish, Irish, French, jazz, classical, etc.

4) Know where your couplers are, and use them. Using a variety of couplers will make your playing sound more interesting.

5) Do not spend all your time studying only examination and/or contest pieces, especially if you want to play in public or at parties. Playing before the general public, including friends and family, means knowing a few pieces that your listeners are familiar with. I recall some years ago watching a well-known and brilliant accordionist performing a piece of Latin American music on the television talent show *New Faces*, and being enthralled by his performance. As soon as the music finished I asked my brother-in-law what he thought, and have always remembered his reply: *"He might be brilliant, but he won't win. The public don't want virtuosity, they want to be entertained."* And so it was – the accordionist didn't win, or even come close. In similar vein is the fact that Max Bygraves, because of his evergreen, popular repertoire, sells as many records as any of the great singers, from Presley to Pavarotti. The point of all this is that choosing the right repertoire is more important than developing a virtuosic technique if you want to entertain the public. (Please note that this is not any kind of a crusade against virtuoso players or their music!)

6) Try to learn some pieces by heart. By doing so, you will end up really knowing your pieces that much better. Learning by heart can be done if you take your sheet music and learn two bars at a time, and a patient approach will pay off.

7) Playing 'by ear' is a great skill to have, and can be learned by sitting on a sofa or a comfortable chair and slowly picking out simple, well known tunes on the treble keyboard. Once you have gone through a tune, find a different starting note and play it in a different key. Here again, a patient approach is necessary.

8) Playing in public gives you an incentive to practise. Doing a tune or two at your local accordion club or folk club is a good way to get experience of playing in front of an audience where your efforts will be appreciated. The same can be said of playing in concerts at a junior school or nursing home. Once you have experienced the atmosphere and pleasure of performing in a concert, no matter how small your contribution, you will feel uplifted and gratified.

9) If and when an opportunity comes along to play in public, if possible take it. Don't put yourself down by thinking that you are not good enough – otherwise you could easily spend the rest of your life waiting for the day when you are ready! As Mark Twain, the famous 19th Century American novelist (and accordion player) once said: *"Twenty*

years from now you will be more disappointed by the things you <u>didn't</u> do than by the ones you did,"

10) Once you have started playing in public, you will need to build a large repertoire, and a lot of well-known pieces will be required. This means looking beyond music specially composed or arranged for accordion, and looking at books of tunes arranged for organs/keyboards. Music books such as *101 Hits for Buskers*, plus similar titles, published by Wise, will be very useful, as will books in *The Easy Keyboard Library*, published by IMP. These books offer lots of famous numbers, and include chord symbols. Building a repertoire will, of course, take time – so, once again, be patient. *"Rome wasn't built in a day"* is an old saying, but true when applied in the context of musical development.

11) When playing in public, put on a confident attitude and refuse to be over-awed by a place or situation. Go out on stage and act as if you own the place! I remember many years ago appearing in a Folk Night concert one evening at a school where I taught, and openly expressing anxiety about how the audience would react to me – half expecting and fearing the worst. A teaching colleague called Mike Neill, an experienced singer/guitarist also on the bill, wisely pointed out to me *"most people in the audience don't know a crotchet from a bottle of ketchup, so why worry?"* Of course, he was right, and there really was nothing to worry about – and the audience were actually very appreciative of the fact that some of the teachers and pupils were there to put on some entertainment.

12) If playing for others, practise your pieces a lot so that you can go out and relax and actually enjoy what you are doing. Preparation of the right kind will make this possible. Another point is – if at all possible - to smile while you are playing. This can be achieved with practice, and will enhance your rapport with your audience. Someone very wise once said that *'A smile is the shortest distance between two people."* How True!

13) If you find yourself playing for dancing, you will need to play in a steady tempo – whatever the style of music or dancing. Keeping a steady tempo is a skill in itself, requiring much practice. Actual experience of dancing is very useful indeed for anyone who plays for dancing, enabling the musician to appreciate the subtleties of tempo and movements.

14) Playing for dancing, also for concerts, is likely to involve playing tunes in medleys. If you are putting tunes together in medley form, it is generally a good idea to vary the key signatures as this will help to prevent a monotonous sound for everyone, including the musicians. Changing couplers every now and then similarly helps to keep your music varied, and prevents monotony setting in.

15) Listen to other players whenever you can, in performance or on CD/cassette. These do not necessarily have to be other accordion players – there is much to learn about performance, repertoire, instrumentation and stage presentation from guitarists, pianists, organists, jazz

bands, orchestras, etc. For example, Harry Hussey, accordion entertainer and master improviser par excellence, bases his left hand technique on how guitarists provide accompaniment. There is a lot of benefit to be obtained from listening to/observing other musicians.

Rob Howard (June 2003)

Ahvennainen, Veikko   Finland is a country where the accordion is popular and playing standards are generally high. It is therefore surprising that relatively few Finnish accordionists travel abroad or are known in other countries. An exception to this, however, is Veikko Ahvennainen, an accordionist who has played in Britain, the USA, Russia, plus numerous other places. He plays a 5-row accordion, and is as equally at home with traditional folk dance tunes as he is with classical music by the great composers. In America, Ahvennainen became friendly with fellow concert accordionist John Molinari, and recorded several LPs on the record label owned by Molinari. These records subsequently spread Ahvennainen's musical reputation in the USA and Canada, and also in Britain through Malcolm Gee's Accordion Record Club. Veikko Ahvennainen has appeared in Britain, principally at Caister in 1991, where his superb playing is almost matched by his witty and dry sense of humour. Ahvennainen looks basically very serious, and his humour takes people by surprise, and is all the more effective for it. This writer has a vivid memory of him conducting a master class at Blackpool, and whilst singing and playing the song *Over The Waves*, commenting in his very broken English: *"I not Pavarotti"* in such a droll manner that the onlookers all fell about laughing. He had a timing only possessed by the best comedians.

Selected discography: *Best of Pietro Frosini* – an LP made using a 1930s accordion to add special authenticity; *Accordion Variety Concert; Bach-Handel; Metsakukkia* – a CD containing Finnish traditional tunes plus two pieces by Pietro Frosini.

Alexander Brothers, The   Jack and Tom Alexander turned professional in 1958, and have purveyed their selections of Scottish songs (on vocals & accordion) with great and consistent success ever since. They have travelled abroad, appeared on television and radio, and made a large number of recordings and videos. Their repertoire and style is very much the impression the average tourist has of 'Bonnie Scotland' – full of mist, haggis and heather! Tom Alexander was an All-Scotland Accordion Champion in1958, and he occasionally makes solo appearances in accordion clubs where his brilliant playing is heard to full effect. Tom's solo accordion CD *The Flying Scotsman* is a mixture of Scottish and other accordion music, and has been critically acclaimed.

Selected discography: *At Your Request* (1975); *Tribute to Sir Harry Lauder* (1986); *Flower of Scotland* (1990); *Best of the Alexander Brothers* (1992); *The Flying Scotsman* – solo accordion recording (2001)

Video: *Song of the Clyde* (1992)

Amplification   *The author is indebted to Charlie Watkins, Britain's leading authority on the subject of accordion amplification, for the following article: -*

Accordion Amplification: The Art of being Heard

The delightful and innate problem with the sound of the accordion is its own individuality and characteristic sound format.

Were the response curves, attack and general ambience changed to make it comply with that accepted as the norm, it would be as easy to amplify the accordion as it is the guitar, piano or voice, etc.

But likewise, this change of character would distance it from those who love the sound as it is and would send us all looking for what we have lost with all its nuances of mellow, delicate and singular acoustic 'flavours' and, yes, irregularities too.

So we are left with an instrument capable of extreme tonal facets. A power potential curve exceeding that of most other instruments. A response of 'attack' potential that would leave keyboard amplifiers gasping in dismay and inadequacy.

Start at the beginning, and acknowledge that, as is the way of the world, we accordionists have also inherited the 'not so perfect' sound source.

For instance, played on its own as a solo instrument it's fine in the front room or a secluded and sparsely populated area, everything is fine.

Given an audience of 50, a hundred or more, and the deficiencies begin to show through.

Given again the high level of ambient noise and chatter from a Barn Dance or Ceilidh gathering or pub and you'll begin to see what I mean.

YES! I mean NO! You can no longer hear the qualities and character that I've been rabbiting on about.

Your serried, compacted battalions of internal reeds, abundant in number as they are lacking in size and individual power output are now sadly behind in audibility.

Compared with the power and authority of the great, wooden clarinet reed for instance or the percussive impact of the piano or double bass strings with their great length we are absolute non-starters. Add to that the shortage of strength in your left arm to pump multiples of these reeds into life shows through – the heavier bass reeds grabbing most of the energies which should be shared by the floating, delicate outputs from the treble reeds which your right hand multiplies copiously to generate the exquisite chords which give the accordion its great mellow and influential characteristic.

Listeners at the back of the audience are

Watkins 'Song Bird ' Accordion Amp.
100 watts output. Six inputs. Specialised Accordion channel . Hi Fi or vocal channel. Four Midi (or other instrument) channels. Soft coned 10" speaker and treble horn.

Jack Emblow, Harry Hussey, Frank Marocco and most leading players use them so I suppose it's all right. Weight 11 Kgs.

in dismay. They are unable to hear anything but scraps of what you are trying to get through to them.

When this happens you've got one of two options open.

Stop playing at those venues, or get an amplifier.

Let's assume you go for an amplifier.

Choose one that is small and powerful. The chances are that, like me, you are past your heavyweight lifting days.

Don't decide, or be advised, that *'an amplifier is an amplifier is an amplifier'* because it's not. No way.

If you finish up with an amplifier which has been designed to pander to, and capture, the guitar market – you'll have a hard coned, harsh and 'toppy' sound and output which, when faced with your delicate accordion wave forms will be at a loss to know what to do with them.

Forget 15" speakers (with their associated weight and size) because a 15-inch cone won't do it for you, despite what the salesman says.

Don't go for outputs in excess of 100 or 150 watts because it's extra weight and doesn't do anything for you.

Remember that the frequencies and minute harmonics being generated by your accordion are absolutely essential to the beauty of the accordion sound genre.

Overpower them or leave them underpowered and you'll have lost it. Believe it or not.

Illustrated is a specific and dedicated accordion amplifier. Made by me, I'm afraid, but you don't have to buy it if you don't like it.

In which case go looking for a good voice style amplifier, or similar flat response *Hi Fi* type of unit. You won't find what you want in the guitar, keyboard, or general amplifier areas – that way lies disaster.

Having got your amplifier, don't tear into it and assume that now you've done *your* part, now it's down to the magic of the amplifier, so plug it in and away you go!

It doesn't happen like that.

First you need an internal microphone of "pick up" or a stand-alone microphone.

There are several accordion mics on the market and millions of the stand alone sort, so if you go for one of *them* you'd do well to remember that you'll be best served with a studio type condenser with a strong pick up sensitivity.

None of your Shure SM 58 or Beyer highly directional much vaunted and equally hopeless units.

Always use a 'protected' circuit breaking plug board. Study the sounds and tonal setting, which emanate from the FRONT of the amplifier – not the back. (That's an entirely different sound)

If and when you get a whistling sound, that's because you're in or you have to much Treble set on the control or because your pick up or mic is inadequate. Get rid of *that* for a start – very audience stressful.

If your audience or venue is particularly large take an output from your amplifier and plug it in to the house system (in which case make sure the operator of that knows what he's doing).

Try to arrange your amplifier to be to your side and slightly facing in to you so that you get your ear on the sound, which the audience is getting from the *FRONT* of the amplifier. This technique, you'll find is also very stimulating to your playing performance.

Now you're in with a chance to let your audience *HEAR* the best sound there is – that of the ACCORDION.

Charlie Watkins, W.E.M. (London, September 2003)

Anderson, Alistair Born in 1948. Originally finding fame as a member of the *High Level Ranters*, a song & dance band specialising in the folk songs and dance tunes of their native North East of England, Anderson became a high profile solo artist featuring the English concertina and Northumbrian pipes. He recalls that when he announced that he was giving up his career as a school-teacher to become solo concertina player back in 1972, people who knew him thought he was mad. When asked years later how he managed to establish himself as soloist, his reply was a simple *"You just go out and do it. The only thing you can do is be prepared to play anywhere in the country."* A virtuoso on the concertina, Alistair Anderson has set new standards on his instrument, and is always in great demand at folk clubs and festivals in this country and abroad. In 1974 produced a tutor plus accompanying LP for the English concertina. Since then, Anderson has occasionally given workshops at folk festivals and been a tutor at specialist summer schools, passing on some of his vast expertise to others, especially young people.
Selected Discography: *Concertina Workshop* (1974); *Alistair Anderson Plays English Concertina* (1981); *Lookin' for Apples* (1981); *Steel Skies* (1982); *Grand Chain* (1988)

Anderton, Sir James In the late 1960s, while serving as Assistant Chief Constable of Leicestershire, James Anderton became friendly with Francis Wright, then Principal of the British College of Accordionists. In 1972 Anderton became Chairman of the BCA's newly established Governing Council. He then steered the BCA through the legal processes required to establish the College as a Company Limited by Guarantee, and as a Registered Charity. In 1977 Anderton became Chief Constable of Greater Manchester, after which he then became Vice President of the BCA, and then President in 1984. During his tenure as Chief Constable of GMP, Anderton became a highly controversial figure for his outspoken views on law and order, homosexuality, drugs and many other subjects, and his name was seldom away from the media. He had an especially difficult relationship with the ruling Labour Council in Manchester, and his high media profile only eased off when he retired from the police in 1991, the year he was knighted for his services to law and order. In 1992 Sir James Anderton and his wife became Patrons of the BCA, and Albert Delroy succeeded him as President of the College.

Antonio Antonio, real name Tony Lowe, was a pupil of Adrian Dante, and a regular performer in hotels and restaurants in London in the 1970s to 1990s. He used a Musettina electronic accordion, and was a highly competent musician. His repertoire mainly featured Continental and Latin American music, though he was actually more versatile than that. In 1983 he recorded *Restless Fingers*, a solo LP of the sort of music he played in his work, and Adrian Dante produced this on his Caravelle record label. In 1997, Tony Lowe was tragically murdered in his own home.
Discography: *Restless Fingers* (1983); track listing – *Cin Cin Polka, Cuballero, Caprice, Marsala Bella, Simple Et Musette, Samba Polka, Restless Fingers, Luci E Ombre, Dark Eyes, Interrogation, Bouquet, Valse Des As.*

Back-strap A back strap is a piece of leather, or substitute material, used to hold together the straps of an accordion across the shoulder blades or the lower back. Its main functions are to increase stability of the instrument and to take some of the weight off the back and shoulders. Many players find the use of a back-strap essential, and this simple accessory is easily obtainable via any accordion dealer.

Bandoneon The bandoneon is a free reed instrument closely related to both the accordion and concertina. The instrument takes its name from its 19th Century inventor, Heinrich Band, a German who came from the town of Krefeld. The bandoneon became widespread first in central Europe and later it became popular in Argentina where it is primarily associated with that country's fascination with the tango. The bandoneon exists in several button key versions, and in both chromatic and diatonic sytems. The most well-known and accomplished bandoneon player in recent times is Argentina's Astor Piazzola, a world travelled exponent of the tango. In London, however, Albert Delroy – better known as a musette accordionist and composer – was also a skilled bandoneonist.

The picture shows Andy Banks wearing a special 4-row Shand Morino owned by the late Will Starr

Banks, Andy Born in Wick in the north of Scotland, but resident in Birmingham for so long that his accent is 'Brummie' rather than Highland Scots, Andy Banks is a devotee of the Shand Morino 3-row accordion. The article on the **Shand Morino** found in this book has been prepared and contributed by Andy.

Andy Banks plays traditional music, is essentially self-taught, and reckons that the only teacher he has ever had was Jimmy Shand himself! This came about some years ago when Andy was travelling through Fife, and decided he would try to locate the great man, who lived in Auchtermuchty. He found Shand's address by asking the attendant in a petrol station, and soon afterwards found himself receiving a two-hour virtual 'masterclass' from the Scottish legend. Jimmy Shand made some simple playing suggestions that Andy says improved his playing standard incredibly, leaving him wondering why he had never thought of these things himself! Andy's main contribution to the accordion scene is his long-term dedication to the Midlands-based Club Accord, stretching back to the mid-1970s, not long after the club's formation by Malcolm Gee. Lots of people come and go as members of accordion clubs, but it is people such as Andy who are the real backbone due to an unstinting loyalty and interest.

Barbour, Freeland Piano accordionist in the original line-up of Silly Wizard, Perth-born Freeland Barbour went on to form the Wallochmor Ceilidh Band in 1977 together with Sandy Coghill on three-row button accordion. This band was innovative in featuring two lead accordions rather than the usual practice of 1st and 2nd accordions, extra amplification and a slightly faster tempo than average. The Wallochmor's first LP *Looking for a Partner* sold well, and was followed by other recordings. Some years later, Barbour formed another ceilidh band, The Occasionals, and more recording and performing success followed, beginning with a CD titled *Footnotes*. Apart from his band work, Freeland Barbour has performed extensively in Scandinavia and the USA, and he has worked for many years in record production. He has also been a BBC radio producer of programmes such *Take the Floor* and *The Reel Blend*, to name but two.

Barwell, Hugh (Born 1948) York-based Hugh Barwell has played accordion gigs of various kinds for more than two decades, some using midi sounds and others using purely acoustic accordion. He was originally a bassoon player, attaining all eight grades on that instrument and playing in a youth orchestra. An interest in the music of the Beatles led Hugh to take up the guitar, and studying French at university also led him in the direction of the accordion. More recently, an interest in electronics and computers has facilitated knowledge of accordion midi systems, and Hugh has now written four books offering help to would-be midi accordionists.
Books: *Overview of the Roland RA-800; User Guide for the Roland RA-800; Guide for the Roland RA-90; Guide for the ORLA XM600.* Telephone: 01904 656 857; e-mail address: hugh@hbarwell.freeserve.co.uk

Bass Keyboards The majority of piano accordions and Continental chromatic accordions use Stradella bass keyboards, though in recent years there has been an increase in number and availability of these instruments fitted with free bass left hand systems. A few instruments are also made featuring both Stradella and free bass left hands, and these are known as converter systems. The Stradella bass is also to be found on British Chromatic button accordions. There are variations of both the Stradella and free bass systems, though these are rarely to be found on instruments sold in this country.

Melodeons and diatonic button accordions, other than British Chromatic models, have diatonic left hand configurations using only a small number of bass buttons that are completely different to Stradella or free bass systems. See also **Free Bass** and **Stradella**.

Bassetti Bassetti is an alternative name for a free bass accordion, commonly in use until the 1980s, but rarely used since.

Bavarian Bands The establishment of *bierkellers* and holiday camps in the late 1940s spawned the formation of Bavarian bands, also known as 'Oompah bands.' These were generally small combos that played sing-along music and used comedy routines, often with a fake, over-the-top Bavarian persona and they often poked fun at German mannerisms. The routines and repertoires of these bands tend to be similar, frequently offending both political correctness and the race relations laws – often simultaneously! Some Bavarian bands have developed from the ranks of brass bands, generally recognisable by having more players than the three, four or five piece outfits that have set themselves up primarily to play 'Bavarian' routines. The writer recalls watching the bemused faces of some Germans in the audience at Caister Accordion Festival in 1986, as the front man of the Karl Braun Oompah Band went through his comedy routine, dressed like the German Kaiser and with a string of giant fake sausages draped around his shoulders! The average Bavarian band features an accordionist, a tuba or sousaphone player and a front man, whose job it is to sing, make jokes and get the audience singing and joining in the fun. The Manchester-based *Baron Wolfgang Bavarian Band*, led by the late Stan Walker, claims to have been the very first of the British bands in this genre. This band played 28 consecutive summer seasons for Butlins and Pontins at their holiday camps. Well-known accordion luminary Barry Dawson is another fine musician who worked as a Bavarian-type entertainer, as does Jersey-based accordion/vocals entertainer, Steve Roxton. Malcolm Gee regularly used Bavarian bands at his festivals, principally to provide lightweight accordion-led entertainment as counterpoint to the serious accordion artistes on the bills. In 1984, Malcolm Gee produced a record by *The Bavarian Steinswingers* on his ARC label, playing music minus their comedy routine. In the 1990s, the steady closure of many *bierkellers* across the country and a drastic decline in the number of live music acts booked by the holiday camps has greatly reduced the work for Bavarian bands, though many continue to play in social clubs and for private functions.

Bayan Until the Perestroika & Glasnost years of the late 1980s, very few people outside the USSR had either seen or heard of a Bayan accordion. The thawing of East-West relations, however, led to Russian musicians becoming well known on this side of what used to be, to recall Winston Churchill's famous phrase, *The Iron Curtain*. The word 'bayan' is actually the Russian word for accordion, but the Bayan (button) type of accordion has its own sound, with a wide musical range that can sound very resonant – suitable not only for Russian traditional folk music, but also the classics. The layout of the treble keyboard is similar to a B system Continental chromatic, and many instruments also feature a convertor bass system, facilitating a tremendous range of music.

Russia's Oleg Sharov, through his constant touring involving appearances at accordion clubs and festivals, has done more than anyone to popularise the Bayan accordion. Another Russian-born Bayan player becoming well known in this country is the London-based Nikolai Ryskov. A book called *The Art of Bayan Playing* (available in English, German or Russian), published in 1985 by Friedrich Lips, arguably the world's foremost expert on the subject, has done much to raise the profile of Bayan accordions and its playing technique worldwide.

Be a Better Player *Rosemary Wright, who has more experience than most at teaching music and the accordion, wrote some excellent articles for the Accordion Times on the subject of improving one's playing. An abridged version of these articles is presented here, with kind permission of the author.*

Introduction.

It is never too late to start aiming for perfection. Even if you will never reach Virtuoso standard, you will get far more out of your playing if what you are doing is correct. Observance of good habits will make new pieces so much easier to learn, and will thus give you greater satisfaction and enjoyment.

A word of warning, though. The quest for perfection must never become a misery or an obsession. You must still enjoy the practising and playing that you do, and should not be too disappointed when perfection is not achieved. I assume, therefore, that you are anxious to improve, wherever possible, upon your present capabilities, without aiming for a higher standard than you can, at this stage, reasonably achieve.

There is a lot of truth in the saying that *"Every person is an individual"*, but at the same time there are certain faults and problems which occur all too frequently in many people's playing, and it is my intention in this series to cover the main aspects of accordion-playing. If you find that you already do what I suggest, then this should be of some reassurance to you.

Accuracy of pitch and timing.

Have you ever heard the late Les Dawson's piano playing, or listened to the Portsmouth Symphonia? If you have, then you may well believe that playing the right notes is not really important! Not so. Whether you play from music, or *'by ear'*, you should always try to keep to the composer's ideas, and this includes playing the correct notes in the correct timing and rhythm.

One reason for playing the wrong notes can be the use of faulty fingering. The other main cause is incorrect reading. Granted, any of us can make mistakes like that, but, on the whole, by being as careful and observant as possible when learning a new piece, we should be able to get very near to the truth. Here are a few *"dos"* and *"Don'ts"*:

1) DO notice the key signature before you begin, because it is essential to the tonality of the piece.
2) DO remember that accidentals apply throughout the bar, unless cancelled during that bar (even advanced players forget!).
3) DO check bass notes and chords.
4) DO listen to what you play. Your ear should tell you whether it sounds right or wrong.
5) DO look at the time signature also before beginning to play, and ensure that you understand the note values used. (Remember – a crotchet does not always equal one beat).
6) DO learn a piece slowly before trying to play it quicker.
7) DON'T start a piece at one tempo, then speed up or slow down as passages vary in difficulty. It is best to play the whole piece at the speed at which the most difficult passages can be played with ease – not very exciting, perhaps, but worthwhile in the long run.
8) DON'T be satisfied with *"just anything"*. By not playing accurately, you are failing to portray the composer's ideas authentically.

Use your bellows correctly.

Does the sound of an accordion being played badly make you cringe? Well, next time this happens to you, don't just reach for your earplugs. Ask yourself instead, *why* it sounds bad, and the answer is nearly always that the player has little or no idea of bellows control. Sometimes I wonder whether people who claim to dislike the accordion do so because they have heard the instrument (regardless of the keyboard system) played in this manner.

The bellows are, of course, essential to the generation of sound, since they cause air to be passed through the reeds in order to produce the notes that are played (this is comparable to the function of the lungs of a singer or wind-instrumentalist). Furthermore, control of the bellows also affects phrasing, dynamics and articulation, yet far too many players – and teachers – give it such a low priority. Is it any wonder that examiners and adjudicators criticise faulty bellows control more than anything else?

I seem to have acquired a reputation for being very particular about good bellows control (ask my pupils!), but I honestly believe that whatever type of music you play on the accordion, it will sound so much better if you handle the bellows properly. Obviously, it makes sense to acquire good habits right from the start, but if there is still room for improvement in your own bellows control, then it is not too late to change your ways! You don't need to be an expert or a 'serious' player to bother about bellows control, because by following these simple guidelines, anyone can achieve success: -

• Bellows direction should be changed tidily i.e. *never* during a note (unless specifically requested by a composer for a special effect). A jerky sound must be avoided at all costs.
• Bellows direction should be changed, as far as possible, *between*

phrases, since this is more musical. It is always wise to mark the bellows changes on the music.

- Bellows direction in an introduction needs some thought, since the first subject proper should be commenced with an outward bellows movement.
- At the end of a study or piece, the bellows should be closed, or almost closed. This not only shows clear musical thinking, but also looks tidier.
- Where regular changes cannot be made, such as in polyphonic playing, the bellows changes must be made discreetly, and where they can least disrupt the flow of the music.
- Good co-ordination between fingers and bellows in achieving effective articulation is essential.
- It is worthwhile experimenting with the bellows to discover the dynamic range of the instrument. Obviously, the harder one pulls, the louder the sound. A crescendo or diminuendo effect needs practice to achieve a _gradual_ change of volume, likewise, a very soft start to a note can only be achieved by pressing down the note _before_ pulling the bellows just enough to produce a sound.

Articulation.

Articulation is the manner in which the notes themselves are played, and is necessary to give definition to your playing. It is comparable to the vocal inflections in speech. Usually, it is clearly indicated by signs over or under the notes (dots, short lines, slurs, accents, etc), which direct us to join notes smoothly, or detach them, or emphasize them, and so on. (_'Touch'_ refers to the actual physical action involved in articulating the notes, and since it can only be applied to keyboard instruments, it does not have exactly the same meaning as _'Articulation'_).

Sometimes articulation details and phrasing slurs are shown. The former, placed below the notes, should be observed as instructions for playing the notes themselves, whereas the large slurs (above the notes) indicate how the music is divided up, and thus, where to change the bellows.

Phrasing.

This enables us to make sense of the music, and to give it shape and meaning, for the benefit of both players and listeners. Phrases in music are comparable to sentences in literature, although they are usually equal in length. They are often clearly marked on the music by large slurs, and will help to give both a balanced idea of the piece generally, as well as a good indication of bellows movement. Remember that phrases do not always begin on the first beat of a bar!

A further aid to good interpretation is the shaping of a phrase, using dynamic contrast. Where no specific instructions are given regarding dynamics within a phrase, it is advisable to make a slight gradual increase in volume (crescendo) leading to the most important note in the phrase (climax), then to _'round off'_ the phrase with a slight decrease in volume (diminuendo). Again, careful control of the bellows is essential here.

Dynamics.

Variations in volume add further interest to a performance, and this is governed by bellows control. The harder you pull or push the bellows, the louder the sound produced, and as I have mentioned before, you need to experiment to know your instrument's capabilities.

The range of dynamics within a piece should be taken into account, and kept in proportion. They are relative to each different piece; for example, *'mf'* could be the loudest volume in one piece, but the softest in another, and they would vary slightly if measured in decibels.

'Crescendo' and *'diminuendo'* need care, because the change in volume must be gradual and consistent. Accordionists tend to find the *'diminuendo'* harder, but it is worth persevering to achieve an effective *'easing off'* of pressure on the bellows.

Where no dynamic indications are given, this is no excuse for an expressionless performance. Instead, as with phrasing and articulation, you should try to work out a few ideas for yourself. It is often suitable to get gradually louder as the pitch ascends, and softer as it descends.

Pace does not permit me to detail the signs used for articulation and dynamics, but reference to a book on the Rudiments of Music will give adequate guidance, and a tutor book will explain their application to the accordion. You will no doubt have realised that the foregoing three aspects of interpretation are very much inter-related, and that all are dependent on good bellows control.

Now for some guidelines: -

1) A piece must be expressed, whatever its tempo, and its style and character need to be taken into account. Slower pieces call for more sensitivity and feeling, but faster ones need expression in order to avoid monotony.

2) Ensure that you know every term and sign on the music of the piece that you are playing. Ignorance is no excuse for an inadequate interpretation.

3) Don't think that instructions regarding the interpretation and expression of a piece don't matter. It matters enough for composers to indicate their intentions, therefore these should be observed. If, however, you are playing *'by ear'*, try to imitate the way in which you have heard the piece played, as well as aiming for the right notes.

4) Try to find out as much as possible about the origins and genre of the piece. In, for example, dances or ethnic music, it is helpful to know about such characteristics as speed, rhythmic features, melodic clichés, and its origins (e.g. a dance to ward off evil spirits!). The aim is to make the piece sound as authentic as possible.

5) The correct registration should be used. If your instrument does not have a particular register, then choose the next most similar alternative. Avoid playing everything on the *'Master'* coupler. Make use of your couplers.

6) Ensure you understand which repeats are required, and how they affect the piece.

7) Always play in a positive (but not aggressive) manner, in other words, as if you mean what you are playing, and are not afraid of expressing yourself. If you can convince your audience of your interpretation, then a few wrong notes will be over-looked in the excitement of the moment.

(Self-conscious players should regard performance as *'larger than life'*, and pretend that the instrument is speaking for them, rather like a ventriloquist's dummy!).

8) Never associate *'loud with fast'* or *'soft with slow'*, because this does not always follow.

9) *'Rubato'* playing is often hated and feared, since not only does it not always come naturally to the player, but it also results in there being more than one acceptable interpretation. The term means literally *'robbed time'*, and the idea is that some bars are played a little faster and others a little slower than the strict-time tempo, but the whole passage should take the same length of time to play as it would in strict time.

Post script.

The intention of this series has been to give some guidance on how to get the best out of your accordion playing. Success does not always come easily, but it can be yours if you make the effort, and have the determination to succeed. Happy playing!

Rosemary Wright, Accordion Times, 1988/87

Bellows There is a point of view held by many people in the musical world – usually non-accordionists – that the accordion's sounds are produced solely by the instrument's reeds, directed by couplers choices via the compression of air from the bellows. In other words, the accordion produces a sound that is entirely mechanical.

The truth is very different. One only has to hear someone playing the accordion without any consideration for phrasing to realise that it is the correct use of the bellows that really creates the quality of sound and intonation that constitutes good music. Correct bellows control is vital to creating the sounds that the player wants – plus levels of volume, emotional quality and feeling – and is a skill that needs much thought and practice.

At its most basic level, bellows control involves pulling outwards/pushing inwards for either two or four bars at a time, maintaining consistency throughout the piece. Changes of bellows direction need to be made cleanly between the bars, and should not occur *during* notes. This will result in an evenly balanced sound, avoiding the 'gasping' heard when no bellows control at all is observed.

The most effective use of the bellows comes, however, when the bellows direction changes due to the phrasing that exists in the music. This is what really creates the musical sounds the accordionist should be looking to produce. Bellows control can, in fact, be compared with the breathing of a singer, to whom phrasing should be all-important. It follows that the one thing an accordionist should <u>not</u> do is to break the phrasing i.e. change bellows direction part way through a phrase. The music produced by breaking the phrasing is awful, and to be avoided at all costs. One of the accordion world's all-time legends, Toralf Tollefsen, owes a large part of his reputation to the fact that when he phrased music, he used his bellows in similar manner to the way a skilled violinist uses the bow to create flowing phrases and beautiful sounds. Tollefsen never just pulled and pushed the bellows, he *moved* the bellows with the degree of subtlety or drive that the music required – raising the use of an accordion bellows to an art form.

Best, Julie Carlisle's Julie Best is a product of the Ronmar Accordion School, and one of the finest piano accordionists around today in this country. She has a highly skilled and disciplined technique, and excels at many styles of music. A bank manager by profession, Julie has played duets with her teacher, Ron Hodgson, and they are arguably the foremost accordion duet in the country at the present time. Julie and Ron have played at clubs and festivals in many parts of the country. Julie has also occasionally worked as a solo artiste, but remains best known for her duet playing. See also **Hodgson, Ron**.
Selected discography: *Magical Accordion Duets* (1990s) – a three part series; *Gin & It* – a solo CD of accordion classics (2002).

Beynon, Ivor Welsh-born Ivor Beynon ranks amongst the finest teachers and most dedicated personalities that the accordion scene in this country has ever produced. Writing in the *Accordion Times* in November 1993, he recalled the following: -
  "I started playing the accordion during my school days, and by the time I was in my early teens I was giving concerts throughout the Principality, including the Swansea Empire. At first I received lessons from Luther Owens, a dance band pianist, long before the BCA or NAO were even thought of. In my mid-teens I heard of the BCA, and travelled regularly to London for a course of lessons at the College.
  My first interview was with the then Principal, Professor Eustace St. George Pett, who although a professor at one of the London music colleges, found time to devote some of his energies to being Principal of the BCA. His two books, Just Music, and More Music, were among the first to be published with accordionists specifically in mind. I have vivid memories of Prof. Pett – always elegant, with a buttonhole flower, and I shall always be grateful to him for placing me with that excellent musician, teacher and gentleman, Conway Graves. Little did I realise at the time that many years later we were to become firm friends, and it was my good fortune to have him as the senior member of the teaching staff at the BCA when I was appointed Principal. It was at the BCA, situated in Store St in those days, that I also had the privilege of meeting Frank Skilton, Matyas Seiber (a.k.a. GS Mathis), and Captain James Reilly, the father of harmonica virtuoso, Tommy Reilly, and Dr Otto Meyer, without whose vision, foresight and endeavour there would not have been a BCA or NAO.
  In those pre-war days, 24 Store St was not only the Head Office of Hohner Concessionaries Ltd, but also the base for everything to do with accordion and harmonica playing – the BCA and Accordion Times. It was here also that I heard a brilliant player called Louis Cabrelli.

On completion of my course with Conway Graves I returned home to Swansea, inspired and fired with ambition. Shortly afterwards an Accordion Contest was arranged locally, and my band was placed second to an excellent band from Cardiff – Joe Gregory's (there were only two in the section!), and I learned a great deal from this experience. A year later I organised BCA examinations in Swansea, and Captain Reilly officiated as adjudicator and examiner on both occasions.

Activities were curtailed by my being called up for army service in 1939, but even during the war my accordion playing continued. I have spent virtually a lifetime working for the musical advancement of the accordion and its players, and one of my dreams was realised when, well after the war, I became a member of the London Sinfonietta."

Ivor Beynon was at the forefront of the movement from the post-war period for practically the rest of his life, and his *Ivor Beynon School of Music*, based in Kingston-on-Thames in Surrey produced lots of fine players such as Sylvia Lee, Cyril Pasby, Sylvia Wilson, Jerry Mayes, Phyllis Gillingham, Eddie Moors and Chiz Bishop, the greatest British Champion of them all. *The Ivor Beynon Accordion Method*, published in the 1980s, is still available, and is a lasting memorial to a great teacher.

Ivor Beynon passed away in May 1998, and his service to the accordion movement in this country cannot be praised too highly.

Bishop, Chiz (1927-2000) Portsmouth's Charles 'Chiz' Bishop once said in an interview for the *Accordion Times*: *"I was born at a very early age in 1927, and as a direct result I was one year old in 1928! My parents – one of either sex – soon noticed my ability to play on the linoleum, and forthwith decided that I should be set to music. In 1935 I found a 48 bass job in my Christmas stocking (I had big feet!). In 1937, I was given a 120 bass model and commenced proper lessons."* He was a very quick learner, making rapid progress. That same year he entered and became area champion of Hampshire, Dorset, Wiltshire and West Sussex, then, as he put it, *"became something of an infant phenomenon"* by beating fifteen other (and older) finalists in winning the All-Britain Advanced Solo Championship at the age of ten!

During this period, Chiz began having weekly lessons at the British College of Accordionists, travelling from Portsmouth to London by train each Saturday. Also having accordion lessons at the BCA was George Shearing, the famous blind jazz pianist. Chiz would accompany George to their lessons, and home again, and they became great friends. Once his parents picked up George at the

10-year-old Chiz Bishop receives the Championship Trophy from Haydn Wood, November 6th, 1937

station, Chiz followed a weekly ritual of going off to the cinema to watch the latest cartoons. Watching cartoons was to become something of a lifelong pleasure for Chiz, who always enjoyed the antics of Tom & Jerry, Popeye, etc.

In the 1938 All-Britain Championships, Chiz was edged out in a close contest, losing the Advanced Solo title to Sonny Drinkwater, from Brixton. This was the only occasion in what was to become a long and distinguished competitive career that Chiz Bishop finished second to anybody.

The onset of war in September 1939 interrupted Chiz Bishop's title aspirations for quite a few years, and by 1945 he was serving in the Royal Artillery. By the time he was back in 'Civvy Street' it was 1949 and ten years had passed since Chiz had done any serious playing. The formation of the NAO in 1949 and the advent of the first post-war *Accordion Day* inspired him to make a competitive comeback, and in 1951 Chiz entered and re-won the Advanced Solo title plus the relatively new Virtuoso Championship. He had enlisted Ivor Beynon as teacher, and set his sights on winning the world title. The fact that Chiz never managed to win the world crown is testimony to the incredibly high standard of the overseas competition in the 1950s and 60s.

On the home front, Chiz continued his dominance at *Accordion Day*, winning national championships again in 1952 and 1953. After a hiatus lasting a few years, Chiz launched a comeback to the championships, winning Virtuoso titles in 1959, 1960, 1961 and 1962. In fact, every time Chiz entered the All-Britain Virtuoso section, he came away with the title – an unbeaten champion!

In the January 1993 edition of *The Accordion News*, the question **Chiz Bishop - where are you now?** (asked in a previous issue) was answered in a letter to the magazine by the man himself: -

"This is a question I have often asked myself. 'Where am I? What am I doing here? Why don't women dance backwards any more?'

It all seems directly related to 'Where have I been?' As many of your more mature readers will recall, I dropped out of the accordion scene after my last concert in Southend, for Jerry Mayes, around 1965/66. I was having a lot of trouble with a damaged shoulder, and the weight of the instrument on the shoulder straps made the pain so intense I was having blackouts. I tried the instrument in a clamp, but it just wasn't the same.

I transferred to organ and sold my Morino V1 (which I still regret) and played as resident organist in many venues, doing both lounge and concert work. I also played with dance bands, pit orchestras, jazz groups, cabaret backing, as well as developing writing and arranging skills, and teaching, of course.

Also about this time I met someone whom I had admired from afar from some time... we only ever met on Accordion Day once a year and had hardly spoken, but it transpired that she echoed my feelings after all so we eventually married. Our trophies share the same cabinet at last!

In 1976 I put a band together with my wife Sylvia (Bennet) and we flew to the Mediterranean and worked on a cruise liner for nine months, coming home for a three-week break before setting off to the Caribbean for four months. A couple of weeks at home, then back to the Med. It was fairly hard graft but very pleasant, so we kept it up for a few years, and then returned to a house we had bought in Gosport and began to put down roots. I had been Musical Director on the ship, playing my Hammond B3 and piano with the band in the main ballroom, while Sylvia was solo organist in the lounge. We met many great people, and made a lot of lasting friends and have many happy memories of those years.

Back home, I was soon busy arranging and orchestrating music for anything from a trio to a 16 piece swing band. I was staff manager to the Manhood High School Showband in Selsey, writing arrangements for Ray McVay, sending music all over the world as well as playing in local bands and teaching.

Sylvia bought me a 120 bass accordion as a surprise Christmas present, and although I appreciated the thought, it couldn't match up to my beloved Morino, though it was fun trying out some of my old repertoire before letting one of my beginners have it."

Chiz played piano with the Jim Haimes swing band, and this band continues to use many of the fine arrangements produced by Chiz.

Chiz Bishop occupies a special place in the history of the Virtuoso Championship of Great Britain – he was the equivalent of the unbeaten 1950s World Heavyweight Boxing Champion, Rocky Marciano – always a winner. When it came to *Accordion Day* contests, Chiz Bishop was a formidable competitor, and he won the All-Britain Virtuoso Championship a record seven times, plus three Advanced Solo titles – a total that seems unlikely to be beaten, especially when you consider that he won his first national title in 1937 and the last one in 1962 – over a twenty five year period!

Chiz passed away peacefully on November 22nd 2000. November 22nd also rather fittingly happens to be St Cecilia's Day – the patron Saint of music.

Blair, Gary Glasgow's Gary Blair – the son of the late Jimmy and Lola Blair - is famous for his Scottish ceilidh music, as anyone who has been present at the Saturday evening dance at the Scarborough UK Championships will testify. He is, however, far more versatile than probably most people realise, having been classically trained and also capable of playing/performing in many international styles. Gary is also a worthy candidate for nomination as Britain's most popular accordionist, either at home and abroad, should ever an election be held on this topic. He has become well known in many countries such as the USA, Canada, Iceland and France – where he has appeared at the Chartres Festival. Gary is a regular at accordion festivals in this country where his energetic playing for dancing, and his charismatic style of teaching at Scottish music workshops, have made him a perennial favourite.

Gary Blair began learning the accordion at the age of eight, and was soon entering competitions and winning titles, eventually becoming the All-Britain Under 17 Champion (Bell Trophy) at the NAO Championships held in Margate in 1978. Not surprisingly, he also played in the Jimmy Blair Accordion Orchestra, and became MD after his parents passed away. However, Gary's substantial solo commitments led to the disbanding of the orchestra, as a new era in his life dawned involving appearing at clubs, events and festivals at home and abroad. He has been the organiser of the NAO South of Scotland Festival, and had adjudicated several times at the UK Championships.

Apart from playing, Gary is also an accordion enthusiast, with a lot of friends and connections in many places, plus a great knowledge of the instrument's repertoire, history and great players of past and present.

Gary has made or appeared on lots of recordings over the years, some of which appear in the discography below. For some years he recorded anonymously as the Star Accordion Band, a title coined by the record company, performing popular selections via multi-tracking plus rhythmic accompaniment. This sort of recording was primarily aimed at 'the masses' by the recording company and sold on a cut-price label.

On his most recent recording *Still Steamin*,' Gary shows off the capabilities of his new Cooperativa accordion on a wide range of music from many countries.

Selected discography: *Full Steam Ahead*; *Missing Time* (1999); *Still Steamin'* (2003).

Blair, Jimmy (1921-81) One of the truly great 'names' of Scottish, indeed British, accordion history, Jimmy Blair is one of the most significant figures in the development of both the accordion movement and the field of Scottish country dancing. His large accordion school and orchestras and long-term work on behalf of the British College of Accordionists, British Association of Accordionists and National Accordion Organisation were pivotal to the growth of the accordion scene that exists today. In the immediate post-war years, Jimmy was an innovator with his various activities that today many people take for granted, and his contribution should be noted and celebrated.

In the 1920s, Jimmy began playing his father's melodeon, moving on to the 3-row British Chromatic – at that time a new accordion system, and then to the 5-row Continental chromatic. During this period, Jimmy was also a talented artist, winning the City of Glasgow Award of the Year in 1938.

When war was declared, Jimmy joined the Glasgow Highlanders, and later took part in the D-Day landings in June 1944. Jimmy was engaged in some very fierce fighting as the Germans put up stiff resistance, and he was later awarded the *Croix de Guerre* by the French government, France's highest award and the equivalent of our own *Victoria Cross*. Many years later, in September 1981, Jimmy Blair and his accordion orchestra returned to the region to play concerts, and he was feted as a hero.

Jimmy's war service was also responsible for him taking up the piano accordion, and in an article in the magazine *Accordion Review*, he later had this to say: -

"From the day I landed in France, one of my objectives was to capture an accordion, but it was not until we reached Holland that I managed to find one.

I had been sent on a reconnaissance patrol to see if the Germans had left a village. They had, and to my delight they had left a full-sized piano accordion behind in one of their positions. Although we were in a forward position, my Company Commander, a Canadian, insisted on having a party at Coy. HQ that night, and the Germans must have thought we were trying a new secret weapon as I had little or no experience of the piano keyboard!

Every spare moment after that was spent mastering that keyboard. I had two tutors (one in Dutch, the other in German) and after a few months I could read them quite fluently – five words a minute!

During the subsequent period of Occupation, I studied piano under a German Professor from the Berlin Conservatoire, and when the war ended and I was demobbed I decided to remain on the piano accordion, and sold the chromatic".

In 1946, the war over, Jimmy Blair, however, discovered the Uniform keyboard accordion that had recently been invented in America by New Zealander John Reuther. Jimmy had joined the recently formed British Association of Accordionists, and the BAA actively promoted the Uniform system through the pages of its magazine, *Accordion Review*. Jimmy played both Uniform and a piano accordion for several years, and for a period was an enthusiast for Reuther's instrument. Jimmy taught others to play this now defunct system, and even formed a small Uniform keyboard band. Another venture in the late 1940s was the formation in Glasgow of the very successful Scotia Accordion Club, whose motto was *"Practice, and still more practice"*.

Jimmy founded his accordion school in Glasgow in the late 1940s, and for years to come his orchestra and players (including his son, Gary) would win many prizes and championships. In the 1970s, the Jimmy Blair Orchestra would become a dominant force in the NAO national championships. The orchestra also played concerts in France, Belgium and Canada. Jimmy was married to Lola, also an accordionist and teacher, and they had four sons. Lola took over the orchestra after Jimmy died, though she too succumbed to cancer not long afterwards.

By the early 1950s, Jimmy ran his own dance band and became one of the leading names in the Scottish country dance world, playing strict tempo tunes – including some of his own compositions such as *Jigtime Polka*. His band became regulars on the Scottish ITV programme *Jigtime* in the 1950s and 60s, and he regularly recorded country-dance music on the Phillips Fontana label. In all, he recorded about eighty LPs and EPs.

Jimmy Blair will always be associated with Scottish country dancing, and with the acoustic piano accordion, although in the 1940s and 50s he had for a time played the Uniform keyboard system. In 1979, at the All-Britain Championships in Scarborough, one of the Friday evening pre-competition features was a display/demonstration by Hohner Ltd of their latest product, the Hohner Electravox. The demonstrator was a German accordionist called Kurt Geluck, who spent some time showing the variety of electronic sounds that this state-of-the-art, wonder of the age instrument was capable of producing. Eventually, somebody suggested that Jimmy should have a go on the Electravox, and he took over from Herr Geluck. The large audience of curious bystanders watched with interest, then amusement, as Jimmy played a standard piece of music with lots of electronic sounds, then gradually switched off the electronics one by one until finally, he finished up playing Scottish tunes acoustically!

Jimmy sadly died from cancer on November 9th 1981, and his ashes were buried at the *"Cross-road of Rest,"* between Cheux and Argence in Normandy. Antoine Lepeltier, MP for the Calvados region, said: *"During the Battle of the Odun, Jimmy, who was a sergeant, was engaged at this spot with his men, but they certainly didn't regard it as the cross-roads of rest then!"* One of the locals, Albert Grandais wrote a book called *The Battle of Calvados*, in which Jimmy's part in the action is re-told. Monsieur Grandais had this to say: *"With his division, our friend Jimmy took part in all the major battles of the European Theatre, but remained attached to this, the cross-road of rest, where so many of his companions fell, and it was always with great emotion that he regularly came back to visit with us."*
Selected discography: *Highland Party* – a 1965 LP containing a typical Scottish country dance selection.

Blue, Jimmy (1930-2000) Originally from the West of Scotland, Jimmy Blue was a farmer who became a semi-professional, then a full-time professional accordionist as part of the Ian Powrie Scottish Dance Band in the 1950s. When Powrie emigrated to Australia in 1966, the band was then taken over by Jimmy.
Jimmy Blue played the Shand Morino three-row button accordion, and his playing was incredibly neat, slick and smooth sounding. He taught himself to play, using *The Mathis Method* (written by Matyas Seiber), and joined Ian Powrie in 1952.

By 1960, the Ian Powrie band was appearing regularly on BBC television's White Heather Club, and the following year the band turned full-time professional. The line-up was Ian Powrie (fiddle), Jimmy Blue (accordion), Mickey Ainsworth (2nd accordion), Pam Wilkie (piano), Dave Barclay (bass) and Arthur Easson (drums). In 1961 the band began a long association as Andy Stewart's 'backing group,' and can be heard on the singer's many recordings. In the early 60s Andy Stewart and the Powrie band broke all box office records in their seasons playing at the Glasgow Empire, a venue made notorious by the often-quoted show business saying, *"If they liked you, they let you live."*

After the Ian Powrie band became the Jimmy Blue Scottish Dance Band, further success followed with recordings and tours of America, Canada, South Africa and Rhodesia. In 1969, Jimmy and his band appeared in the film *Country Dance*, filmed in Ireland, and starring Peter O'Toole and Susannah York. By 1970, Andy Stewart/Jimmy Blue had become residents on *Scotch Corner*, ITV's answer to the *White Heather Club*.

Jimmy and his wife Joan became involved in the 'Box & Fiddle' club movement in Scotland in the early 1970s, and Jimmy served the movement for many years as a festival adjudicator and also as Chairman of the National Association of Accordion & Fiddle Clubs.

Selected discography: *Favourite Scottish Dance Music Vol 1* (1971)

Bodell, Larysa Having taken up the piano accordion at the age of 7, Larysa (the stepdaughter of Ray Bodell) made fast progress and in 1999 obtained her LBCA and ABCA (TD) diplomas as well as becoming 13 & Under UK Champion. It was whilst at the Baltic Festival in April 1999 that she decided to change to button key accordion, influenced by the wider range of repertoire available. Her competitive successes include:

2001
- 2nd prize winner in the Junior Classical Section at the International Accordion Festival in Reinbach, Switzerland
- Winner of the Fylde Coast Musician of the Year.

2002
- NAO UK Senior Recital Champion
- NAO UK 17 & Under (Bell Trophy) Champion
- 4th Place prize winner in the Anthony Galla Rini Classical Section – Accordion Teachers' Guild Festival, Florida, USA
- 7th place prize winner in Junior Classical Section at the CMA Trophee Mondiale World Championships, Belluno, Italy
- 8th place prize winner and finalist in Junior Classical Section at the CIA Coupe Mondiale, Copenhagen, Denmark
- In 2002, Larysa was awarded the Francis Wright Memorial Scholarship in order to pursue her further musical studies.

- 1st prize winner in the Junior Classical Section at the International Accordion Festival, Montese, Italy
- NAO UK Virtuoso Champion, Scarborough
- 3rd prize winner at the Escaldes-Angdorgy International Accordion Festival, Andorra

Over these years, Larysa has attended master classes in various countries including France, Croatia and Lithuania with some well-known artistes and teachers such as Jacques Mornet, Alexander Dimitriev, Domi Emorine and Roman Jbanov.

As well as a competitive player, Larysa is becoming a well-known concert accordionist, having performed at numerous clubs in the UK, festivals including the International Accordion Festival in Blackpool, Pakefield Accordion Festival, and the National Accordion Fun Festival in Paisley, Scotland. She was also invited to play at the Las Vegas Accordion Convention in 2002 as a guest artiste.

Bodell, Ray Ray Bodell gained all the grades and diplomas of the British College of Accordionists by the age of seventeen, then attained Diploma status of Trinity College of London and the London College of Music including a fellowship diploma for a research paper on the educational recognition of the accordion. He was the first, and so far only, accordionist to win all four major National Accordion Organisation solo championships i.e. Junior, Bell Trophy, Advanced and Virtuoso, and also represented this country in the Coupe Mondiale and other international competitions. In recent years he has concentrated on private teaching, conducting master classes and promoting the interests of younger players. Ray Bodell has served several times as Chairman of the NAO, and presently is Executive Director of the BCA. With his wife Anna, Ray also currently owns and operates Charnwood Music, specialist purveyors of music for the accordion.

Brannelli, Gina Living in Fleetwood near Blackpool where she and other family members run the *Accordion Exchange & Music World (UK)*, a large-scale accordion retail business, Gina is one of the best-known personalities in the British accordion scene. The Manchester-born daughter of Florence & Jack Brannelli, both star accordionists in their day, Gina is without doubt one of the most flamboyant yet highly gifted musicians around today in this country. She has worked for many years with her late husband, Norman, as **Gina & Romany Rye** – an act featuring electronic/acoustic accordion plus percussion with vocals, presenting a broad range of popular and exotic Latin/Continental/accordion standards – on the Cunard QE 2 cruise liner, and in clubs and theatres. Prior to this, Gina was a student of the pianoforte at Manchester College of Music where she attained Associate and Licentiate Diplomas. She also had studied the accordion, and in turn won BAA British & Commonwealth and the CMA World Championships, after which she turned professional. In recent years Gina has built up a large and successful teaching studio in Blackpool, where her students of accordion and piano are consistently high achievers. In addition, in 2003 she became Chairman of the NAO, yet still finds the time to play gigs in this country and America, and run her business interests. Gina's achievements in the accordion world are matched only by her warm and outgoing personality.

British Association of Accordionists Formed in 1946, by Desmond A. Hart and Adrian Dante, the British Association of Accordionists organised regional and national accordion championships, and also introduced a graded examination syllabus. At the same time, Dante's Modern Accordion Publications issued the bi-monthly magazine *Accordion Review*, edited by Desmond A. Hart. In 1950, *Accordion Review* was expanded in size and coverage to become *Accordion World Review*. These magazines included a lot of well-written technical articles on a wide range of topics concerning accordion playing, plus many general music features such as extensive biographies of the great classical composers. A couple of articles from *Accordion World Review* are reproduced in this book by kind permission of Mr Adrian Dante.

The annual BAA national championships were for many years held at St Pancras Town Hall in London, but eventually moved around the country and were held in Glasgow, Manchester, Birmingham and other cities. These festivals were large-scale affairs, attracting large numbers of entries, and playing standards were always high. During the 1950s and 60s, the band competitions were largely dominated by the Barnsley Accordion Orchestra (MD Horace Crossland) and the Coatbridge Accordion Band (MD Chick Kelly), from Glasgow.

Winners of the BAA Open British Championship qualified to take part in the CMA version of the World Championships. In 1952, James Reavey, winner of the BAA title, won the CMA World Championship – becoming the first British accordionist to win a version of a world title.

In 1947 and 1948, the BAA ran All–England Championships, at Lewisham Town Hall, London, in addition to its British Championships.
The All–England Championship solo winners were:

September 1947 – Gwenda Wilkin (Junior Under16) and Horace Crossland (Open)

October 1948 – Gwenda Wilkin (Junior) and Gwenda Wilkin (Open)
A similar All–Scotland event in 1948 resulted in Alastair McAllister (Junior), Jeanne McCloy (under 20) and Archie Duncan (Open) winning the major solo titles. From 1949 onwards, the BAA ran regional festivals that were broadly similar to the NAO system.

The BAA staged an *International Accordion Festival* on Saturday November 8th 1947 at the Central Hall Westminster, especially notable for the debut in this country of Italy's Gorni Kramer and Beltrami Wolmer. Kramer & Wolmer were a phenomenally good duo that made a great impression, and their superb playing can still be heard today on an LP available from Adrian Dante. The all-star evening concert, watched by an audience of 2,000 people, also featured spots from newly–crowned BAA Open Solo Champion Frank Clarke, from Blackburn, and each of the pre-war All-Britain Advanced Solo Champions – Peter Valerio, Alice Swindells (by then known professionally as Alice Dells), Chiz Bishop and Sonny Drinkwater.

The BAA organised many all–star public concerts in the late 1940s and throughout the 1950s, and these tended to feature Continental accordion stars such as Marcosignori, Aimable, Pepino Principe, Tony Murena and Yvette Horner, and the BBC often did live radio broadcasts. Adrian Dante had a flair for organising and promoting on a large scale, as evidenced in the poster below:-

The BAA championships took place annually until the early1970s, when the organisation folded due to Adrian Dante's business commitments as an agent/impresario coinciding with a dwindling number of administrative personnel within its ranks.

British College of Accordionists Founded in 1935 by Dr Otto H. Meyer and Albert Davison MA, Mus.Bac (Cantab), the BCA was based at 24 Store St, London until 1955 when the college moved to 112 Farringdon Rd, London. The BCA was at first an institution for teaching playing technique and musical theory, running courses, setting and administering graded examinations, and acting as an authority on playing standards. The BCA set up its own practical and theory syllabus, along similar lines to the longer established eight grades and diplomas of music authorities such as the Associated Board. The BCA, originally called the 'British College of Accordion Playing,' adopted its present name in 1936, and its first Principal was Eustace St George Pett. The BCA's staff included Matyas Seiber, Captain James Reilly and Conway Graves. Many well-known accordionists studied at the BCA during its London years.

In 1964, with Leslie Law as Principal, the BCA moved to Leicestershire under the chairmanship and patronage of Francis Wright, becoming almost exclusively an examining body. Mr Wright introduced a new constitution, reformed the BCA's structure into a body that set and administered grade and diploma examinations in regional centres across the UK and Malta. The BCA has a Teachers' Advisory Council, made up of teachers representing all parts of the country. The members meet once a year to put their views to the Governing Council of the College.

Since its foundation in the 1930s, the BCA has awarded over 100,000 grade certificates and around 400 Diplomas. The BCA has since moved home a couple of times, and its present address is: 112 Countesthorpe Road, South Wigston, Leicestershire LE18 4PG; telephone 0116 278 4094. The BCA also has its own web site, and the address is: www.britishcollegeofaccordionists.co.uk

Button Key Accordion This phrase describes an accordion that has buttons on both left and right hand keyboards, and such instruments are generally divided into two main types – chromatic and diatonic, which can be additionally subdivided. For further information, see also the sections **Continental Chromatic Accordions** and **Diatonic Accordions**.

Burch, Marion Taught to play the accordion by the late Martin Lukins, and a member of his championship winning Advanced Orchestra, Marion Burch later became a teacher of both chromatic and piano accordion systems. She has directed accordion orchestras of her own, tasting success at the UK Championships on several occasions, and has organised concerts for charity involving star players. In 1995 she recorded a cassette of French musette music, in aid of charity. Marion has been the MD of weekend orchestras for children at accordion festivals.
Discography: *Marion Goes Continental* (1995)

Burke, Joe A legend in the field of Irish traditional music, Joe Burke was the Senior All-Ireland Champion in 1959 and 1960. Since then he has travelled extensively, playing his trademark Paolo Soprani BC two-row button accordion wherever Irish music is popular. Resident in New York since the 1970s, Joe Burke has remained faithful to the mainstream style of Irish music and, as such, is regarded by his countrymen as a father figure of the genre. Joe Burke, whose familiar bushy beard makes him look rather like a member of The Dubliners, is also a superb flautist, and has recorded a CD using the flute.
Selected Discography: *A Tribute to Michael Coleman* (1975); *Joe Burke* (1978); The *Traditional Music of Ireland* (1982); *The Tailor' Choice* – Joe Burke uses the flute only (1983); *Happy to Meet, Sorry to Part* (1986).

Burns, Tito   (1921-2002) London-born Tito Burns was the first of this country's jazz accordionists, and in the years immediately following the end of World War Two in 1945, became one of the great broadcasting names through presenting and also performing on the weekly BBC radio programme *Accordion Club*. In the 1930s Tito had entered accordion contests, and then played professionally with Felix Mendelssohn and Lou Preager, two well-known names of the time. After war service in the RAF, Tito Burns began playing his own style of bebop jazz in London nightclubs, fronting his own sextet. He was a musician with a great flair for jazz, and had lots of ideas for presenting his music. In the 1950s, Burns was voted *Best Jazz Instrumentalist* several times in polls conducted by *The Melody Maker* newspaper. By the 1960s, Tito Burns had also become a theatrical agent, and as his agency work grew, he withdrew from playing and eventually gave up music altogether. As an agent, he was very successful indeed, and handled the affairs of many leading show business names, including Cliff Richard and The Rolling Stones. To accordionists, however, Tito Burns will always be remembered as the man who pioneered jazz accordion in the 1940s and 50s. He was married to the singer Terry Devon.

<u>Selected discography</u>: *Bebop Spoken Here* (1948)

Burton is a town in South Derbyshire that has a special place in the accordion history of this country. In 1935, accordionists Les Beckley, Stan Kersey and Ron Wildsmith founded the West Burton Piano Accordion School, and this was the start of a long tradition of accordion teaching, performing and competing that has continued right up until the present day. For many years Burton Town Hall was the venue for an NAO area festival, and Burton-based accordionists such as Marian and Stan Schofield, Pauline Simpson, Wendy Freeman, John Chilton, Karen Street, Jennifer Robinson, Karina Fodden, Julie Patrick and Alison Johnson have featured consistently at local festivals and the UK Championships from 1935 right up until the present time.

Cabrelli, Louis (1915-1988) A native of Dundee, but of Italian parentage, Louis Cabrelli was one of Scotland's first piano accordion star players. Although born in Scotland, Cabrelli did not belong to the traditional dance music scene, but was a concert performer of standard, popular and classical music. He began playing the diatonic two-row button accordion as a boy, but switched to the piano accordion when his father brought him one back from a visit to Italy. He taught himself to play, and developed a formidable technique, from endlessly listening to records of Pietro Frosini, and the brothers Pietro and Guido Deiro.

Louis Cabrelli was 'discovered' by the Capaldi Brothers when he was introduced to them after their accordion double act at a theatre in Dundee. Young Louis began touring the variety theatres in the early 1930s, but quickly tired of living out of a suitcase and went home to Dundee. Charles Forbes, who owned a music shop in Dundee, made arrangements for Cabrelli to live in London and study at the British College of Accordionists. Cabrelli studied the classics and also developed a sponsorship connection with Hohner, who made a special Morino for him in 1937. By this time, Cabrelli's star was in the ascendancy to the extent that he was the chief guest soloist at the All-Britain Championships' evening concert on November 6th at the Central Hall, Westminster. His programme that night included Rimsky-Korsakov's *Flight of the Bumble Bee*, Chopin's *Valse in C sharp minor*, and his own arrangement of *Variations on Over the Waves* (Rosas). By this time, Cabrelli was regularly playing concerts in many countries, and also making records. In Germany in 1938, however, his 'card was marked' by the Gestapo for gesturing at a portrait of Hitler, and whilst there he was ordered not to play any music written by Jewish composers such as Gershwin and Mendelssohn. In August 1939, Hohner's London Managing Director, Dr OH Meyer, awarded Louis Cabrelli a Gold Medal and Diploma of Merit *"for his outstanding contribution to the musical development of the piano accordion."*

When war came less than a month later, on September 3rd 1939, Cabrelli's life changed forever as he gave up music, and went into the family ice cream business, and was then interned as an 'enemy alien' when Italy took Hitler's side. In fact, Louis Cabrelli virtually gave up the accordion altogether and did not play at all for many years, until the 1970s when he renewed his interest and began teaching the instrument privately.

Scottish dance band legend and button accordionist Jimmy Shand knew Louis Cabrelli well, and said this of him: *"He was a musical genius, and when he played it sounded like three men playing!"*

Cann, Bob (1916-1990) Bob Cann was brought up on a farm in the Dartmoor area, and came from a family where everybody seemed to play something – melodeons, concertinas and harmonicas. He grew up steeped in traditional country-dance music, and played the melodeon from an early age. A regular at folk clubs, festivals and country- dances, Bob Cann was both a player and caller whose band, The Pixies, was popular and respected in the West Country. Bob graduated from the two-row melodeon to the Club Model accordion, an instrument rarely encountered in this country. He was a master at playing English country-dance music, and in 1989 was awarded the British Empire Medal (B.E.M.) by the Queen for his lifetime contribution to country-dance music.
Selected discography: *'Proper Job'* (1999) – this 28 track CD contains recordings made between 1952 and 1988, and features extensive notes on the man and his music.

Cajun Cajun music is a style of music originating from Louisiana in the USA. In 1755, the British expelled the French speaking population from Acadia, Nova Scotia, Canada. The French speakers resettled in Louisiana, thousands of miles to the south and in a much sunnier, hotter climate. The name Cajun is itself a phonetic mispronunciation of Acadian. These settlers took their French language folk music with them, and for many years Cajun (together with its later black derivate, **Zydeco**) remained exclusive to Louisiana and the eastern region of Texas, yet was virtually unknown to most of the rest of the world. Since the 1980s, due to an explosion in interest in various forms of what is generally termed World Music, Cajun music has become well known and popular in Europe and much of the rest of North America. In Britain, Cajun bands from Louisiana have appeared at folk festivals and folk clubs leading to the formation of Cajun bands, clubs and festivals in this country. Recordings, music books and Cajun accordions have become easily available, and the Cajun style is now here to stay, as it were. There are now tutor books and videos on sale in this country for those wishing to learn how to play Cajun style accordion.

The fiddle was the lead instrument of Cajun music until the arrival from Germany of the diatonic button accordion in the late 19th Century. Button accordions were taken to America by immigrants from Germany, Poland, Italy and other parts of Europe in the 19th Century, and the Cajun communities in Louisiana were quick to appreciate the instrument and appropriate it for their own music. Cajun bands have always favoured the one row accordion (what the British refer to as a melodeon), with fiddle, guitar and rub-board percussion frequently used in support. Apart from bass guitars, Cajun remains mainly an acoustic form of music (unlike Zydeco, where electric guitars and keyboards have become commonplace). Cajun music is essentially dance music, largely featuring two steps, one-steps and waltzes plus some blues rhythms. The Cajun style has been influenced considerably by Country & Western over the last half century, with some bands incorporating the steel guitar into their line-ups. Song lyrics are usually in French, but the French language has endured two hundred years separation from its motherland and will seem strange to anyone who has studied and knows some French.

To many accordionists brought up within the worldwide mainstream accordion tradition and familiar with the music of Toralf Tollefsen, Charles Magnante, Marcosignori, etc, the sound and unusual rhythms of a Cajun band is likely to be something of an acquired taste, if appreciated at all. In 1988, Malcolm Gee decided the time was right to add a Cajun band to the performers' roster at Caister Accordion Festival, but met with pure disaster. The band were put on stage following the Friday evening concert, but were not allowed a sound check before they went on, with the result that their sound was harsh, unbalanced and much too loud. The main hall emptied in record time as around 900 people went off to bed early, many of whom were cursing Cajun music as being something quite horrible! People who are gradually exposed to Cajun in normal circumstances, however, often quickly become hooked on this fun, care-free style of good time music.

The Cajun tradition has produced its own stars, many of whom have become well known outside Louisiana. These include the likes of Nathan Abshire, Austin Pitrie, Iry Le Jeune and the Balfa Brothers – all major stars in the post-World War Two era. More recently, top name accordionists have included Michel Doucet, Wayne Toups, DL Menard and Marc Savoy. Marc Savoy deserves a special mention as a noted accordion manufacturer in addition to being a successful performing and recording musician.

It is interesting to note that Cajun music, which existed for so long in an insular society in probably the poorest American state, Louisiana, has not merely survived all the other more recent American forms of music which have grown up around it (e.g. Rock n' Roll, Jazz, Rhythm & Blues, Country & Western, Bluegrass, Gospel, Soul), but has evolved, prospered and now spread to other places. The reasons are probably that Cajun (and Zydeco, too) has been willing to adapt to, rather than resist other forms of music, and draw influences from them whilst retaining its indigenous character – in short, Cajun has often re-invented itself, thus appealing to each new generation in different ways. It seems as if the accordion-led sounds of Cajun will go on being popular with its adherents for many generations to come.

Selected discography: *The Rough Guide to Cajun & Zydeco* (1997) – produced by World Music Network – features selected recordings made by a variety of artistes, and serves as a good introduction to the Cajun and Zydeco styles.

Camilleri, Charles   In the 1950s, 60s and 70s, Maltese-born Charles Camilleri was a star performer on piano accordion, and a frequent visitor to Britain, performing on Accordion Day and in numerous other high profile concerts. He made records, composed for the accordion, and appeared on radio and television. Since the 1980s, Camilleri has moved into the classical world as a conductor, composer and arranger, and has been much less in evidence in the accordion world. He has, however, kept in touch with the British accordion scene, and has occasionally visited accordion festivals. His name nowadays crops up occasionally on Radio 3 and Classical FM.

Selected discography: *Spectacular Accordions* (1960)

Capaldi, Renaldo   (Born 1938) *Renaldo Pietro Capaldi, known to his friends as Ron, is a member of a large extended family of musicians. Apart from a long career as a very fine professional accordionist, Ron was the editor/publisher of the Accordion Times from 1986 to 1990, and was renowned for maintaining high standards of journalism and presentation in this magazine. He is also known to many as an examiner for the British College of Accordionists, and as an adjudicator at festivals. In the following short autobiographical sketch, Ron Capaldi writes about his life and musical career: -*

"I was born in Gloucester on 13-4-38, and in 1940 moved to Evesham, Worcestershire. In 1945, I was diagnosed as an insulin dependent diabetic, and complications from this were to seriously affect my life and work. At the age of eight I started piano lessons with a local teacher. I wanted to learn the accordion, but in those days diabetics were thought of as being semi-invalids and my father (ex-professional accordionist Carmino Capaldi of *'The Capaldi Brothers'*) thought the accordion would be too heavy for me, particularly as we only had his 120 bass instrument to hand.

A year later, he capitulated, and I started to have tuition from him on his accordion, using two different tutor books, by Pietro Deiro (to whom I owe my middle name), and by Charles Magnante. Progress was slow because of a whole series of illnesses, including Yellow Jaundice, Pleurisy, and Bronchial Pneumonia – all of which were considered quite serious for a diabetic in the late 1940s and 50s. In October 1953, I was admitted to Romsley Hill Sanatorium with tuberculosis in both lungs, and was there for two and a half years.

When I was eventually discharged, I was classified as disabled and told (at age 18years) that I would not be going to work, so I simply got dad's Morino out of its case and started studying and practising.

BCA exams were designated slightly differently in those days, but I started with the equivalent of Grade 3 and took all Theory and Practical exams to their highest levels. Most of these were passed with Honours, and I also collected a Silver Medal on the way.

June 1st 1963 – I got married! My first ever-female pupil was my bride, and 40 years later – still is.

On the 20th November 1963 I took the A.B.C.A. Teachers' Diploma, which I passed with Honours, and on the next day I successfully took the Performers' L.B.C.A. Diploma. The only person prior to me who had ever done this was James Sexton. The British College of Accordionists at that time was situated in Farringdon Rd, London. Ivor Beynon, who was then Principal of the BCA, invited me to join the teaching staff of his private school in Kingston-Upon-Thames. A little while later, I was asked to join the staff of the BCA.

I gave up teaching at the BCA and for the Ivor Beynon Accordion School when a variety agent approached me with contracts. I toured all over the UK for a couple of years, doing clubs and variety theatres. I spent one Christmas Day in a Welsh mining village. My Christmas dinner that day consisted of some cheese sandwiches and a flask of tea 'put up' by my landlady of the previous night's lodgings. I should have been at home with my wife and young son (Paolo). I retired from touring.

We settled in Cheltenham where I opened a tuition studio. I was teaching accordion, piano and classical guitar, which I had studied in my younger days. I was lucky to be able to do a few broadcasts during this period, my first ever radio appearance having been on BBC Birmingham just before I did my Diplomas. I had acquired one of the very first, genuine Hohner Golas in 1965, and so loved this instrument that I made sure I put in some practice every day.

In August 1984 I was engaged by Francis Wright to lecture at a BCA weekend course for teachers and advanced students. During this weekend I suffered a major heart attack, and was taken to Kettering Hospital. I was left in a physically poor state, and it looked for a time as though my playing days were over.

Having recovered sufficiently to resume working, I took over the *Accordion Times* from Francis Wright mid-way through 1986, changing the magazine's format from A5 to the larger A4 size. I had the un-enviable task of trying to follow a series of very capable previous *Accordion Times* editors, and did my best to match their high standards.

I had been thinking for a while of making a purely solo recording. It was to be typical acoustic accordion solos – no electronic sounds, no accompanying instruments, and none of the traditional ceilidh sounds of Scotland or Ireland. I gritted my teeth and got back down to practise knowing that if I was going to do this, it would have to be soon – before my health deteriorated any further. In September 1987 the tape *Pure Accordion* was born. Far from perfect, but as far as I was concerned at the time, the best I could do.

At the end of 1990, I gave up publishing the *Accordion Times*, and the magazine was sold to new owners. From there on, things went rapidly downhill health wise. Renal disease was diagnosed, and they reckon I have about 10% of kidney function. Over a period of two years, I had to have nine operations on my right hand. I can do normal everyday things, but not playing!

I carried on teaching until September 2002, but a series of heart attacks has caused me to give that up.

Throughout my career I have always enjoyed arranging and composing, and have been blessed to have some works commissioned (for classical guitar), and many printed and published.

I have had a lot of illnesses over the years, and although it seems to be all doom and gloom, I don't think of it like that. It's been quite a good life, really".

Renaldo Capaldi, Cheltenham, August 2003

Discography: *Pure Accordion* (1987). The tracks include: *Vivacita, Lucia, On the Sunny Side of the Street, Echoes of Spring, Coquette, La Danza, Granada, Polkette, Return to Sorrento, Hearts Echoes, Nola, Nicolette, Guantanamera, Dark Eyes.*

Caravelle Records *is the title of the recording label specialising in accordion music, founded and owned by Adrian Dante. The Caravelle catalogue includes the following:-*

- **Accordion Tapestry** (LP) – classical favourites performed on acoustic/electronic accordion by Pearl Fawcett.
- **Musette Parisienne** (LP) – musette music played on acoustic/electronic accordion by Pearl Fawcett.
- **Music On The Move** (cassette) – strict tempo dance music on acoustic/electronic accordion and piano, played by Pearl Fawcett.
- **Virtuossimi** (LP/cassette) – Pearl Fawcett and Yuri Kasakov (USSR) perform solo classics.
- **Les Melodies Continentales** (cassette) – Continental specialities performed on acoustic/electronic accordion by Pearl Fawcett.
- **Viva Frosini** (cassette) 12 compositions by Pietro Frosini played on acoustic accordion by Pearl Fawcett.
- **The Two Great Pietros** (cassette) – 12 compositions by Pietro Frosini and Pietro Deiro, played on acoustic accordion by Pearl Fawcett.

- **Marcosignori – The Poet of the Accordion** (cassette) – 12 tracks of light music performed by the maestro.
- **Musettina** (cassette) – 12 Continental pieces played by Delmondi.
- **Twenty Fingers** (LP) - the brilliant Kramer & Wolmer duo.
- **Wolmer Plays Wolmer** (cassette) – Italian maestro Wolmer Beltrami plays 12 of his compositions and arrangements.
- **The Accordion Cassette of the Century** (cassette) – compilation featuring Delmondi, Pearl Fawcett, Francisco Cavez and Luciano Fancelli.
- **Francisco Cavez & his Latin American Orchestra** (cassette) - 12 tracks
- **Café Continentale** (LP) Delmondi performs 12 Continental numbers in brilliant style.
- **Accordiomania** (cassette) - 12 tracks featuring Enzo Toppano, Wolmer Beltrami and the Adrian Dante Accordion Orchestra.
- **Restless Fingers** (LP) - Continental music performed by Antonio (Tony Lowe) on acoustic/electronic accordion.
- **Pietro Deiro – Daddy of the Accordion** (cassette) - 12 classic compositions played by the master himself (recorded 1914-16).
- **Pearl Adriano** (cassette) – Continental music & light classics performed by Pearl Adriano (Fawcett) on acoustic/electronic accordion and piano.
- **Encore Marcosignori!** (cassette) - 12 classic tracks - a master at his craft!
- **Ettore Fantasia** (CD) - 14 tracks presenting the compositions of Eugene Ettore, performed on acoustic/electronic accordion by Pearl Adriano (Fawcett).
- **Allegria Continentale** (CD) - 11 tracks performed by Pearl Adriano (Fawcett), featuring Continental music and popular classics.

Each of the above recordings is listed in the Caravelle catalogue available from Adrian Dante, 2 Bence Close, Darton, near Barnsley, South Yorkshire S75 5PB; telephone 01226 382 976; e–mail: pearladriano@hotmail.com

Castelfidardo The northern Italian town of Castelfidardo, home to most of the Italian accordion manufacturers is very much the 'Mecca' of the accordion world. The firm of Paolo Soprani began making accordions in Castelfidardo in 1863, and many other manufacturers followed suit by opening factories in the town. In 2003 there are no less than 28 accordion manufacturers situated in the town, including many famous names such as Gabbanelli, Vignoni, Pigini, Guerrini, Allessandrini, Fantini, Cooperativa, Ballone Burini, Borsini, Brandoni, Castagnari, Tombollil, Zero Sette, Beltuna, Bugari Armando and Victoria. Castelfidardo now houses its own accordion museum, and in October the town is the venue for an international accordion competition. For several years the town has attracted visitors from all over the world, including regular annual organised trips from Great Britain.

Cassidy, Jimmy Accordionist Jimmy Cassidy has played professionally for many years, prior to which he held no less than six All-Scotland championships. He was taught piano accordion by Bill Wilkie, and made rapid progress due to his natural flair for music coupled with exceptional sight-reading ability. Jimmy also studied the piano at Perth Academy, and later adapted to the electronic keyboard, and one of his musical influences is Harry Stoneham, the great electronic organist. Apart from appearing in Scotland's *Box & Fiddle* clubs, Jimmy Cassidy has  also travelled extensively and was at one time Musical Director in the prestigious Sydney Opera House, in Australia. He has made recordings since the late 1960s, and is a musician of great all-round flair and technical ability. Apart from being widely known as a fine exponent of Scottish music, Jimmy also excels at the French musette style, and his latest CD *Accordeon Continental* (a recording that also features Billy McGuire) underlines this point emphatically. Selected discography: *Jim Cassidy* (1986); *Accordion Excellence* (1999); *Accordeon Continental* (2003). Jim also appears on the video *A Night With the Accordion Champions* (1999); also featured on this first-class live show from The Salutation Hotel, Perth are Wayne Robertson, Peter Bruce, Davie Stewart and Johnny Duncan.

Cassotto An accordion with reeds in cassotto has some of its reeds fitted into what is called a 'tone chamber,' and this special feature produces an extra quality resonance and mellow sound – especially useful for classics or jazz. An instrument with cassotto reeds is, however, generally more expensive than the basic reed, non-cassotto accordion.

Chemnitzer concertina In Chemnitz, Germany in 1835 Carl Uhleg devised and developed what has become known as the Chemnitzer concertina, a free reed instrument that is related to both the concertina and the bandoneon. This system was used in Germany and other parts of central Europe, and was taken to America by migrants during the 19th Century where it remains popular today with those who like to perform ethnic music. This cousin of the accordion was little known in this country until Brian Erickson from Wisconsin, USA, appeared as a guest at Caister in 1991, playing in a style and with a sound that was new to most of the festival-goers.

Choosing an Accordion *The accordion is a very versatile instrument, capable of adapting to a lot of international musical styles and traditions. The very wide range of instruments available, piano or button keyed, and coming in many different shapes, sizes and sound possibilities, makes choosing an accordion a* *tricky problem, especially for a beginner. The purpose of this article is to present some of the considerations when one is looking for an instrument.*

1) There is the question of size. Generally speaking, you should look for an accordion that is not too large, bulky or heavy. An accordion that is too large and/or heavy for you is disadvantageous in that it will be hard for you to control your playing, and it will also be a nuisance to transport around. Also, a too large/heavy instrument instrument may well cause or aggravate back, shoulder or arm problems, especially if you are likely to play standing up. Since the early 1990s, many of the manufacturers have introduced several high quality 72, 80 and 96 bass instruments to cater for a growing consumer demand in smaller, lighter and less bulky accordions.

2) What type of sound do you want? If you like classical music and/or jazz, straight tuning is preferable to musette. If, however, you want to play Scottish, Irish or English folk dance music, musette tuning is better than straight tuning. The same is true if you intend to play French, Italian or other Continental styles.

3) How many treble voices do you need? A four-voice accordion will be heavier than its three-voice counterpart, but it will also have a more powerful sound. If you are hoping to play in public places such as dance halls or restaurants, a four-voice accordion will be best.

4) Some accordions are highly decorative to look at, whilst others have a plain finish. It is all a matter of personal taste. To one person a colourfully decorated accordion is a thing of beauty, but to the next, the same instrument appears gaudy. Beauty is very much in the eye of the beholder!

5) Piano or button accordion?? Although the piano accordion has been the main choice for most people in this country for almost a hundred years, in the last twenty years an increasing number are choosing the chromatic button systems. If you choose buttons, there are two alternative systems to consider, the B and the C arrangements. Supporters of the B system believe that the way the scales are set out matches the shape of the hand most naturally; those who prefer the C system claim that the arrangement of buttons is advantageous for those who have played a piano keyboard.

6) If you are primarily interested in playing Irish traditional music, many people in Ireland will insist that the BC-tuned two-row button instrument gives a more authentic sound plus better/more correct ornamentation than any piano or Continental accordion. The BC button accordion is, however, less versatile than the piano/chromatic systems. It all depends how much you are 'into' Irish music.

Rob Howard (May 2003)

Clay, George   In the post-war years and through the 1950s and 60s, Birmingham's George Clay was one of this country's leading accordion teachers and best known luminaries. In July 1952, he founded the Birmingham Accordion Club, and no less than 142 people turned up on the opening night. His Birmingham Accordion School had studios in Birmingham, Coventry and Wolverhampton, and his pupils achieved many awards at the NAO national championships. One of his most notable successes was Pamela Deakin, Virtuoso Champion in 1956. He also wrote many interesting articles for the Accordion Times, one of which is reproduced in the section **Magnante, Charles**, - a review of a concert given by the maestro in New York.

Club Model is the name given to a diatonic accordion that has two rows of treble keys, plus a shorter treble row containing extra sharps and flats; this instrument also has a diatonic bass, usually with eight buttons. The Club Model originated in Germany and is found in Southern Germany, Austria and Switzerland. This type of accordion is rarely seen in this country, though the late Bob Cann, a Dartmoor-based country-dance player, was a fine exponent of this allegedly difficult system. Over the years, the name Club Model has been incorrectly used by some as a label for any kind of diatonic button accordion or melodeon. See also **Cann, Bob**.

Coleclough, Johnny (Born Manchester 1933) Johnny Coleclough acquired his first accordion in 1940, and during the war he played in the air raid shelters, but to his dismay most of his audience stayed outside saying that they would rather listen to the sounds of the bombs dropping than his playing! This did not deter him, however, and at fourteen he was a Carol Levis 'discovery.' He become a professional musician with Orlando's Orchestra after National Service in the RAF, eventually switching to the electronic accordion in the 1970s, featuring this instrument daily at Blackpool Tower for seven summer seasons. Johnny's musical career has also seen him performing in Scotland, Germany and Spain. Later, Johnny became resident accordion plus vocals entertainer (billed as *Johann & His Band*) at the Piccadilly Bierkeller, Manchester. A highly experienced stage performer, Johnny has in his time played gigs with musicians as diverse as Count Basie and Mantovani. He recalls coming home from work to receive a telephone call asking him to fill in that evening with Mantovani for a concert at Belle Vue, Manchester. On arrival, Mantovani instructed John that he wanted *"the musical score to be played exactly as written, so that it sounds just like the records and with absolutely no twiddly bits!"* This concert was also a turning point in his life when Johnny decided that he would, to use his own words, *"never suffer stage fright again."* He recalled that early on in the concert, the orchestra were playing the tango *Hernando's Hideaway*, and the arrangement called for the accordionist to play solo phrases in answer to the main theme played by the whole string section numbering around sixty. Surrounded by dozens of high-class musicians – the cream of Mantovani's finest – he wondered what on earth *he* was doing amongst *them*?! Finding himself charged with what felt like an awesome responsibility of fitting in vital solo phrases in the company of such excellent musicians was a fantastic experience but also a learning curve.

In the mid 1990s, Johnny became Vice President, then President of Stockport Accordion Club. He has also become a popular and inspirational leader of workshops for busking and stage presentation at accordion festivals, and has made numerous appearances as guest artist at accordion clubs where his lively presentation and ebullient personality have made him a great favourite. (See also **Strange, but true…**)

Comhaltas Ceoltori Eireann, CCE for short, is a non-denominational and international organisation that exists to promote Irish traditional music in all its forms via group music classes and competitions. Competitions are organised on a county and provincial basis in Ireland, and on a regional basis in Great Britain and the USA, and the age categories range from under 12 to over 18.

In Britain, there are four annual *Flead Cheoil* (Gaelic for *"Feast of Music"*) regional competitions – London, Midlands, Northern and Scottish. Winners and second place competitors qualify for the All-Britain finals, which is in itself a qualifying stage for the international All-Ireland Fleadh, held annually in August.

The CCE considers the various free reed instruments as separate entities. There are thus separate sections for the piano accordion, two-row button accordion, melodeon, concertina and harmonica. Those who play the 3-row British Chromatic or 5-row Continental chromatic compete in a special 'miscellaneous instruments' section.

In Britain, the branches of CCE are usually to be found in large cities – London, Manchester, Liverpool, Leeds, Birmingham, etc. Group classes for instruments generally include the piano accordion and two-row, where one can learn to play Irish music in the traditional style.

See also the section **Irish traditional music**.

For further information contact CCE, 32 Belgrave Square, Monkstown, Dunlin, Eire; telephone 010 353 (0) 1 2800 295. CCE also has its own website.

In Britain, there is Comhaltas Ceoltori Eireann website that can be located via a general web search, including an e-mail address fleadhman@aol.com

Competing at Accordion Festivals
The following article was written by Gerald Crossman, an experienced adjudicator.

Part 1: What adjudicators listen for.

Some points are obvious, some might not be quite so. Here are a few, but first let me emphasise that adjudicators are not demons with horns breathing fire. They are friendly, human, understanding, fair and knowledgeable, qualified and experienced.

For what are they listening? There are many things. There is not only accuracy of notes, but also their correct length and proper observance of rests. Nice 'clean' playing is called for. In addition are the presentations of expression, dynamics, phrasing and various marks (legato, staccato, etc), style, artistry and interpretation as well as good bellows control and observance of coupler or registration changes. If coupler markings are not included in a piece of music, then the judges will take note of the competitor's choice of tone colours and be swayed accordingly.....for the better if suitable and effective. The following of metronome markings on copies, (showing tempo, i.e. speed) is watched as is strict adherence to a tempo, e.g. as in a march or a waltz, without slowing or rushing. When exact speed markings are absent, adjudicators notice chosen tempos. Musicianship of competitors is particularly demonstrated during 'out of tempo' (ad lib) music.

If judging a combination of players, the adjudicators are listening for, in addition to the above, togetherness and balance of sounds, and the quality of the ensemble. They also watch, in the case of bands and orchestras, how well the musicians follow a conductor's indications.

'Own choice' competition pieces are expected to be of the grade for the section concerned, otherwise marks can be affected adversely. Adjudicators are certain to observe any visual faults, too, of competitors, such as the way of holding the instrument, bellows movements, position of arms and hands, also fingering. Beneficial comments regarding these would probably be written to help players

Part 2: Competitors at a Festival.

Arrive at the playing venue in good time. Remember that very cold weather outside can affect the tone of your accordion. The tone should recover after the accordion has been inside for a little while.

Loosen the fingers on the instrument before your performance is due if it is possible, but don't play so that the sound of your accordion will encroach into the adjudicating area. You might even have to avoid using the bellows. However, a convenient or special room is often provided for a last minute warm-up or rehearsal.

Try not to get tense during the time preceding competitive playing. Endeavour to relax. Some deep breaths could help. Wash your hands to refresh them just prior to your section.

Pause for a few seconds before beginning to play in front of the adjudicators in order to 'settle down.' It will also help to prevent a false start, which can disturb composure. Be comfortable, ensure you have undone the bellows at both top and bottom, see that you have set the desired commencing couplers, and make certain your fingers are placed on the correct starting keys. Be in possession of a clear mind!

Play accelerandos, rallentandos, crescendos, diminuendos, pauses, breaks and so on in musical fashion. Pay attention to fortes and pianos. Be the master of your instrument. Playing should be well controlled and, where called for, nicely rhythmical. Music that is out of tempo (ad lib i.e.- at will), gives you the freedom to demonstrate your ability of interpretation to the adjudicators.

If you know your test pieces well, you'll have confidence in yourself. However, never be over confident. You're liable to lose concentration, and this can cause errors. If you happen to make a mistake during your playing, don't keep thinking about it and don't worry. It's not so terrible!

Concentrate on what you are doing at the time. Your attention should not be diverted otherwise further mistakes could follow. Naturally, you want to play to the best of your ability. **If a slip occurs, carry on without hesitation**. Consider your performance after you have finished. You can choose to either sit or stand whilst playing your pieces.

To my way of thinking, it does not matter whether you read the printed music or play from memory when performing for adjudicators. Some famous concert artistes have the music in front of them during a recital. At festivals, someone to turn music is usually present if required, and a music stand should be to hand. It might be practical and convenient to have the pages of a test piece joined together side by side in strip form to eliminate or reduce turning over. You need to purchase two copies for doing this.

A final word in this part regarding your finishing bars…don't fizzle out during the last few notes of your piece. Have a respectable ending to a respectable performance.

Now, a *Final* final word….Create stage presence by having a pleasant personality whilst playing as though you are enjoying the experience. Judges and audience will appreciate this.

Part 3: Preparation BEFORE a Festival.

It is, of course, important to prepare your pieces well for any festival. There are proper ways to practise or rehearse. Not much use is served by just playing the music over and over again. Analyse any problems to help you rectify them. Compositions should always be studied slowly and carefully at first, bar by bar, phrase by phrase, section by section, gradually building up the whole, and up to tempo.

Good sensible fingering is essential, likewise, practise with separate hands. Aim to understand your pieces, and capture intended moods and atmosphere.

When you select an 'Own Choice' piece be sure that it is a) of the appropriate grade; b) within your capabilities to perform it; and c), you feel comfortable with it. The competitive grade for which you enter should be the one equal to your ability.

In good time beforehand, check that your accordion is in reliable playing condition. It is very disturbing to have sticking keys, couplers that don't work properly, reeds emitting strange sounds, reeds that don't stop making themselves heard whilst you are playing, reed blocks coming loose, leaking bellows, and so on. Examine straps, buckles and brackets, especially on older instruments. It's like an MOT on a car!

Always keep your accordion clean, and that includes the keys. You'll feel and play better, and prevent your fingers sticking or skidding.

When you leave home to compete in an Accordion Festival make sure you have with you all the music you require (no unauthorised photocopies or manuscript copies). If reading music, don't leave your reading glasses behind if you need them. You can hardly forget to take your accordion! I remember a violinist who once went to a broadcast session with his violin case, and when he opened the case in the studio, yes you're right, the violin wasn't in it!
Gerald Crossman, *The Accordion Monthly News* (1990).

Composing and Arranging Music *Ken Farran, an accordion teacher and player from Warrington, has composed and arranged music for solo accordion and for accordion band. In 1998, he wrote a couple of articles for the magazine Accordion Profile in which he discusses the issues involved in composing and arranging music.*

Composing & Arranging

Have you ever thought of trying your hand at composing or arranging? You never thought you could do it? Well, this is not a textbook on how to do it, but more of a prod on getting you interested, and giving you something to think about.

Of course, you must be able to write the dots on the stave, as it were. I know playing into a computer can do it, but this does have its limitations, and often needs tidying up, as, *"You only get out what you put in,"* and this can often be harmonically wrong.

In composing and arranging, invention (as in producing something new) is crucial, as we only have thirteen notes to work with. Without some spark of creative ability, no one can hope to invent. Some do not know that there is a small spark waiting to be fired. It does not matter how small it is, because it can turn out to be a blazing inferno of creative talent and a source of immense pleasure.

To produce/write music of real artistic merit, one cannot avoid the need, no matter how talented, for careful study of music in both its academic and artistic fields, and in painstaking experiment. Composing or arranging is an art form and **not** a piece of trivia – many people can paint a wall, but could they paint a picture?

The beginner in music writing must have some standard as a guide, and should not be discouraged if first attempts fail. Some established music writers will say you need to be Grade V1 plus to write 'Good Music', but Mozart was only 6 years old when he started composing seriously; Bizet was 17, Mendelssohn was 10, Beethoven 12, and Schumann was 7. The list is almost endless. They, of course, had a "special gift" – most will never aspire to these great heights, but just think of the immense pleasure you can have and maybe give to others, just by trying. Most artists will never be a Van Gogh, but they can have great satisfaction in painting.

Listen to as much good music as you can – more so in the field you wish to specialise in composing or arranging, so that an insight can be gained into the methods used by others. The wider your tastes, the greater the benefit. A lot can be learned from symphonies, ballads, operas, jazz, pop, etc. Deliberate copying of music is obviously wrong, and will get you nowhere. Good musicians will spot fakes. Okay, so where or when do we get inspiration to write music? Most composers don't wait for it – sometimes music has to be written even when there is none! Film, television and theatre music is often required, on demand, at very short notice. Some famous composers like Mozart and Rossini often waited until the day before a performance before writing.

The budding composer or arranger should not be satisfied with simple tunes, but should try to put to music some thought that is in the mind. Listen to music that shows emotion and, if possible, read the score. Typical are Tchiakovsky' *1812 Overture*, Brahm's *Lullaby* and Beethoven's *Pastoral Symphony*. There are countless examples to be heard on Classic FM radio. There are many examples in modern music as well. The professional music writer will often work to a timetable – even a 9am to 5pm office hours' routine – others will work in the afternoon or evening. Amateur writers will not be able to work on that scale, but the point is, the professional will prefer to work in long slots as the mind needs to unwind and thoughts collected before serious writing begins. It is also beneficial to listen to the type of music you want before putting pen to paper e.g. if you want to write a march, then listen to a few marches, not for musical ideas but to get yourself in the mood.

Can you sing – or hear music in the mind – from a score, without an instrument? If not, you will have to use an instrument to hear your ideas - ideally, a keyboard, as chord formations can be seen and heard, and keyed to ideas. Some music writers don't use any instruments, and can hear the sounds of both melody and harmony, and even counterpoint. Some have 'sketch books' (books of blank stave) and use them when inspiration strikes, often away from home, then draw upon it sometime later on. It is worthwhile trying to develop the ability to 'sight sing,' and practise writing ideas in a sketchbook. (Beethoven had no option. He became deaf, but still wrote some of the world's best music).

The essence of a good composition or arrangement is a good easy, natural flow where the listener is either at ease or is caught up in the emotion portrayed. Music writing is like poetry – full of drama, emotion, punctuations, etc, which can all be brought to life on whatever instrument is used.

What key do I write in? Well, a beginner in composing or arranging would do better to stick to the keys of C, F and G in the early stages, but should not get entrenched in those keys as the music could be very mundane and very predictable. Having said that, the average player does not like to go beyond three sharps or three flats! One obvious thing to bear in mind when setting a key is its range – is it too high or too low? If you use too many ledger lines, you could be putting it out of range of many of the smaller instruments and a few singers.

I once read in a book in the late 1960s, that certain keys have emotions that are different to others. It is well known that major keys often portray happiness, whilst minor keys express sadness. Here is a small sample of some keys that the book mentioned:-

MAJOR		MINOR	
C	Bold, vigorous	C	Gloomy, sad
D	Majestic	D#	Tragic
Eb	Dignified	E	Restless
G	Pastoral	G	Melancholy
Ab	Dreamy	G#	Sorrowful
Bb	Bright, graceful	A	Tender, noble
B	Energetic	Bb	Funereal

Fascinating subject, isn't it?

Once you get into composing or arranging, be adventurous, BUT learn the rules (there are so many), but don't let them stifle your creative ability. Many of the great composers in the past broke or bent the rules of music (others would say they broke new ground) to get the result they wanted, and these broken rules eventually became the new rules for the future. Do not be misled; these composers knew what they were doing. It was not done through ignorance.

Ever thought of syncopation in your music? Syncopation, either in composition or arrangement. Used in the right place and not overdone, syncopation can add an extra twist and charm to the whole piece. It is often thought of as being something modern, but was well known and used to great effect by Bach and Handel.

To take ideas from another composer and make it appear as your own work is theft, and heavy fines can be levied. Variations – transcriptions and arrangements of other composers' work is quite legitimate, providing of course that the law of Copyright is observed, as again a hefty fine can be given. Copyright in a musical work exists for seventy years after the composer's death. The same applies to an arrangement of the classics: as an example, if I make an arrangement of a work by Mozart, then the Copyright of the arrangement will last for seventy years after my death. There is no exclusive Copyright in a title. The field of Copyright is a complex issue, so advice is best obtained from legal sources.

Once you have become proficient in either composing or arranging, what do you do next? Acceptance by a publisher may be exciting, but care is needed when form filling, as Copyright could unwittingly be signed away to the publisher. Any payments would then be on a Royalty basis (a percentage of sheet sales), but – would you know how many copies had been sold? What would you think to publishing your own music? Would you know if your music were good enough to sell? Publishing your own work could involve a great deal of work and expense for possibly little reward. This would involve your own type setting costs if you did not have a computer and a laser printer, plus printing costs and advertising in a variety of magazines. A lot of things need to be taken into account before any action is taken. You are the only one who can decide. This might seem a far cry from when one thought: *"I only want to write music."*

The ability to compose or arrange music is a great thing that ought to be encouraged. It is also very satisfying even if one does not go to the trouble of getting it published. The accordion needs more good music. The accordion world has too many accordionists, but not enough musicians!! True or not, do yourself and others a favour – study music – play music, and write music.

Your music lessons are important, as you progress from simple music writing to the more advanced forms of musical expression. Some musical bodies argue that arranging is harder than composing, and that it is an arrangement that 'sells' the composition. It is true that a simple tune can be transformed into something of beauty by good arrangement. (If you feel confident, try making a 16 bar – four-part arrangement of Three Blind Mice). It is of immense value to be able to study chord progressions in a hymnbook, or chorale music by Bach. The knowledge gained will be a valuable aid to composing and arranging. Just looking at progressions or even playing them can be confusing; one has to be able to analyse what has been done, and why (ask your teacher). Music lessons are important. Studying the work of some 'Great Composers' can enhance musical sounds.

Ken Farran, Accordion Profile, 1998.

Compton, Tony Cockney born Tony Compton has an accent that makes him sound like a cast member of BBC TV's Eastenders, and is in fact from the East End of London, where he learned to play the piano accordion as a youngster. He was taught by Don Destefano, and has been grateful ever since for the very sound tuition he received. Tony was once resident accordionist at a restaurant in London frequented by Charles Kray, elder brother of the notorious Kray twins. Looking back on the 1950s and 60s, Tony recalls that the gangs run by the Krays and their equally infamous rivals, the Richardsons, were the law in parts of London, and that it may well be the case that the police today would gladly like them back on the scene to restore law and order! The Krays and their like threatened and killed other criminal types, and would not tolerate the muggers, yobs, child molesters and burglars we hear so much of nowadays.

Tony Compton made his first broadcast on Radio Luxembourg at the age of sixteen, and then went on to entertain regularly at the Savoy and Hilton Hotels in London's West End. He has also played in such shows as *Piaf, Cabaret, Cider With Rosie, Lark Rise To Candleford*, etc, in theatres, jazz clubs and has even performed a concerto with a symphony orchestra. He has recorded background music for television commercials and Capitol Radio.

By the early 1980s, Tony had become a demonstrator for Hohner, promoting the electronic accordion, and in 1984 made an LP showcasing the acoustic and electronic sounds of the Hohner Vox 4, then a 'state of the art' instrument.

Tony Compton is one of Britain's most accomplished accordion entertainers, with a penchant for playing jazz. He is also, however, very experienced at playing for strict tempo dancing, and has recorded albums of specialist dance music. Since the 1980s, he has frequently teamed up with Jack Emblow and their performances of 'easy listening' plus some jazz, punctuated with humorous and musical anecdotes, have become great favourites in accordion clubs. The Emblow/Compton combination were guest performers at the inaugural Chartres Accordion Festival in northern France in 1989.

Tony has occasionally written musical articles for accordion magazines, and some of his writing has been reproduced, with kind permission, in this book – see **Jazz**.

Selected discography: *Bell Accordions Presents Tony Compton Playing the Hohner Vox 4* (1984); *Flying High* (1987 jazz LP with Jack Emblow); *Country Style*, 1986); *Sentimental Journey* (2000); *Days Of Wine & Roses* (2003).

Concertina A small hexagonally shaped button keyed instrument, originally designed and patented in 1829 by Charles Wheatstone in London. The buttons are fixed on both sides of the instrument, and there are two main types – The English system in which each button plays the same pitch note on both push and pull of the bellows, and the Anglo German system (developed in Germany) in which the direction of the bellows changes the pitch of each button. Unlike accordions, which have developed almost beyond recognition since the 1820s, concertinas have undergone relatively few changes since Wheatstone's time. The English concertina was originally intended to be used as an alternative to the violin in concert orchestras, though this aspiration never came about.

For those interested in the subject, *The Concertina Maintenance Manual*, written by David D. Elliott, is a well-written and illustrated exposition of the internal mechanisms of the English, Anglo and Duet concertina systems. Written in 1997 and from *Mally Publications*, this book also contains a large number of useful contact addresses for concertina players. For concertina repairs, the reader is advised to contact Chris Algar, The Music Room, Hobgoblin or West Country Accordions – see the section called **Accordion Retailers in the UK**.

The International Concertina Association, founded more than fifty years ago, exists to promote the instrument and represent its players. The ICA publishes a quarterly newsletter, *Concertina World*, and full details of news and activities are to be found on a website, and their e-mail address is: ica@johnwild.demon.co.uk. The co-ordinator for the ICA's activities, newsletter and website is Somerset-based Wes Williams (telephone 01963 440010).

Continental Chromatic Accordion The Continental chromatic accordion has buttons on the treble side, and the pitch of the keys is not affected by changes in bellows direction; the average model has a Stradella bass for the left hand. Most Continental chromatic accordions have five rows of treble buttons, and these are arranged so that the keys progress diagonally in semitones. Continental chromatic instruments, widespread across Western Europe for almost a hundred years, are becoming better known in Britain and Ireland. There are two main categories, as follows:-

1) The C system has the C button in the first/outer row, and the pitch then progresses upwards in semitones diagonally, outside to inside rows (in a right to left direction). A variation of the C system is the French system, which is outwardly notable for its stepped treble keyboard; situated behind, out of sight, are the couplers.

2) The B system has the B button in the first row/outer row, and the pitch then progresses in semitones from inside to outside rows (left to right direction) – an opposite configuration to the C system.

Conway, Mario Born and resident in Cardiff, Mario Conway, five times All-Britain Virtuoso Champion in the 1970s, holds the distinction of being the first person to gain a music degree from a British university using the piano accordion as a main instrument, having obtained a Bachelor of Music, first class honours. This was later followed by study for a Master of Arts Degree in 20th Century Music.

Essentially a classical musician, Mario Conway has appeared as guest at many accordion clubs, festivals and concerts, both in Britain and in Europe. He has appeared at the Royal Festival Hall, the Edinburgh Festival, and with the Welsh National Opera.

Mario Conway has also been a committee member of the National Accordion Organisation and a highly respected adjudicator at festivals, including the UK Championships. An LP, *Conway* was released in 1980, issued by the late Malcolm Gee on his ARC label.

Coppard, Sue Wiltshire's Sue Coppard is an accordionist with an extraordinary talent for composing music in a multiplicity of international genres. Her compositions are all self-published, and demonstrate this lady's remarkable talent for writing original music for accordion in styles that traverse the world. Sue plays solo accordion gigs and has a repertoire that includes popular songs, film and show numbers, cocktail and dance music from the 20s on, evergreens of all vintages, folk, gypsy, classical, opera, swing, and an extensive selection from France, Italy, Germany, Spain, Latin America, Greece, Yugoslavia, Russia,

Romania, Hungary, Vienna, Scotland and Ireland. She has appeared at festivals, and is the organiser of the White Horse Accordion Club.

Another of Sue's passions is organic farming and the organic movement. In 1971 she began a worldwide organisation known by the acronym *WWOOF* – see below.

Discography: *Magic Carpet* (1990); *Carried Away...* (2003) – two recordings consisting entirely of Sue's compositions – for details telephone (01225) 866 679.

WWOOF stands for *World Wide Opportunities on Organic Farms,* and is an international exchange network where bed, board and practical experience are given in return for help on organic farms. WWOOF provides opportunities for organic training, changing to a rural life, cultural exchange, and being part of the organic movement. WWOOF has its own website: www.wwoof.org; e-mail hello@wwoof.org ; telephone 01273 476 286.

Couplers (a.k.a. Registers or Switches) Couplers are tab controls found where the grill meets the front of the treble keyboard, used to activate the various reed combinations that produce certain sounds. The couplers usually feature patterns of dots that indicate which reeds are playing, and the more dots showing, the greater the sound. Some accordions have a slide coupler along the outer edge of the treble keyboard; this puts on the 'master' coupler i.e. all the available reeds are played together. Most accordions of 48 bass and over also have some couplers on the bass side, giving choices of sounds from the left hand reeds.

Most music written or arranged for accordion includes coupler suggestions, and these help to provide 'colour' and add extra interest. It is a good idea to make use of the couplers, even if your music has no coupler suggestions, to give a tonal 'edge' to what you are playing. For music where there are no coupler suggestions, you will need to experiment, but this will help to give you a better overall sound. The worst option is to continually play everything using the same coupler, whatever that may be, as your sound is likely to become monotonous, especially if you are playing a number of pieces lasting for more than a few minutes. Some players actually do play everything on the same coupler, but this is not making the most of an instrument.

A lot of people tend to favour one or two couplers, and generally ignore the rest. This is a mistake, particularly if you play music from a wide range of styles and types. Find uses for your couplers, as this will enhance your overall sound and widen your musical scope. Don't be one of those accordionists who do not even know what couplers they have! They are the ones who, when playing in an accordion band, are fumbling when the MD asks everyone to put on, say, a 'violin,' or a 'bandoneon' coupler – and eventually have to be guided to the right tab. Get to know what voices your instrument is capable of producing.

ACCORDION LORE.

23. COUPLER REGISTRATION. (I)

DEVISED & DRAWN by *G. Romani*

The early type of Accordion which we now call "Melodeon" became widespread around 1870. It had one row of ten treble keys, two bass keys plus the vital air release valve, and was in one key, being single action. Each button produced two sounds on the in or out movement of the bellows. They were fitted with 1, 2, 3 or 4 "Stops" which enabled the player to select the reed sets built into the instrument.

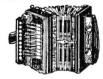

"10-key Melodion,
Three sets reeds,
Rich tone, 9-fold
bellows....10/6.
Post, 9d.extra."
[From a Mail order
catalogue ,c.1895.]

By 1900, the larger uniform tone three-row Chromatic Button-key Accordion was extant, but strangely only one reed switch was fitted, usually as a small lever behind the treble keyboard.

Similarly, the first piano-keyed Accordions (c.1910) had either no coupler system or just one, operated by a slide on the edge of the keyboard.

This continued to be the norm up to the 1930's, but by the end of the decade, Push couplers had replaced the slide mechanism.

A few top-class instruments had more than one treble coupler, and a bass coupler was also fitted.

Hohner "Morino"
41/120/4, 2 Treble,
1 Bass Couplers.
Price: £66.
['Accordion
Times', Aug.1939.]

With the revival of the industry after World War II, multi-coupler instruments became the norm, the treble couplers being operated by a series of tabs between the keyboard and the grill, and similar bass couplers between the bass buttons and the bellows, as on the great majority of accordions today. . .

Crucianelli
41/120/4
Multi-coupler.
Price: £400.
[A.T. 1953]

The range and effect of these various registers and couplers depends in the first instance on the actual reeds fitted to that particular instrument. To understand this properly, it is necessary to know the way in

which the maker has organised the reed sets, and we will go into this in detail in the next "Accordion Lore".

First, we must explain the way Coupler Registration is indicated in notation.

Up to the 1930's, composers and arrangers simply indicated "Coupler on" or "Coupler off" either in plain words or by the following signs:-

C = Coupler on.   Z = Coupler off.

In American music of the period we find:-

R = Register On.   * = Register off.

With the advent of multi-coupler instruments, more elaborate systems had to be devised, all of which varied from country to country, creating no little confusion. . .

In 1953, at Copenhagen, the International Confederation of Accordionists (C.I.A.) set out a new system of registration which has been universally accepted. In this system a circle divided into three segments is used to indicate the Treble reeds in order of pitch:

Superoctave (4')[8va higher.]

Normal Pitch (8')

Suboctave (16')[8va lower.]

The reed sets sounding are indicated by Dots in the various segments, e.g.

= 1 Reed at Normal Pitch.

= 1 Reed at Suboctave Pitch.

= 3 Reeds at Normal Pitch. etc.

[To be continued. . .]

ACCORDION LORE

24. COUPLER REGISTRATION (II)

DEVISED & DRAWN by *G. Romani*
© 1987.

The range and scope of the Coupler Registration available on any particular instrument depends on the number and range of the reed sets provided by the maker.

Dealing solely with the TREBLE KEYBOARD in the first instance, the following categories will be found.

1. 1-voice Models. Usually restricted to small 8- or 12-bass instruments with a limited treble range, only one set of reeds at normal pitch is used.

2. 2-voice Models. These can occur in two formats: (a) Octave-tuned, i.e. one set at Normal (8') pitch and one set at Suboctave pitch (16') sounding an octave below Normal, giving: or (b) Vibrato-tuned, i.e. one set at Normal pitch, the other set also Normal but tuned slightly sharp, giving:

3. 3-voice Models. Two types here also: (a) Octave-tuned, having Superoctave (4') set (an octave higher than normal), Normal (8') and Suboctave (16') sets, giving:

(b) Vibrato-tuned, with two sets at Normal pitch (one set slightly sharp) and a Suboctave set, giving:

4. 4-voice Models. Again two types: (a) Superoctave (4'), Normal (2 sets, one tuned slightly sharp) and Suboctave (16'), giving:

(b) Normal (3 sets, one exact, one slightly flat, one slightly sharp) and Suboctave (16') giving:

5. 5-voice Models. Only one type here, with Superoctave set, Normal (3 sets, one exact, one flat, one sharp) and Suboctave set, giving:

These are the main forms of Treble reed layouts normally found, but others may be found on special instruments.

The Coupler Registration used in notation is that for the 5-voice model. Therefore, if your own instrument has a lesser number of reed sets, you will have to make a substitution in some cases. For instance, if the music requires ⊕, and you have a 4-voice model (Type 4a), then you have to use ⊕ in lieu.

Or, if ⊕ is required, and you have a 3-voice model (3b), then only ⊖ can be used, since you have no Superoctave set.

The following table will make this quite clear, as it shows what registration should be used to realise the notated fore-going.

Of course, it must be remembered that the fore-going shows the possibilities available, some manufacturers organise the coupler mechanisms in varying ways, sometimes duplicating the coupler tabs, or, sometimes, for the sake of increasing the number of coupler tabs, making use of the sharp normal set on its own or in combination with other reed sets, creating a most unmusical "out of tune" effect.

A much better effect obtainable on some instruments is the placing of some reed sets "in cassotto", i.e. in a special tone enhancing chamber, giving the single reed a more rounded sound than the ordinary open reed sets. Usually, the Normal (8') set ⊖, and the Suboctave (16') set ⊖ are "in cassotto".

In the final analysis, every player must know the musical possibilities afforded by his particular instrument and utilise these to the best effect in the interpretation of the music he or she plays. Judicious use of the varying tone colours available on the modern accordion can enhance the performance in no uncertain way.

In the next "ACCORDION LORE", the possibilities and effect of the Bass Keyboard couplers will be examined. . .
(To be continued. . .)

TABLE OF INSTRUMENTS AND COUPLER REGISTRATIONS POSSIBLE

NOTATION & 5-voice	Four-voice (a)	(b)	Three-voice (a)	(b)	Two-voice (a)	(b)	One-voice

Your accordion will have a certain range of couplers to choose from, depending on whether it is straight-tuned or musette-tuned. There are some accordions that feature both straight and musette tuning, called 5-voice instruments offering a full and exceptional range of couplers. Although the player has a very wide range of reed combinations at his or her fingertips, these instruments tend to be heavy and bulky, making the 5-voice a generally unpopular choice with most players.

A skilled and experienced player will use the couplers to make tonal changes, and these are often done with subtlety. For example, on the 1972 LP *Accordion Showpieces*, Gervasio Marcosignori makes many coupler changes to match changes in mood, but the changes are mostly imperceptibly made yet add constantly to the musical patterns heard by the listener. A case in point is the piece *Preludio e Fuga,* on which Marcosignori makes no less than seventy changes on the bass registers in about three minutes, yet the listener never hears the changes being made – only the variations produced in the music.

Crossland, Barry   In the early 1950s, Barry Crossland (taught by his father, Horace) became a regular competitor in area and national British Association of Accordionists' festivals, winning four North Midlands titles (1950/51/53/54) and achieving second place in the Open Solo Championship in the 1953 and 1957 BAA British Championships at St Pancras Town Hall, London. In May 1954, Barry was the BAA's representative in the World Junior Championships in Naples, Italy, achieving a creditable 4th place. Looking back, Barry recalls:-

"On New Year's Eve 1948 I played my first ever gig with dad's six piece band in Doncaster – still in short trousers! When the shops opened on January 2nd 1949, I bought myself a suit with long trousers out of my earnings, for six guineas. Not bad, considering a miner's wage was then about £5.10 shillings a week.

In October 1954 I travelled to Naples to compete in the World Junior Championships, with the Australian accordionist Lou Campara, who had just finished his British tour. He was on his way home and had planned to visit his parents in Italy.

On the morning of the competition I arrived at the venue at about 9am to find a young chap positioned in the foyer, distributing signed photographs of himself, which also carried the inscription 'World Champion'!! The chap was Giacomino Bogliolo, the Italian competitor, and obviously very, very sure of himself. And you know what? He went on that day to wipe the floor with the rest of us! He really <u>was</u> a brilliant player, and well worth his win. The next time I saw him was a few years ago when he turned up as the MD of the band backing the Italian entrant in the Eurovision Song Contest."

Barry Crossland joined the RAF for his National Service in 1955/57, after which he worked in his father's music shop in Barnsley. He began playing the bass guitar in show bands and drifted away from playing the accordion. Over the years, the bands he worked with backed Frankie Vaughan and Marty Wilde.

In 1991, Barry retired from playing bass guitar and has since become involved in teaching the accordion.

Crossland, Horace (1914–86) The son of a miner, Horace Crossland began playing the accordion at eighteen, and became a founder member of Bell's *Alhambra Accordion Band* in the 1930s. By 1939 he had formed his own accordion band, and during World War Two became a member of ENSA, entertaining the troops. In 1947, Horace Crossland won the first All-England Championship at a festival organised by the British Accordion Association. This win made Horace the first post-war national accordion champion, two years before the NAO was formed and the All-Britain Championships were resumed. Mr Crossland's greatest contribution to the accordion world was his work as a teacher and bandleader. His pupils included Pearl Fawcett and Heather Smith, both outstanding accordion champions, and his bands were regularly successful in BAA competitions. In 1959, he opened a music shop in Barnsley dealing in accordions and concertinas. In the years prior to his death on October 27th 1986 at the age of 72, Horace Crossland was Musical Director of the highly regarded *Barnsley Accordion Sinfonia*, whose repertoire included several of their conductor's compositions. His son, Barry, is an accordion teacher, and based in Scarborough.

Crossman, Gerald Born in London in 1920, Gerald Crossman plays piano accordion, piano and organ, and has been one of Great Britain's premier accordion luminaries since he first came to prominence in the late 1930s.

From a musical family, Gerald began piano lessons at the age of five, and took up the piano accordion at twelve. His progress on both instruments was rapid, and one of his piano teachers was the famous concert pianist, Edward Rubach. Gerald's cousins were clarinet/saxophonist Joe Crossman, guitarist Sid Jacobsen, and Jock Jacobsen, drummer with Lew Stone. During his

schooldays, his best friend was Michael Anderson, the film director well known for such movies as *Around the World in Eighty Days* and *The Dam Busters*.

By the late 1930s, Gerald was teaching the piano and accordion. He was already a professional musician, and had played two summer seasons in a hotel in Cliftonville, Kent; a hotel in London's Tottenham Court Rd; Lyons Corner Houses; and had appeared as a solo accordion act in charity concerts at several West End theatres. In 1938, he made his first recordings, with musical direction by George Scott-Wood.

The outbreak of war in 1939 initially meant involvement with ENSA shows, but in April 1940 Gerald joined the RAF, eventually finishing the war stationed in India.

Once the war was over, Gerald's musical career moved up several gears and he became involved in a wide range of activities including concerts, radio broadcasts, recordings, studio session work, composing, film music recording sessions, and on both BBC and Independent Television. His work involved both accordion and piano, and was extremely diverse. For example, he made broadcasts of light classics with orchestras using both instruments, accordion broadcasts from Radio Luxembourg, and French-style accordion solos broadcast from Paris. Gerald appeared several times on the BBC radio show *Accordion Club*, and in 1952 formed the *Gerald Crossman Players* (signature tune, Gerald's own composition *A Night in Montmartre*), which performed on the morning BBC radio shows *Morning Music, Bright and Early* and *Music While You Work* until 1966. Members of the *GCP* included, at various times, Reg Hogarth, Ivor Beynon, Brian Dexter, Jack Emblow, Henry Krein, Albert Delroy, Victor Parker, Tommy Nicol and Emilio (Emile Charlier).

In the post-war years, Gerald played on Cunard ocean liners Queen Mary and Caronia, docking in New York where he met the great accordionists Pietro Frosini and Charles Magnante. He also met John C. Gerstner, editor of the US magazine *The Accordion World*, which the featured several articles written by Gerald. Another highlight was a voyage to Argentina, working as a musician on the Royal Mail Line cruiser *Andes*, where Gerald was thrilled to see and hear enthralling tango orchestras featuring bandoneons.

Gerald Crossman has played with and alongside a list of stars that reads like a show business *A to Z*, including Joe Loss, Ted Heath, Eric Robinson, Nat Temple, Lou Praeger, Billy Cotton, Edmundo Ross, Sidney Torch, George Scott-Wood, Primo Scala, Matyas Seiber, Mantovani, Frank Chacksfield, Ron Goodwin, Norrie Paramor, Cyril Ornadel, Tommy Cooper, Roy Castle, Bob Monkhouse, Morecambe & Wise, Sir Ralph Richardson, Sir Harry Secombe, Jack Hawkins, Charlie Chaplin, and even the legendary Marlene Dietrich, for whom he provided piano accompaniment.

Gerald has had a long term involvement with the British film industry, and has composed and played music for many films, used on the soundtracks of movies such as *The House of the Arrow* and Tommy Steele's *Tommy the Toreador*. He can be heard as the pianist on the sound version of Chaplin's 1923 film *The Pilgrim*. Occasionally he has made cameo appearances playing the accordion e.g. *The Magnificent Two*, with Morecambe & Wise.

In 1968, Gerald married Miriam Offner, and in the 1970s he returned to playing on P& O cruise liners, touring the Mediterranean, West Africa, the West Indies and also Scandinavia. During this time he also provided the solo piano accompaniment for seasons of silent films at the Academy Cinema in London's Oxford St.

In addition to playing, Gerald Crossman has written and arranged a great deal of music amounting to a hundred plus compositions, including such perennially popular pieces as *A Night In Montmartre* and *Granada Mia*. Many of his compositions have been recorded, such as the bright novelty piece *Out of the Wood*, recorded by Stanley Tudor on the Odeon, Manchester, Wurlitzer theatre organ (CD, *Powder Your Face With Sunshine*, produced by the Lancastrian Theatre Organ Trust, 1997). His *Festa Rusticana* was used as the test piece in the 1951 All-Britain Championships for both Advanced and Virtuoso sections, and is published by Charnwood. He has also written two accordion tutor books i.e. *Melodyway Piano Accordion Tutor*, and *Latin American Rhythms*.

Mr Crossman is also exceptionally knowledgeable about the accordion and music in general, and is a prolific writer with over two hundred published articles to his credit, and his lucid and always educational style of writing has graced many accordion magazines worldwide, including our own *Accordion Times* and *The Accordion Monthly News*. A few of his magazine articles are reproduced in this book, with kind permission of the author and publishers.

Within the accordion world, Gerald Crossman is an Honorary Vice-President of the National Accordion Organisation, has been a Council Member of the British College of Accordionists, and has served many times as an adjudicator at the All-Britain Championships. His instruments have included a Hohner Atlantic 1V and a Dallape Artist Model, and he has previously used a Settimo Soprani and Hohner Organola 11.

At the time of writing, Gerald Crossman is still an active musician, and the last word on his remarkable life and career belongs to him: *"I have thoroughly enjoyed my professional life. With the variety, I wouldn't have done anything else."*

Cunningham, Phil Originally from Edinburgh, but later living on the Isle of Skye, Phil Cunningham on piano accordion and his brother Johnny on fiddle were key members of the 1970s and 80s folk band, Silly Wizard. Their intuitive duet instrumental breaks during songs and their tune sets were amazing, as was their finger flashing virtuosity on jigs and reels or sensitive playing on slow airs. Phil's solo work was equally impressive, and the recordings made by Silly Wizard exist to prove the point. The modern-styled, breathtaking and exciting solos by Phil Cunningham on Scottish and Irish dance tunes have caused him to be labelled variously as *"A nuclear Jimmy Shand"* and *"Jimmy Shand meets Jimi Hendrix"*! The Cunninghams later played together in the band Relativity before going their separate ways. In the 1990s Phil Cunningham teamed up with fiddle maestro Aly Bain, and they have since made many television and radio appearances together, plus many recordings.

Most of Phil's concert appearances have been in folk clubs and festivals rather than on the accordion scene, yet he is without doubt one of Britain's foremost accordion talents. In 2002, Phil Cunningham was awarded the MBE for his services to traditional music.

Selected discography: *Silly Wizard – Live Wizardry* (1988); *Airs & Graces* (1986); *The Pearl* (with Aly Bain 1999); *The Ruby* (with Aly Bain, 2000); *Another Gem* (with Aly Bain, 2001); *Spring All Through The Summer* (with Aly Bain, 2003).

Tune book: *The House in Rose Valley Vol 1* (2001) contains 54 of Phil's compositions.

Videos: *Silly Wizard Live at Center Stage* (1988); *Another Musical Interlude –* a live recording made at the Eden Court Theatre, Inverness (2000)

Currie Brothers, The Jim, Tom and Liam Currie are a trio of brothers who play accordions and stringed instruments to high standards, and are commonly acknowledged as one of the Scottish accordion scene's best live acts. They excel at Scottish traditional music, but also are superb at everything from *Tico Tico* to *Orpheus in the Underworld*. As if that were not enough, they also sing – presenting programmes that promise something for everybody. The really surprising thing is that they have not to date appeared at any of the accordion festivals south of the border.

Selected discography: *By Special Request* (1982); *Versatility* (1994)

Dante, Adrian (Born 1914, real name Dante Adriano) An 'Elder Statesman' of the accordion world, London-born but Italian raised Adrian Dante has been a player, teacher, composer, arranger, writer, publisher, organiser, agent and impresario with a long and exceptional track record of success in each of his diverse activities. In the pre-war years, Dante was a professional accordionist, making countless radio broadcasts both with his quartet and as a soloist. He was the first accordionist in this country to broadcast the compositions of Pietro Frosini, and also the first to perform *The Flight of the Bumblebee* in public. In  arranging and performing classical music on the accordion in the 1930s, Dante was ahead of his time, and many of his ideas about music have since come to be regarded as standard practice.

In 1931 he began teaching the accordion, and in the post-war years after 1945 founded the Accordion Development Centre based at 131 Hampstead Rd, London NW1. The ADC employed many well-known teachers such as Percy Holland, Eddie Harris, Francis Cava and Albert Delroy. Many of his pupils have become high-class accordionists, including Gerald Delmondi, Antonio (Tony Lowe), Gina Brannelli and, most notably, Pearl Fawcett.

In 1946, Adrian Dante and pre-war All-Britain Championships organiser Desmond A. Hart founded the British Accordion Association, an organisation that set up and ran its own regional and British national accordion championships. Dante also published his own magazine, *Accordion World*, in the 1940s, followed by *Accordion World Review* in the 1950s/60s and 70s. See also **British Association of Accordionists**.

Dante is the proprietor of *Caravelle Records* and *Modern Accordion Publications* (a.k.a *M.A.P Editions*), both specialising in Continental accordion music. He has made the recorded music of Pearl Fawcett, Delmondi, Antonio, Kramer & Wolmer, and others, available to the public. Dante knew the composers Pietro Frosini and Guido and Pietro Deiro intimately, and has written extensively about each in British and international accordion magazines over the years. He has also acted as an impresario, bringing international-class accordionists such as Gervasio Marcosignori, Yuri Kasakov (USSR), and Italy's famed Kramer & Wolmer to Britain for tours. Adrian Dante's outstanding work in promoting Continental and classical music on the accordion is a major contribution to the worldwide accordion scene, and is ongoing.

Dawson, Barry (1919-2003) London-based Barry Dawson (birth name Harry Wingfield) was a professional accordionist for more than fifty years, and his music took him around the world, playing in Europe, Hong Kong, Dubai and on cruise liners. He composed music for the accordion, and broadcast on BBC radio several times.

Barry Dawson was originally a journalist, but when war broke out in 1939, he enlisted in the army and rose to the rank of sergeant. After demob in 1945, he used what money he had to buy a 120 bass piano accordion, and set about developing a solo music act entertaining in restaurants, clubs, variety theatres and whatever else he could find. He could also sing and play the trumpet, and these were incorporated into his performances; these talents became especially useful when, in the 1960s, he became a Bavarian-style entertainer in the London bierkellers. Barry was keen on French musette music, and this was a style he was often booked to perform in various places.

Sometimes Barry would start off a gig by playing the trumpet with his right hand, and accompanying himself with the accordion basses. He claimed that with this technique he could immediately lower the tone of any pretentious function, such was his slightly anarchic sense of humour!

With his journalistic background, Barry was also an excellent writer and his erudite articles appeared in the *Accordion Times* on and off from the early 1950s until the late 1990s. He was also had an outgoing personality, and was closely involved with the people who ran the NAO from 1950 onwards. Barry passed away on July 5th 2003 at the age of 84.

Deakin, Pamela (Born 1936) Pamela Deakin, from Warley, Staffordshire, was one of this country's greatest competitive accordionists in the 1950s, winning three All-Britain Championships amongst a host of titles. She began studying the accordion seriously under George Clay in 1950, the famous Birmingham teacher. Her progress was rapid, and within three years she was a national champion, winning the All-Britain Amateur Championship in 1953, and again in 1954. In 1955 Pamela achieved a creditable eighth

place in a strong field of 21 competitors at the Coupe Mondiale World Championships held in Brighton. Her greatest achievement came in 1956 when she won the All-Britain Virtuoso Championship, though her second attempt at the world title was less successful than her first, finishing fifteenth. Since her competitive career ended, Pamela Deakin has been a popular and respected accordion teacher in the Midlands.

Deiro, Guido (1886-1950) Elder of the two Deiro brothers, Guido Deiro is largely remembered for his composition *My Florence*, and this is grossly unfair when Guido's life, career and achievements are considered. A prolific recording artist, performer and composer, Guido also was the first to introduce the piano accordion to the American public when he appeared on stage at The American Theatre, San Francisco, in 1910.

Born in Italy in 1886, Guido worked as a miner before becoming a full time musician. He emigrated to the United States in 1908, a year after his brother, and took up the piano accordion. He began an illustrious stage career in 1910, and signed a recording contract with Columbia in 1911. His debut recording was *The Sharpshooter's March/Cirrirribin*, which sold well and was soon followed by a series of other records such as *My Treasure (Tesoro Mio)/Variety Polka, Ave Maria/Miserere, Dill Pickle's Rag/In the Land of Harmony, La Spagnola/Dolores*, plus many more. As the second decade of the 20th Century

progressed, Guido and his brother Pietro, who was under contract to Victor Records, became big selling recording artists, but only once did they duet together on record – in January 1914- on *I Love Her, Oh! Oh! Oh!/Mammy Jinny's Jubilee*, issued by Columbia. Pietro's records were by now outselling those by Guido, and the rivalry between the recording companies prevented any further scope for cooperation.

Guido Deiro really was a true pioneer of the piano accordion, and even claimed to have devised the name itself. He was the first to make records (1911), the first to play on stage, and he was the first to play on radio (in Detroit, 1922) or appear in a film (1921), using a piano accordion. As if that were not enough, he was the first accordionist to perform on the American vaudeville circuit, the first to write a hit song (*Kismet*, theme song of a Broadway musical, 1911) and the first to play the piano accordion in a sound motion picture (*Vitaphone* in 1928; shown on the TCM cable/satellite channel in 2002). Later in his life, in the 1930s, he wrote a tutor book – *The Royal Method for Piano Accordion, by Guido Deiro*, followed shortly afterwards by a follow-up *Volume 2*.

Being the handsome celebrity that he was, Guido had many female admirers and was married no less than four times. Although legend has it that he was married to Hollywood film star, Mae West, this is incorrect. Mae West appeared in a stage show in 1914 that required her to sing and play the accordion, and Guido was hired to back her from the wings while the famous lady mimed and sang. This led to Mae and Guido living together for four years, and he must have readily responded positively to her much-quoted request of *"Come up and see me sometime"*!

The advent of 'the talkies' in 1927 meant both the demise of silent films and also the vaudeville circuit, and a gradual decline in the stage careers of both Deiro brothers plus their friend, Pietro Frosini. The rapid growth in radio, however, more than amply compensated as a new outlet for their talents, and Guido's career carried on successfully until he died on July 26th 1950 in California. (See also **Strange, but true…**)

<u>Compositions</u> include *My Florence, Deirina Mazurka, Polka Variata, Queen of the Air.*

Deiro, Pietro (1888-1954) The younger of the Deiro brothers is sometimes referred to, with much justification, as '*The Daddy of the Accordion*', due to his widespread, high profile promotion of the piano accordion in the early years of the 20th Century.

Like his brother Guido, Pietro worked as a miner before turning to music for a living. He emigrated to the USA in 1907, and switched to the newly introduced piano accordion. Pietro joined the vaudeville circuit and signed for Columbia Records, although soon afterwards he switched to the rival Victor label, and his recordings began to consistently outsell those of his older brother. Pietro had already become a prolific and successful composer of music for the accordion, and his talent for composition was to raise his profile considerably in the accordion world and establish his long lasting reputation. In March 1914, for example, his composition *Pietro's Return/Danube Waves* proved to be a big seller, both in terms of record and sheet music sales. Even today, almost a century onwards, *Pietro's Return* is played and recorded by accordionists – testimony to the enduring quality of the great man's work. Accordionists similarly frequently perform another of Pietro's early compositions and recordings, *Beautiful Days*, today, and an orchestral arrangement also is played often and enjoyed by audiences in many countries.

After vaudeville declined, in 1928 Deiro set up the *Pietro Deiro Headquarters* at 46 Greenwich Ave, New York – a business famous amongst accordionists, and later run by his son Pietro Deiro Junior. This business later relocated to 133 Seventh Ave South, New York.

In 1952 the famous American comedian Jack Benny was in England for a performance at the London Palladium, and a strike called by the US Musicians' Union meant that his team of accompanists – including the legendary Pietro Deiro – could not appear. Thus it was that London accordionist George Booth found himself on stage with Jack Benny, filling in for the great Mr Deiro. Afterwards, George and Pietro met up backstage, socialised and played music together.

The great Pietro Deiro passed away in 1954, but his son, Pietro Junior, who became an accordion luminary in his own right, carried his work forward.
Selected discography: *Daddy of the Accordion* – a cassette featuring Pietro Deiro playing several of his own compositions in the early years of his career. *I Padri della Fisarmonica – vol 1* – a 23-track compilation, including some own compositions (2002)
Selected compositions: *Tranquillo Overture, Trieste Overture, Beautiful Days, Pietro's Return, Cubanera, Quick Silver, Pyramid, Abundance, Chanticleer, Lido Mazurka, Dora Mazurka, Rumbero, Loreto, Buenes Aires, Romanola, Concerto in A.*

Dells, Alice Known originally as Alice Swindells, Macclesfield's Alice Dells travelled all the way from her home town to a music shop, Mameloks, in Manchester, every week for accordion lessons with the late Sid Baxter (remembered as the composer of *Gypsy Mood*). In 1936 Alice achieved fame within the accordion world by becoming the second All–Britain Champion, at the Central Hall, Westminster. Winning the national title opened up a career as a professional accordionist that took Alice not only around this country, but also all over Europe and the Middle East. She recalls the following: -

"I was lucky to have piano tuition, but the accordion took over – much as I loved the piano. Fortunately I had a very good teacher – though it took my dad a whole year to find Sid Baxter. Dad attended one of Sid's 'Accordion Nights', which he enjoyed tremendously.

However, war took over, and Sid was called up. I eventually joined ENSA – the Entertainments National Service Association. What lovely people I had the fortune to tour with, and wonderful people to stay with. I cannot describe the kindness we had bestowed on us. After touring Britain, there followed marvellous tours of Egypt, North Africa, Lebanon, Palestine and Iraq. Music and entertainment speak all languages.

Iraq was a very quiet country then, and when we pulled up outside the

Hotel Semeramis, I though we were in a back alley! However, the hotel was beautiful inside.

After the Middle East, the ENSA party toured Denmark, Germany, Austria, Italy, Holland and France – where I was very honoured to play in Lourdes at the Grotto (Schubert's Ave Maria). This was not a professional engagement.

Back in England I played in theatres and cabaret venues all over the place, though I never made it to the London Palladium, just the London Casino and Collins Theatre, Islington. Away from London – all the 'posh' theatres, and the 'dumps'!

I've always played solo, and then had to, as needed, add a little vocals due to theatrical agents requiring this. I can only wish every accordionist good health to enjoy playing their music."

Alice worked with many well-known show business names of her era, including vocal duo Anne Ziegler & Webster Booth, pianists Rawicz & Landauer, and the great radio comedy star Jimmy Clitheroe. When she appeared with Rawicz & Landauer, Alice recalls that Maryan Rawicz, a brilliant classical pianist, surprised her by admitting: *"I always wanted to learn to play the accordion, but never found the time."* Now retired from performing and also from teaching the accordion, Alice still lives in Macclesfield.

Delmondi, Gerald Often referred to simply as 'Delmondi', Gerald Delmondi's hey-day was the 1950s and early 60s when he was a regular performer of Continental and Latin American music on BBC Radio's Light Programme. Coached by Adrian Dante, Delmondi's music is characterised by its dynamics, expression and subtle phrasing, and he was regarded as an outstanding Continental-style and jazz accordionist, much in demand in restaurants in the London area and on the radio, working both as a soloist and with his own quartet. Delmondi also taught the accordion in the 1950s and 60s. Although Delmondi's playing career has petered out since the 1980s, his records remain to show that he was indeed one of the greats of his style and era.

Selected Discography: *Dancing Through Europe* (1960); *The Italian Accordion* (1965); *Café Continentale* (1980).

Delroy, Albert A specialist at performing French musette and Latin American music, Albert Delroy's regular weekday morning broadcasts on BBC Light Radio were heard and enjoyed by millions in the 1950s and 60s. Delroy was an authority on the French musette scene and also knew a great deal about the many different varieties of accordion systems, and as such was a prolific contributor for many years to the *Accordion Times* and other publications. Although best known as a piano accordionist, Albert Delroy could also play

both the chromatic button accordion and the bandoneon, and both to a high standard. He wrote music, much of it in the musette style, and also made recordings. In the 1980s, Charnwood issued two compilation cassettes, and also were responsible for making available much of Delroy's sheet music. In 1992 Albert Delroy was appointed President of the British College of Accordionists.
Selected discography: *Accordion Heritage* (1987); *Delroy Encore!* (1988)

Deuringer, Hubert Born in 1924, Hubert Deuringer learned the piano accordion, clarinet and saxophone as a teenager and made his first broadcast on accordion during World War Two while serving in the German army. Once the war was over, Deuringer began a career as a professional musician that saw him emerge quickly as one of Germany's finest post-war accordion talents. Specialising in swing music and jazz, he played as a soloist, formed a trio, a quartet and a quintet, and also performed with orchestras. In 1960/61, Deuringer recorded two LPs in duet with compatriot Klaus Wunderlicht on Hammond organ. Forty years later, these recordings came to the attention of Nigel Ogden who played selected tracks on his programme, *The Organist Entertains* on BBC Radio 2. The Deuringer-Wunderlicht LPs were subsequently released on a CD titled *Swing & Happy* in Britain, and became available via mail order from MSS Studios (telephone 01341 422115). The German Monopol label, covering his career from 1945 to 1995, has issued a four CD compilation of 88 of Hubert Deuringer's recordings and titled *Accordeon a la carte*. This CD set shows just what an accomplished accordion artist Deuringer was in his heyday, and is available in this country from MSS Studios, a Welsh-based mail order company on 01341 422 115.

Diatonic Accordion The word diatonic is used frequently in reference to accordions, and refers to those instruments in which the pitch of a note changes according to a push or pull of the bellows. Listed below are the three most common systems:-

- **DG diatonic** – two rows of buttons on the right hand (treble) keyboard, with the outside row set in the key of D major, and the inside row set in G major. The bass usually (but not always) has eight buttons, set in a diatonic configuration. The DG instrument is called an accordion in Ireland, but in England is generally known as a melodeon – widely used in Morris dancing and also in English country-dance bands.
- **BC diatonic** – the outside row is set in the key of B major, and the inside row is set in C major. The right hand scales of each row are a semitone apart, giving this instrument a wide range on the treble side. The bass side usually contains eight buttons, in a diatonic configuration. Throughout the 20th Century the BC accordion has been widely used in Irish traditional music, and when many Irish people mention the accordion they visualise the BC instrument first and foremost.

- **BCC# diatonic** – the outside row is set in B major, the middle row is set in C major, and the inside row in C sharp major. Since Jimmy Shand had a customised model made for him in the early 1940s by Hohner, this kind of instrument normally has had a Stradella bass system on the left hand rather than a diatonic keyboard (see also **Shand Morino**). The BCC# diatonic accordion, known commonly as a British Chromatic system, is therefore really a hybrid instrument.

Dingle, Ken Ken Dingle began playing piano accordion in 1946, and was self-taught until 1950 when he studied in London with Percy Holland. By the 1960s, Ken had formed an accordion orchestra in the West Country and regularly competed in the annual NAO regional festivals and All-Britain Championships. He and his wife Anne were founders of South East Cornwall Accordion Club, and promoted the accordion vigorously for many years in their area. Ken was particularly keen and skilled at composition, and wrote scores of short pieces for accordion. In the 1980s he began a project to record (on cassette) and also publish his many compositions as sheet music, and these were privately made available under the name *Kenzone*. In the late 1990s, his compositions were revived, and Ron Hodgson's *Eden Music* reissued the sheet music, and the cassettes on CD. Ken Dingle's excellent compositions cover a wide spectrum of styles popular with accordionists, and they survive as his legacy to the accordion movement.
Discography: A series of three CDs, each titled *Take Note*, was issued in 1999 from the 1980s *Kenzone* cassettes. These CDs feature Ken Dingle playing a total of around fifty of his compositions. John Nixon did the re-mastering, and the sheet music was re-issued by Ron Hodgson (see **Hodgson, Ron**).

Doris, Malachy Using piano accordion plus occasional vocals, Malachy Doris has pursued a successful career in Ireland for over forty years. He has made a large number of recordings, some with the four-piece *Malachy Doris Ceilidh Band* and others as a soloist, mainly on cut-price record labels, often to be found on market stalls. An accordionist with a straightforward, unflashy approach, Malachy Doris' style concentrates on putting the tune across in a way that appeals to the casual listener, a formula that has proved to be very successful. Malachy Doris' recordings, because of their widespread availability, have spread his name and his easy listening music to the general public in Ireland and Britain, and he has done much to help keep the accordion popular for many years.
Selected discography: *Irish Dance Time* (1980); *Continental Accordion* (1984); *The Best of Irish Dance – The Malachy Doris Ceilidh Band*; *Accordion Gold* (2002)

Double Octave An accordion with double octave tuning normally has four sets of treble reeds; this includes tremolo tuning, and one set of reeds tuned an octave lower and another set tuned higher than normal pitch. The presence of the higher octave pitch reeds – often called a piccolo reed – makes an accordion with double octave tuning particularly useful in playing classics or jazz, or in accordion orchestras.

Dry Tuning and Wet Tuning are alternative terms sometimes used for straight and musette tuning.

Duncan, Archie (born 1927) Introduced to the piano accordion at the age of ten, Archie Duncan found himself part of a Scottish Command Concert Party entertaining the troops during World War Two. In 1946 he joined the army for two years and gained further experience playing with unit bands, after which he began to study the accordion more seriously.

Between 1948 and 1952, after which he turned professional, Archie entered Scottish, British and World Championships organised by the British Association of Accordionists, becoming the Scottish Open Champion four times during this period.

His first solo radio broadcast was with the BBC in October 1953. In 1954, he formed the *Archie Duncan Quintet*, and thereafter was involved in broadcasts for many years after that. From 1961 to 1965, he was principal accordionist with the Scottish Variety Orchestra. During the 1960s Archie appeared on the television programmes *The White Heather Club* and *Degrees of Folk*. In 1966, he was selected to play and record the theme music to the BBC television thriller *The Dark Island*, composed by button accordionist Ian MacLachlan. Since then, of course, *The Dark Island* has become probably the most played and recorded Scottish number of all-time (eclipsing even *The Bluebell Polka*) – but Archie Duncan did it first!

In the 1970s, Archie Duncan made two excellent LPs, and has since pursued a career as highly regarded session accordionist. He also happens to be the uncle of present day accordion star, Gary Blair.
Discography: *High Level Accordion* (1972); *Three Faces of St Andrew*

Duncan, Tom Scots born Tom Duncan was a Chief Superintendent in the Lancashire Police, and a keen amateur accordionist in his spare time. However, once he had retired from the 'day job,' Tom began to involve himself more fully with the accordion. He set up the Wyre Accordion Club, and then organised the first of his annual Easter Saturday Wyre Accordion Festivals at the Marine Hall, Fleetwood. He then went a stage further, organising weekend *International Accordion Festivals* – very much in the style of Malcolm Gee's Caister events – with the first one taking place at Pontins' Middleton Towers holiday camp at Morecambe in 1995. The following year the festival re-located to Pontins at Blackpool, in the Spring, and has been there ever since. Tom's festivals have presented many world-class stars such as Danielle Pauly, Frank Marocco, Peter

Soave, Oleg Sharov and Dermot O'Brien. He has also been keen to present younger players to the public – a cause dear to his heart.

In 1997, Tom Duncan joined forces with Heather Smith as joint editor and publisher of *Accordion Profile*, a monthly magazine. This A5-sized publication has, to a large extent, continued the style and flavour of the late, lamented Malcolm Gee's *Accordion Monthly News* of the 1980s.

At the UK Championships in Scarborough in May 1999, Tom Duncan received a Special Award from the NAO for his dedicated service to the accordion movement.

Never one to seek the limelight, and preferring to watch events on stage from the sidelines, Tom Duncan decided in 2003 that the time was right for him to step aside from organising his festivals. His legacies to the accordion movement are the many opportunities and encouragement he offered to young, up-and-coming accordionists.

Dunn, Fred Swiss-born Fred Dunn plays and teaches both piano and button accordion, functions as an examiner for the British College of Accordionists, and has a number of academic music qualifications obtained some years ago in Switzerland.   He has also composed and recorded literally dozens of Continental-style pieces, of varying degrees of difficulty, and in solo, duet and band arrangements - all of which are obtainable from Fred Dunn's website: - www.madasafish.com/~freddunn

Ear, Training your *The following article was written by Adrian Dante, one of this country's most eminent authorities on accordion playing technique, and reproduced by kind permission of the author: -*

Training Your Ear

Everyone stands in rapt admiration of the accordionist who has the knack of improvising and embellishing an air as he goes along. He may not be much of a musician from the point of view of knowledge and technique; he may not even know his notes and very often doesn't. It makes no difference. His spontaneous playing by the light of nature, inspiration of whatever you care to call it, arouses all the more wonder and envy in the listener. Those who have learnt the hard way look back on their hours and hours of laborious practice and think: "If only I could do *that*!"

Slavish Imitation

Well, you can do that – provided you don't put obstacles in your path by adopting a defeatist attitude in advance. The musical education most of us undergo tends to fill us with paralysing inhibitions and make us slaves to a mechanical technique. In these circumstances self-expression as opposed to slavish imitation is made unnecessarily difficult. Bear in mind that the player who wins applause for his improvisation, for dressing up a melody or adding a few modern breaks, and so on, is using self-expression – and getting a tremendous 'kick' out of it.

There are a few points to clear up which will help you to free yourself from your musical inhibitions and enjoy yourself in the same way. First, please understand that the ability to improvise is NOT a mysterious gift of nature bestowed by the wisdom of Providence on some and denied to others. It can be acquired. It simply is part – an important part – of the sum total of all musical ability possessed to a greater or lesser degree by every performer-interpreter-composer.

Listen to Your Own Playing

The ability to improvise or 'dress up' a tune comes through ear-training in the perception of sound. It follows, therefore, that concentrated listening is an important preliminary. Unfortunately the conventional musical education to which most of us are accustomed does its best to ignore ear training. So much time and energy are devoted to pure technique to achieve correct performance of the printed score, nothing is left for the development of originality, however modest. The average music student's only outlet for self-expression is in the way he interprets – the expression he puts into his playing. To be interested in expression, especially if the student attempts to deviate from the way in which he is taught and from the expression directions printed on the score, is a healthy sign. It means that the student is at least listening very attentively to what he is playing.

Secondly, the power of improvisation is too often regarded as the prerogative of the untutored 'nature boy' or of the learned composer. In the hands of the vast army of middling musicians, it is feared and shunned in case it should prove to be an obstacle to good playing.

All Music Is One in Essence

This is nonsense. To get it out of your head, think of the whole field of music from the humblest to the highest as ONE; think of all musicians from the most limited and primitive to the greatest, as sharing the same quality or talent in different proportions. Skill in spontaneous expression needs training and developing like any other manifestation of artistic expression. A painter or a sculptor is encouraged at his art school and throughout his career to express his *own* ideas; he is expected to do so, otherwise he is dubbed a mere copyist or craftsman. Why should a musical education be kept within such strictly disciplined bounds that it discourages the development of originality?

Finally, without improvisation there would be no creation – no musical masterpieces at the very highest lever, no musical score for you to reproduce or copy in sound every time you play, or attempt to play it. When a composer goes to his instrument, whatever it may be, and tries out a few notes, or a few bars of something that is "in his head" – something that may one day be a great concerto or symphony – is he not improvising? And has he not, in the vast majority of cases, also had a thorough theoretical and practical education in music?

The Great and You

What, then, is the difference between the great composer and you and me and the chap who makes up a bar or two here and there to embellish a simple air played on the accordion? The difference is that in the great one the creative urge – the need and the ability to make new combinations of sound – is so strong that it breaks through the cast-iron swaddling bands of even the worst type of musical upbringing. In the case of the rest of us the creative spark is so weak, it may be stifled without our ever knowing we possessed it.

The composer literally carries music in his head; when he goes to his instrument to try it out, he is merely externalising it. Until he can translate from his head to the instrument and then, through the naming of notes, give the sounds he hears permanence on a musical score, there can be no composition for the rest of us to play.

You too, must carry music in your head by learning to play by ear and from memory. In the first stages of musical creation the composer is playing by ear. The process involved in playing by ear music that has been learnt from a score and memorised, or merely heard somewhere, and in the early stages of composition is the same in so far as the performer has "music in his head" and seeks to externalise it in sound. The means whereby he does this, whether he be great genius or humble strummer is identical: it is in the ear. Only through the use of the ear in attentive listening does one develop a sense of *pitch* and *time*.

Two Kinds of Pitch

Pitch is essentially the ability to distinguish between one note and another. Without the use of pitch, relying on time and rhythm alone (as in the beating of drums), a certain limited and monotonous kind of music is possible. Primitive tribes in various parts of the world have always used this kind of music, and there are many folk tunes today consisting of nothing but variations on three or four notes.

So, to be the admiration or your friends – and perhaps follow in the footsteps of the great – the first thing you have to do is to train your ear in the discrimination of pitch. You will find you cannot do this without singing, humming or, if you prefer, whistling, preceded by attentive, concentrated listening, not only to the playing of others, but to your own.

There are two kinds of pitch, relative and absolute. Judgment of relative pitch is to be able to sing, hum or otherwise reproduce the next note above or below a given note, using the scale tone intervals. If from one given note you are able to build up a whole scale, then your ear is quite discriminating and you have a good sense of relative pitch.

Absolute pitch is less easy; but practice in relative pitch soon develops it. A sense of absolute pitch may be defined as the ability to give to a sound its musical name and key; to be able to say on hearing a single note or a piece of music: "That is B*b* minor," or "That is written in the key of B*b* minor."

Hear It Before You Play It

Now, a player with a pitch-discriminating ear, not only finds it easy to memorise music, but also to indulge his own fancy in little phrases of his own. He finds it easy because the 'music in his head' (which, incidentally, he does actually hear with the inner ear of his mind) is always *in advance* of what he is playing. He hears the sound he is playing *before* he makes them on his instrument.

How otherwise did the great Beethoven write so much immortal music when he was stone deaf? Whatever the instrument being studied the same principles of ear-training apply. It can profitably by linked to eye-training with the printed score in front of the student; but the aim should be to become independent of that score, especially for accordionists for whom printed music is still limited.

Solfeggio Exercises Will Help

For acquiring a sense of absolute pitch there is nothing better than a progressive series of *solfeggio* studies. They will teach you to recognise at a glance the value and pitch of the printed notes, their inter-relationships and their relationship to key. Without this eye and ear training the accordionist is lost in professional orchestral work and has to rely on parts written for other instruments.

Half an hour of *solfeggio* exercises a day, singing by ear from a note struck, later without any note struck, will make a vast difference to the ear training and memory work of any student in a matter of months. Try it and see.

Adrian Dante, Accordion World Review (1955)

Easton, Jim Jim Easton OBE is Scottish-born, but world travelled thanks to his career in the diplomatic service, taking up appointments in France, Italy, Belgium, Yugoslavia, Czechoslovakia, Bolivia and the USA. Before his diplomatic career became the main part of his life, Jim played both accordion and the trumpet, and was a member of an army dance band during his National Service in the 3rd Queen's Own Hussars. He rose to the position of Vice Consul, but since retiring, has devoted time to practising and performing on the piano accordion, and has also composed music for the instrument. He has also written many articles for the *Accordion Times*, and has self-produced two CD recordings.
Discography: *Playing To The Heart* (2000); *Musical Journey* (2003).

Edmondson, Tommy (1934-2001) A lifelong player of the 5-row button accordion, Tommy Edmondson was a skilled country-dance musician, well known in the North East for his playing at ceilidhs and at the Rothbury Accordion & Fiddle Club, of which he was a founder member. He was also a regular player at the Mull Music Festival. At twelve years of age, Tommy was encouraged by Jimmy Shand, no less, to practice his newly acquired accordion, and took the great man's advice to heart – becoming good enough to play gigs in the bands of Angus Fitchett and Andrew Rankine whenever these bands came to his area. Tommy has been immortalised as the man who plays the theme music (*The Trumpet Hornpipe*) for the long running BBC television programme, *Captain*

Pugwash. Sadly, the end title credits the programme's music to Johnny Pearson, the BBC staff music conductor, and with no reference to Mr Edmondson. Equally sadly, Tommy Edmondson was paid only 30 shillings (£1.50p in today's money!) for the recording session – a deal that excluded him from royalties. *Captain Pugwash* has been shown for many years – with lots of repeats - in several countries worldwide, and one can only wonder how much the accrued royalties would have added up to!

Electronic Accordion, The   In the 1970s, the widespread emergence of the electronic accordion in this country tended to elicit all kinds of responses from people, ranging from great excitement at what was perceived to be a 'new dawn' in musical sounds from an instrument whose sound had changed little for decades beforehand, to downright hostility at what others considered to be a gaudy, second-rate imitation of an electronic organ. The first electronic accordions, such as the Cordovox, were reedless and actually did sound like organs; later instruments combined traditional reeds with electronics. The fact that the player could use either reeds or electronics or combine both features made possible a very wide range of sounds, making electronic accordions useful and common in show bands, bierkeller bands and for solo pub/club entertainers. The disadvantage of these instruments was their weight plus the extra gear that had to be carried around. The popular model used in this country has been the Elkavox. The arrival of midi in the 1990s has seen the electronic accordion superseded by a newer system with greater musical potential. See also the article on **Midi**.

Electronium   The Electronium was the ancestor of the electronic accordion. It was designed by René Seybold in 1950, and manufactured by Hohner in Germany. The Electronium was actually an electronic organ in the shape of an accordion, and carried no reeds. For a long time, the accordion world was sceptical about the Electronium, and eventually the instrument evolved into the electronic accordion, which also possessed reeds and functional bellows.

Emblow, Jack   As far as the general public is concerned, Jack Emblow is undoubtedly the most listened to accordionist in Great Britain as a result of over forty years playing on the soundtracks of films, radio and television programmes, plus many advertisements used on TV and in the cinema. Jack's accordion has been heard countless times on the theme and incidental music of BBC television's *'Allo,'Allo*, and *Last of the Summer Wine*, and ITV's revival of *Maigret* and the early series of the BBC's *Bergerac,* to name but four of the many TV shows featuring his music. His film credits include and go right back to *Whistle Down The Wind*, starring Hayley Mills and Alan Bates, and Cliff Richard's *Summer Holiday* in the early Sixties.

In 1959, Jack was signed up by the late Cliff Adams as accompanist for a new programme called *Sing Something Simple*, due to broadcast for a short season on BBC radio's Light Programme. That 'short season' went on every week for the next 42 years! *Sing Something Simple* became a radio 'institution', finishing in November 2001 following the death of Cliff Adams.

Jack Emblow has been a professional musician throughout his working life, beginning as a member of the Al Podesta Accordion Band in the 1940s. He toured the country's variety theatres, but by the mid-1950s had moved into the world of recording studios as a session musician. Jack has featured on the recordings of other accordionists, including Jimmy Shand and Dermot O'Brien. Of the latter, he recalls playing second accordion when Dermot O'Brien was recording a version of *The Carnival Of Venice*, but the rehearsal was not going well. O'Brien and his backing band, *The Clubmen* plus Jack, spent a long time practising the piece but it would not come out right. After a frustrating time in the studio, the musicians decided to have a break and all went to the nearest pub for a pint or two. An hour later, suitably refreshed with some 'amber nectar', they went back to the studio, donned instruments, and when the red light in the studio shone, produced a spot-on version of *The Carnival of Venice* – the last track on the LP *The Laughing Accordion*, by Dermot O'Brien & His Clubmen (plus anonymous 2nd accordion part by Jack Emblow).

In 1973 Jack Emblow, Ernie Shear (banjo), Roy Davey (vibes), Pete Collins (bass) and Geoff Lofts (drums) were recruited and put together by the BBC as a session band – *The French Collection* – whose brief was to play well known tunes in a bright, lively style as interlude music on the late Ray Moore's Saturday morning shows on Radio Two. Such was the impression made on listeners, a series of *French Collection* LPs followed, presenting tunes everyone knows in a snappy, lively accordion-led sound. Early publicity for these records stated that: *"This all too depressing world needs cheering up from time to time, and nobody is better qualified for that none too easy task than the French Collection."* That sentence sums up the music of the *French Collection*.

Jack has made a lot of recordings in his own right – some solo, others as part of *The French Collection*, and one LP – a jazz album called *Flying Home* - was made in 1987 with fellow accordionist, Tony Compton. In the 1960s, Jack made a series of four musette-style LPs for EMI under the pseudonym, Adriano. These were made-to-order pastiche recordings of French musette music, and have now become collectors' items. Jack Emblow also made several recordings backing the Cliff Adams Singers in the *Sing Something Simple* style. There were also many EPs and singles released in the late 1950s and 60s of music performed in French and Continental styles. Tracking down Emblow recordings is no easy matter, and it would take the investigative skills of Sherlock Holmes to make a complete list of the many LPs, cassettes and CDs featuring the music of this great accordionist!

Jack Emblow's long-term connection with EMI as a session musician inevitably means that he has featured on the recordings of many famous singers, including artistes as diverse as Donovan and Elton John, folk-rock chart toppers The Strawbs, and the eccentric ex-model, Grace Jones. He also played on The Beatles' *All You Need Is Love*, a Number One hit record in Britain and the US in July 1967. Jack can also be seen playing on the video version of *All You Need In Love*, as part of a huge backing studio orchestra under the direction of George Martin.

Jack has owned several accordions, both straight and musette tuned, but is known to favour the Excelsior straight tuned with cassotto model he bought in New York many years ago. He believes that the tight compression found on the American-made Excelsiors allows the player to achieve good intonation with very little effort, especially useful for a jazz musician such as himself. On the other hand, he is not keen on the sound of musette instruments, despite having made many recordings in that style. To Jack's ears, a musette instrument gives an impure sound, and his preference is for the sort of straight, mellow tone heard on his jazz recordings or *Sing Something Simple*.

Apart from his studio work, Jack Emblow has established a reputation as an outstanding jazz musician, appearing in jazz clubs and at jazz festivals in this and other countries. For several years, in the 1970s/early 80s, he worked in a small combo, alongside trumpet player, the late John McLevy. Since then, Jack has played and recorded regularly in a highly successful quintet led by ace jazz guitarist, Martin Taylor. This small group has been popular and much admired around the country, presenting a modernised version of the sort of jazz pioneered by Django Reinhardt/Stephane Grappelli's *Quintet of the Hot Club of France* in the 1930s.

Jack Emblow has made many guest appearances in accordion clubs, and also at such festivals as Caister, the All-Scotland Festival in Perth, and in France at the Chartres Accordion Festival. In recent years, he has worked extensively with electronic accordionist, Tony Compton – with whom he has a special musical rapport – but still occasionally appears as a solo accordionist.

Little known is the fact that Jack has arranged and composed music for accordion, and in the early 1960s wrote *Jazz Accordion* - a tutor book about learning how to play jazz on the accordion. One of his compositions, *Tango Musette*, was recorded and appears on the French Collection compilation CD *Enjoy Yourself*; and his arrangements of the Gershwin classics *I Got Rhythm* and *Summertime* were published by Charlie Watkins.

In 2002, after several years serving as an Honorary Vice President, Jack Emblow was elected Honorary President of the National Accordion Organisation of the United Kingdom – a fitting honour indeed for the man known to so many as 'The Guv'nor.'

Selected discography; *Ritual Fire Dance* (1964); *Sur Le Pavé* (1965); *The Last Time I Saw Paris* (1966); *Under the Bridges of Paris* (1968); *I Love Paris* (1971); *Happy Music Party* (1973); *The French Collection* (1974); *Travelling With The French Collection* (1975); *I Love Paris* (1985); *Flying High* – made with Tony Compton (1987); *Spirit of Django* (1990); *Enjoy Yourself* (1991); *Paris Musette* (1997); *Café de Paris* (1997)

English Connection, The *In this autobiographical piece, John Nixon, a master of the English concertina, tells about his life in music (see* also **Nixon, John***):*

The English Connection
Recollections from John Nixon

My father, the late Jack Nixon, was one of five children who lived with their parents in a village just outside Bolton in Lancashire. The village (Little Lever) was surrounded by, on one side, the church where I was christened, the Leverhulme Park, a river, Ramsden's pub, a very lofty railway viaduct, and just beyond that, a monster canal viaduct which, like the railway viaduct, crossed the valley high in the sky. Further round was a steep grassy bank on top of which was a terrace of cottages. In the centre of this terrace lived a man who was to have a big influence on my father's life (and subsequently mine).

The man was a musician who played a Wheatstone Treble Aeola (which had glass keys), and other instruments such as Musical Glasses and a Musical Saw. I think his name was Abraham. My father, as a boy, used to climb the grassy bank and sit outside Abraham's house to listen to his music. Abraham soon encouraged my dad into his home to listen properly, and this led to dad being taught by Abraham to play the concertina.

My dad's family were not interested in hearing a youth practising scales in the house, so dad had to practice in the coal shed outside. Of course, when his ability was recognised locally, the family became very interested. Dad saved his money until, at age 19, he bought a new Wheatstone Aeola Treble (the one that I still play).

My father married and they set up home around the corner in Radcliffe Road in two rooms above a butcher's shop (which is where I was born in January 1927), just a couple of hundred yards along the road from where the steeplejack and media personality Fred Dibnah lives today. The shop is currently a chip shop.

We moved to Bridgeman St, Farnworth, which is where, at the age of four, dad taught me to play a Wheatstone Treble of the learners type, which had rosewood ends and white bone keys, except C naturals which were coloured red. I have a similar model still, which, with reeds removed, has been used by a number of actors in various TV productions that I have played in. When I was almost six years old, my dad bought me a second hand Wheatstone Aeola Baritone for ten guineas, and that is the one I use mostly nowadays.

Dad took me along to a Bolton Concertina Band rehearsal when I was six. This was in the basement of Queen St Mission in Bolton, and dad, who was the lead concertina, introduced me to the band's conductor, Albert Jennings (who also conducted the Black Dyke Mills brass band), and it was agreed that I be allowed to join the band. I was handed a Wheatstone Baritone, which had been tuned by the local expert (Dick Lord, I think his name was) so as to be playable in Horns in F parts directly, using standard English fingering. I played many concerts with the band, and the highlight came on January 18th 1935, one week before my 8th birthday. It was a broadcast from the old BBC Manchester studios in Piccadilly. I remember such programme items such as a Selection from *The Maid of the Mountains, Lustpiel Overture,* and *The Entry of the Gladiators* march. I can, for some obscure reason, remember that each player was paid 5 shillings, except the drummer (not part of the normal line-up), who received 7 shillings & 6 pence.

About this time, dad formed his Quintet, which enjoyed success with many concerts and broadcasts from Manchester. In those days, the BBC used to audition folk in their own homes as well as the studios, and I can remember a visit to our home in Bridgeman St by BBC men Mr DG Bryson and a Mr McNair, who auditioned dad's Quintet. Initially, the Quintet consisted of dad leading on Treble, Charlie Pollitt 2nd Treble, Wilf Wallace on Baritone, Bert Dingsdale on Double Bass, and Jim Howarth on Cornet. An excellent pianist called Arthur Prescott later replaced Jim Howarth. The popular programmes they played included *The Grasshopper's Dance, Cuckoo Waltz, Old Comrades March, Belpheger March,* and most popular of all, the *Intermezzo* from *Cavaleria Rusticana.*

During the 30s, dad also played many solo spots around Lancashire and Yorkshire, usually accompanied by a pianist. He eventually arranged the piano parts for me to play on my Baritone and, as a duo, we were quite busy by the late 30s, playing in clubs, schools and pubs, etc. Each year dad would book our one week holiday in Morecambe at Mrs Law's boarding house in Queen's Square, and he also arranged for the two of us to play at the Phoenix Club in Lancaster for three evening spots. This engagement each year paid for our family holiday.

A very significant contribution to improving my sight-reading came as a result of borrowing large volumes of complete pianoforte works of all the great composers, from Farnworth Public Library. By now, I had developed the ability to read the bass clef parts of piano music on my Baritone, and each free evening (after my father had bathed and eaten – his day job was an Iron Moulder), we would play all the music available from the library, playing some of the more difficult parts over again until we were satisfied with our performance.

I was given an opportunity to go to the BBC studios in Manchester to audition for the Children's Hour programmes, and although I passed the audition, I wasn't allowed to broadcast until I was twelve years old, and even then I had to have a licence from the local authority.

Eventually, in 1940, I did play the first of many solo spots on Children's Hour, accompanied on piano by that great musician, the late Violet Carson – later to become famous as Coronation Street's Ena Sharples. I remember playing *Tosselli's Serenata,* Heyken's *Stanchen Serenade,* and Sousa's *Stars and Stripes Forever* march. I was also called upon to perform the musical parts of actors in a number of radio plays for the Children's Hour.

Just prior to this, in the late 30s, dad bought me a trumpet and I eventually played it with his Quintet, and also with the local Salvation Army Band and the Farnworth Old Brass Band.

When the Second World War came along, members of the Bolton Concertina Band and dad's Quintet dispersed for the war effort, and never reformed after the war ended. I sold my trumpet and borrowed money to buy an alto saxophone, with the intention of getting the concertina into a dance band. In fact, the saxophone (and clarinet) took over as I was in demand to play lead saxophone at the (then) Bolton Palais and Bury Palais. During the resident band's holidays, I took my own band into each ballroom for a fortnight.

Even though I had, you could say, made it with the saxophone and clarinet, I still wanted to push the concertina forward to play with other instruments. One evening, whilst playing for dancing with a quartet, I used the concertina for a waltz and played through the stand microphone so as to be heard above the other instruments. A man came to me and said he could provide me with a much better sound with a personal amplifier and a small microphone fitted to each end of the Baritone. After he tried various combinations, I was kitted out properly and that opened up a whole new opportunity to develop my playing in dance bands and with jazz groups. I shortly afterwards moved to the South-West, and the amplified Baritone was heard in just about every establishment in the Bath, Bristol and Warminster district, including the radio and television studios of TWW and the BBC. I was very busy playing for dancing in large and small bands, and became a member of the Tony Mockford Quintet at the Grand Spa Hotel in Bristol for some years. Tony loved the sound of the Baritone and wrote many special arrangements for it within the Quintet. The guitarist with this band, Bill Parnham, had previously been a member of the Mantovani Orchestra.

I later moved to the West London district of New Denham and developed a long lasting BBC and ITV television connection for session work, and also obtained many engagements to play in orchestras for the recording of film scores, notably with the London Symphony and Wren Orchestras. The noted French composer, Philippe Sarde, first wrote for the English concertina in his score for the Roman Polanski film, *Tess* and he said that he liked the sound of the concertina because it was different. He scored the concertina for four films, which were recorded in London or Paris.

I had the pleasure of playing alongside the great Jack Emblow during a jazz session in Marlow in 1972, and that was the first of many enjoyable sessions in or around West London.

I had become conscious of the fact that I had gradually used the English concertina in an ever-enlarging sphere of music, and this was something that dad did during the 1930s. This has been done in the company of quite famous musicians such as Michel le Grande, Paul McCartney, Henry Mancini and Barbara Streisand, and I feel sure that my father, and the man who taught him so many years ago, would have been pleased and even proud to have witnessed such a wide acceptance of the English concertina. I hope that others can further this, and that the very many players whose main interest lies in the English folk idiom will take advantage of any tuition available, to spread their abilities to take in classical, jazz and dance music, in addition to the folk music of other countries.

My father taught me to play the English concertina, but even more, he taught me to appreciate all forms of music and how to listen to them properly.

John Nixon, September 2000

English Country Dance Music and the Electronic Accordion *The author of this book used a Giulietti electronic accordion in a ceilidh band during the 1980s, and wrote the following article as a means of exploring the instrument's possibilities in the genre of English country dance music: -*

English Country Dance Music & the Electronic Accordion

English country-dance bands nowadays come in various types and instrumental line-ups, and over recent years there has been a tendency for electronic accordions, keyboards, bass guitars and electric guitars to be regularly and effectively featured alongside the more traditional acoustic instruments such as fiddles, banjos, melodeons, concertinas and accordions. This may not please the purists in the English folk dance world, but electronic instruments are seemingly here to stay.

Since the 1980s, the electronic accordion has been used to good effect for country-dances, barn dances or hoe-downs (the names are interchangeable for basically the same thing!). The purpose of this article is to look at some of the possibilities that the electronic accordion has to offer when played for a hoe-down (or whatever name you choose for English folk dancing).

The first point to make is that an electronic accordion can give a band a full and very rounded sound. The fusion of acoustic and electronic voices in the treble, together with the powerful electronic bass provides tremendous drive and lift to dance music, when played properly. The most useful electronic voices are likely to be the flutes, vibrato, percussion, piano, clavichord and string bass. These can come together in various combinations according to the type of dance the music is chosen for, and are best used in conjunction with acoustic voices: in country-dance music the function of electronic voices is to supplement, and not replace, acoustic accordion sounds.

English country-dance music is actually an eclectic genre, which covers tunes in 2/4, 4/4, 6/8, 9/8 and 3/4 time signatures from England, Scotland, Ireland and North America. There are also American square dance tunes, and music from the 16th and 17th centuries collected by John Playford and known collectively as *'Playford'*. Tunes from the French Canadian folk tradition, parts of Europe and even sing-along evergreens from the likes of Max Bygraves (especially useful for the old-fashioned barn dance) are often found in the repertoires of modern-day country-dance bands. Gone are the days of about forty years ago when the playing list would most likely be largely tunes of English origin.

The broad variety of present day folk dance repertoire makes the sound possibilities of an electronic accordion very useful indeed. For instance, in American tunes such as *Golden Slippers, Liza Jane* or *Oh, Susanna*, the combination of piano and clavichord (or honky-tonk piano, if available), added to musette treble and piano bass makes a super sound configuration. If a mandolin effect is available, that too will be fine. On Playford tunes, a different approach is required, in keeping with music of the Elizabethan and Stuart eras. Acoustically, straight reeds such as violin or bandoneon couplers coupled with clavichord or oboe or 4-foot flute, or possibly a guitar effect, will give the most suitable mix of sounds. On the other hand, a set of English, Irish or Scottish jigs requires a musette treble with no more than supplementary light sounding flutes plus piano. The left hand will use piano and bass, but the treble is most effective when set largely acoustic.

All the examples cited here are suggestions based on practical experience, and should not be regarded as definitive: they are meant to demonstrate some of the many possibilities in this genre. The important thing to bear in mind is that electronic voices should be chosen for effect, and this requires some experimentation. In typical dance tunes used for longways sets such as *The Rakes of Mallow*, acoustic musette is coupled with 8' 4' 2' flutes plus percussion, plus piano and vibrato in the treble – with acoustic low reeds plus bass plus piano. This tune, because of its staccato sound, would have one or more percussive sounds to provide some extra sparkle. On the other hand, a tune such as *The Girl I Left Behind Me* would use the same registration minus any percussion due to the legato nature of the melody. When playing hornpipes, percussive effects are a good idea – especially on a tune such as *The Sailor's Hornpipe*.

Some electronic sounds are of little or no use in folk dance music. These include strings, the 16' flute and sustain. A rhythm box is also not useful – in folk dance playing, it is often necessary to alter tempo. Having said that, the electronic accordion has enough combinations of sounds to add an interesting fresh dimension to what was once strictly the domain of acoustic purism.

Rob Howard (written in 1985, revised in 2003), Accordion Times

Enzo, Roberto An Italian who originates from Lido di Jessolo, near Venice, Roberto Enzo, a very talented piano accordionist, was twice the CMA Junior World Champion, and then twice runner-up for the CMA version of the senior world title in the 1970s and 80s. In his formative years as a musician, Roberto Enzo played regularly in an orchestra in St Mark's Square, Venice, entertaining the tourists. During his National Service in the Italian army, he drove a tank and was seriously concerned that the physical demands of tank driving would endanger his hands for playing the

accordion. Happily, his hands survived, and he went on to resume his career as a professional accordionist on discharge.

In 1990, he met and married a Scottish tourist, and promptly re-located to Glasgow – an event in his life that was also to herald a completely new phase for him as a musician. Soon after moving to Glasgow, Roberto visited *Rolston Accordions*, seeking contacts for employment as either an accordion teacher or a player. Robert Rolston recalls with amusement how Roberto, whose command of English was at that time somewhat limited, came into the shop asking if he could be employed as a teacher giving accordion lessons. The shop staff misunderstood Roberto's question and were convinced that he had come in wanting accordion lessons for himself! Once the communication problem was cleared up, it was not long before Roberto was a teacher for *Rolston Accordions*, playing regularly in restaurants around Glasgow, and improving his English.

Before moving to Scotland from Italy, Roberto Enzo had been a virtuoso accordionist, using an acoustic accordion and playing largely classical music and accordion classics. In Glasgow, however, he had a considerable change in musical direction – switching to midi, broadening his repertoire, and becoming a vocalist. In fact, Roberto Enzo re-invented himself as an all-round instrumental/vocal entertainer. He has appeared as guest artist at several accordion clubs and festivals in Britain, and is without question the best Italian musical entertainer residing in Great Britain today.

Discography: *My Accordion* – accordion classics & specialities (1993); *Souvenir Italiano* – volumes 1,2 & 3 (1996); *Robert Enzo Plays* – 16 instrumentals in Italian/Latin style, and all tracks composed & performed by Roberto Enzo (1997); *Romantic Moments* (1998).

Famous People who have played the accordion or related instruments include:

- **Jerry Allen** – American jazz organist and a legend of the electronic organ world.
- **Idi Amin** (1923-2003) - infamous and eccentric dictator of Uganda from 1971 to 1979. Amin is believed to have caused about 400,000 deaths in Uganda during his rule, and disappeared following an uprising, later turning up in Saudi Arabia.
- **Robert Beatty** – Canadian-born Hollywood film actor of the 1950s/60s.
- **Kevin Bowyer** – an internationally acclaimed classical organist, his recordings are occasionally played on BBC Radio 2's *The Organist Entertains*.
- **Benny Andersson** – member of Sweden's 1970s 'Super Group' Abba, now working as a professional accordionist. Anderrson also composed all of Abba's many hit songs.
- **Ronald Binge** – accordionist with the Mantovani Orchestra, and creator/arranger of the characteristic Mantovani cascading strings sound; most famous as a composer of such well-known light classical pieces as

Elizabethan Serenade (for which he won an Ivor Novello Award), *The Watermill* and *Sailing By*. A biography: *Sailing By – The Ronald Binge Story*, written by Mike Carey, was published in the year 2000 by Tranters, Payne St, Derby (telephone 01332 341 982). This book is an excellent read for anyone who is interested in the music of the 1930s to the 1950s, and comes complete with a full list of the many compositions and recordings made by Ronald Binge

- **Ward Bond**. Hollywood and television actor from the 1940s through to the 60s, Ward Bond is remembered by many as Major Seth Adams in TV's *Wagon Train*, and for major roles in such classic movies as *Gentleman Jim, The Quiet Man, The Searchers* and *It's A Wonderful Life*. In the latter film, Bond is featured in the last scene playing the accordion as the character Clarence gets his wings from heaven!

- **Jackie Brown** – World Flyweight Champion, 1932-35, Manchester's Jackie Brown was a crowd pulling, extrovert personality well known for playing his piano accordion in his dressing room to all and sundry both before and after his fights, and in public houses where he also sang. Made a fortune from boxing, but spent or gave it all away!

- **Chic Calderwood** – British Light-heavyweight Champion, 1960-66, from Craigneuk, Scotland, who once fought an exhibition bout with the legendary Muhammad Ali at Paisley Ice Rink. Calderwood played piano accordion, and was well known for playing at parties and social events. Killed in a car accident in Scotland, 1966, shortly after unsuccessfully fighting for the world title in Puerto Rico against Jose Torres.

- **Charlie Chaplin** – the great comedy star of silent films and later 'talkies' such as *The Great Dictator* played the accordion as a recreation. His daughter Jane Chaplin, in an interview for the *Los Angeles Times*, recalled: *"He had an old accordion, very heavy. He'd put it on his shoulders, strap himself up, and play these old English songs. The more we clapped, the more he played, and the more we got to stay up late!"*

- **Jacques Chirac** – President of France since 1995.

- **Martin Day** – BBC television producer when not playing button accordion in a Cajun band. Regular member of the *Ragin'Cajuns*.

- **Charles Dickens** (1812-1870) - world famous 19th Century English novelist whose works include *Oliver Twist, Nicholas Nickleby, Great Expectations, David Copperfield* and *A Christmas Carol*. Dickens was a keen accordionist in his spare time, and in 1852, on a tour of the USA where he gave readings from his works, in a letter home (dated Tuesday March 22nd) he wrote: *"I have bought another accordion. The steward lent me one on the passage out, and I regaled the ladies' cabin with my performances. You can't think with what feeling I play 'Home, Sweet Home' every night, or how pleasantly sad it makes us."*

- **Bruce Forsyth** – host of TV's *Generation Game*, but also a singer and musician.

- **Connie Francis** – American singer of Italian parentage who had hit records in the late 1950s such as *Who's Sorry Now* and *Stupid Cupid*. As a teenager, Connie appeared on American TV singing and playing the accordion, after which she went professional. The first advice her manager gave her was to drop the accordion from her stage act, as it was considered passé – advice that Connie heeded.

- **Mahatma Gandhi** - peaceful and charismatic campaigner for India's independence who was assassinated in 1948. As a young man, Gandhi played the English concertina.

- **Benjamino Gigli** (1890-1957) – legendary Italian tenor, who achieved fame and fortune in America, starring at the Metropolitan Opera in New York for 12 seasons from 1920 onwards. Gigli played the accordion as a recreation.

- **Valery Giscard d'Estaing** – former President of France. In 1973, when serving as Finance Minister and also at the time a rising, high profile politician and personality, Giscard agreed to play his accordion live on French television, giving the instrument's image a great boost. The following year, Giscard was elected President, and did much in the cause of the poor, women's rights, business expansion and the stimulation of exports.

- **Simon Gledhill** – winner of several NAO championship titles on piano accordion in the late 1970s/early 80s whilst a teenager, now a world travelled celebrity theatre organist, noted for his performances and recordings on Wurlitzers in the USA and often heard on BBC Radio 2's *The Organist Entertains*.

- **Tord Grip** – soccer coach from Sweden, and right hand man to England football manager Sven Goren Ericsson.

- **Mike Harding** – comedian, folk singer, writer, actor and presenter of *Folk On Two* on BBC Radio 2. Famous for his 1970s hit record, *The Rochdale Cowboy*, Mike Harding is a multi-instrumentalist who plays both piano accordion and concertina.

- **Thomas Hardy** (1840-1928) – novelist and poet from Dorset whose works include *Tess, The Mayor of Casterbridge* and *Far from the Madding Crowd*. Hardy played the button accordion, but preferred to play the fiddle, and was renowned for playing at country-dances. Hardy's musical side is celebrated on stage and CD by The Yetties.

- **Rolf Harris** – versatile Australian entertainer, musician, singer and artist with such chart topping songs as *Tie Me Kangaroo Down*, *Sport* and *Two Little Boys*. See **Harris, Rolf**. Rolf made the news in 2002 when his accordion accidentally caught fire on stage during a performance! (See **Strange, but true…**)

- **Jascha Heifitz** (1901-87) – Lithuanian-born but raised in America, Heifitz is regarded by the classical music world as the greatest violinist of the 20th Century. Away from the concert hall, however, Heifitz liked nothing better than to play the piano accordion for relaxation.

- **Peter Honri** – concertina playing member of a famous Music Hall family, seen and heard performing in an episode of *Dad's Army* called *The Godiva Affair*.

- **Geoffrey Hughes** – Liverpool-born actor who played Eddie Yeats in *Coronation St*, Onslow in *Keeping Up Appearances*, and Vernon Scripps in *Heartbeat*.
- **Jean-Michel Jarre** – French showman famous for his colourful synthesizer and laser-light shows, Jarre often includes a musette accordion within his performances.
- **Pete Jolly** – American jazz pianist; occasionally uses accordion in his performances.
- **Ron Kiefel** – American professional cyclist; 1984 Olympic Bronze medallist & US team captain; seven times *Tour de France* competitor.
- **Bert Kampfert** – German bandleader and composer who was once a member of an accordion orchestra. Kampfert wrote such well-known songs as *Spanish Eyes* and *Strangers in the Night*, and was also the first person to record The Beatles in 1961/62.
- **Francis Lai** – composer of film music e.g. the score from the movie *Love Story*.
- **Howard Leader** – actor who played the German officer with the eye patch in some episodes of *'Allo 'Allo*, and who later became a regular member of Esther Rantzen's team on BBC's *That's Life*.
- **John Lennon** – in the 1950s, before he became famous with The Beatles, John Lennon was an enthusiastic player of the accordion and the harmonica. Years later, in June 1967, Lennon borrowed Jack Emblow's Hohner Gola during a break from recording *All You Need Is Love*, and entertained all present in the studio. A photograph was taken of John Lennon playing the Gola, and this appeared in the press at the time. The original photo (wherever it is!?) probably would now have a high collectable value, such is the market for Beatles' memorabilia.
- **Barry Manilow** – American singer/pianist. In the much-criticised 1984 BBC television programme *The Accordion Strikes Back*, a short clip from a live performance showed Manilow poking fun at a time earlier in his life when his mother apparently coerced him into having accordion lessons. The anecdote provoked a furious reaction from viewers who accused him of demeaning the accordion. The clip may have been taken out of context as Barry Manilow has before and since often featured the accordion in his performances, and has demonstrated that he is actually a skilled player.
- **Richard Nixon** – US President, forced out of office by the infamous 1974 Watergate scandal, played the accordion. His two daughters were also accordionists.
- **Eamonn O'Neal** – Granada Television producer and GMR local radio personality. Eamonn, a cousin of the American Hollywood movie star Ryan O'Neal, plays an Elkavox and specialises in Irish traditional music. He made an LP of dance music in 1979 called *Mind the Step*. Eamonn acted as MC at the Evening Concert for the 1988 and 1989 NAO North West Area Festivals at Stockport Town Hall, and played as accompanist for the Lally School of Irish Dancers – one of the support acts to chief

guest artiste Jack Emblow (see also the section **Strange, but true...**).

- **Ross Perot** – American Senator and former Presidential candidate Ross Perot is a keen amateur accordionist in his spare time.
- **Edith Piaf** – legendary French songstress whose songs such as *La Vie En Rose,* Je *Ne Regrette Rien, Milord* and *L'Accordeoniste* have given her everlasting fame. Piaf could play the accordion, but did not accompany herself on her recordings.
- **HM Queen Elizabeth the Second** – had accordion lessons in the 1940s.
- **Donald Shaw** – keyboard player with Celtic Folk Band *Capercaillie.* Donald Shaw won the 1984 All-Britain Advanced Championship at Buxton.
- **George Bernard Shaw** – (1856-1950) – Irish-born playwright, writer and novelist who also played the English concertina, Shaw is arguably the greatest dramatist in the English language since Shakespeare. His plays include *Pygmalion, Arms and the Man, Caesar and Cleopatra, Androcles and the Lion* and *Major Barbara.* In 1888, writing under the pseudonym Corno di Bassetto, Shaw had this to say: *"There are people who desire to enjoy music socially; to play together, to explore the riches of concerted chamber music for the mere love of it, and without any desire to expand their lungs or display their individual virtuosity. Yet they are too old to learn the fiddle.... The difficulty is fortunately easy to solve. The instrument for them is a concertina...."*
- **George Shearing** – blind jazz pianist; composer of *Lullaby of Birdland.* Shearing studied the accordion at the British College of Accordionists in London, and in the 1940s played the Uniform system keyboard.
- **Shuldham–Shaw, Pat** – One of the English folk dance world's greatest composers, Pat Shaw wrote *Margarets's Waltz* – a tune that has become popular with Scottish accordionists in recent years. See the article **Shuldham–Shaw, Pat**
- **Nicholas Smith** – actor who played Mr Rumbold in the hit BBC TV comedy series *Are You Being Served?* Rumbold was seen playing the accordion in some episodes.
- **James Stewart** – Hollywood actor, the star of *It's A Wonderful Life* and many other movies. Has made more movies than any other actor. Jimmy Stewart once played accordion on BBC TV's *Parkinson* show.
- **Donald Thorne** (1900-67) – popular cinema organist who took up the accordion, and in the 1930s wrote a tutor book for piano accordion.
- **Mark Twain** – 19th Century American novelist, especially famous for writing *Tom Sawyer* and *Huckleberry Finn.* Twain not only played the accordion, he wrote a short story called *Accordion Essay – The Touching Story of George Washington's Boyhood.*
- **Reg Varney** – comedy actor best known for ITV's *On The Buses*; also a pianist, Reg Varney played professionally in variety theatres and has played accordion and piano live on television.
- **Geoff Wheel** – a forward, capped 32 times, in the all-conquering Welsh Rugby Union side that won the Grand Slam in the early 1980s. Has

appeared on local radio playing accordion and discussing the NAO festival in Swansea.

- **Prince William** – in 1995, the elder son of Prince Charles and the late Diana, Princess of Wales, had accordion lessons from Cyril Pasby during his time at Eton.
- **Eric Winstone** – 1940s and 50s big band leader. Eric Winstone was also the composer of such famous swing music pieces as *Caravan, Oasis* and *Stagecoach*.
- **Bernard Wrigley** – comedian, folk singer, occasional actor on stage, television and cinema (credits include *Coronation St*, *Emmerdale* and *Brassed Off* – playing the trade union leader). Bernard Wrigley often uses a bass concertina to accompany his songs.
- **Klaus Wunderlicht** – German electronic organ star on Hammond and Wersi organs.

****

Farran, Ken Warrington-based piano accordion player, teacher, composer, arranger, and Musical Director of the Weaver Valley Accordion Band, Ken Farran has made a substantial contribution to the cause of the accordion. Ken was once a cornet player in a Salvation Army band, and is a highly skilled, trained musician. He occasionally plays French-style gigs as 'André Dumas', and as a solo accordionist he has appeared in shows such as two theatrical productions of *Piaf*, on television in an episode of *Hetty Wainthrop*, and on the radio. He also frequently works in a duo alongside his wife, Wendy (Beautemont), and they have played on the Orient Express, at the Oasis Holiday Centre as well as in prestigious hotels and restaurants. Ken Farran has been an orchestral workshop MD at accordion festivals. Ken has long been involved with the NAO and has served as an adjudicator at NAO area and UK competitions. Currently he holds the position of Deputy President.

Ken started playing the accordion at five years of age, and as a young boy went along to gigs with his father's band. His dad played a Delfini 120 bass in a six-piece accordion band, and sometimes, young Ken played his Alvari 48 bass during the interval, to the amusement of the dancers. Later, Ken took lessons and the BCA exams, and for a short time was taught by Conway Graves.

At the age of 15, Ken played on Radio Luxembourg's *Opportunity Knocks*, hosted by Hughie Green. By 1950, he had a dance band of his own, and he had also joined the National Accordion Organisation, taking part in concerts. By the 1970s, he had become an NAO committee member, and in 1984 became General Secretary and co-ordinator for the All-Britain Championships. Subsequently, Ken became in turn, Vice President, then Deputy President of the NAO. His wife Marion carried on as Secretary but died in 2000.

In the year 2000, he was given an Award of Merit for services to the accordion.

Ken has taught the accordion and brass instruments since 1956, and in the 1970s became a member of the Teachers' Advisory Council of the British

College of Accordionists. In 1977 he was invited to teach accordion at the Manchester School of Music, and in 1981 started an accordion school in Warrington at Dawson's music store. He has also taught accordion part-time at Salford Technical College and with Wigan Education Authority.

In 1982 Ken formed the Weaver Valley Accordion Band. Around this time he had also begun to arrange and compose music, some of which he has published himself. The WVAB have played in numerous contests and concerts, and have toured Germany and Holland.

Apart from the accordion, Ken has also been a choirmaster and has conducted a performance of Handel's *Messiah*. He has also played violin, clarinet and guitar. One of his favourite sayings is that *"There are too many accordionists/instrumentalists, and not enough musicians"*.

Fellowes, Douglas Douglas Fellowes fulfilled many roles within the accordion movement such as player, teacher, organiser, adjudicator, but above all was a great enthusiast for the instrument. At various times in his life he was an administrator with the National Union of Miners, Secretary of the Musicians' Union, and a professional musician. Douglas was also the driving force behind Barnsley Accordion Club, and was known to many as an adjudicator at NAO festivals. Douglas was liked and respected by all who knew him, and when he died aged 78 in February 2003, he was mourned by many and sadly missed.

Festivals The accordion movement in this country has a long history of staging festivals, dating back to the 1880s when contests were held for players of button accordions and melodeons. The advent of the piano accordion in the late 1920s led to the organisation of local and national championships from 1935 onwards, and for more details the reader should consult **Accordion Champions of Great Britain/United Kingdom** – 1935/03 or the article titled **Accordion Day**.

One of the most recent large-scale weekend festivals held at a major venue in this country was the London Accordion Festival, held at Wembley Conference Centre on the 8th/9th December 2001. The Festival Director was Romano Viazzini, who assembled an all-star cast including Gervasio Marcosignori (Italy), Frederic Deschamps (France), Frank Marocco (USA), Jerome Richard (France), Vladimir Zubitsky (Russia), Djorde Gajic (Yugoslavia), Gary Blair, Keith Dickson's KODA, Jack Emblow, David Lukins, Owen Murray, David Farmer, John Leslie, Romano Viazzini, and many others. This festival also featured the BBC Concert Orchestra, and one of the concerts was broadcast on BBC Radio 3, compèred by Richard Baker. The staging of this festival was a huge gamble, following on from a series of accordion events in the preceding weeks that included the inaugural Pakefield and Bridlington festivals and the Coupe Mondiale, staged in Harrow. This sequence of festivals, all within the space of a couple of months, probably detracted from attendances at all these events – especially the London Festival.

Non–competitive accordion festivals where the main activities are workshops and concerts are a relatively new development in this country, and the credit for this idea belongs to the late Malcolm Gee. In November 1982, Gee organised a weekend festival at the Pontins Sands Bay Holiday Centre, near Weston–Super–Mare. The success of this venture eventually led to Malcolm Gee staging an annual Autumn Accordion Festival at the large Caister Holiday Centre, near Great Yarmouth. The popularity of Caister inspired others to stage non-competitive festivals in such places as Morecambe, Blackpool, Ayr and St Audrie's Bay in Somerset.

When Malcolm Gee died suddenly in 1997, Robert and Loretta Rolston stepped into the breach and ran the Caister festival. In 2001, however, the Caister site was redeveloped, and the Caister organisers were forced to look elsewhere. Loretta Rolston, now in sole charge, took her Caister team to Bridlington, staging a non–competitive event at the Spa Complex and using the local hotels. In the same year, Heather Smith and Tom Duncan staged a non–competitive festival at the Pontins Holiday Centre at Pakefield, situated close to the former Caister site. The festivals at Bridlington and Pakefield, plus the now long–established St Audrie's Bay event held in July are all faithful to Malcolm Gee's famous rallying call that this sort of event should be a *"total indulgence in accordions"*.

Flutina is the name given to the very first design of accordion, the first model of which was patented by Cyril Damien on May 6th 1829 in Vienna. Damien's instrument played chords on the right hand and bass notes on the other side, and was intended for accompanying singing. He called the instrument an 'accordion' – roughly translated as a 'chord machine'. In 1831, Pichenot Jeune in Paris designed a 16 <u>single note</u> – not chorded (8 key diatonic) flutina that played tunes, and he referred to this development as a 'clavier melodique'. This instrument is the true ancestor of what became known later in the 19th Century as the melodeon, from which the names derives. The original flutinas had paddle-like buttons and worked on a diatonic principle (each button produces two notes, sounded according to push or pull of the bellows). Not many flutinas have survived, and they have a substantial collectable value.

Folk Camps *If you enjoy camping, play an instrument and like folk music, the chances are that taking part in a Folk Camp will be of interest to you. Folk Camps are organised in many parts of the British Isles, and also in France. Details of Folk Camps can be obtained from Capers Folk Activity Holidays, 18 Roughmoor Cottages, Taunton, Somerset TA1 1HA; telephone 01823 270 754; e-mail info@folkcamp.com. There is also a website, found easily by typing Folk Camps into a general wordsearch.*

The following article, reproduced with kind permission of the Accordion Times, is an account of a fortnight's holiday spent on the French Folk Camp at Daoulas, Brittany in August 1988.

Putting the tent and cordial in Entente Cordiale!

It was the prospect of sun, beaches, fresh air, music and dancing which lured the Howard family to try out a Folk Camp holiday in Brittany this year. Marj and I, and our daughters Jane and Helen, packed our borrowed tent and drove all the way from rainy Stockport to sunny Daoulas for a fortnight of what the advertising leaflet called *"putting the tent and cordial in Entente Cordiale!"*

Most people reading this will no doubt be unaware of what a Folk Camp has to offer. The basic idea is that people interested in folk music, song and dance share a campsite and share their interests. Each week of the Folk Camp has an experienced leader, warden, caterer and musician to plan activities and ensure the day-to-day running of the camp. Everybody is expected to lend a hand at some stage with the chores, though folk activities of one kind or another fills most of the time.

At Daoulas, the mornings were given over to music and dance workshops, the afternoons to sunbathing on the beaches or sightseeing, and the evenings to a nightly ceilidh. Plenty of games, dancing and singing, plus other activities, were arranged for the children, and such was the rural position of the campsite, no babysitters were necessary.

From an accordionist's point of view, it was a happy coincidence that for each of the two weeks of the camp, the appointed musicians were accordion players, and excellent ones too!

Dave Roberts, from Southampton (country dance player, classically trained pianist and music graduate), was the 1st week's musician, and Jack Brothwell (music teacher from Swindon), was the 2nd week's musician – both knowledgeable musicians and experienced country dance players, well able to inspire the rest of us to join in the fun. It was the job of the musician to lead the morning workshop, oversee the dance workshops, and to play for the nightly shindigs.

Rob Howard accompanying Tanya, a young Irish dancer

Dave Roberts played a red coloured 80 bass Orfeo piano accordion. His morning workshops were concerned with the general principles of playing for country dancing, such as keeping a steady tempo, providing lift in the right places, how to start and stop properly, how to play cleanly – correct phrasing, proper time value of notes, and paying attention to rests. His often-repeated request to *"hear daylight"* referred to observing the rests, and was, of course, intended to try and make the music sound better.

On one of the days, Dave held an accordion workshop – the purpose of which was to explore ways in which single note bass runs can enhance the effectiveness of folk dance tunes. As he put it himself: *"The notes are all there, all you have to do is experiment and find them."* Dave gave all present a couple of sheets each, with two tunes containing bass runs he had worked out himself. The tunes were the *Fairy Dance* and the *Trumpet Hornpipe* (a.k.a. *Captain Pugwash*), and the bass arrangements were effective and thought provoking. Dave was not a man to simply theorise on music, however – every night he demonstrated his ideas and technique when playing for dancing.

Jack Brothwell played a two-row melodeon. A man of seemingly limit-less energy, Jack would lead the evening ceilidh well into the small hours, and still be up to lead the morning music workshop with renewed enthusiasm. A man of many talents, Jack not only played his beautiful Castagnari melodeon with great skill, but also proved himself as a dance caller, singer, Morris dancer and linguist. He had recently published a book of country-dance tunes, and many of these tunes were used at various times in the second week. The book is called *Follow the Band*, and presents simple but effective two part arrangements suitable for a wide range of instruments. This book,

and another one called *Playford Style* by another melodeon player called Dave Brown, formed the basis of the material used both in the morning workshops and nightly ceilidhs.

Asked about his role as a musician, Jack said: "My general aims on Folk Camps are to include as many people as possible in as much music making as possible. I try to encourage people to join in and not worry about their ability. Most people are sensitive enough to realise when to play quietly or drop out now and then. When people do join in, I try to make sure the music is of a suitable standard, and concentrate on playing it well. As far as *Follow the Band* is concerned, these are tunes that are enjoyable to play, but technically not too demanding, and therefore suitable for workshop and band use."

The fortnight at Daoulas passed all too quickly, though the memories have lingered on. The beautiful countryside and the many picturesque villages, many looking like the set of *Maigret* or *'Allo, 'Allo*. Sunbathing in hot temper-atures and swimming in the Atlantic during the afternoons were followed by the great evening meal prepared specially by local cook, Denise le Bars. We had a kite making competition and a grand massed test flight, with some weird and wonderful designs taking to the French skies. In the evening dances there were moments that stick in the mind, such as the occasions when Dave Roberts would *"do a Les Dawson"* and suddenly change key in the middle of a tune out of sheer devilment, leaving everyone, especially the rest of the band, wondering what was happening. Playing in the band at nights was in itself enjoyable and memorable. Seeing Jack Brothwell simultaneously calling the dances whilst playing, sometimes also in French for the benefit of visiting locals, was quite amazing. The sight and sound of people leaping around for dances such as *Sir Roger de Coverley* make brilliant memories. A local button accordionist, known to us only as Jacques, came into the camp one evening and taught us all some

Breton dances. The grand tours we did in the local towns, performing our British folk music, song and dance for local audiences was a great experience, as were the Bal Folkloriques (ceilidhs) held in the open air in market squares. All in all, a great holiday, and thanks to all concerned for all the fun we had.

Rob Howard, Accordion Times, January 1989

Folkworks Since the late 1980s, the North-East based *Folkworks* organisation has been responsible for setting up courses, concerts and summer schools specialising in all aspects of vocal and instrumental folk music for young people. Folkworks has done a great deal to raise the consciousness of young people towards folk music (and the accordion and other instruments), and has taken its enthusiastic approach into schools in many parts of the North-East. The Youth Summer School in Durham attracts about 100 participants, and in recent years the tutors have included many of the best musicians around such as Freeland Barbour, Karen Tweed, Alister Anderson and John Kirkpatrick. Accordion, melodeon and concertina workshops are all featured alongside other instruments, and standards of tuition and playing are high. *Folkworks* is an Educational Charity based in Newcastle and serving mainly the Northern Counties of England, although its work and influence is gradually extending further afield. Contact Folkworks at 69 Westgate Rd, Newcastle upon Tyne, NE1 1SG; telephone 091 222 1717.

Foster and Allen Mick Foster (piano accordion) and Tony Allen (guitar/vocals) have been one of Ireland's most commercially successful accordion-based acts ever, with record sales of over eighteen million worldwide. Their appeal transcends Irish music, and their repertoire includes ballads, love songs, evergreen favourites and Country & Western. The result is that Foster & Allen are not perceived as an 'Irish' act, and are followed by the general public at large – anyone, in fact, who enjoys melodious singing and playing. Mick Foster won the 1964, 1968 and 1970 All-Ireland piano accordion titles at the Fleadh Cheoil (Irish traditional music festival), and he usually plays some accordion solos in concerts and on recordings. He has made solo recordings, usually of Irish traditional dance music. This immensely popular duo originally based their style on Scotland's Alexander Brothers, but quickly established a name for themselves when their record company had the foresight to release as a single *A Bunch of Thyme*, which was a chart topping hit in 1984 both in this country and in Ireland. Follow up singles, *Maggie* and *After All These Years* were also big selling records, and Foster & Allen had the distinction of performing on BBC TV's Top of the Pops – featuring the accordion, of course. Since those heady days of the mid-80s, the duo have become internationally successful consistently filling theatres wherever they play, and producing to date 22 best selling albums and at least eight videos.

Selected discography: *The Worlds of Mick Foster & Tony Allen* – a double CD featuring solo albums (1988); *Traditional Irish Favourites* – Mick Foster (accordion) & Richie Daly (piano) (1999); *Songs That Sold A Million* (2002); *The Very Best of Foster & Allen* (double CD) (2003)

Tune book: *Mick Foster's Favourite Accordion Tunes* – 24 accordion arrangements include *The Bluebell Polka, Happy Hours, Haste to the Wedding, High Level Hornpipe, Jacqueline Waltz, Life in the Finland Woods, Sorrento Thoughts* and *The Oslo Waltz.*

Free Bass The term free bass means a bass keyboard made up entirely of single bass notes, and with no fixed chords. Since the 1980s, there has been a considerable expansion in the spread of free bass instruments worldwide, and they have become commonplace amongst accordionists who have serious aspirations in classical or modern music. Until the 1980s, free bass instruments were often called Bassetti accordions.

Free bass accordions come in three types i.e. those with only single bass notes; instruments known as 'converter' systems, featuring both complete single note basses plus a conventional Stradella bass, controlled by a switch enabling either bass system to be used; accordions with a Stradella bass system plus three or four extra rows of single bass notes.

French Musette July 14th – Bastille Day – in France is the one-day in the year when the accordion player – the *accordeoniste* – really is the kingpin of entertainment in cities, towns and villages throughout the nation. Throughout the rest of the year, however, the French maintain an ambivalent attitude towards the instrument that foreigners always associate most closely with their music and culture. You can go into the large supermarkets or record stores and find lots of CDs by French accordionists, and record sales are perennially high, yet lots of French people will hotly deny actually liking accordion music! This is somewhat similar to the situation in Britain regarding Cliff Richard inasmuch as few people admit to liking Cliff, and amongst the under 35s it is most 'uncool' to be a fan, yet his concerts always sell out and his record sales have been massive for more than forty years. As far as the accordion in France is concerned, its image problem seems bound up with the fact that it is perceived as being the instrument of the lower classes – the proletariat (the so-called *"poor man's piano"* syndrome). Conversely, in China, the supposed link between the accordion and the working classes has led to the instrument being officially government sponsored and held in the highest social esteem.

The accordion has been popular in France virtually since its invention in 1829 by Cyril Damian in Vienna, Austria, and French craftsmen have manufactured instruments since the 1830s. The style we today call French musette, however, has its origins in the early/mid 19th Century when regional immigrants began to arrive in Paris in large numbers from the Auvergne, bringing their local 'musette' folk music and dance with them, at first played on pipes. The pipes were soon superseded by diatonic button accordions, introduced by Italian immigrants, and superseded yet again after 1900 by the more recently developed chromatic button accordion. Immigrants from Belgium, and gypsy communities – 'les manouches' – added their own tunes and accordion and guitar music styles to what had become an expanding song and dance music genre emanating from and especially popular with the working classes. Dance halls (known as the bal musette) and cafes were the places to play, hear or dance to the developing 'bal musette' style, pioneered by the likes of Emile Vacher, Adolphe de Prince, Louis Ferrari, Belgian-born Gus Viseur, and the Italians Tony Murena and Joseph Murena. There was also the Peguri family: Felix Peguri who arrived in Paris in 1890, and set up in business as a maker and repairer/tuner, and his three sons, Charles (1879-1930), Michel (1882-1958), and Louis (1894-1972). All were first class players and composers, and Michel Peguri is especially remembered for composing *Bourrasque* and *Aubade D'Oiseaux*. Incidentally, a lot of musette compositions from the pre-war period carry the name Jean Peyronnin in addition to the composer's name, and the reason for this is that Peyronnin was a highly trained pianist who was responsible for writing down the tune on paper, and creating an arrangement in the process.

By the 1930s, as in England, the accordion was living through a golden age, with accordionists enjoying great popularity not only for 'bal musette' dance music but also as accompaniment for such great vocalists as Jean Sablon, Charles Trenet, Edith Piaf, and many others. Fortunately for future generations, the most popular accordionists and singers of the 1920s and 30s – including each of those mentioned above in this paragraph – made recordings that we can enjoy today. See also the section: **Musette**.

As in Great Britain, the advent of war in 1939 adversely affected accordion activity and when peace came six years later, the public's musical tastes were changing, and the accordion's golden age period was over. Nonetheless, the post-war era has seen the rise of many brilliant accordion stars, such as Yvette Horner, Emile Prud'homme, Jo Privat, Aimable, Joss Basselli, Andre Verchuren (who somehow during the war miraculously survived the horrors of Dachau concentration camp), Marcel Azzola, and many, many more. The work of Maurice Larcange with his accordion school deserves special mention, producing literally scores of accordion stars of the future in the musette style. The inception of the Chartres Accordion Festival in 1989 has boosted the accordion in France, and given scope for overseas players to attempt to make their mark with French audiences.

For as long as anyone can remember, many British accordionists have had an interest in playing musette numbers, and sheet music has been readily available for many years, as have recordings by French accordion players. It is also happily the case that various opportunities exist on this side of the English Channel for accordionists with a repertoire of French musette music e.g. there are French themed evenings to play for; French restaurants; every November, in England there are Beaujolais events; there are also theatrical shows such as *La Cage Aux Folles, Gigi* and the stage version of the BBC television comedy *Allo, Allo.*

A number of British composers have written interesting pieces in the musette style, most notably Albert Delroy whose music such as *Chanson de Paris, Chateau de Chillon, Paris Accordion* and *Aubade Java* really captures the nuances and flavour of France. Several of Delroy's musette compositions have been used for competition purposes in NAO festivals over the years, as has *C'est La Vie* (a musette java) composed by the late Barry Dawson. The 1960s BBC television version of *Maigret*, with its famous musette pastiche (composed by Ron Grainer, and played by Reg Hogarth), no doubt inspired many a would-be musette accordionist. Even forty years after *Maigret* appeared on TV screens in this country, the theme tune is still played – and recognised. The later theme from BBC TV's *Allo, Allo,* (composed by David Croft, and played by Jack Emblow) is another popular pastiche of the musette style, as is the theme from the 1980s ITV version of *Maigret* (composed by Nigel Hess, played by Jack Emblow). For those interested in learning musette pieces or acquiring CD recordings from France of musette accordionists, Croydon-based Trevani has the best and widest selection; for videos of French musette players, Charlie Watkins (WEM) has an excellent variety to choose from – see the section: **Accordion Retailers in the United Kingdom**. Some of the larger supermarkets in France have record departments, and these usually include extensive ranges of CDs featuring musette accordionists.

Frosini, Pietro (1885-1951) Born in Catania, Sicily, Pietro Frosini is one of the legendary names of the accordion world, and his compositions continue to be played and enjoyed around the world.

Pietro Frosini meets Adrian Dante. New York, 1949

Pietro was taught to play the diatonic button accordion by his father as a young boy, and at seven became the proud owner of an instrument with 37 treble and 33 bass buttons.

In 1895 young Frosini studied the clarinet, cornet and musical theory at the Municipal Conservatory of the Arts in Catania, and his talent on clarinet and accordion was soon recognised in his hometown and beyond. Unhappy with the lack of acceptance for the accordion, Frosini turned down a government scholarship to the more prestigious Royal Conservatoire in Milan. In 1902, Frosini instead journeyed to Malta to join the British Royal Navy, playing the cornet in the military band and travelling to many countries. One of the countries Frosini visited with the RN was Great Britain, and one of the band's performances was given in the presence of HM King Edward VII.

On discharge from the Royal Navy, Frosini returned to Sicily before moving back to Malta, where he was 'discovered' by American talent scouts working for the Orpheum variety circuit. Soon, Frosini was heading off to the New World in search of fame and fortune.

Frosini arrived in Fresno, California in 1905 and made a living playing in the Vaudeville theatres. He made his first recordings on wax cylinders, then on gramophone recordings. Once in the USA, Frosini commissioned a New

York-based accordion maker called Bernadonna to construct an instrument for him, designed to his specification. Frosini received the new accordion in the Spring of 1906, and began a professional career which lasted for half a century, and in which he never missed an engagement. In 1911, Frosini made his first trip to Britain as a professional accordionist, and one of his many performances was given in the presence of King George V.

In 1909 Frosini began a long recording career. In 1914, Frosini recorded his arrangement Italian Fantasy, an imaginative medley of well-known tunes, and later recalled: *"I was playing a magnificent version of the Italian Fantasy. When I got to the last page of the score, where the bellows shake section begins, there was a crash on the window of the studio in which I was recording. A base-ball had shattered the glass! After I had calmed down, those of us present all laughed at the incident and resumed making another recording of the fantasy."*

In 1920 Frosini married Alfrida Larsen in Philadelphia, and she was to be a great inspiration and support to him, especially when he was overtaken by ill heath later in life.

In Milwaukee in 1922, Frosini gave his first performance of his arrangement of Richard Wagner's *Pilgrim's Chorus*, and his rendition drew tumultuous applause from both the audience and the accompanying orchestra. After the concert, some of the orchestra members went backstage and confronted Frosini, one member saying: *"You must have some mechanical gadget playing inside that accordion. No accordionist can play that piece alone."* They asked him to dismantle the accordion to see for themselves, and the maestro duly obliged. A Sherlock Holmes style inspection revealed that all was indeed above board, and Frosini went home that night a legend in the eyes of his fellow musicians.

The Vaudeville theatres began to disappear when silent films gave way to the 'talking pictures' in 1927, and Frosini's career also underwent a change of direction as he moved into radio broadcasting in 1931. Frosini became a regular on American radio, and millions nationwide heard his music. In 1938 he made some memorable appearances at the famous Radio City Music Hall in New York, mesmerising his audiences with such pieces as his arrangement of *The Carnival of Venice*.

In 1939, Frosini moved into a more serious mode of music with the publication of the Frosini Master Series – compositions such as *Rhapsody* (numbers 1, 2 and 3), *The Russian Fantasy* and *Brittania Overture*. These longer pieces are likely to be of interest to the serious concert accordionist.

In March 1942, Frosini gave a recital at Carnegie Hall, New York, and the review in the New York Times described him as: *"a musician of great sensitivity, a virtuoso, a veritable poet of the accordion"*.

Unfortunately, Pietro Frosini's last few years were spent in poor health, including badly failing eyesight, though he did his best to carry on with his music and his teaching, mainly thanks to his indomitable spirit. Frosini died on September 2nd 1951, aged 65, and his legacy to the world are his many wonderful compositions, a priceless heritage, which reflect the joyful and spirited nature of this great Italian American musician.

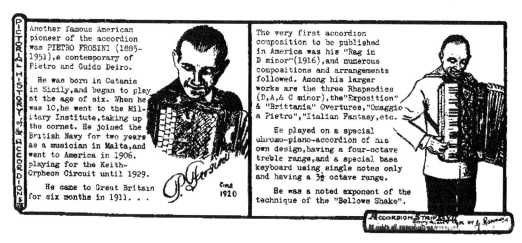

Another famous American pioneer of the accordion was PIETRO FROSINI (1885-1951), a contemporary of Pietro and Guido Deiro.

He was born in Catania in Sicily, and began to play at the age of six. When he was 10, he went to the Military Institute, taking up the cornet. He joined the British Navy for two years as a musician in Malta, and went to America in 1906, playing for the Keith-Orpheon Circuit until 1929.

He came to Great Britain for six months in 1911. . .

P. Frosini Circa 1920

The very first accordion composition to be published in America was his "Rag in D minor" (1916), and numerous compositions and arrangements followed. Among his larger works are the three Rhapsodies (D, A, & C minor), the "Exposition" & "Brittania" Overtures, "Omaggio a Pietro", "Italian Fantasy, etc.

He played on a special chromo-piano-accordion of his own design, having a four-octave treble range, and a special bass keyboard using single notes only and having a 3½ octave range.

He was a noted exponent of the technique of the "Bellows Shake".

ACCORDION STRIP XVII ... or L. Romani

Discography: *Pietro Frosini – Original Recordings 1920-1935.* A digitally remastered CD of solo recordings was released in 2002, and the fifteen tracks include: *Dizzy Accordion, La Mariposita, Jolly Caballero, Olive Blossoms, Love Smiles, Bel Viso, Hot Fingers, Silver Moon, Frosini Symphonic March, Swedish Italian Mazurka, Cordinella, Serenata Primavera, Gauchos On Parade, Rag in D Minor* and *Bel Fiore*.

Selected compositions: all of the above plus *Sicilian Serenade, Loveliness, Omaggio A Pietro, Sweepstakes, Celestial Whispering, The Brave Matador, Valse Chromatique, Accordiomania, Fragrant Flowers, Musette Mazurka, Spaghetti Tangle,* plus more than a hundred other pieces.

Gajic, Djorde Yugoslavian-born Dr. Djorde Gajic began playing accordion at the age of six, and was soon recognised as a prodigy – giving solo recitals and appearing on radio and television. In 1988 he began studying in Moscow at the Russian Academy of Music (formerly the Gnessin Institute), eventually becoming a Doctor of Music in 1995. Now resident in Glasgow, Djorde Gajic is one of the foremost accordion teachers and virtuoso performers currently living in this country. Unlike many virtuoso accordionists, however, he has not moved over to the button system, and has continued to play the piano accordion. He has made many appearances at accordion festivals, and his fantastic technique can be seen and appreciated on the video of the 1995 Caister Festival.

Galla-Rini, Anthony (Born Manchester, Connecticut, USA, January 18th 1904.) From Italian parentage, Anthony Galla-Rini played the cornet from the age of four, and the accordion from six. He appeared in Vaudeville theatres from the age of seven, and later studied the theory of music and the art of conducting. As a teenager, Galla-Rini began both to teach the accordion and to write music for the instrument. He developed into a serious concert artiste, performing at venues across America, including New York's Carnegie Hall on many occasions. He has also toured Britain and Europe, playing in London, Manchester, Sheffield and Glasgow.

Galla-Rini composed his first concerto for accordion in 1941, and a second in 1976. He has also arranged many of the great classics by JS Bach, Chopin, Tchaikovsky, Verdi, Handel, Brahms, Beethoven, and others, for accordion.

This great accordionist/composer/arranger has worked extensively in Hollywood for many years, and *Hans Christian Anderson, Rhapsody in Blue* and *High Noon* are just three of the many films where his playing can be heard.

One of Galla-Rini's most high profile pupils is Jorgen Sundequist, the Swedish concert artiste who is well known in Great Britain. Galla-Rini has taught, lectured and directed master classes and workshops for longer than anyone else in the accordion world, and at the time of writing (in 2003), is still in business. His long-term contribution is truly without equal.

Gee, Malcolm (1940-1997) Midlands-based Malcolm Gee was a pharmacist-turned- publican whose hobbies included travelling, motorbikes and anything to do with the accordion. During a trip to Australia in the mid-1970s, Malcolm began to play the piano accordion, and on his return home to Kidderminster decided to further his growing interest in the instrument. Disappointed to find no organised accordion activity in his area, in 1976 he founded Club Accord as, to use his own words, *"a focal point for accordionists in the West Midland"*. As Club Accord quickly grew in numbers and importance, he organised a recording session for several of the club's leading players, the results of which were issued as the LP *It's All Accordion To What You Like,* in 1979. This LP led to Malcolm establishing the Accordion Record Club, a mail order catalogue service offering records and cassettes by accordionists from around the world. The result of this was to enable enthusiasts in Britain and Ireland to become familiar with a very much wider range of accordion music and players than had hitherto been possible. The ARC was wound up in the early 1990s due to Malcolm's increased commitments at his pub, *The New Inn*, situated in Arley, near Bewley.

In 1983 Malcolm Gee began the publication of a mail order magazine, *The Accordion Monthly News*. Developed from the monthly Club Accord newsletter, the *AM News* quickly caught on and became the accordion movement's main form of national and international communication, with subscribers and correspondents in many parts of the world. He was very proud of his success at bringing accordion players and enthusiasts together, and his lead was the catalyst for the magazine *Accordion Profile* that picked up where Malcolm Gee left off, as it were.

As one of the British accordion scene's greatest ever innovators, Malcolm Gee was the first person to organise a weekend festival dedicated to the accordion. A festival aptly described by Malcolm as *"A total indulgence in accordions",* took place at Pontin's Sands Bay, Weston-Super-Mare, on November 8th/11th 1982, featuring Mario Conway, Neil Rowan and The Bavarian Steinswingers as chief guests. The success and special atmosphere of this inaugural festival led to a succession of what became known as Autumn

Accordion Festivals, based at Caister Holiday Centre, close to Great Yarmouth. In 1986, Malcolm scored a great coup for the accordion movement by persuading the legendary Toralf Tollefsen to emerge from retirement and appear as chief guest.

The energy and commitment Malcolm Gee applied to the concept of the non-competitive accordion festival led to a series of successful Caister Autumn Accordion Festivals in the 1980s and 90s, and other similar events such as his Spring Accordion Camp in Arley, Worcestershire and St Audrie's Bay in Somerset. These events, apart from making celebrity guest accordionists accessible to enthusiasts, did a great deal to improve communication and foster friendships between accordion players, teachers, organisers and enthusiasts nationwide.

Malcolm married in 1990, but wedded bliss was short-lived and he and Maddie separated in an acrimonious split. The failure of his marriage, business worries, plus Malcolm's intense nature had a debilitating effect on his health.

In January 1997, en route to Scotland, Malcolm Gee suffered a major stroke, and died in hospital the following day. He single-handedly provided the British accordion scene with a shot in the arm when it needed one most, and his legacy proved to be the concept of the non-competitive accordion festival and the growth of accordion clubs around England and Wales, facilitated by Malcolm's exceptional drive, energy and infectious enthusiasm. We may never see his like again.

Glenn, Gordon Gordon Glenn is one of Britain's finest full-time professional accordionists, and his smooth and silky style, plus wide repertoire of standards, light classics and accordion specialities, is very popular wherever he appears. An advocate of the acoustic, Stradella bass accordion, Gordon Glenn is a solo musician whose only gimmick is his perfectionist approach to his performances. Gordon's music has taken him to many countries over the years, and especially memorable highlights of his travels include visiting the Pyramids in Egypt, Field Marshall Rommel's HQ in Tunisia, and the huge war graves ceme-  teries in North Africa – the latter making a lasting impression on him. Apart from music, Gordon has worked as a TV 'extra', appearing in all kinds of programmes, such as Brookside where he was a jury member during the 'Jordache trial' episodes. Most notably, he appeared in the first episode of the BBC comedy series *Dinner Ladies*, in a speaking role as Victoria Wood's father, and also playing the accordion. A veteran of variety theatres, clubs and cruise liners, Gordon Glenn also likes to appear at accordion clubs and festivals.
<u>Discography</u>: *Moments of Musical Reflections* (1995)

Grainger, Murray Educated at Manchester Grammar School and the Royal Academy of London, Murray Grainger B.Mus (Hons) LRAM, has studied accordion with Professor Owen Murray. He represents the younger generation of accordionists through his teaching at Chetham's Music School, Manchester, and his involvement with the children of Bank's Lane Junior School in Stockport, where the Fosbrooks music and dance teams (whose MD is the very energetic and visionary Liza Austin-Strange MBE) are based.

As a performer, Murray has impressive credentials with appearances in the BBC Henry Wood Promenade concerts, the Edinburgh Festival, Cheltenham Festival, Chichester Festival, Celtic Connections Festival, Sidmouth International Folk Festival and the Interceltic Festival at Lorient in Brittany. Murray's classical training and interest in folk music has given him a broad musical base, and he has worked with the Hallé Orchestra, the BBC Symphony Orchestra, the Scottish Chamber Orchestra, Northern Sinfonia, the Scottish Ballet Orchestra, Almeida Opera, and the folk band, Whistlebinkies. He has also made broadcasts using the accordion on BBC Radio Three and BBC Radio Scotland. The instruments used by Murray include both piano accordion and 5-row chromatic free bass.

Murray recently formed a duet partnership with fellow accordionist Amy Thatcher (see also **Thatcher, Amy**), and their repertoire is an eclectic mixture of original and traditional music from Britain, Ireland and overseas; in 2003 they released their first recording, *Paper Bird*.
Discography: *Paper Bird* (2003)

Griffiths, Jack Welshman Jack Griffiths played piano accordion from a boy in the 1920s, and then through the so-called 'Golden Age' of the 1930s when instrument sales were at an all-time peak and accordion clubs, bands and players seemed to be everywhere. This era instilled Jack Griffiths with a love for the accordion that motivated him later in life to become an organiser par excellence. In the 1980s, Jack Griffiths founded Swansea Accordion Club, and for many years was the driving force behind his club with his prolific report writing in accordion magazines and tireless organisation/promotion of events. He then became the organiser of the annual NAO area festival, variously called 'The All-Wales Accordion Festival' and 'Accordion Day In Wales'. People with the drive and dedication of Jack Griffiths are few and far between in any walk of life, and when he died in 1991 he proved to be a hard act to follow.

Handle, Johnny Born 1934. Johnny Handle plays piano accordion, piano, guitar, fiddle and Northumbrian pipes; he also sings, composes and tells stories – a true exponent of the Geordie folk tradition. He performs solo and also as a long-time member of the *High Level Ranters*, and has been recording since the early 1960s. Handle was a miner, then a teacher, and now is a full time performer – one of the best all-rounders and most entertaining musicians in the folk club and festival scene. His performances and recordings include songs, accordion pieces, ragtime piano solos, monologues, humorous stories, etc – some self-composed and the rest from the rich Geordie cultural tradition.

Selected discography: *Northlands One* (1985); *Northlands Two* (1985); *Gateshead Revisited* (1990); *Handle With Care – the songs & tunes of Johnny Handle* (2001); *Six of the Best* (2002) – a recording of self-composed piano rags.
Tune book: *The Johnny Handle Manuscripts Volume 1* – a varied collection of compositions (1992)
The Northumbria Anthology: In 1999, Johnny Handle was appointed researcher and coordinator of *The Northumbia Anthology* by Newcastle University's Music Department, the result of which was a 20 CD set of songs in the Geordie *"Tyne to Tees"* tradition. Contributors include Johnny Handle, Alex Glasgow, Vin Garbutt, Sheila Armstrong, Sting, Jimmy Nail, Alan Price, Lindisfarne, Robson Green, Ed Pickford, Bob Fox, Benny Graham, Tim Healy, Owen Brannigan, Kevin Whateley, Denise Welch, The High Level Ranters, and many others. For details, e-Mail: info@mawsonwareham.com

Hanger, Jean Based in Harlow, Essex, Jean Hanger is a long established teacher of both piano and chromatic button accordion systems. Moreover, she is a great enthusiast for the accordion and organises the Harlow Accordion Club, and is a regular at all the main accordion festivals in this country plus Chartres in northern France. Jean's never flagging enthusiasm has resulted in her area becoming a frequent venue for concerts, and the establishment of a band.

Harmonica Also called a mouth organ, a harmonica is small reed instrument related to the accordion. It consists of a graduated series of metal reeds mounted in a small rectangular metal or wood frame, and each reed has a channel to conduct air from or to the player's mouth. As with accordions, there are diatonic and chromatic models in which each reed chamber produces either one or two notes, depending on the type. The pitch of a harmonica is determined purely by the length, width and thickness of the numerous vibrating reeds.

Germany's Friedrich Buschmann is credited with inventing the harmonica in Berlin in 1821. A number of modern composers such as Alexander Tcherepnin, Darius Milhaud and Ralph Vaughan-Williams have written special works for the instrument, and the two best-known solo harmonica players in this country to date have been the American-born Larry Adler, and the Canadian-born Tommy Reilly. Both Adler and Reilly elevated the status of the harmonica to the concert hall stage, and did countless broadcasts and popular recordings. See also **Adler, Larry** and **Reilly, Tommy**.

Harmonica players and enthusiasts are likely to be interested in knowing about *The Encyclopedia of the Harmonica*, a book published in the USA in 1998 written by Peter Krampert. This exhaustive survey of the worldwide harmonica scene contains no less than 900 articles on players, bands, techniques, resources

The harmonica scene in Britain is well organised through the National Harmonica League, and from the 1930s to the 1960s was closely linked to the National Accordion Organisation and *Accordion Times* magazine. The NAO *'Accordion Day'* used to include All-Britain Championship sections for the national harmonica championships. The NHL's President is Paul Jones, former lead singer with Manfred Mann, and it publishes its own magazine, *Harmonica World*. The NHL has its own website, easily located via a general word search, and its e-mail address is: nhl@harmonica.co.uk

Harmonica Maintenance *The harmonica, like any other instrument, needs looking after if it is to stay in good condition. Douglas Tate, 1963 All-Britain Solo Harmonica Champion and later a festival adjudicator wrote the following article about the basics of harmonica maintenance: -*

Looking After Your Harmonica

Any musical instrument needs maintenance from time to time and the harmonica, of course, is no exception. There are a number of regular attentions which may be carried out which will prolong the useful life of the instrument and make it more pleasant to play.

But please note: As with any delicate mechanism great care must be taken when handling and dismantling the harmonica. Never attempt to tamper with the brass reed plates or reeds. Experts set these with great care, and carelessness in handling can undo this work.

When first commencing to practise it is a good idea to warm the instrument by blowing very gently. Never heat directly in front of a fire, etc., as this will ruin it. Harmonicas settle down after a few hours 'running in' playing. At first, the tone can be difficult to control; this is a function of 'running in,' and it soon becomes manageable.

Sometimes it will be noted that the button-return spring squeaks. Light oiling can cure this. Take the two screws out of the mouthpiece and remove it and the slide movement completely. You will see the spring coiled round a steel rod at the right-hand end of the instrument at the bottom of a round hole. Place one drop of oil on the coil of the spring; if you use more, the oil may swell the wood of the body.

At this stage, it may be as well to clean the mouthpiece and slide-piece. **Never** use an abrasive polish. Soap, water and a toothbrush are all that is necessary. When each piece has been removed, rinse very thoroughly to remove any traces of soap. You will notice a film of tarnish on the cover plates and mouthpiece; don't attempt to remove this as it helps the instrument to move in the mouth more freely.

Reassemble in this order: Lay the harmonica on its rear edge on a table so that the holes are uppermost, spring towards the right. Put the flat lower plate of the slide movement on the mouthpiece. If you feel the edges of the holes, one side feels sharp; this should face the wood. Next, place the two pieces of plastic tubing in the two round holes at either end, making certain that they bed down into the recesses.

Next, put the slide on. Thread it over the spring, which fits into the small hole at the button end. With the button to your right, the last hole on the right of the slide should be towards you. This is so that, with the button released, the exposed holes are away from you, or on the top layer. Having done this, set the slide down so that the two pieces of plastic slide in the slots.

Next, place the folded plate, with the slot to the right, over the other two pieces so that the plastic goes through the two end holes, and the small metal tongues engage with the bottom plate. Now put the mouthpiece on, making certain that the small nick in one end goes to the button end. Screw the mouthpiece down reasonably tightly. If the slide movement is now very stiff, release by about one eighth of a turn or less. It will soon loosen up considerably as soon as the slide becomes moist with playing.

Very occasionally you may find that, due to excess moisture in the harmonica, the white plastic flaps over the blow notes stick to the reed plates. The best thing to do in this case is to remove the cover plates and very gently wipe the underside of the flaps with blotting paper, being careful not to interfere with the reeds on this side of the plate.

You will notice that the flaps consist of two pieces of plastic; these are glued together at the fixed end but should be free along the length. Part them with a needle and dry out any moisture. Replace the cover plates, making certain that the front edges fit into the slots on the reed plates. If, for any reason, a flap falls off it may be re-fixed with Durofix cement or similar glue.

If anything else goes wrong with your harmonica, or you have any doubts about your ability to follow my instructions, it would be better to consult any of the businesses in the section **Accordion Retailers in the United Kingdom**. It is far better to pay a few pounds to get a reed tuned or replaced than to try it yourself and ruin a good instrument.

To keep your harmonica out of the repair department, note the following rules: -

1) Never play after having eaten until you have thoroughly washed out your mouth.

2) Always play with your head slightly up so that not too much saliva flows into the instrument.
3) Never tap the instrument on any hard object to remove moisture, always on the palm of your hand.
4) Never over-blow your harmonica.
   If you obey these simple rules your harmonica should last indefinitely.
   Douglas Tate, Accordion Times, March 1967

Harris, Eddie (1919-96) Eddie Harris had a long career as an accordion teacher, including many years at the British College of Accordionists during the BCA's time in London, until 1964. He organised and conducted the BCA Orchestra during the 1950s, and was an ever-present figure at accordion events, most notably the All-Britain championships, from 1935 onwards. A composer and author of *Theory of Music for Accordionists*, Eddie Harris was President of the National Accordion Organisation. He was one of the founding fathers of the accordion movement in this country, and was fittingly awarded the NAO Award Emeritus in 1995 for his lifetime contribution to the organisation. One of the true 'founding fathers' of the present day accordion movement in the United Kingdom.

Harris, Rolf (Born 1930) Born in Perth, Australia, Rolf Harris uses a piano accordion in his stage act and also on some of his recordings. As a teenager, Rolf was a strong swimmer, and was the 1946 Australian Junior Backstroke Champion. In 1952 he arrived in London to study art at the City & Guilds School in Kensington, where he met Alwen whom he later married, and in 1956 Rolf had paintings exhibited at London's Royal Academy of Art. Rolf wrote and recorded *Tie Me Kangaroo Down Sport*, which in 1960 was the first of many hit singles. From 1966 onwards Rolf became a regular host of his own television show on BBC, one of his guests being virtuoso accordionist Gervasio Marcosignori, from Italy. In recent years, Rolf's art programmes and *Animal Hospital* shows have sustained his popularity with all ages. In 1968 he was awarded the MBE, and in 1971 and 1995 he was the subject of television's *This Is Your Life* – one of very few people to be featured twice. In 2002, Rolf made the headlines when his accordion caught fire on stage - for more details see the section **Strange, but true...**

Hartley, Ken Blackpool-based Ken Hartley is one of the most talented but underrated players on the British accordion scene, and is also one of the great

comedians. As a one-time student of the famous American accordionist Joe Biviano in New York, Ken has a brilliant two handed technique that is equally at home playing accordion classics, popular music, Latin music and jazz. On stage, Ken usually plays a 48 bass instrument, but gets the most amazing music from a small instrument that only seeing and hearing is believing! His music is usually accompanied by his infectious sense of humour, and he soon has his audiences in fits of laughter. Ken Hartley plays in restaurants, and appears in accordion clubs and also occasionally does jazz workshops at festivals.
Discography: *Los Muchachos* (2000) – a privately produced CD featuring jazz and Latin American music on alternate tracks.

Helixon A helixon is a diatonic accordion, normally with four rows of treble buttons tuned to the major keys of F, B*b*, E*b* and A*b*. The bass keyboard has about fifteen buttons, with a particularly distinctive and resonant tone. The helixon is popular in Switzerland and the Alpine regions of Austria, where it is used for the regional folk music indigenous to these places.

Hill, Noel An Anglo concertina player from West Clare, and arguably the Irish traditional scene's finest exponent of this instrument, Noel Hill has become very popular in America, where he spends much of his time. Hill's 1988 LP *The Irish Concertina* is a 'tour de force' of great playing throughout; now available on CD.
Discography: *Ignoc Na Grai* – recorded with button accordionist Tony MacMahon (1986); *The Irish Concertina* (1988); *Noel Hill & Tony Linnane* (1988).

Hinchcliffe, Harry Keighley-based accordion teacher/performer/contest organiser Harry Hinchcliffe has been one of the busiest and hardest working people in the British accordion movement since the 1980s. His Craven Accordion School always has lots of students, supports the northern NAO festivals, and frequently produces prize winners – including Harry's sons, Paul and Daniel.
In the 1990s, Harry assumed responsibility for organising the NAO North Central Festival, and this annual event has grown in size and stature under Harry's enthusiastic generalship.

Hodgson, Ron The accordion scene in this country has produced some very talented and accomplished people over the years, and at the forefront of these is Carlisle's Ron Hodgson – player, conductor, teacher, writer and festival organiser. Ron started playing at seven years of age, and passed all eight BCA grades with distinction marks. As a competitive accordionist, in 1957 he went on to achieve second place in an international competition in Moscow. Ron and his wife Margaret also achieved second place in the Advanced Duets section that year in the NAO Championships. During his National Service days, Ron played in the army dance band in Germany, and was featured in shows with the late, great Danny Kaye. After demobilisation, he formed his own dance band, and was featured on both BBC radio and television. He founded the Ronmar School of Music, and the Ronmar Accordion Orchestra, and these long-running institutions have been renowned for their consistently high playing standards. In recent years, Ron has been closely involved with the running of the Caister and Bridlington accordion festivals, and has contributed musical articles to the *Accordion Times & Monthly News*. His considerable teaching expertise has been distilled into a series of three tutor books, which can be used with or without a teacher. These books have been published through *Eden Music*, Ron's own publishing company. He has struck up a highly successful duet partnership with Julie Best, one of his pupils, and they have performed and recorded with considerable critical acclaim.

Selected discography: *Magical Accordion Duets* – volumes 1, 2 & 3 (1990s): these recordings present a wide range of accordion classics from many parts of Europe and the British Isles – excellent performances and arrangements throughout.

Eden Music: The *Eden Music* catalogue contains over 140 solos and duets composed by Ken Dingle and Ron Hodgson, and at least 49 band/orchestral scores – from Grade 3 to Grade 8; the Ron Hodgson Accordion Tutor Course, parts 1, 2 & 3; CDs and cassettes. Telephone/fax: 01228 522466; e-mail: ronhodgson@beeb.net

Hohner The German company founded by Matthias Hohner in 1857 produced harmonicas, then accordions a few years later, that were exported in large numbers to many countries. In this respect, the vigorous export marketing policy of Hohner instruments was much more go-ahead than any of its rivals – including the Italian companies. The result was that throughout much of the late 19th and 20th Centuries, M. Hohner Ltd outsold all its rivals worldwide.

In 1930 Dr Otto H. Meyer was appointed head of the Hohner operation in the UK, just as the accordion craze in this country was getting under way, and the company's accordions and harmonicas were soon selling in large quantities – ahead of all competition. The establishment of the British College of Accordionists, *Accordion Times* and the annual All-Britain Championships (all from 1935 onwards) were all made possible by the sponsorship of M.Hohner Ltd, and personally piloted by Dr Meyer. Thus it was that the Hohner Company virtually controlled the British accordion movement throughout the 1930s. Photographs of leading accordionists from the 1930s, 40s and 50s tend to show a prevalence of Hohner instruments, and it was not until the late 1950s that the Italian accordion manufacturers gradually began to catch up and make serious inroads into the British market, thereafter diminishing Hohner's sales superiority. In 1964, the BCA moved from its London home, where it was situated as a part of Hohner's HQ in Farringdon Rd, to Leicester. The new-look BCA was thereafter under the independent control of Francis Wright. From 1965, Mr Wright also assumed responsibility for organising the NAO All-Britain

Championships, thereby lessening the influence of Hohner in the domestic competitive scene. Hohner's financial interest in the Accordion Times ended when the magazine ceased publication in 1974. The revival of this magazine in 1982 came via Francis Wright, and without involvement from Hohner.

In 1950, there occurred a major schism within the World Accordion Championship movement when several national bodies, including the British Association of Accordionists, broke away from the CIA to form the rival CMA. This came about due to discontent about the alleged extent of Hohner's involvement – perceived by some as control – in the Coupe Mondiale World Championships.

Since the 1970s, the Hohner Company has diversified into manufacturing other musical instruments, and has in recent years begun a commercial operation in China the world's largest potential market for accordions and related instruments.

Holland, Percy (1916-94) One of the generation of accordionists who came along during the 1930s, Percy Holland became a highly skilled player by the time war broke out in 1939. He joined the army, was posted to the Far East and was unlucky enough to be taken prisoner by the Japanese. Part of his story as a F.E.P.O.W. is told in this book, in the section **World War Two**. In common with many others, his experience at the hands of the Japanese had a long-term adverse effect on his health, though after the war he went on to become one of London's finest accordion teachers. In the 1950s, Percy taught at Jennings'  Accordion Centre, 100 Charing Cross Rd, London, and also at the shop owned by Toralf Tollefsen and Nils Nielsen. Percy Holland was highly regarded both as a teacher and as a person by his many pupils, who included the player/prolific composer Ken Dingle (also featured in this book).

Holter, Geoff A fully trained accordion tuner and repairer, Geoff Holter worked for Bell Musical Instruments Ltd for many years, managing the firm's Darlington branch until its closure in 1990. Since taking over the former Bell's shop, *Geoff Holter Accordions* has emerged as a company with a highly reputable name for sales, service, and repairs. The firm is present at most accordion festivals, maintaining a high profile across the British accordion scene.

Holmes, Ian One of Scotland's great post-war players, Ian Holmes, from Dumfries, began studying the piano accordion under Alex Carter at the age of thirteen. In 1956, he joined Bobby MacLeod's band on second accordion, and in 1960 took on a similar role with Andrew Rankine, before forming his own band in 1962. Ian Holmes has also played as a soloist, and in 1957 won the Senior Scottish Championship at the All-Scotland Championships in Perth. At this festival he won the Jimmy Shand Shield, presented by the great man himself. Ian also plays the 5-row button chromatic, and has recorded using both types of instrument. He has a particular interest in the music of Scandinavia and Switzerland, has also composed music in these genres, and has made authentic-sounding recordings (using the 5-row).

Selected discography: *It's Grand To Be Irish* (1966); *Sounds Scandinavian* (1988); *Ian in Switzerland* (1997)

Book: *The Dumfries Collection* – 41 original compositions (1998)

Horner, Yvette Looking at present day pictures of Yvette Horner, it is hard to believe that she has been playing since the 1940s, and was the World Champion in 1948. Yvette Horner has actually sustained two musical careers in France, as musette accordionist and also as a classical concert pianist. Her accordion style is always relaxed and smooth, and her recordings always sound fresh and bright: one is left with the impression that she could not make a bad recording if she tried! Sometimes she diverts from musette to play/record other styles, as on *Paris Broadway*, a CD featuring famous film and show tunes. For many years, Yvette was the official musician employed by the organisers of the Tour de France, and was seen on French television performing at various stages of the race. She has appeared several times in this country, in concerts organised by Adrian Dante. Despite having suffered a stroke in recent years, Yvette still occasionally plays in concerts and at festivals, and her recordings are widely available in France – and they also occasionally find their way into the larger record shops in this country. Yvette has a great belief in the power of music to lift the human spirit, and once said that if music was banned, society would need a lot more psychiatric hospitals.

Selected discography: *Paris Musette* (1972); *Tangos, Pasos, Valses* (1978); *Preferences* (1992); *Reine de Musette* (1994); *Paris Broadway* – Yvette Horner with the Jazz Orchestra from the Paris Opera (1995).

Hulme, Brian (Born 1939) Brian Hulme, from Oldham in Lancashire, began playing the accordion in 1953, and had lessons with Bert Thornton. He also had piano lessons, eventually becoming adept on both instruments, and with a penchant for playing jazz.

Brian remembers, back in the 1950s, going on holiday to the Isle of Man and volunteering to take part in a talent contest run by the famous bandleader Ivy Benson. He played *Simonetta* (composed by Martin Lukins), backed by the Ivy Benson all-girls band, and recalls: *"Most of the people who entered were singers, but a lot of them were not very good. Ivy Benson was ruthless with them, interrupting some after just a few moments and calling out, 'Thank you...next please!' I got a good reception probably because I was doing something different, the only one playing the accordion, but I didn't win the contest. Still, I can always say that I played with the Ivy Benson band!"*

After a conventional round of doing BCA examination grades and competing in NAO area festivals, Brian became a semi-professional pianist/accordionist in a trio, playing for weddings and other functions. For a living, Brian served in the Merchant Navy, worked in engineering, and finally ended up as secondary school teacher – now retired. Since the early 1980s, he has played accordion many times in restaurants and hotels, and has also appeared as a guest in accordion clubs. In the late 1990s Brian found himself in demand for television work, playing the accordion in the ITV programme *Hotel Getaway*, hosted by Matthew Kelly, and an episode of the remake of *The Forsyte Saga*, in which he appears as a Parisian accordionist in a café scene playing musette music as a backdrop to the storyline.

In the summer of 2003, Brian suffered a stroke and is, at the time of writing, making a recovery and determined to play music again.

Humour When Ken Dodd was once asked why his home city of Liverpool seems to produce so many comedians, he famously replied, *"You need a sense of humour to live in Liverpool."* Sometimes accordionists must feel that they need a sense of humour to play the accordion, especially when people try to describe the instrument – usually gesturing with both hands in a pull and push motion! In keeping with the idea of not taking ourselves too seriously, here are a few jokes about the accordion: -

- What's the difference between an onion and an accordion?
  No one cries when you chop up an accordion.

- What do you call a Parisian accordionist who jumps in the river?
  In Seine.

- What do you call an accordionist with a mobile phone?
  An optimist.

- What's the difference between an accordion and a trampoline?
  You take your shoes off when you jump on a trampoline.

- Why are there camels in Egypt and accordions in Italy?
  The Egyptians had first choice.

- What is the range of an accordion?
  Twenty yards, if you have a good throwing action.

- Why do some people automatically hate the accordion?
  It saves a lot of time.

- What do you call twenty accordions at the bottom of the ocean?
  A good start.

- What do you get if you drop an accordion down a mineshaft?
  A flat miner.

- What's the difference between an accordion and a concertina?
  A concertina takes less time to burn.

- If you drop an accordion, a concertina or a melodeon off the top of a block of flats, which one would hit the ground first?
  Who cares?

- Who was that musician I saw you with last night?
  That was no musician, that was an accordion player.

- What is the difference between an accordion player and a terrorist?
  Terrorists have sympathisers.

- What song is most frequently requested of accordionists?
  Can you play "Far, Far Away"?

- What would you have been if you had not become a musician?
  I would have become an accordionist.

- What is the definition of perfect pitch?
  Dropping an accordion into a dustbin without it touching the sides.

- How do you make a million pounds playing the accordion?
  Start with two million.

- "Good morning, I'm the accordion tuner."
  "But I didn't send for you."
  "No, but the neighbours did!"

- What do a music lover and an accordionist have in common?
  Absolutely nothing!

- What's the difference between a car engine and an accordion?
  A car engine can be tuned.

- The accordionist had been playing away all day, when there was a knock on his door and he found a man standing there.

"I live next door to you," the man explained. *"Do you know I work nights?"*

"No," said the accordionist, *"but if you hum it, I'll play it."*

- Recommended minimum safe distances between street musicians and the public

  violinist .... 25 feet
  a bad violinist ....100 feet
  guitarist .... 50 feet
  electric guitarist ....100 feet
  accordionist... 60 miles

However, none of these jokes about the accordion is quite as insulting as the following definition of a bodhran: -

A taut pigskin, played by an un-taught pig!

Hussey, Harry Harry Hussey began playing the piano at the age of 5 and the accordion at 14, both by ear. For his 14th birthday, Harry was given a 48 bass piano accordion and within three months was proficient enough to be semi-professional, playing in pubs in the Kilburn district of London. A chartered surveyor by profession, Harry developed his highly skilled accordion playing as a semi-pro for many years, and since retiring from the day job, has been playing full-time around the country's accordion and jazz clubs and festivals. Harry has never read music, but is a master improviser – able to produce sophisticated versions of practically any style of music, almost instantly. His ability to improvise, coupled with his vast repertoire amazes most people when hearing Harry for the first time. He also has great energy and vitality, and can seemingly play for hours at a time. On top of all this, Harry must be one of the very few accordionists anywhere who goes to play concerts minus a prepared programme, and who then will perform for the entire evening just taking requests from the audience!

Backed by drummer George Carroll and bass guitarist Doug Inkpen, Harry is a regular and immensely popular performer at accordion festivals in England, usually in informal situations in restaurants and evening bars. Here again, Harry will play for hours on end, and the pleasure he derives from entertaining like this is clearly obvious. Best known as a jazz accordionist, Harry has played with the likes of George Chisholm, Frank Marocco, John Nixon and Jack Emblow; he has also performed alongside such stars as Matt Monro, Norman Wisdom, Rolf Harris and Anthony Newley.

In 1989, Harry Hussey belatedly

began a recording career. With concertina player John Nixon, plus discreet backing on drums from Wally McKenzie, two cassettes of jazz favourites were issued – *Harry Hussey meets the English Connection* and *Reeds At Play*. In 1994, Harry was playing in a pub one evening in the London area and he became aware of being watched very intensely by a large and scary looking man. During a break, the man – a stranger to the pub – came over and Harry was disconcerted by the man's somewhat intimidating manner. The stranger, however, had connections within the recording industry and had been so impressed with Harry's music that he wanted to do a deal and get him into a studio. The deal involved recording not one but a series of several CDs called *Absolute Accordion*, and manufactured in Belgium by the Kuys Leisure Group. The first CD issued was titled *Play it again, Harry*, featuring a variety of music, including some jazz. Since then, Harry has also recorded a double CD *Harry Hussey and the Windsor Quartet*, and *The Harry Hussey Trio*, volumes one and two. The latter two CDs were made with Messrs Carroll and Inkpen, and present jazz selections in the style heard in the bars during the evenings at accordion festivals.

Selected discography: *Harry Hussey meets the English Connection* (1989); *Reeds At Play* (1990); *Absolute Accordion: Play It Again Harry* (1994); *The Waltzes* (1995); *Harry Hussey and the Windsor Quartet* (1997); *The Harry Hussey Trio* – volumes 1 & 2 (2002).

Improve Your Playing

Variety is the Spice of Music
some advice from Gerald Crossman.

Accordionists playing the popular standard evergreen numbers as solos can make their performances more interesting for themselves and their audiences if they employ one or more of the following suggestions.

The selection of ideas below is for providing musical colour and variety of style whilst playing a tune, as well as encouraging originality. If playing for dancing, then strict tempo and rhythm must be maintained.

1. Change couplers (registers) as appropriate.
2. Play in an octave different from the one you've just been using.
3. Alter the expression, phrasing and other marks on repeats, to provide another interpretation.
4. Follow a section or a chorus of single treble notes with double notes and/or chords, or vice versa. When playing chords, be careful not to cover any melody that should be predominant.
5. On a repeat, put some variation (contemporisation) to the melody and perhaps after the harmonies if you are capable of doing this. Simpler melodic variation can be achieved by changing the values of notes and rests.
6. Thin out the number of accompanying chords. Play mainly the essential

harmonies, keeping a rhythmical feel when this is required. The inter-minable oom, cha, cha, is liable to get rather monotonous.

7. Change key where musically practical, usually at the beginning of a later chorus or section.

8. Perform a first chorus *ad libitum* (Latin: usually abbreviated to ad lib, meaning: at pleasure, at will, freely – not in tempo) then in rhythm after-wards (straight rhythm or perhaps a Latin American rhythm). Ideal material for this treatment is old French standards like *La Vie En Rose* and *Autumn Leaves*, also the Italian *Arriverderci Roma* and *To Be Or Not To be* (*Anima C'ore*). You could also play a first chorus using one rhythm, and then change the rhythm for a later chorus, possibly chang-ing the tempo, too.

9. Double the rhythm in music that is suitable for doing this e.g. eight in a bar instead of four, thus creating an exciting effect. An alternative is triplets.

10. Change the rhythm e.g. from three in a bar to two or four in a bar, or vice versa. Examples of well-known items where this has been done are *Lover* and *Fly Me To The Moon*. Try playing the middle section of *I Could Have Danced All Night* as a bright waltz. See how you can get into it from the preceding phrase, and out of it to the phrase that follows.

11. Don't spoil a good tune by making an arrangement too complicated. I think you would agree that *Laura* is an example of a good tune.

12. Good imaginative introductions, bridge (linking) passages if desirable between choruses, and codas can all help enhance your arrangements.

13. Finally, stay within your technical abilities if playing to audiences, and when in doubt, leave out! Unashamed simplicity is often effective and acceptable.

Gerald Crossman, The Accordion Monthly News, 1989

Internet The establishment of the internet (or worldwide web) has enabled accordionists to spread information about themselves internationally, and there are many interesting web sites to visit. Several of the world's leading players either have their own web sites (try typing in names on a general search engine such as www.google.com) or can be found on accordion-related sites. The largest website for the accordion is called *Accordions Worldwide*, whose address is: - www.accordions.com. This website gives information about instruments, manu-facturers, events, recordings, festivals, composers, music, schools, orchestras, magazines, plus more. It is available in seven languages, including English, French, German, Italian, Spanish, Russian and Chinese, and is a truly interna-tional operation.

Irish Traditional Music Since its introduction into Ireland in the late 19th Century, the accordion has made a lasting impact in Irish traditional music. The two-row diatonic button instrument was the first type of accordion to reach

Ireland, and many purists to this day insist that this is the best choice (especially in B/C tuning) for playing Irish dance music. This is because of the diatonic accordion's capability for achieving the required 'lift' and facility for playing triplets, ornamentation, turns and cadences which are essential features of Irish dance tunes. The piano accordion, three-row British Chromatic and five-row continental chromatic have all found their way into traditional music and become commonplace since the 1930s, but none of these later imports has actually supplanted the longer established two-row B/C instrument.

Although much of it is dance music, Irish traditional music is also a highly melodic art form with a deep-rooted emotional quality as part of its attraction. The music can be considered as three component parts i.e. dance tunes (reels, hornpipes, marches, polkas, jigs, slip jigs and waltzes); slow airs – often evocative or haunting; and songs which can be about love, politics, history, travel, joy, sorrow, or indeed any combination of these things. The musical score of *Riverdance*, made internationally famous by Michael Flatley, is a case in point: a musical collage of various rhythms illustrating different and wide-ranging moods. The popularity of Irish music at home and abroad has continued to thrive despite the rapid urbanisation of many parts of Ireland and the passing into history of the *Quiet Man* image of the famous 1951 John Wayne film.

Many musicians and listeners regard Irish music as an art form. The best players are usually those who not only achieve correct ornamentation and good style, but can also work out their own variations on tunes, sometimes re-composing whilst playing. Many of the best accordionists are not content to play standard rhythmic accompaniments but will use the bass side notes to add to the melody line in various ways. An example is Martin O'Connor, a two-row player who once played with *De Danaan* before embarking on a solo career. O'Connor's two handed skill on the B/C accordion is outstanding, evidenced on his excellent CD recordings such as *Perpetual Motion* and *Chatterbox*, the latter with all the music composed by the artist in Irish style. In his De Danaan days, O'Connor recorded a remarkable version of Handel's *Arrival of the Queen of Sheba* – successfully defying the alleged limitations of the two-row accordion.

As already implied, accordions have played a significant part in the field of Irish folk music. Towards the end of the 19th Century, as traditional Irish pipes were experiencing a decline, the one and two-row button accordions (known in England as melodeons) grew to prominence, being relatively inexpensive and easy to learn. By the 1920s the button accordion, especially the two-row B/C type, had found general favour with traditional musicians, and this has remained the case to this day. When many Irish people refer to *'the accordion'*, they tend to think of the two-row instrument rather than any other kind of accordion.

Since the 1940s other types of accordions have become commonplace in Ireland. Three-row and piano accordions are nowadays as much in evidence as the perennial two-row, the much improved and faster playing action of modern piano keyboards now being fast enough to cope with the ornamentation of Irish music. In recent years even the 5-row continental chromatic has found its way into Irish music making, these instruments now being imported from abroad in greater numbers.

Although Irish music is well suited to, and originally intended for, solo performance by voice or instrument, Ireland has long been famous for its ceili (also spelt ceilidh) bands. The large ceili bands – eight or so musicians playing in unison on accordions, fiddles, flutes, banjos and percussion – emerged in the 1920s. One of the first was *Dan Sullivan's Shamrock Band*, and more modern ones include the *Gallowglass, Kilfenora, Bridge, Tulla, Athlone* and *Donal Ring Ceili Band*. Each band includes one or more accordions, with the *Gallowglass* band being led by Pat McGarr on Hohner Atlantic 1V piano accordion plus Brendan Breen on second box using a 5-row Borsini. The *Gallowglass* band were the most commercially successful and universally well known of the ceili bands due to their radio and television appearances in Ireland plus their massive worldwide record sales, dating back to the 1950s through to the 1990s. They were All-Ireland championship winners in the ceili band class in 1953/54/55, and then vacated their crown to concentrate on a professional career. Their long career came to a grand finish in 1993 with the release of a video *The Gallowglass Ceili Band – Together For One Last Re-Union*, issued by Apollo Video, and featuring no less than 150 costumed Irish dancers.

Solo accordion players emanating from the Irish traditional music scene include such star performers as Dermot O'Brien, Seamus Shannon, Joe Burke and Fintan Stanley. It is interesting to note that these four all play different systems – piano, three-row, two-row and 5-row accordions, covering the main types of instrument now to be found in Ireland. The most commercially successful of these is Dermot O'Brien, a musician who began his playing career in a ceili band but went on to become a solo artist playing and singing Irish music around the world. Although nowadays not regarded as part of the main-stream of Irish traditional music, Dermot O'Brien has probably done more than anyone to spread the accordion music of Ireland internationally.

The Irish community in the USA, especially on the East Coast and Chicago is large and influential, and tends to have the expatriates' zeal for the culture of a far away homeland – especially with regard to music. It is hardly surprising, therefore, that a number of Irish Americans have become excellent accordionists e.g. button player Billy McComiskey from New York, and James Keane (piano accordion) from Chicago. The all-female band *Cherish the Ladies*, featuring Joanie Madden on button accordion, are all outstanding musicians whose recordings have become best sellers in this country.

How best to learn Irish traditional music has always been a matter of keen debate. The strong emotional character plus the problem of achieving correct ornamentation spawns the commonly held point of view that this music cannot actually be taught, and can only be instinctively learnt. It is certainly the case that many fine players of Irish music have never had any formal tuition but have 'got into' the style by listening to others and participating in informal sessions in pubs or joining ceili bands and learning from the bottom up, as it were. There is, furthermore, the point of view that standard musical notation cannot adequately express the manner in which the music should be performed.

Having said that, a huge amount of Irish music is now in print including a number of tutor books giving advice on performance using diatonic and piano accordions. Many excellent Irish accordionists have been taught music in a formal sense yet have nonetheless become highly proficient at playing their nation's traditional music, confounding the view that playing 'by ear' is the correct way to learn. In recent years video tuition has become another option for learning Irish music, with tapes for the two-row button accordion by such skilled players as John Williams and PJ Hernon becoming available.

In the late 1940s there developed a need for a central co-ordinating body in Ireland to organise activities for musicians, dancers and singers. This resulted in the emergence of Comhaltas Ceoltori Eireann, a Dublin-based organisation that is non-political, non-sectarian and seeks to actively promote Irish culture in Ireland and abroad. It organises teaching and competitions for all relevant instruments, singing and dancing, and stages entertainment shows. Its most well known events are the 'Fleadhanna' (music festivals) held in Ireland and Britain during the spring and summer months. The All-Britain finals, staged in a different place each year, qualifies the winners to participate in the All-Ireland Fleadh Cheoil (pronounced FLAD KAYOAL), the most prestigious event of all. This is a mighty feast of music, song and dance lasting for at least three days towards the end of August, with attendances regularly reaching 100,000 per day. The All-Ireland festival caters for approximately 4,000 competitors, plus about 10,000 performers of various kinds – huge numbers, requiring a lot of forward preparation. Each year this event is held in a different town, and visitors are drawn from many parts of the world. Competitors come from expatriate Irish communities in various countries as well as from the homeland itself, and the first non-Irish born accordionist to win the Senior All-Ireland championship was the American James Early (on piano accordion) in Buncrana in 1976. For anyone interested, the HQ address of Comhaltas Ceoltori Eireann is C.C.E., 32 Belgrave Square, Monkstown, Dublin, Republic of Ireland. CCE also has a British-based website. (See **Comhaltas Ceoltori Eireann**)

Irish dance music fulfils several purposes. The ceili – the social dance – is perhaps the most obvious. Set dancing, involving groups of four couples per dance, is usually done to lively and lengthy tune medleys. Some musicians such as the three-row accordionist Matt Cunningham specialise in playing for set dancing, performing at clubs and festivals. There is also the highly impressive-looking step dancing of the competitive Feis (pronounced FESH), where teams or solo dancers perform intricate steps in which the legs alone play a part. In competitions, the accompaniment is more than likely provided by an accordionist, often with piano backing. Some accordionists have developed accompaniment to art-level standards; outstanding in this genre are the Glasgow duo Gerry Conlon & Seamus O'Sullivan. Their highly polished music is heard to great effect on a series of CD recordings issued by Bryan's Room Recordings; e-mail gerry@zetnet.co.uk The step dancer performs a pre-set routine to the lively tunes played, but does not otherwise respond to the music – an expressionless face being the norm! The outwardly serious outlook of those who participate in step-dancing is at odds with the spontaneous fun of ceili dancing, and the origins of this curious dual nature of Irish dancing lies somewhere in Irish history, religion and folklore.

The greatest collector of Irish tunes was Francis O'Neill, Chief of Police in Chicago, and also a noted flautist. O'Neill compiled a book containing 1,859 dance tunes and airs which was published in 1903 as *O'Neill's Dance Music of Ireland*. Often referred to as *'the bible'* and still widely in use a century later, this was the first and as yet the greatest attempt to gather and classify on paper the heart of the traditional repertoire. For those who may be interested, O'Neill's book is easily obtainable through music shops. There is also a version of the same book called *O'Neill's Music of Ireland*, but this contains purely fiddle settings of the same repertoire.

No article about Irish traditional music would be complete without discussion of the airs composed by Turlough O'Carolan (1670-1738), the blind harper. O'Carolan (also known as Carolan) composed over two hundred tunes – some lively, some slow and haunting, but all of them beautiful and uniquely structured. O'Carolan's music was composed as he travelled around the homes of wealthy patrons, and most of his pieces are dedicated to the people he met and the places he visited. This music is not dance music – though some of the tunes have occasionally been adapted into dance settings – and is generally played for concert performance, enduring in the repertoires of folk and classical musicians for two centuries. Although written as harp music, the O'Carolan pieces translate well to the accordion and can be made to sound very effective indeed. Dermot O'Brien included *O'Carolan's Receipt for Drinking* on his 1992 CD *Irish Tapestry*, and *O'Carolan's Concerto* on his 1974 LP *Dermot O'Brien*. O'Carolan's music seems to evoke an age now long gone in Irish history, and his tunes were apparently much admired by Beethoven, the first person credited with writing them down on paper for posterity.

The popularity of Irish traditional music is spread internationally across the English-speaking world. To play Irish music well on the accordion (no matter what type of button or piano system), especially with its characteristic ornamentation, is not easy and requires much skill and practice. With its continual growth and development, Irish traditional music is a living tradition and a challenge for those who take it up.

Jazz *Jazz has been a relatively small but significant part of the British accordion scene for most the 20th Century, going back to the mid-1920s when George Scott-Wood went to America where he met and played with the legendary band leader Paul Whiteman, and other jazz musicians. Since George Scott-Wood's heyday in the 1930s, the accordion scene in Britain has produced a few notable jazz exponents such as Tito Burns, Martin Lukins, Jack Emblow, Tony Compton, concertina players John Nixon and Simon Thoumire, Harry Hussey and the Scotsman, John Huband.*

Is it possible to learn how to play jazz? Opinions in the music world are divided on this matter. Some people believe that the musical principles behind what is accepted as jazz can be studied and applied, but others hold the view

that playing jazz comes essentially from the heart and requires a creativity from within that cannot be taught.
In the following article, Tony Compton has this to say: -

LET'S PLAY JAZZ

"Please can you teach me to play jazz?"
"Sorry," I reply – *"No!"*
"Well, who taught you?"
"Nobody," I replied.
"Well, what is jazz then?" They ask.

I tell them that there are *many* definitions. For example, *The Oxford Companion to Music*, by Percy A. Scholes, has a four-page definition! Collins Dictionary, on the other hand, simply says *'syncopated, discordant music'*! An illustrated Chambers Dictionary, now over forty years old, doesn't even list the word. And as a sixteen-year-old music student, I was told by the Head of the Music Department (a highly qualified musician with a doctorate): *"Jazz is decadent, young man, give it up. You will never get anywhere with it, it's rubbish!"*

Thank goodness times have changed, and jazz is now accepted as a truly individual art form.

I personally think Fats Waller hit the nail on the head when replying to the question: *"What is jazz? Lady, if you've got jazz, then you know what it is."*

Many accordion students like to listen to jazz but I feel that they are frightened to venture away from their straight classical training. I am a firm believer that you don't have to improvise to play jazz. My own feeling is that phrasing is most important, and my advice to a student is to take a simple tune and play it as written. Then, play it again and alter the phrasing. I would imagine that some music teachers would call this syncopation. Add a few dots here and there, take off a few dots, slightly alter the value of some notes, and leave a few spaces. Many jazz musicians often say that it's not what you play that's important, but what you leave out.

Another piece of advice I sometimes offer is to listen to jazz musicians, not necessarily accordionists. Dizzy Gillespie was a great influence on my playing, and even now when playing jazz I try to do things on the accordion that a trumpet player might do. For example, the treble keyboard is just as nimble as a trumpet or tenor saxophone and one should remember that the bellows could be used to accent notes in the same way as horn players do. I always refer to the bellows as the 'lungs' of the instrument.

I feel it is equally important to listen to the greatest instrument of them all – the voice, and here I must mention Tony Bennett, Ella Fitzgerald, Mel Torme, countless others, and of course, the governor himself, Frank Sinatra. All of them superb re-phrasers.

The accordion is a wonderful instrument as it is capable of putting down a strong, sustained chordal backing as well as playing single notes. Again this is illustrated by listening to Art Van Damme, Frank Marocco and, of course, our own Jack Emblow.

There are many academic tips that can be given by more highly trained musicians than myself, and they could explain chord structures and progressions, etc. I'm afraid I always rely on my ears. People often ask: *"What was that chord you played in the so-and-so bar?"* My stock answer is usually *"An augmented 98th with a flattened 12th!"* I rarely know what chords I play but if they sound good I play them.

Jazz is a feeling that should come from within. The true jazz musician can play his or her instrument completely on their own with no accompaniment, and they should be able to feel the rhythm section ticking away inside themselves, and they should be able to communicate this feeling to their audience.

In conclusion – but really there is no conclusion. Like all fascinating subjects, it is an ongoing thing to be explored and improved upon by the individual.

Keep experimenting! Keep swinging!

Tony Compton, Accordion Times (1987)

Gerald Crossman, one of Britain's greatest accordion talents and a highly versatile musician offers the following advice for those interested in investigating the principles involved in playing jazz: -

…AND ALL THAT JAZZ
by Gerald Crossman

In the simplest and briefest terms, jazz is generally defined as a class of music that features improvisation and rhythmic syncopation.

In this article I'd like to give some general comprehensive advice (light reading as well as slightly technical) concerning all styles of popular (often 'evergreen' or 'standard') dance music improvisation, which can be classified under different categories such as Dixieland, swing, funk, and so on. Ragtime, much associated with the piano, is normally played as written.

Improvisation of music is playing impromptu or extempore in melodic fashion around the notes of the harmonies of a piece, and embellishing or incorporating suggestions or variation of the given melodic themes or phrases, performed in appropriate stylish manner (hopefully!). It is instant composition. A few players with little or no musical knowledge are able to do this in some mysterious way. I once knew a policeman who could, and he didn't know a sharp from a flat. He had perfect pitch, but this perfect pitch can be confusing when performing on transposing instruments such as saxophones, clarinets, trumpets, etc. However, the majority of players require study and example.

A good knowledge of scales, chords and arpeggios is fundamental. One needs knowledge of notes and fingering of all types of scales, and one also needs to know how the various kinds of chords are constructed in order to become familiar with the notes of each chord. Arpeggio fingering is important, too. A fine all-round technique must be acquired as is necessary for fulfilling a top performance of any style of music.

Study of harmony is concerned with the chords (combinations of musical sound which complement melodies) and their classification, and includes the rules of progression and resolution, voicing and also cadences. A thorough understanding of the subject enables a player to alter the harmonies of any piece being played in order to provide interesting changes of sound colour here and there, thus giving opportunities to demonstrate personal invention. In addition, the mysteries of modulations are dispersed.

Listening to jazz players' improvisations provides models and standards, though eventually the acquisition of an individual style is preferable to copying. Note that the melodies are usually played straight early in a piece, and likewise towards the end.

Get some recordings of clarinet player Benny Goodman (whom, incidentally, I had the pleasure of meeting), saxophonists, trumpet players, pianists (such as Earl Hines, Nat King Cole, Oscar Peterson and George Shearing). In particular, look out for the recordings of that master American accordionist Art Van Damme. Other American jazz accordionists to look out for are Leon Sash (on button accordion), Joe Mooney, and Ernie Felice, plus the Dutchman Mat Mathews. The music of these artistes was recorded many years ago, but because of its quality it still remains fresh and makes interesting listening.

Find sheet music arrangements of jazz pieces, and gain ideas and inspiration from the shape of the phrases. Carefully examine effective introductions, every fill-in, bridge passage, modulation and coda (ending). When any good arrangement is played it ought to sound natural, also rhythmical when in tempo, not forced or artificial. A feeling of spontaneity should prevail, even when playing from printed notes. Try writing an arrangement of a non-copyright number such as *When the Saints...*

Aural training is important and indeed indispensable in order to develop one's ear and learn recognition of all types of intervals and chords. The knowledge and consequent ability gained from this will be used continuously during extemporisation.

Beginners at improvisation can start their attempts in the simplest fashion – playing mainly single treble notes around the notes of a tonic chord, such as C major (C, E and G). This exercise could feel strange at first. Be rhythmical, weave a nice melodic line and try to be imaginative. Use a steady tempo at first and keep strictly to it. Include some passing notes, some double notes, and the occasional C chord. Hear what is about to be played whilst performing, and co-ordinate the ears and fingers. Remember the points already made. Be, and look, relaxed. Reflect this in the wrist and fingers, for the playing then benefits and the effect is transmitted to the listeners. Proceed to the chord of C6 (C, E, G & A). The next suggested step is to make similar efforts on the dominant 7th chord G7 (G, B, D & F), after which the subdominant F major (F, A & C). Practise in every key possible, minor as well as major. Good fingering is important throughout.

If confidant so far, progress to a piece which can be simply harmonised with only two chords (e.g. the first eight bars of *Sweet Sue* in the key of G and their repeat only need D7 in bars 1, 2, 3, 4 and G or G6 in bars 5, 6, 7 and 8). Try a piece with three chords (e.g. the first eight bars of *Lady Be Good* in G, needing G in bars 1, 3, 4, 7 and 8; C7 in bar 2, and D7 in bars 5 & 6). See how well everything can be linked together smoothly and musically. Let the sounds flow. Gradually increase abilities by playing tunes requiring more harmonies, but don't cram in too many notes, i.e. don't be too busy. For the moment, let tasteful economy be the motto!

In later stages familiarity with advanced chords should be acquired. There are chords with the added this and that, diminished and augmented whatsits, flattened so and so's, chords of the ninth, eleventh, thirteenth and also suspensions, as well as other such intricacies like chromatic chords. Sounds more complicated than it is but it.comes quite naturally once one gets into the swing.

Gerald Crossman, The Accordion News, 1992 (abridged version)

Jenkins, Brian   In the 1950s, Manchester's Brian Jenkins was taught the piano accordion by the late 'Pip' Walker at Reno's music store, and then by George Harris, proceeding through the BCA grades and attaining a high standard of performance. He was, however, also a brass band player and eventually this took precedence over the accordion in his spare time away from the day job with British Aerospace, Chadderton. Brian played and conducted within the brass band world, then re-discovered the accordion in the early 1990s when he first attended a practice of the *Clifford Wood Accordion Orchestra*. In 1996, Brian became MD of the *Stockport Accordion Orchestra* during the band's transition from the *CWAO*. Later, he also became involved with the *Tameside Junior Accordion Band* and the *North West Accordion Orchestra*. The Stockport Accordion Orchestra, as it became known, frequently uses Brian Jenkins' arrangements that are characterised by his brass band influence. In recent years, he has been a popular and respected MD of the weekend orchestras at the Blackpool and Pakefield festivals.

Jones, John   (Born 1942) Manchester-born but Macclesfield based John Jones is a relative late-comer to the accordion. John only took up the accordion seriously in 1988, when he joined the recently revived Clifford Wood Accordion Orchestra, using a Ranco bought in 1936 by his late father. In 1991, John began busking in Macclesfield, collecting money for the local hospi-tal's Scanner Appeal. This led to him playing and collecting for a long list of charities, most notably the Alzheimer's Society, the British Red Cross, David Lewis Centre for Epilepsy, East Cheshire Hospice, Francis House Children's Hospice,
Macmillan Nurses, Marie Cure, and the Multiple Sclerosis Society. He has also made three music cassettes, all proceeds of which were donated to various

charitable causes. To date, John Jones has collected in excess of £125,000 for good causes, and in the process has become one of Macclesfield's most well known citizens – a common sight playing in the town's market centre and hospital. He also plays frequently in retirement homes in and around his area, and is a regular and stalwart member of the Stockport Accordion Club and Orchestra. (See also **Strange, but true...**)

Karklins, George Egons 'George' Karklins was born in Riga, Estonia, and came to Britain after the Second World War. Amongst other musical accomplishments, George was an excellent jazz accordionist, and he was a regular performer at both North Staffs Accordion Club and Club Accord in the late 1970s and throughout the 1890s. At Club Accord, he became well known for his off-the-cuff duetting with Harry Swingler, and the pair of them contributed to the 1979 LP *It's All Accordion To What You Like*. George was a regular performer at trade stands at accordion festivals, instantly recognisable with his black beret, and was sadly missed when he died in 1989.

Keen, David David Keen was once a competitive accordionist, winning many titles, and regularly competing each year at '*Accordion Day*'. He has been an accordion teacher, and has conducted orchestras, and then he became heavily involved in the administration side of the competition scene. For many years, London-based David was a key committee member of the NAO, serving as Chairman and editing the organisation's own magazine known as the *NAO Accordionist*. Eventually, differences with the NAO led to him breaking away and the *NAO Accordionist* was renamed and re-invented as the bi-monthly magazine *Accordion World*.

Kirkpatrick, John (Born London, 1947) John Kirkpatrick is one of the folk world's biggest names, having appeared as a main guest at all the best known folk festivals both as a solo performer and as a member of such high profile bands as *Steeleye Span, The Albion Band* and *Brass Monkey*. Kirkpatrick plays Hohner one and two row melodeons, Casali three row B/B/C# diatonic accordion, and the Crabb Anglo GC concertina; he is also a composer, dancer and a fine singer, steeped in traditional English folk song, dance and Morris music which are his main interests. A prolific recording artiste, Kirkpatrick has, to date, featured on more than two hundred recordings – some vocal/instrumental, others purely instrumental. His 1985 LP (now available on CD) *Three In A Row,* one of the best selling folk recordings of the year, is an entirely solo recording using one and two row melodeons and three row accordion, plus several of John K's own compositions. Track number 4 is the old accordionists' favourite, *Blaze Away*, a tour-de-force performance that demonstrates Kirkpatrick's incredibly dextrous and much admired two-handed technique, very rare amongst diatonic accordionists. The CD, *One man & his box*, made in 1998, is another recording that shows John K's capabilities as a solo performer. This recording, using 3-row button accordion, one-row melodeon and Anglo concertina is a 20-track programme of tunes and songs typical of what John does in a solo gig in a folk club. The penultimate track is *The Bells* (a.k.a *The Bells of St Mary's*, thanks to the great Bing Crosby), an instrumental using the Anglo concertina, is quite a show-stopper in live performance, as John swings his instrument round and over his head in a wide circle to create a peeling church bells effect.

In 1999 John Kirkpatrick produced two tuition videos *How To Play The English Melodeon*, featuring one and two row instruments and using English folk and Morris dance tunes as the genre for teaching/learning purposes. A third video, sub-titled *The Masterclass*, completed the series. This video set, offering a lucid explanation with well-structured demonstrations of how to play/improve playing techniques, is likely to prove to be a long-lasting contribution to the melodeon from a genuine master of his craft. The videos, published by Mrs Casey Records, PO Box 296, Aylesbury, Bucks HP19 9TL, have all proved to be best sellers.

Somewhat overlooked is the fact that John Kirkpatrick is also a skilled and imaginative composer of tunes and songs, most of which are within the English folk genre. Composed on diatonic instruments, many of the dance tunes reflect the idiosyncrasies of these systems and so have a value-added 'character' as a result. An example is the jig *Jump At The Sun*, a lively tune that is great for getting dancers to leap around the floor. By way of contrast, the air *As The Sun Was Setting* is a beautiful melody that demonstrates the composer's musical sensitivity. Kirkpatrick also has a quirky sense of humour, such as in the song *Welcome To Hell* in which the lyrics tell of how a deceased accordionist arrives in Hell whilst a similarly deceased harpist is admitted through the gates of Heaven. Most of Kirkpatrick's compositions have been published in tune and songbooks.

Kirkpatrick's status within the folk scene made him first choice for the BBC as presenter of two series of weekly radio programmes in the 1990s, titled *Squeezin' Round The World*, shows which focused on accordion music and personalities from folk traditions in many parts of the world. Although these programmes tended to view the accordion largely in the context of folk and world music, one show centred on the life and music of Jack Emblow, including an in-depth interview with the maestro.

John's most recent project has been to collate 101 traditional English tunes together (all playable on a DG melodeon) that are all suitable as dance music, in a book called *John Kirkpatrick's English Choice*. All the tunes have also been recorded on two CDs, *Orlando's Return* and *Garrick's Delight*. These CDs and the book are published by Dave Mallinson, and can be obtained via the web site http://www.mally.com

In recent years, John Kirkpatrick has made appearances at accordion clubs and the Pontin's International Accordion Festival at Blackpool, thus introducing his music and instruments to mainstream accordion audiences.

For a list of John's available recordings or to join his mailing list, please send a stamped and addressed envelope to Squeezer, P.O. Box 531, Craven Arms, Shropshire SY9 5WB. John's web site is: www.johnkirkpatrick.co.uk

Booking: John Kirkpatrick can be booked via Speaking Volumes (sole agent), telephone 01905 611323; fax: 01905 619958.

Compositions: *Opus Pocus* (tune book); *What Do You Do During The Day?* (songs).

Tune Book: *John Kirkpatrick's English Choice* (2003).

Videos: *How To Play The English Melodeon* (Volumes 1& 2; Vol. 3 – *The Masterclass*).

Selected Discography: *Jump At The Sun* (1972); *Morris On* (1971); *Plain Capers* (1976); *Going Spare* (1978); *Facing The Music* (1980); *Three In A Row* (1985); *Blue Balloon* (1987); *Sheepskins (1993); A Short History of John Kirkpatrick* (1994); *Earthling* (1994); *Force of Habit* (1996); *Welcome To Hell* (1997); *One Man & His Box* (1998); *Orlando's Return* (2003); *Garrick's Delight* (2003)

Korbakov, Alexander (Born 1962) Russian-born Alexander 'Sasha' Korbakov first visited this country in the early 1990s, and was an instant success with his lively traditional music, virtuosic skill, colourful costumes, easy charm and good looks. The late Malcolm Gee introduced him to British audiences at Caister, after which appearances at accordion clubs and other festivals followed in quick succession. Since his first visits, Alexander (known to many as Sasha) has acquired a more modern and upmarket Bayan accordion, in place of the vintage model he originally played, and has also revised his repertoire to include classical pieces. Lumic Productions made a 90-minute video in 1995 in which Alexander Korbakov is seen playing with the Severn Valley Steam Railway as a backdrop; Malcolm Gee also interviews him, and there is a concert given in a stately home. He is a popular accordionist, who is likely to make many more visits to Great Britain.

Krein, Henry For several decades, from the 1930s through to the 1990s, Henry Krein was a much admired accordionist, and his long-standing connection with the BBC meant that his music was heard by radio audiences across the country – especially for his Sunday evening Grand Hotel broadcasts. Henry was part of the *Gerald Crossman Players* in the 1950s, regularly broadcasting music with a

154

Continental flavour. He was also a familiar figure at recording sessions, and – as a keen motorcyclist – would travel across London with his accordion on board. Jack Emblow recalls travelling as a passenger with Krein, weaving in and out of the London traffic, and being really relieved on arriving at their destination in one piece!

Kulvietis, Joe (1929-2001) Lithuanian-born Juozas (Joe) Kulvietis came to England during the war years to escape from both Nazi and Soviet oppression. He played the accordion, and set himself up as a teacher in the Huddersfield area. In the 1980s, Kulvietis served as organiser of the NAO North Central Festival in Huddersfield, and also occasionally organised concerts featuring overseas players, most notably Toralf Tollefsen's final stage appearance in 1988.

Laurie – Graham and Brian Brothers Graham and Brian Laurie, from Paisley near Glasgow, together founded an accordion school in the early 1980s that quickly grew in size and became well known for high standards of tuition, playing and performance. In 1987, the G & B Laurie bands entered the NAO UK Championships for the first time, winning trophies and in subsequent years became the dominant force in the band/orchestra side of the national festivals. In 1988, the various G & B Laurie orchestras made the first of several triumphant visits to the NAO North West Area Festival at Stockport Town Hall, where their professional approach to playing and high standard of appearance made a strong impression on festival organisers and public alike.

In 1999, Graham and Brian went their separate ways, but their respective newly formed schools have continued their winning ways at local and national festivals.

Leslie, John The proprietor of the Kilburn-based retail business *Accordions of London*, John Leslie, is a man of many talents. Apart from his high profile business interests, he is an accomplished player (with a long track record of being heard on radio or television advertisements, and such radio programmes as *Breakfast Special*, the *Charlie Chester Show* and *Round Midnight*), a most accomplished teacher (with many pupils winning accordion championship titles), and is also the patriarch of a family that includes several children who have become excellent accordionists. As if all that were not enough, John has composed music, conducted workshops and master classes at festivals (most recently being at St Audrie's Bay), made recordings, and has served as the UK adjudicator at the world championships since the 1970s.

Leveson, Les Les Leveson's love affair with accordions started while he was listening to a street musician in London at the age of eleven. His first accordion was a 24 bass Hohner, and he later progressed to a 120 bass Pancotti (Excelsior). Mr Phillips, a piano teacher, who played with the De Groot Orchestra, taught him. War service interrupted his tuition, but not his playing, during which time he played a Hohner 'liberated' from a bierkeller in Germany. Once the war was over, for Les it was back to improving his playing skills.

About 1950, the trusty Pancotti was overhauled by Bruno Allodi, with whom a lifetime association began. Les played in clubs and pubs, and formed the Les Brown Trio. In the 1970s he was invited to join a Russian dance group called Troika, and became their Musical Director under George Orloff, who submitted Les' name to the Inner London Education Authority to take over his Adult Education evening classes. This continued for some ten years, and from those classes came the Buttons & Bellows Band.

In 1986, Les took early retirement from the day job and was fortunate to go to work part-time with Emilio Allodi, son of Bruno, and this proved to be an invaluable experience – learning the skills and techniques of accordion repair and maintenance.

He moved to Lincoln in 1988, where he helped to establish the Lindum Accordion Club. Les has been a keen supporter of the accordion festivals, including Weston-super-Mare, Blackpool, St Audrey's Bay, Caister and Bridlington. The annual pilgrimage to Caister presented the opportunity to take over the Beginners and Elementary Orchestras, much encouraged by Ron Hodgson.

Les continues with teaching the accordion (he likes to think his forte is with beginners) and accordion maintenance.

Lukins, David Uxbridge-based David Lukins comes from a true accordion background, with father Martin Lukins achieving near-legendary status amongst accordionists of his generation, and mother Dorothy Lukins leading a series of orchestras through many NAO national accordion championships finals. It is little wonder that David has aspired to be the son and heir to the Lukins family accordion heritage, and he has revived many of his father's compositions and arrangements in his repertoire. David also plays the vibraphone, and still occasionally features this instrument in his performances, by way of contrast with the two accordions (straight and musette tuned) that he uses. David has become a frequently booked guest at accordion clubs and festivals around the country, and his performances are always eagerly looked forward to. He and wife Angela (also an accordionist) have a son Andy, who looks set to carry the Lukins musical name and accordion reputation into the future.

156

Lukins, Martin London-born Martin Lukins was born on August 10th 1923. He started piano lessons at the age of 5, and the piano accordion at 12. In 1937, at 14 and after only two years study, he played the accordion on BBC radio's Children's Hour. This was the first of nearly 1,000 radio and television appearances by this outstanding accordionist in a show business career in which Martin Lukins performed with or alongside the likes of Frank Sinatra, Phil Silvers, Gracie Fields, Bob Monkhouse, Ken Dodd, John Hanson,  Moira Anderson, Charlie Chester, Bill Maynard, Frankie Vaughan, The Bachelors and Morecambe & Wise – a real name dropping celebrity list!

Just before war broke out in 1939, Martin's fledgling playing career received an unexpected break when the musical director of a variety show, in which he was appearing, walked out in the middle of a week at the Grand Theatre, Bolton. *"They gave me the job although I was only 17,"* recalled Martin years later. *"I also carried on with my solo accordion spot. It meant I was getting two salaries for the rest of the tour, which included the Shepherd's Bush Empire, now the BBC television studios."*

During the war, Martin Lukins joined the RAF, becoming a member of the RAF Central Band, and remaining in the service until 1952. While in the RAF he was admitted to hospital in Uxbridge, his hometown, with high fever and tonsillitis. *"I was sweating blood because I was supposed to be at the Lime Grove studios on the Saturday night,"* he recalled. *"I sneaked out, did the television show and then crept back in again! If anyone found out, they made no mention of it."* He was doing so well at this time that he was driving into camp in a big car while the Wing Commander came in on a bicycle! *"It became obvious I would have to leave, so I bought myself out,"* he said.

In 1947, the newly constituted British Association of Accordionists introduced its own national championships and in 1950 Martin Lukins decided to enter, winning the first of three consecutive BAA Open Solo titles. Some years later, in 1959, he won a competition called the World Oscar for accordion playing in Pavia, Italy – his pinnacle in the field of competitive playing.

In addition to a long and very successful playing career, Martin Lukins made many recordings (on both acoustic and electronic accordions, and also on piano) and was also a much admired composer and arranger. His compositions and arrangements for accordion were for many years played by up and coming accordionists looking for interesting and musically challenging material.

Yet another feature of Martin's life was his long involvement in teaching the accordion, and running accordion bands/orchestras. He ran no less than six different accordion schools in different parts of London, and appeared on television with one of his accordion orchestras.

In his later years, Martin Lukins emigrated to Perth, Western Australia. By this time, persistent back trouble had forced him to give up the accordion, and henceforward he switched exclusively to playing the piano. Martin Lukins passed away on October 18th 2002 in Perth, and was mourned by all those who remembered his fabulous music.

Magnante, Charles (1905-86) Many good judges regard America's Charles Magnante as the greatest accordionist of all time, and his arrangements and compositions are held in similarly high regard. Magnante's music is, for many accordionists, the high water mark of sophistication, and his passing in December 1986 caused universal sadness across the accordion world.

Magnante was a founder member and President of the American Accordionists' Association on three occasions – 1950/51, 1955/56 and 1969/70. He was also a composer whose works include *Accordiana, Accordion Boogie* and *Waltz Allegro*. He arranged music by the great classical composers such as Chopin and Tchaikovsky, and was generally considered to be a concert performer par excellence. He also wrote tutor books – *The Charles Magnante Accordion Method* – that were highly rated by teachers and students, and sold in many countries.

Magnante was known and greatly admired in Great Britain, and his compositions and arrangements are sought after and played right up to the present day. It is a pity that his recordings and tutor books – all quality products – are not currently available.

A report of a concert by Charles Magnante, given on Sunday 27th March 1955 at the Steinway Hall, New York, appeared in the *Accordion Times*, written by Birmingham accordion teacher George Clay, and is reproduced here with kind permission of the magazine: -

Magnante the Magnificent!

"Magnante was introduced onto the stage and glanced around at the now packed hall, where people were standing along the walls and lined up at the back, and a few youngsters were even forced to sit on the steps leading up to the stage. That such a crowd had attended made him very happy, quite obviously, and as he said, 'Perhaps next time it will be necessary to hire Madison Square Garden.'

His first item was the *Toccata in D Minor*, by JS Bach. He played it faultlessly; secondly came the *Sonata Pathetique Opus 13*, by Beethoven, and although the accordion itself is not of the percussive quality that is usually associated with this sonata when played on the piano, Magnante's interpretation brought out all the tragedy of this great composer's life.

The *Warsaw Concerto*, composed by Richard Addinsell, was played next, and it was difficult to realise that this was originally written for the piano. The moving basses in the left hand were played with several changes of the bass couplers, bringing as much variety into the piece as possible. Two tricky waltzes followed – *Waltz in G flat* and *Waltz in F Minor*, both pieces by Chopin.

Mr Magnante then mentioned that he was going to play a more modern type of music, and his first number, *Flying Saucers*, demonstrated his fabulous technique perfectly. He then asked the children to name some tunes, and proceeded to play variations on these tunes interspersed with the whistle, train effects, canary, aeroplane, all played against the theme of Casey Jones.

He then did an improvisation on a standard 12 bars *Boogie Woogie*, and for his last item of the first half of the programme, played the *Flight of the Bumblebee*, by Rimsky Korsakov. In my own collection of recordings I have never heard anything to compare with this, particularly the last treble chromatic run, which was played in minor thirds.

Before the second half began, Mr Pietro Deiro Jnr, Vice-President of the American Association of Accordionists, was introduced. His first, and most fitting remark was, *'Is there another solo instrumentalist that could perform numbers from Bach to Casey Jones, who could hold our interest such as it has been held today?'*

Mr Magnante opened the second half of the recital by talking about musical interpretation. His discussions on dynamics, phrasing and expression marks, gave him ample opportunity to play dozens of numbers. One of his items, which brought a big laugh from the audience, was *Drama in Music*. To demonstrate this he played the popular *Dragnet* music. This, of course, is a top line television programme in the States, and is always followed by a knock at the door, which precedes the arrival of the police. Fortunately for us that afternoon, no police came in after that!

If ever a person qualifies for the title of *'The Complete Accordionist,'* Charles Magnante would be the obvious choice: tremendous control (he played for nearly three hours), fantastic technique, wonderful musicianship, and an approach to the subject that is quite individual. Off stage, Charles is the most delightful of men, with a ready wit and a serious note when the talk comes round to accordions. There was a queue, which took an hour and ten minutes to disperse, for autograph signing and photographs.

After the recital, Magnante, Pietro Deiro Jnr and I had an informal chat, and after I had congratulated him on his tremendous performance, he calmly said, *'I am sure glad you enjoyed it, George, as I didn't feel too good.'* He had apparently fallen in the morning, and hurt his back, and there were big bruises all across his back and ribs. All this before the most tremendous playing I have ever heard!"

George Clay, Accordion Times, December 1955

Selected discography: *Accordion Pops Concert* (1955); *Roman Spectacular* (1960); *Carnival – in far away places* (1966); *Romantic Accordion* (1972); *They Said It Couldn't Be Done* (date unknown)

Mallinson, Dave Known to one and all as 'Mally', Dave Mallinson has played two and three row melodeons since, as a teenager, he found that he preferred these instruments to the guitar that most people he knew were playing. Mally developed into a highly skilled player, with a strong interest in the country-dance music of Britain and Ireland. He has played extensively in folk dance bands, and has occasionally entered competitive festivals, including the All-Britain Irish Traditional Championships.

Mally's interest in traditional music led him into starting and developing a business from his home in Cleckheaton in West Yorkshire, in the 1970s. He used his considerable playing experience and expertise to write a series of tutors for the melodeon, using country-dance and Morris tunes respectively as the musical source material. These tutor books plus accompanying cassettes were self-published, and this was the beginning of what became *Dave Mallinson Music*, eventually to be based in a shop premises at 35 Bradford Rd, Cleckheaton. Mally's business steadily grew to major proportions, and was regularly represented at most folk and accordion festivals, all over England.

The success of Mally's melodeon tutor books inspired him to publish books of traditional tunes, and the writing and publishing eventually took up so much time that he sold the shop, which now trades as *The Music Room*. Mally's shop had always sold free reed instruments, and *The Music Room* is a main agent for Pigini accordions. There are piano and chromatic button accordions, British Chromatics, melodeons, concertinas, harmonicas – plus a repair/tuning service available.

The American 1960s artist Andy Warhol once famously claimed that everyone has fifteen minutes of fame in their lives, and if this is true then Mally's turn came when his ceilidh band was booked by Yorkshire Television to film a barn dance scene for *Emmerdale*. By the time the episode was screened, Mally was presenting a trade stand at the Whitby Folk Festival, and was unaware that his sequence was on television that evening. He recalls leaving his hotel and walking through the town, and being accosted everywhere he went by people who had unexpectedly just watched him playing music while the Sugdens, Tates, Seth Armstrong, Eric Pollard *et al* were acting out an every day story of country folk. It was fame at last!

Mancini, Rudy Manchester-born, and of Italian descent, Rudy Mancini managed public houses in the centre of his home city where he honed his skills and technique as an entertainer on both accordion and piano. In the 1930s, Rudy played accordion many times at a city centre pub in Manchester called *The Band on the Wall*, which is, to this day, still a very well known venue for all kinds of live music. When Italy joined the Germans by declaring war on this country in June 1940, all 'Italian' men were rounded up the police and arrested as 'enemy aliens'. Rudy was interned on the Isle of Man, but eventually released when he volunteered to join the RAF. During RAF service, Rudy became a member of the entertainment concert parties, making many contacts.

After the war, he played professionally, appearing in shows alongside the likes of Dick Emery, Cardew Robinson and Peter Sellers, and made many radio broadcasts for the BBC in the 1940s and 50s, especially on *Variety Bandbox*. Rudy Mancini was both a good sight-reader and a superb improviser, and he developed a technique and musical sensitivity that was the envy of all who heard him play. Eventually, Rudy Mancini and his wife Pat – after some years running pubs in Manchester – moved to Blackpool where they bought a series of hotels, most notably the large Queen's Hotel. A revered figure amongst northern accordionists, and rated by some good judges as the greatest ever British accordionist, it is a shame that the business interests of this self-made millionaire curtailed his musical career, and no commercially made recordings are available. Rudy was equally talented on the accordion, piano and electronic organ, and was adept at many styles of music.

Mao Tse-tung Why should China's most famous ruler of modern times have an entry in a book all about the accordion, you may well ask? Following the overthrow of Chiang-Kai-Shek in 1949 after a long civil war, Mao's Communist government ruled China with reforming zeal, affecting all aspects of everyday life. In 1966, the ruling party decided it was time to review progress, and make further changes wherever deemed necessary. This period was the beginning of a ten-year period called the *Cultural Revolution*, during which time it came to Mao's attention that the accordion was the musical instrument most closely identified with the working classes (i.e. the *'Proletariat'*). The accordion was quickly elevated to an instrument of high social status in China; on the other hand, the Communist Party reformers derided and poured scorn on the pianoforte, equating this instrument with the rich and wealthy (i.e. the hated *'Bourgeoisie'*). Chairman Mao, never a man to do things by halves, decided there and then that the accordion must become the instrument of the people, and insisted that it must be on the curriculum of every school in China. Where all the teachers or instruments were to come from is anybody's guess, but the fact is that the accordion became the only compulsory subject on the Chinese educational curriculum!

With such a draconian approach and investment, inevitably there would be a breakthrough into the international accordion arena, and in 1989, China entered the Coupe Mondiale for the first time when Jun Chen, Jiang Lin and Wei Yue competed in Switzerland. China has its own accordion manufacturer, Parrot, whose instruments are virtual copies of Scandalli. Two world-class players have emerged from China in recent years, Fang Yuan and Zhang Guoping. Fang Yuan, an attractive and talented young lady from Shanghai (now living in Singapore), was an aspiring concert pianist who was forced to abandon the piano thanks to the ruling party's reforming notions. However, she successfully switched to the piano accordion, eventually becoming a concert artiste of international stature, travelling the world (including Great Britain, where she has appeared at Caister), to great critical acclaim. Mr Zhang, who uses a top of the range Parrot free bass piano accordion, has made recordings, and has toured overseas extensively. He also has performed in this country, and to great acclaim. However, China is still a relatively closed society – unlike the former USSR member countries – and it is likely that there are many more high-class players as yet unseen by the rest of the world, such was Chairman Mao's far-reaching contribution to the accordion world.

Marchell, Tony Accordion entertainer/vocalist from Manchester, using an Elkavox piano accordion and taught by the late Clifford Wood, Tony Marchell has made a full-time living performing in clubs, pubs and bierkellers. Tony Marchell specialises in performing popular and evergreen music, and his repertoire largely consists of medleys of songs through the decades, from the 1930s up to the present day. This genial, all-round entertainer has a wealth of playing/performing experience, and was featured in the evening concert at the NAO North-West Area Festival at Stockport Town Hall in 1993 as chief support to the great Jack Emblow. He is a particular favourite at North Staffs AC, but has yet to be discovered by the accordion festivals.

Marocco, Frank American jazz accordionist Frank Marocco's musical career began in Chicago where, at the age of 17, he won a national music contest. He performed his winning solo with Mark Weber and the Chicago Pops Orchestra, playing before several thousand people in Soldier's Field.

Frank spent the next few years travelling all over the USA with his quartet, playing at top hotels and clubs in Las Vegas, Lake Tahoe and Palm Springs. Eventually, he settled down in Los Angeles.

After a period playing with the Les Brown band, Frank worked extensively with the late, great Bob Hope, both on television and on worldwide tours entertaining US forces. Over the years, Frank has also worked with a huge number of artistes in the show business world, including Frank Sinatra, Dinah Shore, Doris Day, Harry Connick Jr, Liza Minelli, Ray Connif, Burt Bacharach, Dolly Parton, Marty Robbins, Johnny Cash, John Denver, Glenn Campbell, Dudley Moore, Sophia Loren, Bob Newhart, George Burns, Pink Floyd and The Beach Boys, plus many more.

Frank Marocco has done a lot of work in recording studios, especially for films and television. His playing can be heard on the soundtracks of such movies as *The Muppet Movie, Grease, The Addams Family, Charlie's Angels, Austin Powers 3 – Goldmember, The Lion King, Beauty & the Beast, Rocky 3, Indiana Jones & the Last Crusade, Dr Zhivago, Schindler's List* and *The Godfather 2* and *3*.

In 1992, Frank was chief guest (alongside Sweden's Jorgen Sundequist) at Caister Autumn Accordion Festival, and returned to this country in 1997 as guest at Blackpool International Accordion Festival. His superb playing, dazzling two-handed technique, ability to entertain, and warm personality has endeared him to British audiences, and most of his many marvellous recordings are available from Trevani.

Selected discography: *Evergreens* (1992); *Freedom Flight* (1995); *Turn Out the Stars* (1996); *Chicago Accordion Club - Live Solo Concert* (1999); *Appassionato* (2003)

Videos: *Frank Marocco Live in Concert* – two separate tapes, featuring acoustic solos.

MacLean, Calum Calum MacLean comes from the Isle of Mull, and is one of Scotland's most accomplished 5-row Continental chromatic button accordionists. As a boy he played the melodeon and the British Chromatic until he took up the 5-row Continental chromatic at the age of fourteen. In his formative years, Bobby MacLeod, Mull's other great accordion star player, influenced Calum's playing. Years later, in 1970, Calum won the European Championship, and since then has maintained a position as one of his nation's finest musicians. Essentially a solo accordionist rather than part of the dance band scene, Calum is also a  great composer of music for accordion, and he is particularly adept at writing pieces that are pastiches of French musette, Swiss, Latin, Italian, etc. Many of his compositions have been published, and also recorded. The composers Calum MacLean has admired over the years are Pietro Frosini, Pietro Deiro, and Scotland's Ian Holmes. The range of music featured on Calum's recordings is varied and impressive, and his style is much admired.

Discography: *Scottish Accordion Favourites* – Volumes 1 & 2; *Festival Accordion* (1976); *Calum MacLean Plays Calum MacLean* (1989); *Mull Holiday* (2000); *The Tartan Top Twenty* (2002) - this CD features eight reissued tracks from *Scottish Accordion Favourites - Vols 1 & 2*

Books of compositions: *The Calum MacLean Collection*; *Music From Mull*; *Seven Accordion Duets* – all published by *Deeay* – tel.: 01307 64324.

MacLeod, Bobby Scotland's Bobby MacLeod came from Tobermory on the Isle of Mull and played the piano accordion in his own highly successful dance band. Newspaper polls in the 1950s indeed showed that Bobby MacLeod's band was second only to Jimmy Shand in terms of popularity, and MacLeod's record sales and frequent appearances on radio and BBC television's White Heather Club endorsed this assessment. It is sometimes said that in Scotland, histori-cally there are two distinctive styles of traditional dance music: the East coast style and the West coast style, chiefly represented by Jimmy Shand from the 'East coast' and Bobby MacLeod from the 'West coast.' Thus it was that Bobby

Macleod's accordion style, borne out of what the Scots call a Pipe music technique, came to be influential on players from his part of Scotland who rose in the ranks after him in the 1960s up to the present day.

At Christmas 1955, Bobby & his band played for the London Scottish Society Ball, after which the musicians visited a London nightclub. Still wearing their tartan jackets, they were spotted and asked to play by the manager. Bobby & Co. obliged, not with jigs, reels and strathspeys, but with a jazz and swing set. The owner was so impressed that Bobby was offered a residency as a jazz musician, although the offer was gracefully declined.

Bobby MacLeod both owned and ran the Mishnish Hotel on Mull, and by the 1970s had virtually retired from gigging with his band. During the 70s, he took up the 5-row Continental chromatic, and performed and recorded with this instrument, though he continued to also play the piano accordion.

Selected discography: *Bobby's Kind Of Music* (1970); *Maestro MacLeod* (1977); *The Man from Tobermory* (1978)

McGuire, Willie (a.k.a **Billy**) Born near Paisley, Willie McGuire is one of Scotland's best ever players of the 3-row British Chromatic button accordion. Influenced by the late Will Starr, instruments played include a Shand Morino, Paolo Soprani and Fantini. He became the Scottish Senior Accordion Champion in 1987, won at Perth Festival, and has since guested at many Accordion & Fiddle clubs around Scotland. Has also represented Britain at the prestigious Chartres Accordion Festival in France. A stylish musician who excels equally at Scottish and Continental music, evidenced by his fine recordings.

Discography: *Willie McGuire, Scottish Accordion Champion, Reaches for the Summit* (1988); *BOXing CLEVER* (1991*); Accordeon Continental* (made with Jimmy Cassidy, and available as either CD or video, 2002).

Marcosignori, Gervasio Italy's Gervasio Marcosignori occupies a special place in the affections of British accordionists, and his high level of virtuosity has been admired in this country since his first visits here in the 1950s. A winner of the CMA World Championship in 1962, Marcosignori has remained World Champion ever since in the eyes of his many admirers! He has used many instruments, but is forever associated with his favourite – the Scandalli Super VI. Although he has always performed classical music, in the 50s, 60s and 70s, Marcosignori performed and recorded a wide range of Continental and Latin music – and this was the basis of his popularity with many people.

In the 1970s, he moved on to the Transicord and Syntaccordion electronic instruments, demonstrating these instruments in this and other countries. He also began to become much more inclined towards classical music in his concert performances and recordings. A quiet and dignified personality, Marcosignori has performed countless times in this country, and is one of the few accordionists concert promoters *know* will guarantee extra interest and increase ticket sales merely by virtue of his name being added to a concert or festival programme.

Selected discography: *Dancing Continental* (1961); *Record of the Century* (1962); *Accordion Showpieces* (1972); *The Poet of the Accordion* (1991); *Encore!* (1995).

Mayes, Jerry The cause and development of the accordion in this country owes a great deal to a number of people who were trained at the British College of Accordionists in the immediate pre-war/post-war periods. Jerry Mayes, taught at the BCA by Ivor Beynon and Graham Romani, is a case in point, having spent more than half a century as a performer, organiser, teacher and examiner. Based at Southend-on-Sea, Essex, he has attained both ABCA (TD) and LBCA diplomas from the BCA, plus an A.Mus from the London College of Music, and has acted as an examiner of the BCA and the Leicester School of Music (for guitar). Jerry has taught the piano accordion, keyboards, electronic organ and classical guitar, and prepares pupils for all levels of examinations up to diploma level. *"I know people take fright at the idea of preparing for an examination,"* he says, *"but in most cases it's the best way to get to know how to play your instrument properly."* Jerry also runs ensemble classes where pupils play together and acquire the skills of group performance. Apart from teaching music, Jerry has also done a lot of playing and is an ardent enthusiast for the accordion, and he summarised his thoughts thus: *"The accordion has come a long way, and I am so pleased that at last it is being accepted into our national music colleges. There is still a lot to be achieved. Professor Owen Murray has lit the beacon for present and future generations of accordionists to follow. I am convinced that free bass instruments are here to stay. Whatever system of accordion playing you have grown up with, the main thing is to ensure that you have a good instrument to play and that you always aim to play well. Work hard and you will succeed, whatever make and system of instrument you have chosen."* Jerry Mayes has been at the epicentre of the accordion's development throughout most of the instrument's modern history, and his contribution cannot be overestimated.

Maxwell, Jennifer   Carlisle's Jennifer Maxwell began accordion lessons at six years of age, and is taught by Ron Hodgson. She joined the Ronmar Accordion Orchestra at eleven, becoming its youngest member. Jennifer's high-flying progress as a solo accordionist is evidenced by her consistent successes in contests, having so far won an incredible total of over a hundred trophies. This array of silverware must take a lot of display space, not to mention cleaning! The highlights of Jennifer's contest career to date are winning the 2002 Under 15 Solo and

Under 15 Musette Solo UK Championship titles, and the UK Junior Championship in 2003 at Scarborough.

Melodeon A melodeon is a small instrument in which the pitch of the notes changes according to a push or a pull of the bellows i.e. it is diatonic. There are one, two or three rows of buttons on the treble side, and up to sixteen buttons on the bass side, and both sides are diatonic. The melodeon is widely used for Morris dancing and also in folk dance bands. Amongst the various members of the accordion family of instruments, the melodeon is the linear descendant of the first accordion produced by Damian in 1829.

Melodica Briefly popular in the 1960s and 70s, a melodica is an instrument played in the mouth like a recorder but with accordion-like reeds and short piano keyboard. This latter-day member of the free reed family seems to have followed those other 'nine day wonders', the chord organ and the Rolf Harris *Stylophone*, into oblivion.

Mexano's Accordion Band In the mid 1930s through to about 1950, Mexano's Accordion Band toured the cities and seaside resorts of this country, and was one of the most commercially successful of the accordion bands of the pre-war/post-war eras. Founded by Luigi Finella, better known as Lou Mexano, (1915-1994), this band featured ten accordions, sousaphone and drums.

Meyer, Otto (1899-1989) Few people today realise the dominant position in the British accordion scene held by the German company M. Hohner Ltd in the 1930s up until the beginning of the 1970s. Hohner not only sold the most instruments, played by the majority of the leading players and teachers, but in the 1930s were also responsible for setting up the network of accordion competitions culminating in the annual national All-Britain Championships, the British College of Accordionists, the National Harmonica League, and the monthly *Accordion Times* magazine. Each of these initiatives came from Dr Otto Meyer, head of Hohner's UK operation from 1930 to 1967.

Dr Otto Meyer, born in Bradford of a German father and an English mother, worked in the export division of Hohner in Hamburg in the 1920s, rising to the position of Export Manager. His bi-lingual fluency in English and German made him the ideal candidate to take over the developing British operation in 1930, and his pro-active approach to marketing and sales made an immediate impact in raising Hohner's profile in this country. In 1935/36, Meyer spearheaded the various initiatives listed above, and his drive and vision resulted in the establishment of the accordion scene that flourishes today.

Meyer's adroit management skills ensured that Hohner survived the 1939-45 war years when all imports from Germany stopped, and the company's existence in this country was under threat. Deemed by the authorities as an *'enemy alien'* due to his name, parentage and position, Dr Meyer was interned in 1940 for a few months, though released following an appeal to a tribunal.

Otto Meyer spent many years as the Principal of the British College of Accordionists, and in 1949 helped to found the National Accordion Organisation, serving as its first Chairman (1949-58). Eventually he was elevated to the status of NAO Deputy President, and also served the International Confederation of Accordionists (CIA) as its Propaganda Secretary.

Midi *Peter Whiteley, well known for his M.I.D.I workshops at Pakefield Accordion Festival, wrote the following article.*

Musical Instrument Digital Interface

This electronic music system is now the standard worldwide system for electronic music systems. It was developed (in Japan) in order to have a compatible system that could be applied to all instruments as far as is practically possible.

In order to explain in very simple terms how this system is used by, and is applied to the accordion, it is necessary to first of all take a look at an electronic keyboard. The electronic keyboard has three basic component sections, that we will now look at individually: -

1) THE KEYBOARD

The keyboard is fitted with electric switches very similar to a light switch, except much smaller. Every time a key is pressed, the switch attached to that key closes, and an electronic circuit is activated. The function of this circuit is to generate a number, which corresponds to that key. All of these numbers are pre-set, and are peculiar to each particular key.

The note 'Middle C' has the number 60. As we progress up the keyboard in semitones the numbers increment by 1 for each consecutive semitone. Middle C# therefore has the number 61.

Likewise, as we go down the keyboard from Middle C, the numbers decrement by one for each semitone. The note B natural immediately below Middle C therefore has the number 59.

This is the sole function of the keyboard. It is purely the mechanical part of an electronic number generator.

It is at this point that you have to accept that it is possible to send an electronic number down a piece of wire. To go into detail on how this is actually done is way beyond the scope of this article, and would not serve a useful purpose.

Don't forget that we are still discussing an electronic keyboard, and not an accordion.

2) NOTE GENERATOR

The function of this section of the keyboard is to receive the electronic numbers from the keyboard generator, and generate an electronic musical note. The device that carries out this procedure is often referred to as a R.O.M. (Read Only Memory). This is an electronic integrated circuit that receives the electronic numbers from the keyboard, and sends out the corresponding musical note e.g. the R.O.M. receives number 60 and sends out Middle C note.

However, when the key is released it is necessary to send out another number to turn the note off. In actual fact, each time we press a key we send out 3 numbers:

Put very simply (and please don't write to me to tell me this is not exactly correct!):-

The 1st number tells the R.O.M. which note to play.

The 2nd number tells the R.O.M. whether to turn the note ON or OFF.

The 3rd number tells the R.O.M. how loud to play the note.

3) AMPLIFIER

This is the final section of the keyboard, and all it does is receive the notes from the R.O.M., amplifies them and then sends them to the loudspeaker, in order for us humans to be able to hear them.

HOW THEN CAN THIS SYSTEM BE APPLIED TO AN ACCORDION??

Firstly, when we have our accordion modified to MIDI, what we actually have done is this:-

1) Suitable electrical switches are fitted to each key. There are various types of switches available, from spring types (as in burglar alarms) and magnetic types.

2) All these switches are connected to an electronic number generator that is usually fitted inside the accordion.

3) A power supply to power up the number generator, and a cable, is provided to connect our accordion to an EXPANDER or, as the case may be, to an ELECTRONIC KEYBOARD. An expander is simply an electronic keyboard, without a physical keyboard.

You may have already guessed that by connecting our MIDI accordion to an electronic keyboard via the MIDI IN socket, we can actually play the keyboard from the accordion. All we are doing is replacing one number generator with another.

There are a number of expanders about now that have been designed with the accordion in mind. One such expander is the ORLA.

Yamaha have also produced keyboards that have a built-in expander for the accordion. Models 1000 and 2000 are two such instruments.

I hope that this short article has at least gone some way to help us musicians understand the mysteries of modern musical instruments.

Peter Whiteley, Stockport Accordion Club, 2003.

Molinari, John (1912-1989) John Molinari, from San Francisco, California, was in the 'Premier League' of American concert accordionists, possessing a fantastic technique and vast repertoire. Molinari owned his own record label, known as *Accordia Records*, and became well known and popular in Britain and Ireland in the 1980s thanks to the distribution of his recordings by Malcolm Gee's *Accordion Record Club*. He toured Scandinavia and the USSR, and was booked to appear as a chief guest artiste at Caister Accordion Festival in 1989, but very sadly succumbed to cancer a few weeks beforehand.

Selected discography: *Accordion Solos – Volume 5; Accordion Concert; Accordion Variety Concert; Classical Favourites*. Each of these records was issued in the 1970s.

Modern Accordion Publications is the name of a publishing company dedicated to sheet music, written works and tutor books for the accordionist, and was founded in 1946 by Adrian Dante. The *International Accordion Music Catalogue* features a very large number of sheet music titles, including compositions and arrangements by such great names as Pietro Frosini, Pietro and Guido Deiro, Eugene Ettore, Yvette Horner, Luciano Fancelli, Jo Privat, Albert Delroy, Adrian Dante, Gorni Kramer, Beltrami Wolmer, Joseph Columbo, Pearl Fawcett, Charles Magnante, Joe Biviano, and many others.

The MAP catalogue also includes the classic tutor books *Prima Vista – Sight Reading by Adrian Dante*, and *Finger Dexterity for Accordion, by Pietro Deiro*.

For further details, contact MAP Editions, 2 Bence Close, Darton, near Barnsley, South Yorkshire S75 5PB; telephone 01226 382 976; e–mail: pearladriano@hotmail.com

Murray, Owen The son of an accordion teacher, the late Chrissie Letham, Owen Murray has been a keen accordionist since he was a teenager. However, for most of the time he has played the accordion, Owen Murray has been a strong believer and practitioner in the free bass system, together with the development of a repertoire that will extend the accordion's playing scope and its image within the musical world.

Owen Murray studied in Copenhagen, Denmark under the late Mogens Ellegard from 1974 to 1980, at the Royal Danish Academy of Music. His course involved musical theory, harmony, counterpoint, history, aural training, singing, psychology, piano, analysis, as well as an in-depth study of the free bass accordion. He appeared on radio and television in Denmark prior to returning to Scotland.

Over the last two decades, Owen Murray has steadily championed the cause of the free bass chromatic button accordion, and has made many converts to his cause – especially younger accordionists, who are not set in their ways and are receptive to new ideas in music. In 1986 he was appointed Professor of free bass accordion at the Royal Academy of Music in London, the first appointment of its kind in Britain, and has been a pivotal figure in setting up examinations and diplomas for the accordion using free bass. In 1990, the Associated Board of the Royal Schools of Music published his free bass syllabus. Professor Murray's work is ongoing, and his influence on the future development of the accordion scene in this country is likely to be profound.

Murtagh, Dick Manchester's Richard 'Dick' Murtagh was one of the many accordionists who emerged in the post-war period, having served in the army but having been introduced to the instrument prior to the outbreak of hostilities in 1939. Dick played in the variety theatres and clubs, and became a broadcasting accordionist on the popular radio show *Variety Bandbox*, in those far-off days when it was possible to do this with the BBC. Dick Murtagh also had many business interests of various kinds and became a very wealthy man. One of his sidelines was selling accordions, and he owned several shops in the Manchester area – trading under the names *The Northern Accordion Centre* on Queens Road in Manchester, and *Star Accordions* in Sale. His first love was playing, however, and throughout his life he kept up his magnificent technique by playing scales every morning. His great party-piece was the Frosini arrangement of *The Carnival of Venice*, which he delivered with tremendous flair and technical accuracy whenever he performed it.

Musette The word 'musette' refers historically to an old French bagpipe that usually played out of tune, and the term musette later came to describe the French way of tuning accordion reeds so that the instrument deliberately sounded slightly out of tune. This tuning was adopted for the folk music of France and spawned a style of composed music known generally as French musette – see also **French musette**.

Authentic French musette requires an accordion to have three sets of reeds tuned at the same octave: one set is tuned at normal pitch, one set is tuned sharp, and the other is tuned flat. The three sets played together produce the so-called musette tuning. Whilst musette tuning is perennially popular for French, Italian and other Continental styles of light music, it is generally considered out of place in accordion orchestras where the impurity of musette from several instruments played together would create a 'muddy' sound

National Accordion Organisation of the United Kingdom The NAO was founded in 1949, as the result of collaboration between Dr Otto H. Meyer, HJ Bridger and James Black, as a means of administering the regional and national accordion championship festivals of Great Britain and Northern Ireland. In 1950, the NAO was admitted to the International Confederation of Accordionists (C.I.A), thus enabling British representatives to enter the CIA Coupe Mondiale – the World Championships. The first NAO President was Toralf Tollefsen, and Jack Emblow currently holds this office.

The *United Kingdom* (previously known until 1987 as the *All-Britain*) *Accordion Championships* is the NAO's annual flagship event, staged (since 1991) over the May Bank Holiday weekend at the Spa Complex, Scarborough. The NAO national championships (a.k.a *'Accordion Day'*) were originally held at the Central Hall, Westminster, London, until 1965, after which the event was staged in a different seaside holiday resort each year. Since 1991, due to the generous patronage of the town council, the *UK Championships* have been annually resident in Scarborough.

The NAO can be contacted in various ways:-

Telephone: 0116 241 2856 or 0116 278 4094,

e-mail: nao@accordions.com

Web Site: www.accordions.com/nao

National Association of Accordion and Fiddle Clubs In 1963,   Max Houliston started what became known as an Accordion & Fiddle Club at the pub he managed in Dumfries, called *The Hole In The Wall*. This led to the foundation of other A & F clubs in Scotland, most of which were booking guest artistes on a regular basis and thus providing much work for professional accordionists. In 1971, representatives of clubs from Perth, Dundee, Milngavie, Gretna, Straiton, Newcastleton and Galston attended a meeting in Perth, the result of which was the foundation of the National Association of Accordion & Fiddle Clubs. The fledgling NAAFC, under Chairman Mickey Ainsworth and Secretary Ray Milbourne, was set up to co-ordinate and represent the interests of the rapidly growing number of clubs that were springing up all over Scotland.

In 1974, the NAAFC organised its first championships at Mussleburgh, near Edinburgh. From modest beginnings, involving about three-dozen competitors, this annual festival has mushroomed into a large and prestigious event featuring 300 plus accordion and fiddle players. The Musselburgh Festival, as the NAAFC festival is popularly known, is an accordion event on a par in size and status with the NAO UK Championships at Scarborough or the All-Scotland Championships in Perth.

Neary, Paddy Born in the town of Ardee, County Louth, Paddy Neary won the All-Ireland Championship before re-locating to Scotland in the late 1970s. He is often billed as *'Scotland's Favourite Irishman',* and was the chief guest at the 1979 All-Scotland Championships concert (and features on the LP that was subsequently issued of that event). Paddy Neary's fine technique on solo acoustic accordion is heard to good effect on his first LP/cassette, *Paddy Neary's Accordion Magic*, first issued in 1978 and re-issued in 1994 on CD. In the 1980s, Paddy Neary switched to electronic accordion and has since made many recordings. He is particularly adept at using electronic sounds with good taste, and his performances and recordings are notable for the colourful musical images he creates – almost in the manner of an artist creating a portrait from a full pallet of colours and shades.

: *Paddy Neary's Accordion Magic* (1978); *Sounds Like Accordion* (1980); *Memories* (1986).

Nielsen, Nils Born and brought up in Sweden, Nils Nielsen played the chromatic button accordion from being young, and after leaving school worked in Hargström accordion factory in Darlina, learning all the basics of manufacture, tuning and repairs. He came to this country after the Second World War, living in London and doing instrument repairs for Boosey & Hawkes Ltd. In the late 1940s, he joined the Primo Scala Accordion Band, and was the only button player amongst an otherwise all piano accordion line-up. Primo Scala himself – alias MD & pianist/arranger Harry Bidgood – expressed concern that when Nils played, his right hand appeared not to move – one of the differences between a button and piano key player. Harry, always a showman, was forever concerned by appearances, and fruitlessly exhorted Nils to look more animated! Once the Primo Scala days were over, Nils linked up with Toralf Tollefsen in 1955 to open a music shop called *Accordion Central*, 3 Wood Lane, Shepherds Bush. Nils' main function was to look after repairs and tuning, and when Tollefsen sold up and returned to Norway in 1961, he then became a private operator.

Nicholson, Lea In the 1970s, Lea Nicholson was a singer and English concertina player in folk clubs in the South of England. He was, however, interested in a wide range of music and in 1975/76 decided to make a record that demonstrated the wider capabilities of the concertina. The result was an LP called *The Concertina Record*, featuring multi-tracked concertinas on such music as *The Liberty Bell*, JS Bach's *4th Brandenburg Concerto*, and *The Dam Busters*. The cleverness of the arrangements and the quality of the playing and recording has made this LP a tour de force, and a triumph for the concertina. In recent years, Nicolson has been involved in record production as a studio engineer, but his landmark recording has now been released on CD; contact Jamring.com, PO Box 5579, Derby DEI 9DL – tel/fax: 01332 733352.

Nixon, John Born in Bolton, Lancashire. John Nixon's father was the lead concertina player in the 24 strong *Bolton Concertina Band* in the 1920s and 30s. John was taught the English concertina by his father at four and a half years old, and by the age of six had joined the band! In January 1935, the *Bolton Concertina Band*, including seven year old John, broadcast from the BBC on the radio's Light Programme. After that, John made many radio broadcasts, usually on Children's Hour. John became a professional musician in dance bands, using concertina, clarinet and alto saxophone. He became a session musician in recording studios, and also a regular in jazz clubs, becoming friendly with Jack Emblow and the American Frank Marocco. A highly skilled and sensitive musician, John Nixon is one of Britain's finest exponents of the English concertina. As a session musician, John Nixon has appeared on the recordings of many stars of show business, including Paul McCartney, Barbara Streisand, Henry Mancini, Michel Legrande and George Martin, to name just a few. His playing can be heard on the soundtracks of such BBC television programmes as *Kidnapped*, *All Creatures Great and Small* and *'Allo 'Allo*, whilst his film credits include *Santa Claus the Movie, Tess*, and *The Hound of the Baskervilles* – to name but a few examples of John's TV and film work.

In 1984, John played on Paul McCartney's recording *We All Stand Together*, which became a Number One chart hit at Christmas. He recalls that the recording session involved him using treble, baritone and bass concertinas, The King's Singers, the junior choir of St Paul's Cathedral, an orchestra conducted by George Martin, and the legendary 'Macca' himself. John remembers Paul McCartney exhorting The King's Singers to make sounds like frogs, demonstrating animatedly what he wanted!

On another occasion, John was in the studio, again with George Martin at the helm, playing alongside leading French accordionist, Marcel Azzolla, whilst recording a film score. During lunch break, with the studio otherwise empty, John and Marcel, plus a keyboard player had an impromptu jam session, playing jazz together. John wishes to this day that someone had recorded them – a lost opportunity, alas.

Since retiring from the session business, John has played and recorded two cassettes with Harry Hussey and has made a CD solo recording, *John Nixon – The English Connection*. This CD is a showcase for John Nixon's playing and arranging talents, plus his skill as a record producer. Most tracks involve multi-tracking of concertinas and other instruments, creating small group and band effects in a monumental project that must have taken a long time to prepare and produce. In 2002 John was elected as a Vice President of Stockport Accordion Club, and one of his great pleasures is to play impromptu duets with whoever happens to be the guest on Club Nights. See also **English Connection, The**.

Discography: *Kidnapped* – soundtrack LP of ITV series (1977); *Under Milk Wood* – a George Martin produced commercial recording on LP, also featuring Jack Emblow, Tommy Reilly, Harry Secombe, Tom Jones, Philip Madoc, Anthony Hopkins, Aled Jones, Mary Hopkin, Windsor Davies, and others (1988); *Harry Hussey meets the English Connection* (1989); *Reeds At Play* (1990); *John Nixon – The English Connection* (1999); *Just a Little Jazz* (2003).

Norvic Concordia   Established in 1991, Norvic Concordia is an acoustic accordion quintet from the Norwich area with a reputation for performing a broad repertoire to suit a wide range of tastes and occasions. Their line up is Peter Ayres, Kevin Mitchelson, Margaret Ledger, Mary Dent and Warren King. In September 2003 the quintet (on this occasion, a sextet) were guests at

Pakefield Accordion Festival, and made a great impression on their audiences.
Discography: *Purely Accordion* (2002) – tracks include *The Blue Tango; It's All Right With Me; I Will Wait For You; Ecstasy Tango; Medley; La Cumparsita; 'Allo 'Allo; Under Paris Skies; Last of the Summer Wine; Domino; Dancing Madeline; You Keep Coming Back Like A Song/Once In A While; Spanish Eyes; Air from Suite No 3 in D (JS Bach); My Florence; My Fair Lady.*

Nostalgia: The Thirties Accordion Scene *The 1930s was the decade that saw the world slide inexorably towards global conflict, thanks to the increasingly aggressive militarism of Hitler's Germany, Mussolini's Italy and the warlords of Japan. More happily, this decade was also the 'golden age' period for the accordion in Great Britain: public interest, instrument sales, number of players, establishment of clubs, etc, reached record high figures. The All-Britain Accordion Championships, British College of Accordionists and the long-running monthly magazine Accordion Times were all founded in 1935, a high water mark in the development of the accordion scene in this country. The outbreak of war on September 3rd 1939 with Germany, however, led to an immediate halt to the import of new instruments from either Germany or Italy for the next six years, effectively putting an end to what had been a decade of tremendous growth in interest for the accordion throughout Great Britain. In the following article, leading professional accordionist Gerald Crossman looks fondly back at the 1930s accordion scene, through the pages of the contemporary music magazine, Rhythm.*

Accordion Nostalgia

Part One

Whilst rummaging in my loft, I came across some very interesting copies of a long since defunct monthly magazine called *Rhythm*. The oldest issue I have is from half a century ago, May 1934 (Vol. V11. No.80) and it was priced 6d, i.e. two & a half pence. The publisher at that time was a London musical instrument firm John E. Dallas & Sons.

Samuels of Liverpool advertised 120 bass, 4 voice accordions from £12. Casali Verona accordions (same size and voicing) with slide coupler and strong fibre case sold at £23/15s/0d. 3 voice and 2 voice were, of course, cheaper. Scandalli were £27, but their Scott-Wood curved keyboard model cost £34. One could pay about £90 for an instrument. Hohner Concessionaries Ltd took the whole back page of this copy. Hohner accordion prices started at £3/10s/0d. The advertisement included a complimentary letter written by Harry Saville, the piano accordionist in the well-known

Debroy Somers Band, to G. Scarth, Charing Cross Rd, London WC2. The mention of Scarth's Music Shop, which still exists, brings back memories to me of some lessons I had in the back room thereof, my teacher being Frank Skilton. Frank was accordionist in Lionel Falkman's Apache Band, resident in the Brasserie at Lyon's Oxford Corner House. Eventually, I played at all the Corner Houses (and married a girl from there too!).

An advertisement for Coronado accordions had a photograph of Hollywood accordion star Tony Travers with Hollywood film star Gary Cooper, the latter resplendent in cowboy attire and with accordion.

Rhythm, October 1934, showed the latest hits as *Love in Bloom, Cocktails for Two, TwoCigarettes in the Dark, One Night of Love, For All We Know*, and *All I Do is Dream of You*. For two shillings one could buy an album of fifteen well-known standard numbers arranged by Tommy Nicol, who was indicated as being *Accordion Ace of Mantovani's Famous Orchestra*.

The Piano Accordion in One Hour (!!??) for 8 to 24 basses cost a shilling. *How to Play the Piano Accordion* (revised by Dick Sadleir) was for instruments up to 140 basses, and priced at half-crown (2s/6d or twelve & a half pence). Accordion lessons were offered at 2 guineas (£2/2s/0d or £2.10p) per term, 5s/0d (25p) single lesson, duet pupils half fee.

Part Two

Jumping to February 1935, the inside cover presented a fairly young looking George Scott-Wood playing his Scandalli *Scott-Wood* model. In future years, I was to record and broadcast with his accordion band, which included such names as Victor Parker (one of my early piano teachers who used to give me lessons between his silent film performances; later, he played with the Geraldo band and in the Victor Sylvestor Dance Orchestra), Reg Manus, Tommy Nicol, and Don Destefano. Popular songs around this month were *Smoke Gets in Your Eyes, Roll Along Covered Wagon, Man on the Flying Trapeze, I'll String Along with You, Dames, I Only Have Eyes for You, Winter Wonderland, My Kid's A Crooner, Alone,* and *June in January*. A veritable feast! Fine accordionist Frank Gregory was in charge of the Quaglino Quartet appearing at the Holborn Empire in a musical act with vocalist Brian Lawrence and the Carlisle Cousins. Harmonica enthusiasts would appreciate the picture of a young Larry Adler typically performing into an old-fashioned microphone at London's Columbia Recording Studios (now E.M.I.). Hohner advertised two lightweight models – the *Regina* for ladies, and the *Imperial* for children. Advertising Galanti accordions (four set £28, three set £25) is a very youthful and good-looking Delroy. He is described as feature soloist with *Eugene's Magyar Orchestra, Natano's San Romaine Band* and various recording outfits. Post-war, as Albert Delroy, he broadcast with my Gerald Crossman Players and also with his own radio combination. A series of dance records on H.M.V., Columbia and Parlophone were priced at only 1s/6d. Rex and Regal-Zonophone labels were in the shilling market.

Prices of de-luxe plywood accordion cases, announced by Alex Burns Ltd, in *Rhythm* April 1935 issue were: - for the 120 bass model 17s/6d, 80 bass 16s/0d, and 48bass 15s/0d. Cobelle, of Gerrard St, London provided details of their *'piano accordion valet overhaul service'*, and stated that your accordion would be made like new by the specialised service, as follows: - *Treble keys perfectly aligned, all reeds cleaned and tuned, and replaced if necessary. Bass mechanism re-sprung, all palettes re-padded. Bellows cleaned and made leak proof. General finish – Cleaned and rejuvenated.* Send the instrument to them by post or rail and they return it carriage free, packed in a special shockproof container. Prices: - up to 80 bass, £2/10s/0d; up to 120 bass, £2/15s/0d; up to 140 bass, £3 guineas. These prices sound incredible today!

A silvery front page with a picture of King George V and Queen Mary in a theatre's Royal Box heralded the May 1935 Jubilee issue of *Rhythm*. The issue included the music of an accordion solo *The Jubilee Chorus,* written and composed exclusively for *Rhythm* readers by George Scott-Wood. Two popular numbers specially arranged for the piano accordion by Al Davison, M.A., Mus.Bac. (Cantab) F.R.C.O., Principal of the Hohner School of Piano Accordion Playing, were *The Isle of Capri*, and *Roll Along Covered Wagon*, obtainable for one shilling each from the School. Postage was 2d whether for one or two pieces. Each title had two different bass arrangements – an easy one and a more elaborate one.

Part Three

Rhythm for July 1935 introduced us to the song title *Lullaby of Broadway* (the super sensational hit from the First National Picture, *Gold Diggers of 1935*), *Anything Goes* (from CB Cochran's show of the same name at the Palace Theatre), *When I Grow Too Old to Dream*, and *On the Good Ship Lollipop*.

Forward to October 1935! We read in this issue of *Rhythm* that the accordion was THE most popular instrument in Britain, and selling better than any other instrument.

Some details were provided regarding the 1935 *'Accordion Day'* – the first All Britain Accordion Championships, under the auspices of Hohner Concessionaries and *Rhythm*, at the Central Hall, Westminster, on November 16th. Adjudicators booked included Al Davidson, composer Tolchard Evans, Conway Graves (composer, arranger and technical expert, who I knew and greatly respected), musical director Fred Hartley, accordionist Austin Jowett, Eustace St George Pett ARCM, LRAM, George Scott-Wood, and accordionist Frank Skilton. Public admission cost 1s/3d for the whole afternoon and evening (2.45 until 11pm). The Central Hall was the home of the annual *Accordion Day* up until the mid 1960s. Frank Wood successfully organised many of them.

The 100 pages of *Rhythm*, December 1935, were still 6d, but the publisher was now Odhams Press, the editor P. Maddison Brooks, and the over-all layout was different. This magazine contained an *Accordion Section* comprising seventeen pages, which indicated the immense popularity of the accordion. T.W.Thurban wrote on *"Accordion Band Formation and Direction"*, with musical examples; Billy Reid was No.1 in a series *"At Home with the Accordion Aces"*, by Ray Sonin, complete with pictures. Another series started on *"How to Play the Accordion"*, by the editor, who was probably our friend Mr

Thurban; there was a page by *"Squeezeboxer"* on *"Accordion Clubs News and Chat";* Royston Lee reviewed accordion discs.

It is interesting, and sometimes amusing, to read these record reviews. Artists included Roberts and his Piano Accordions (Columbia); London Piano Accordion Band, Scott-Wood (Regal); The Accordion Wizzards (Panachord); and Billy Reid and his Novelty Accordion Band (Decca). Examples of the titles were *All for a Shilling a Day, The Wheel of the Wagon is Broken, South American Joe*, and *Roll Along Prairie Moon.* The breakable 10" and 12" records of the 1930s revolved at 78 rpm, with a limit of about 3 or 4 minutes each side (according to size), and recorded ensemble on wax discs, not on tape. A whole 'take' had to be satisfactory for issue as editing was not then possible.

Part Four

In the December 1935 issue of *Rhythm*, three pages were occupied with results, a report and pictures of the All-Britain Accordion Championships. Names here included Don Bowles of Croydon, Mr H. Thornton of Grimsby, Joe Gregory of Cardiff, Leicester Accordion Club Band (Secretary, Mr L. Croxall), Charles Went of Hornsey Rise, Peter Valerio of Portsmouth (who won the Advanced Solo Championship, and received a cup and gold medal), and chromatic accordion exponent Miss Lorna Martin of London (who was a pupil of Rosa Loader). The photographs placed the feminine angle much to the fore, but accompanying the bevies were well-known bandleader Geraldo, and the German accordion champion Alan Helm. The movement was certainly active! Three pages of music arranged for solo accordion by T.W.Thurban complete the section, titles being *Jealousy* (advanced), Boccherini's *Minuet in A* (intermediate), *Daisy Bell* (easy).

On a personal note – Peter Valerio, mentioned above, was playing with Jack Leonardi's Orchestra at Bobby's Store Restaurant in Bournemouth about three years later, and as Leonardi sometimes used two accordions on his frequent broadcasts, I used to join Peter for these. Sadly, Peter drowned on the South Coast. He was a charming lad.

In *Rhythm* for January 1936, there was an accordion band arrangement of the *Temptation Rag.* The series *At Home with the Accordion Aces* continued, with Mary Honri having the honour this time. Other features included *Accordion Discs Reviewed, Accordion Band Formation and Direction*, and *How to Play the Accordion*; also the solo music for part of *Tiger's Tail*, part of *Wedding of the Winds*, and an easy chorus of *She's a Lassie from Lancashire.*

I am looking through the issue for February 1936. King George V had just passed away. Current numbers were *You are my Lucky Star*, and Shirley Temple's hits from her film *Curly Top.* Plenty of chitchat in the *Accordion Section*! It informed readers that Desmond Hart was a real live wire as Secretary of Chelmsford Accordion Club, and that Peter Valerio's teacher was Mr Harry Hudson of the Portsmouth & Southsea Accordion Club. There was a picture of Ronald Binge, resident accordionist at that time with the Mantovani Orchestra. Ronald created many of the famous Mantovani orchestrations, and was a very excellent musician.

Rhythm, April 1936. The music for *Alone*, from the Marx Brothers' film

A Night at the Opera was published, as was a complete accordion solo *The Ninth Rhapsody*, by TW Thurban. Chris Hayes interviewed the Russian-American harmonica wizard Borrah Minevitch.

Part Five

In the May 1936 edition of *Rhythm*, mention was made that the BBC Television Service would start in July (though it turned out to be at the beginning of November), and a combined radio and television receiver could cost about £60.

Names new in the accordion record reviews included Lou Preager & His Accordion Serenaders, Primo Scala's Accordion Band, American soloist par excellence Charles Magnante (I met him, Pietro Frosini and Pietro Deiro in New York) playing Rachmaninoff's *Prelude in C sharp minor* backed with *Nola* on the Rex label, and young Peter Valerio playing *Merry Widow Waltz* and *Waves of the Danube* on Regal-Zonophone. New at this time was a Settimo Soprani accordion, which had a piano keyboard on the bass side replacing the usual buttons. Selmer was the stockist, price being about £30/10s/0d. Like some other unusual models, this didn't last.

Accordion Championships were held for the first time in City Hall, Sheffield and also in De Montfort Hall, Leicester. Adjudicators for the latter were Eric Little (editor of the *Accordion Times*), Conway Graves and H.Bridger. The premier award at Leicester went to J.E.Jackson of Melton Mowbray, and a special prize for best lady competitor (in those politically incorrect days) was awarded to Mrs F.M.Pepper, of Tilton-on-the-Hill, Leicestershire.

Two months on to July 1936, and we read the story of the *Wonder Boy Accordionist*. This expression used to refer to almost any good young male performer, but in this particular instance, the boy was a remarkable French prodigy by the name of Joe Rossi. He played piano as well as chromatic button accordion. Jack Heyworth, head of a Blackpool musical instrument firm, brought Joe Rossi to England.

Accordion contests were going strongly. First championships to be held in Southsea took place at the South Parade Pier. A solo championships event took place at the Albert Hall, Leeds, and Desmond A.Hart of the Chelmsford AC, organised the Essex Solo Championships at the Pier Pavilion, Southend-on-Sea. The Playhouse Ballroom, Glasgow, and Grimsby Town Hall also saw contests.

Rhythm, August 1936, had 58 pages. Mantovani told *How I use the Accordion*. Accordionists he mentioned included Don Destefano (who later joined Geraldo i.e. Gerald Bright), Tommy Nicol, and Ronald Binge.

Number 10 in the How to *Play the Accordion* series talked about *"That Dreadful Moment"* when someone says *"Play Something!"* and you can't think of anything.

Christmas 1936 saw a double issue of *Rhythm*, 116 pages for one shilling (that's 5p in today's currency!).

Accordion Chat mentioned J.B.Cuvelier, ace Belgian accordionist, who teamed up with accordionist Emile Zigano, born in Liege, but came to England before 1920. When Cuvelier lived in Brixton, South London, he had a very successful business in accordion tuning and repairing, and he attended to my instrument.

Reported was a new accordion – the Ampliphonic Settimo Soprani (with transverse arrangement of short reed blocks) retailing at £52/10s/0d, and distributed by Selmer's. I had one of these, as well as a Dallapé and two Hohner models.

The All-Britain Championships in Westminster on November 7th was described in words and pictures. Catherine Green of Leicester, and Amateur Champion of England, Alice Swindells from the Mamelok Accordion School (coached by Sid Baxter) were featured here, as were those who took part in the massed bands concert. Lord Strathcoma and Mount Royal presented the prizes. In the Intermediate Bands Section, first was Leicester Accordion Club, and second was Madame Courtney's Juvenile Band (a name I knew well). International stars that turned up included German Champion Alan Helm, Hungarian Champion Louis Bobula, European & French Champion Medard Ferrero, Swiss Champions Cily Hebling and Albert Brunner, and Canadian star Johnnie Marrazza.

George S. Harris wrote that Miss Dorothy Holbrook had just formed the first Ladies' Accordion Orchestra in the country. Its premiere was at the Coventry Hippodrome on October 31st.

"The Christmas I Remember Best" had recollections from Marie Honri, Jimmie Turnbull, Lauri Day, Peter Valerio and Tommy O'Hara. Completing the *Accordion Section* was a selection of Christmas music appropriately titled *"A Merry Christmas!"*

Part Six

With the New Year 1937, the price of the January *Rhythm* reverted to 6d. King Edward V111 had recently abdicated, and the Coronation of King George V1 was set to take place on May 12th.

My good friend and exceptionally hard worker for the accordion movement, Graham Romani, received one of his earliest well-deserved mentions regarding a concert by the Band of the recently formed Redhill & District Accordion Club organised by him at Reigate. Club meetings were held on two nights a week.

Pancotti proudly advertised that its Italian firm making its accordions came into existence in 1868 (about 40 years after the accordion was invented).

Let's turn to the next month, March 1937. Plenty of details about clubs – Croydon, Cricklewood, Downham (Kent), Cardiff (the Secretary of which, Phil James, wrote that *"plenty of arrangements for accordion bands can be purchased at any music store"*), Leeds, and Carlton of Forest Gate, London.

The Yorkshire Evening News Amateur Accordion Contest had been held on February 8th at the Albert Hall, Leeds. There was an audience of over 1,000 and 50 players competed. Adjudicators were Captain James Reilly (Examiner for the BCA, and father of virtuoso harmonica player, Tommy Reilly), Henry Crousdon (organist at the Paramount – now the Odeon – cinema, Manchester), and Herbert Thornton (from Grimsby AC).

Part Seven

In the March 1937 issue of *Rhythm*, the PMS Accordion Club, Hackney, was featured: the initials stood for Phillips Music Stores, and Musical Director was Phil Maurice. The PMS club's star performer was Sonnie Drinkwater.

There were plenty of accordionists' photos here – 9 year old Charles Bishop of the Portsmouth AC (later, as Chiz Bishop, to become All-Britain Virtuoso Champion in 1951), four accordionists of the Joe Loss Band (in a Galanti advert), bandleader Maurice Frolic (who was at the Becon Hotel, Crowborough), Harry Roy's Lyricals Dallapé player Len Daniels, and Gypsy Roma posing with her curved keyboard Scandalli.

In an article called *Ark Accordionists*, the Accordion Editor wanted to know why so many players stuck to older pieces such as the *William Tell Overture* or Rachmaninoff's *Prelude*, instead of the more modern repertoire.

In the April 1937 edition of *Rhythm*, the *Accordion Chat* column told that Graham Romani, who had played accordion since 1932, had taken over as MD of the Redhill & District AC. The always very go-ahead Desmond A. Hart had a good plug over two pages regarding his Chelmsford AC.

Records reviewed were by the London Piano Accordion Band, Phil Green (accordion) & George Elliot (guitar) on Parlophone, and Emilio with a *Medley of Hits Parts 1 and 2* on Columbia.

According to a Dallapé advert, Albert Delroy was playing at the famous Santos Casani's Club.

As you will have noticed from these articles, there was always plenty going on in the accordion world in the 1930s – a time of rapid growth for the instrument.

Part Eight – The Final Instalment

In the December issue of *Rhythm*, an article by the Technical Editor described some *"Accordion Innovations"*, and a page of pictures illustrated these. We saw that Ranco made a model with a combined chromatic and piano treble keyboard. Hohner's 'Morino' accordion, costing £66, had recently appeared on the market. It had many new innovations in design. The new 'Basso' by Hohner had a treble keyboard sounding only low bass notes. Scandalli brought out a curved piano keyboard instrument at £62/10s/0d, with seven treble push couplers and two bass couplers.

An unusual Antonio Rocca accordion was built with two treble piano keyboards. It sold for £40. The lower keyboard provided a fixed bandoneon tone, and the upper one had two couplers allowing four tone colours. Frontalini produced a 'multi-coupler' model retailing at £90. This featured eleven treble couplers, the push buttons being placed by the grille. It also had one bass coupler. Multi-coupler accordions were not nearly so common in the Thirties as they are today. Many pre-war accordions did not have any couplers, or had just one treble coupler (slide of wrist push type) for un-coupled or coupled tones.

My apologies to any of those accordion clubs or individuals who have been omitted from this series of articles: the accordion scene in the 1930s was so vast it was impossible to cover everybody and everything from that decade.

(Gerald Crossman, Accordion Times, 1984/85)

O'Brien, Dermot   Born 1933, Ardee, County Louth, Irish Republic. Taught piano accordion by a nun called Sister Malachy at the local Convent of Mercy whilst at school, Dermot O'Brien entered competitions, winning the Hohner sponsored All-Ireland championship in 1954 and 1959 (adjudicator – Ivor Beynon). He played in ceili bands on a semi-professional basis whilst working in the Irish civil service, forming his own ceili band, St Malachy's, in 1956.

Dermot made his very first recording in 1957, a single featuring a set of Irish reels. A copy of this record found its way to the studios of Radio Eireann, Ireland's national radio station, who promptly played the track twice on consecutive days, much to the delight of Dermot and his family. Out for a walk soon afterwards, Dermot was recognised and stopped by a fellow who had heard the radio broadcasts, and whilst congratulating him added, *"but, to be sure, you were better the first time"*!

During the 1950s, Dermot O'Brien was one of his country's stars in the sport of Gaelic football, a ball game that resembles a cross between hockey and rugby. He captained Louth, his home county, to victory in the All-Ireland final in 1957, and highlights of this match preface the video *Dermot O'Brien Live at Clontarff Castle*.

O'Brien became a full time musician in 1962, fronting his own band as *Dermot O'Brien & The Clubmen*, performing a wide range of Irish, Country & Western, popular music and even some trad jazz. Also a fine singer, pianist, guitarist and trombonist, Dermot O'Brien rapidly became one of Ireland's premier entertainers. Dermot and the Clubmen performed at most of the major venues in Ireland and Britain, including topping the bill in shows at London's Royal Albert Hall. Immensely popular throughout the English-speaking world, Dermot O'Brien has kept the flag flying high for the accordion via his countless personal appearances and perennially high record sales. His recordings since the late 1950s include many fine albums of popular accordion favourites. He is worldwide the most popular and commercially successful accordionist Ireland has yet produced. Few accordionists can match O'Brien's stage presence or his innate ability to entertain.

Dermot O'Brien's accordion style is very much his own, and much admired by others. He has striven to be original, although he acknowledges the influence of Jimmy Shand and Will Starr on his playing. He also has had a long-standing interest in the music of the swing bands, and admits to being influenced by the likes of Benny Goodman, Glenn Miller, Louis Armstrong and the Dorsey brothers. Dermot has occasionally featured and recorded jazz and swing music, and on some of his earlier albums has even played trombone and arranged his *Clubmen* so that they sound very similar to the Dixieland trad sound of Chris Barber's Jazz Band.

By the mid-Sixties Dermot O'Brien had become a high profile recording and media personality in Ireland, and in 1966 hit Number One in the Irish charts with the song *The Merry Ploughboy*. This record went straight to No 1 in the week it came into the shops, and Dermot has since commented that: *"Only three artists have ever had records go straight to the top of the Irish hit parade – Elvis, The Beatles….. and Dermot O'Brien. Howzat!!"* In the late 1960s Dermot hosted his own show on Irish television, running for seven years, and featuring Bing Crosby as one of the guests. During this decade he began to visit America, touring the Country & Western circuit and sharing concert stages with the likes of Johnny Cash, Hank Snow and the late, great Jim Reeves. In America, he also performed on stage alongside the legendary rock n' rollers Bill Haley & the Comets.

Entertaining is *'in the blood'* of Dermot O'Brien, though in the mid-1970s he grew weary of the travelling that is an integral part of being a gigging musician and quit *'the road'* in favour of running a public house in Ireland. After a few months of living the life of a publican, the urge to get back into the music business proved irresistible, and the pub was sold.

Resident in the USA since 1983, Dermot O'Brien has continued to tour parts of Britain and Ireland each year as a soloist, occasionally working with his sister Marie O'Brien, herself an accomplished singer and keyboard player. Dermot appeared with Marie at the 1991 Caister Accordion Festival. In the mid-1990s, Dermot became part of the celebrated Irish cabaret team at the Dublin hotel, *Jury's,* involving summer seasons in Dublin and off-season tours of the USA.

In February 1994, Dermot O'Brien and his wife Rosemarie were caught up in the Los Angeles Earthquake, a major disaster that claimed many lives and caused a lot of damage. Dermot had played a charity concert at the St Louis Convent, Woodland Hills, LA, on the evening before the disaster struck. Dermot and Rosemarie stayed overnight in the convent, and at 4.30am they were suddenly and rudely awakened by a horrendous noise, and saw the walls and ceiling shaking with increasing turbulence. Soon, their bed was *"doing hand-stands"* as they gathered what clothes they could, followed by a hasty exit. The convent was only six miles from the epicentre of the earthquake, and the O'Briens only just managed to grab hold of their gear and escape by car moments before the entire district was reduced to rubble, with considerable loss of life in the process. Dermot later described the incident as the most terrifying experience of his life, and counts himself very fortunate indeed to have emerged relatively unscathed from it all.

It is not very well known that Dermot O'Brien has written a lot of songs and music for the accordion, the latter including such pieces as *Alpine Slopes, Alpine Ski Run* and *The Laughing Accordion.* His Swiss-style pastiche waltz *Alpine Slopes* has been featured and recorded by many British and Irish accordionists, and the sheet music has been sought after in vain for years. Recently, Croydon-based retailer Trevani has arranged and published *Alpine Slopes*, in response to demand.

Dermot O'Brien has his own website which can be found if you type in *Dermot O'Brien Irish Entertainer* on a general web search. Dermot's more recent recordings are available via this website.

The dawn of the 21st Century has seen Dermot O'Brien still playing, recording and making occasional short tours of Ireland and Britain, doing what is for him not so much a job as more a way of life.

Selected discography: *"Dance"...with Dermot O'Brien and his Band* (1964); *The Laughing Accordion* (1966); *Off To Dublin In The Green* (1967); *O'Brien's Cross Roads Ceili* (1971); *Tribute to Scotland* (1974); *Dancing Fingers* (1977); *3 Dimensions* (1979); *Live In America* (1983); *Anything Goes* (1990) *Irish Tapestry* (1992); *Twenty Greatest Accordion Hits* (1995); *Evergreens* (1995); *Sing along Irish Favourites* (1997); *Accordion Cocktail* (2001)

Video: *Dermot O'Brien Live at Clontarff Castle* (1992)

Instruments played include piano accordion, piano, trombone and guitar. Accordions have included a *Scandalli* (George Scott-Wood model), *Hohner Morino, Fratelli Crosio, Crucianelli* electronic (acquired in the USA), and a *Solton* midi instrument.

O'Connor, Martin Galway two-row button accordion player Martin O'Connor, formerly of De Danaan, and now a solo musician, has a level of two-handed skill that has to be seen, or at least heard, to be believed. As a member of De Danaan, his album track contributions on a jazzed-up instrumental version of the Lennon & McCartney number *Hey Jude*, and Handel's *Arrival of the Queen of Sheba*, gave early notice of his virtuosity. Like England's John Kirkpatrick, O'Connor defies all the conventions regarding the supposed limitations of diatonic accordions to produce very sophisticated music from an instrument with relatively few treble and bass keys. His CD *Perpetual Motion* reveals Martin O'Connor is also a composer with a great imagination, and he has written many musically interesting pieces that are melodically strong and with rich harmonies, reflecting the accordion traditions of America, France, Italy, Spain and the countries of Eastern Europe, in addition to his native Ireland. Martin O'Connor has appeared at accordion festivals in Europe, but surprisingly is (at the time of writing) little known on the accordion scene in this country.

Selected discography: *The Connachtman's Rambles* (1979; *Perpetual Motion* (1990); *Chatterbox* (1993); *The Road West* (2001)

Organ and Accordion Weekends Alan Venn, an electronic organist and organ teacher from Bolton, Lancashire, has for a few years organised residential weekend breaks for organ enthusiasts in seaside hotels, featuring professional organists. He then took the concept a stage further by booking accordion artistes alongside the organists, thus catering for enthusiasts of both instruments. All events are held in small but high quality family-run hotels with en suite rooms, catering for up to thirty residential guests. These weekends have proved consistently popular, and each event is quickly booked up and eagerly looked forward to by the regulars. Harry Hussey is the most frequently booked accordionist, though Walter Perrie has also appeared. For further details, contact Alan Venn on 01204 840279.

Ornamentation In traditional Irish and Scottish music, ornamentation plays a key part in giving the music its distinctive national character. In Irish music, the ability to play ornamentation correctly is also a means by which a player's skill is measured.

Pacitto, Steve Of Italian parentage, Midlands-based Steve Pacitto began playing the piano at five years of age, but soon switched to and became hooked on the piano accordion. As a teenager he played accordion in a small group that had the distinction of playing as chief support act to the legendary Glenn Miller & his AEF Band, at Walsall Town Hall in 1944. This was a turning point in Steve's life: *"When I listened to the wonderful chords and solos they pumped out, I thought 'This is for me.' This is what attracted me to jazz and swing music."* Steve has played jazz ever since, and for more than twenty years his music has been characterised by his skilful use of electronic accordion sounds – very much in the style of a jazz organist. Most of Steve's work is within the jazz world, though he does very occasionally appear in accordion clubs. He was one of the contributors to the 1979 Club Accord LP/cassette *It's All Accordion To What You like*, produced by the late Malcolm Gee.

Parkinson, Chris Lancashire-born Chris Parkinson crossed the Pennines a few years ago to live and work in Yorkshire. He is also a free-lance musician well-known for his work in recording studios, and has played melodeon, piano accordion, piano, harmonica, guitar, tin whistle and keyboards on the recordings of many great folk artistes such as Dave Burland, Martin Carthy, Ralph McTell, Mike Harding, John Wright and Alistair Russell, to name just a few.

Chris, a self-taught musician, used to regularly play piano accordion for ceilidhs in the early 1980s, but has diversified into performing in many genres and using various instruments. He became part of the House Band in 1984, and has more recently worked as a duo with singer/guitarist Alistair Russell. Together, they produced a CD of favourite Irish & Scottish music called *Paddy Goes to Huddersfield*. Recently, Chris played on the soundtrack of the BBC television series *Billy Connolly's World Tour of England, Ireland and Wales*.

In 2002, Chris produced a video *Learn to Play Piano Accordion*, aimed at the absolute beginner. He has plans to produce a follow up video for those who want to improve their standard.
Selected discography: *Out Of His Tree* – solo CD(1994); *Parky* - solo CD (1997); *Paddy Goes to Huddersfield* – made with Alistair Russell (2002)

Parnell, Frederick Nottingham's Fred Parnell is probably best known to accordionists as an adjudicator at regional and national accordion festivals. He is, however, a man with a long and very distinguished curriculum vitae within the accordion movement in this country. The first person to become All-Britain Virtuoso Champion in 1950, Fred achieved 8th place in the Coupe Mondiale in

Paris later the same year. Teacher, BCA examiner, NAO adjudicator, NAO organiser, conductor, composer and professional musician – Fred Parnell has more knowledge and experience than most, and remains a key man on the British accordion scene.

Pasby, Cyril Cyril Pasby had a long-time involvement in the accordion world, especially within the National Accordion Organisation, and as teacher. He held both performing and teaching diplomas from the British College of Accordionists, and for many years was the accordion teacher at Eton, the famous public school. At one stage, he taught the accordion to HRH Prince William. For many years, Cyril Pasby served as an NAO festival adjudicator, and as an examiner for the BCA. He was, at different times, Chairman of the NAO and Principal of the BCA. Cyril Pasby passed away on June 16th 2003.

Pauly, Danielle Born in a village in Eastern France, close to the Swiss frontier, in 1959, Danielle Pauly is probably the most popular French accordionist ever to appear in Britain. She began accordion lessons at the age of five, and by fifteen had passed a teaching diploma. In 1978, Danielle graduated from the Conservatoire de Belfort with a diploma in musical theory, and in 1984 became a full-time accordion professional. Since then, she has travelled the world, making many highly successful appearances at clubs and festivals in Britain. With her charisma, photogenic good looks and brilliant musette music, no  concert promoter ever lost money when Danielle Pauly was on the programme! Selected discography: *Fleur de Jura* (1985); *Bon Accord!* – made with Scottish accordionist Neil Sinclair (1989)

Performing in Public *Johnny Coleclough, Stockport Accordion Club President, has a wealth of experience playing the accordion in public. He has played in pubs and clubs around the country, at accordion festivals, in accordion clubs, was resident entertainer for many years at Manchester's Piccadilly Bierkeller, and played the electronic accordion for seven summer seasons at Blackpool Tower. In the article that follows, he gives his thoughts about performing in public: -*

Over the years I have performed many times to the general public, and I have also often spoken to other artistes about their feelings prior to going on stage. Feeling nervous is not something only for beginners – it can happen to players who have been appearing in public for years, but everyone has their own ways of dealing with the problem. There is no doubt in my mind that some people can work themselves up into a high state of tension, and even the most seasoned performer can have 'butterflies in their tummies.' I am convinced that the secret to dealing with this problem lies in positive thinking, and for accordionists who are involved in competitions, the need for positive thoughts is overwhelming. As an aid to positive thinking, consider the following points: -

1) Everyone in the hall is on your side – they are not the enemy. This is <u>not</u> a war!
2) You want to perform, so enjoy it.
3) You're not going to be shot! Anyway, capital punishment was abolished in 1965.
4) You've got your music, and you know what you're doing.
5) Your instrument is working well, and you know your way around it.
6) You've not left the gas on at home.
7) You haven't got a cold.
8) You are on time.

You should always present yourself neat and tidy on stage, make yourself comfortable (I like to use my own seat), undo both top and bottom straps, and concentrate on your playing. If you do make a mistake in your playing, carry on playing. If you want to, you can always start again. If the very worst happens and you have a complete breakdown, don't storm off the stage. Just say you are sorry, and walk off with dignity. It's no shame, and I am sure a sympathetic audience will applaud you. If you are playing to a non-accordion audience, most of the above applies, but remember – most important of all – in playing a musical instrument, <u>you are doing something that they cannot do.</u>

Johnny Coleclough, Manchester, June 2003

Perrie, Walter One of Scotland's most charismatic players, Stirling-born Walter Perrie began accordion lessons at the age of seven, then went on to win the All-Scotland Junior Championship at Perth in 1966. He came second in 1967, then won the crown again in 1968, by which time he was already embarking on a semi-professional career appearing in accordion clubs and in theatres. Once Walter had been through university, he became a full-time professional accordionist for a couple of years, and in 1976 toured Canada and the USA with the White Heather Show, Kenneth McKellar topping the bill. In 1978, Walter released an LP, which sold many thousands of copies, and in 1979, he played in a concert in New Jersey, headed by Andy Stewart.

Apart from music, Walter Perrie was also an academic high achiever, graduating from St Andrew's and Stirling Universities with B.Sc, M.Sc and Ph.D degrees in Physics and Nuclear Physics. After a couple of years playing the accordion professionally, he began a career as a nuclear physicist, working variously for British Nuclear Fuels and universities. This led to Walter leaving

Scotland to live in North Wales, and later in the Chester area, where he resides at the time of writing.

Since the late 1980s, Walter has resurrected his playing career, on a part-time basis, and has been a guest at many accordion clubs far and wide. In fact, he reckons to have played in accordion clubs everywhere from the Orkneys to Jersey, and at a few accordion festivals, too. His flamboyant style of musette music greatly enhances his stage performances, and is always popular with audiences.

In 1994/95 Walter held office as President of the Wyre Accordion Club, in Lancashire, and since 1997 has been a Vice President of Stockport Accordion Club. Discography: *Scotland's Accordion King* (1978)

Piano Accordion In 1822 and 1829 respectively, Friedrich Buschmann and Cyril Damien are credited with the invention of their different designs of the accordion. These instruments were button accordions, and it was not until 1852 that the first piano accordion appeared. Jacques Bouton in Paris designed this, and from 1863 onwards Paolo Soprani in Castelfidardo, Italy, began to produce piano accordions for commercial sale. The piano accordion took a long time to catch on with the public, however, and it was not until the early years of the 20th Century that it began to become the preferred choice amongst accordionists. This came about due to the tango craze in dance halls across Europe, when dance band pianists discovered a need to use an accordion sound for authenticity. The average pianist then opted for the piano accordion to meet this particular demand, and this instrument suddenly found itself in the ascendancy within the accordion world.

The piano accordion is really the accordion of the English-speaking world (apart from Germany), and in the USA the brothers Guido and Pietro Deiro pioneered it on the concert stage with great success. In Britain, it was George Scott–Wood who is credited with introducing the piano accordion to the general public in 1927, sparking a craze that mushroomed across the country within just a couple of years (see **Scott-Wood, George**). To this day, the piano accordion is the standard choice for most people in Britain or the USA who take up the accordion. As most teachers and available tutor material specialise in the piano accordion, this country is likely to remain faithful to this system – at least for the foreseeable future.

The average full size standard piano accordion has 41 piano keys, plus a 120 bass Stradella bass, though other sizes and specifications exist.

Playing for Others: *Rosemary Wright has a wide experience of performing in public, and has also acted as an examiner for the BCA and adjudicator in NAO festivals. She has vivid memories of both playing whilst being examined, and also of being an assessor of others. Rosemary has been a concert performer on the accordion many times, and as such, is better qualified than most to discuss the topic of successful stage presentation. In the following in-*

depth article (first serialised in the Accordion Times in 1982/83), she writes very much from the heart.

Playing For Others

If you play a musical instrument, you are sooner or later going to play for other people to listen to. The circumstances under which one plays (whether for one's teacher, family or friends, or in a concert, competition, examination or audition) may vary to some extent, but the psychological effect upon the performer is basically the same.

Musicians usually like to be gregarious, but solo playing is really quite different from playing with other people in that –
a)   one is completely responsible for one's performance,
b)   one has to make direct contact with whomsoever is listening,
c)   one is the centre of attention.

I think most people will agree that the biggest enemy of the solo performer is FEAR, which manifests itself in various ways, otherwise being known as 'stage-fright' or 'nerves'. Basically, it is really fear of any or all of the above-mentioned points, and this can soon turn what should be an enjoyable experience into a real-life horror story.

Is there a cure for nerves?

Unfortunately, there is not. Every performer feels nervous to some extent (although it does not always show), basically because one is acutely aware of the situation – or possibly due to guilty conscience caused by insufficient preparation!

The best thing one can do is accept the state of nerves as an essential part of performance, and come to terms with it as such, so that it does not get the better of one. One must try to discover the root cause of one's fears about solo performance, and if one cannot eliminate them, at least accept them, thus taking a more positive attitude to the situation.

My own experience

Having played in public since the age of five, I have reached the conclusion that one's nerves become more acute with increasing age, a trend that runs parallel with one's development as a human being. This usually starts to happen at the age of about twelve, when adolescence begins. Young children never seem to have 'nerves' as such, simply because they are too young to fully appreciate what performance is all about. At the same time, though, they lack the necessary sensitivity for performance usually present in more mature people – something that this latter group should try to turn to its advantage. Of course, we all know that grown-ups are not supposed to have 'nerves,' but it always amazes me how those who are confident in their own walk of life can turn to jelly as soon as someone listens to their music-making.

Next, I propose to deal with the importance of positive thinking and adequate preparation for a good performance, and then go on to analyse the various situations in which one finds oneself playing for other people, and how best to cope with them. I hope that it will be of interest and benefit to players of all standards and ambitions.

Adequate Preparation

No doubt this would seem to be an obvious requirement: after all, how can one give a good performance of a piece one does not know well enough?

If one is practising for a specific occasion, one should always begin preparation in good time in order to be 'on top' of the piece. Never leave it to the last minute. It is no good saying, *"It will be alright on the night,"* when one cannot play the piece confidently before then.

It is not necessary to be a virtuoso player to give a musical rendering of a piece, so one should ensure a thorough understanding of its character, form and melodic shape, and try to make it 'say something' by the use of appropriate dynamics.

Positive Thinking

This may be easier said than done, but – assuming one has done a little afore-mentioned preparation – what is there to fear?

Of course, the fact that one is under stress when performing can make one reluctant to face up to the responsibility and attention that go with it. There is that terrible feeling of, *"Suppose I make mistakes?"* which can haunt one so much that, by the time of the performance, an encounter with Dracula or a group of hungry lions would be far more preferable!

For those wanting to give a disastrous performance, I can guarantee success if they (a) think in terms of making mistakes, and (b) allow their nerves to get the better of them. If, however, this is not so, then my advice is to tell oneself, *"I can and will play well. I know I can, because I have practised."* One should always try to appear calm, and avoid unnecessary tension. (A little bluffing may be needed, but it usually works).

It is only natural to feel more self-conscious when playing for knowledgeable musicians, or people important in one's own life, but this should not unduly distract one. It is best to concentrate on the musical aspect of what one is playing, and let the audience (however large or small) listen and look, if it wishes.

Making A Start

Let us assume that some friends or relatives are visiting you at your house. Being interested in your musical progress, they say, *"Go on, give us a tune!"* Of course, this is an informal occasion, in a relaxed atmosphere, but you can still feel under stress. Having digested what I have said already, though, you should not worry too much – especially if you apply these *'do's'* and *'don'ts'*: -

1) Do *"have a go."* It may seem like the longest five minutes of your life, but the sense of achievement will make it well worthwhile.

2) Do choose a piece of music well within your capabilities. An easy piece played well makes a better impression than a difficult one played badly; besides, no one judges your playing on the grade of difficulty.

3) Do have at least one piece ready for just such an occasion. It saves a great deal of embarrassment, and you should then be able to play with more confidence.

4) Don't start by making excuses or apologies, or a description of your nervous state. This only spoils your listeners' enjoyment, and certainly will not make you feel any better. Avoid thinking about nerves or mistakes – after all, does an athlete like Sebastian Coe run a race with every intention of falling down before he finishes?

5) Don't make your own judgment on your performance. You are not playing for yourself, so let your listeners form their own opinions. Of course, mistakes happen (hopefully as few as possible!), but – provided the flow of music is maintained – they will not mar the listener's overall enjoyment of the piece. You, too, must enjoy the experience of playing for others, so save the criticism for when you practise.

Further to this last point, the famous American accordionist, the late Pietro Deiro, considered that too often players are really *'back stage performers',* in that they play well only when practising. He attributed this to being under-critical when practising, and over-critical during performance (the latter resulting from one's increased awareness that people are listening).

Another situation where one plays for others is at a concert. The type of concert can vary from a formal gala evening to an informal performance for charity, but the general psychology, as I have outlined it, remains the same.

One usually has advance notice of such an event, thus giving time to prepare a suitable piece or pieces for performance. Remember – if such an opportunity comes your way, then take it!

Concert Performance

Anyone who has played in a concert will tell you that there is more to it than simply going on stage and playing your chosen item(s). A good performer makes it all look so easy, but spare a thought for the blood, toil, tears and sweat of practice and preparation which achieved it.

Let us assume that our performer has chosen to play a piece well within present capability, and has begun preparation in plenty of time. Having mastered the basics (notation and timing), it is then necessary to strive for a good musical interpretation.

But it doesn't stop there. To play well in familiar surroundings (e.g., at home) is one thing. To do so elsewhere, in front of strangers, in the company of our old enemy – FEAR – is quite another. Our performer is bound to feel an increased awareness of the situation – this is but human – but if wisdom is allowed to dictate, this will be turned to advantage and used to add inspiration to the performance.

Whenever I offer advice on this subject, people seem unable to believe that I have been through all the stages of 'nerves', but I have – and have had to make the effort to come to terms with them. I may not appear to be doing an impersonation of a jelly when I play, because outwardly I try to appear quietly confident. In actual fact my stomach is often gyrating in its own time – and my long skirt comes in very useful for hiding my knocking knees!

At times like these I am often tempted to wonder whether it is worth such agonies, but when I think of all the time and effort involved in learning a piece, it does seem an awful pity not to let others hear it. If anything, to back off from the challenge at this late stage can leave one feeling a sense of loss at the opportunity wasted.

It is always wise to avoid last-minute panics, so ensure that what you will wear is clean and still fits, that you know the time, date and place of the concert, and that transport is arranged. Try also to avoid over-tiredness.

Having attended to these details – go ahead and enjoy your concert!

Stagecraft

Having discussed the psychological aspects of playing for other people, I would now like to say something about the importance of good presentation and etiquette in performance, or, as it is sometimes called, 'stagecraft'. This is not the exclusive preserve of professionals and virtuosi. We know they have to 'sell' themselves, but so do all performers – including rank amateurs. Furthermore, attention to this vital aspect will help overcome last-minute 'nerves'.

"Remember that the audience hears with its eyes," said the great accordion virtuoso Pietro Deiro. What he meant is that no matter how well you play, the whole effect is easily ruined by poor stagecraft. It is worthwhile to recall performances you have seen and heard, and to consider which aspects of the performer's behaviour you liked or disliked. Surprisingly enough, good presentation and showmanship can make up for any musical shortcomings.

Points to remember

First of all, a presentable and respectable appearance should be ensured. If you have a choice of dress, then scruffy jeans are not recommended. Make sure also that you can play and move around comfortably in your chosen outfit.

Movement whilst on stage, or deportment, can also make or mar your performance. One should appear quietly confident, and do so with poise and dignity. This can be achieved by moving steadily, keeping the head up, avoiding a sheepish facial expression and, if sitting to play, not turning to look at the chair first. There is nothing worse than the performer who rushes on and off the stage, as if anxious to get the terrible ordeal over with as quickly as possible!

Mannerisms, which both look ludicrous and detract from the performance, are to be strenuously avoided. You may not realise that you are doing them, but the audience soon does. One of the commonest, perhaps, is foot tapping, which not only looks bad, but sounds bad, too. Watching the fingers constantly is inadvisable, because it conveys to the audience your lack of confidence. If you play from memory, it is best to look towards the rear of the hall.

You might think that pulling faces and throwing yourself about looks sophisticated and artistic, but in fact it looks most ridiculous. The energy is better spent on the performance. If you cannot smile when playing, then it is better to keep a straight face.

If good stagecraft seems un-natural to you, try to think of it as being 'larger than life'. Performing on stage is really a form of acting, and will thus differ from one's everyday behaviour.

Finally, a word about courtesy.

It is only polite to respond to audience appreciation. To bow when applause is given, and to smile, will cost you nothing but will complete the rapport between yourself and your audience to a highly satisfactory degree.

The accordion teacher

If you are taking regular musical tuition, you may not think of your teacher as 'other people' for whom you play. This is because you have the opportunity to get to know him or her, and, in time, to build up a suitable relationship.

In actual fact, your teacher is one of the most critical listeners you may have. You are aware that he knows and understands what you are playing, but then you are seeking his guidance to develop and improve this. A good teacher should point out any faults in your playing, but, at the same time, should be able to explain how to correct them. Sometimes, he has to be cruel to be kind, but this is because he really wants you to do well, and does have your best interests at heart. When he does have to comment on any faults, this should not be taken as a personal slight or insult. At the same time, he should make you feel that it is worthwhile to persevere and improve, and give you some encouragement to keep trying.

A teacher should be tolerant of a few slips and mistakes. He does not expect a concert at every lesson. As I have said previously, mistakes are inevitable, but one should try to make as few as possible, and these are better made in the lesson than during an important performance. Besides, if you never make mistakes, you cannot really learn the correct way to play, so try to turn any mistakes to your advantage, and learn from them.

How often do you learn and practise work set in a lesson, and think you have mastered it, only to find that nothing goes as it should at the next lesson?

"But I could play it alright at home," you say, apologetically. No doubt this is true, but, once again, the 'back-stage' mentality creeps in once again. As with concert preparation, you should try to be more self-critical during practising. Don't be satisfied with half of a job – just because nobody else can hear whatever went wrong. Pretend that your teacher is still listening, and try to imagine what he would say about your playing. It is best to aim for perfection by concentrating initially upon achieving accuracy in notation, timing, and playing technique, and then, as these become easier, to consider the musical demands, e.g., phrasing and dynamics.

The ultimate aim of every teacher, apart from teaching you to play the accordion, is to ensure that you eventually achieve musical and technical independence. If you are then prepared to show off this knowledge and ability to others, he will have succeeded admirably.

Examinations

Whether you really like the idea of them or not, examinations create yet another situation where one plays for others.

Examinations are useful as a yardstick of one's ability, and give the opportunity to have this ability assessed by an independent authority. They also give one something to aim for – and a feeling of achievement when successful. A word of warning, though. In a world where examination qualifications are necessary for obtaining jobs or opportunities for further education, music examinations should definitely not be regarded as the be-all and end-all of tuition, but simply as the means to an end.

The main difference between examinations and concerts is that one is now playing to someone who understands what he or she is hearing, and who is giving an assessment of one's playing. Awareness of this can, in itself, cause stress, which – if not carefully handled – can easily undo all the good work done in preparation.

Much of what I have said previously regarding adequate preparation, both musical and psychological, holds good for examinations. Make sure you know the requirements for your grade, and that you have adequately covered them. This is particularly true for the first section of the examination, namely 'Scales and arpeggios', during which time you are settling down, and therefore at your most nervous.

Over the years, I have observed many examination candidates, whether as their teacher, their examiner, or as the steward responsible for the organisation. I find, on the whole, that adults suffer with nerves more than do children. Of course, this is natural, but – as I have said before – more attention to the musical requirements, and less to that jittery feeling, will often overcome any uneasiness in the situation. Some candidates seem to delight in giving graphic descriptions of their nervous state, an ability that serves only to unsettle other candidates – and does nothing to earn extra marks.

As a teacher, I am a firm believer in the music examination system if used properly. I like my pupils to take examinations, but never force them to do so, especially the adults, who do not usually learn a musical instrument for the purpose of taking examinations. When one's pupils turn into self-styled masochists, however, they tend to miss the whole point of examination work altogether. You can only do your best, and provided you have prepared to the best of your ability, then you have nothing to fear.

Concluding thoughts

It seems as if I have written a great deal about the performer's number-one 'bête-noire' – nerves, and given various pieces of advice on how to survive when other people listen to one's playing. I consider this to be very necessary, since practically every performer has some psychological 'hang-up' in such a situation, but many do not know how to come to terms with it, or are afraid of having such fears, and may eventually give up the idea as a bad job.

One should never be content with such defeatist attitudes as *"I always get nervous at concerts,"* or *"My mind goes blank when I start to play on stage."* Try, instead, a little do-it-yourself psychoanalysis, to discover the root cause of your fears, and aim to break the vicious circle of thought that brings about that state.

"How do I make a Grade Two piece sound like a Grade Eight piece?" someone asked me recently. In other words, *"How does one make an easy piece sound really good?"* The answer is to choose a piece you can play well, play it with confidence, and try to achieve a good interpretation. Playing from memory can help, too. The average audience tends to notice how good your playing sounds, rather than the grade of difficulty of your repertoire. Furthermore, you should never allow yourself to be overawed by the musical expertise of your listeners, or by the grandeur of your surroundings.

Don't ever feel that only advanced players should play in public. You don't have to be a virtuoso to play well in front of others. A simple piece played well can be just as enjoyable as one built on pyrotechnics. Obviously, the sooner you become accustomed to being listened to, the less likely you are to become a 'back-stage performer' (rather like the person who can only sing in the bath!)

Those who feel that they lack the necessary confidence to play a solo in public might well prefer to try playing with other people, whether it be in a duo, group or band. Apart from the musical benefits, there is a great deal of satisfaction to be gained from making good music, whilst sharing the responsibility of its production with others.

In reading my articles, your reaction to some of the situations might well have been *"That's just how I feel!"* Perhaps my advice has helped you to overcome your problem, but even if I have only reassured you that you are not the only one who feels as you do, then I consider that my efforts have been worthwhile.

The Accordion Times (1982/83).
Reprinted with kind permission of Rosemary Wright.

Prince, Ingrid In 1976, Ingrid Prince was one of the people who helped the late Malcolm Gee to found Birmingham's Club Accord, and she was a regular member for several years. In 1979 Ingrid contributed the track *Dizzy Fingers* to the LP *It's All Accordion To What You Like*, produced by Malcolm Gee as a showcase for Club Accord's senior players, and in 1982 she reached the pinnacle of her career as a competitive player by winning the All-Britain Advanced Championship.

In recent times, Ingrid has been teaching again, and offers tuition on both chromatic and piano accordions, and on either Stradella or free bass. She can be contacted on 0121 458 2781.

Privat, Jo (1919-96) George 'Jo' Privat was born in one of the poorer parts of Paris, and always retained a 'man of the people' image throughout a life that saw him mix with all levels of society. Jo Privat began playing the chromatic button accordion as a young boy, and by the age of twelve was playing regularly in the cafes and dance halls in downtown areas of Paris. By 1936, he had graduated to the Balajo dance club in the famous Rue de Lappé, the heart of the musette areas of pre-war Paris. He was resident at the Balajo for forty years, eventually becoming a part owner.

Jo always had an affinity with gypsy musicians – 'les manouches' – and his style was closely aligned to the jazz music of the famous *Quintet of the Hot Club of France*, led by Django Reinhardt & Stephane Grappelly. In the late 1980s, he recorded *Jo Privat, Son accordeon, et Les Manouches de Paris* – a brilliant CD in which the accordion maestro joined forces with some really fine gypsy guitarists and violin players to produce a *tour de force* of music in the Reinhardt/Grappelli mould, including some of Django's great compositions such as *Nuages, Minor Swing* and *Chez Jacquet*.

Jo Privat was one of those musicians whose life and career overlapped

both the great pre-war days of the Bal Musette period, and the modern era dominated by the likes of Yvette Horner, Marcel Azzola, Danielle Pauly, Andre
Verchuren, Alain Musichini, and so on. He knew and worked with many of the
earlier 'legends' such as Emile Vacher, Michel and Charles Peguri, Gus Viseur,
Louis Ferrari and Emile Prud'homme. His son, Jo Privat Junior, has continued
his father's musette and jazz style in similar vein.
Selected discography: *Jo Privat, Son accordeon, et Les Manouches de Paris*
(1987)

Pollard, Betty Betty Pollard from Ashton-Under-Lyne near Manchester, came
to the accordion comparatively late in life, but made up for lost time by not only
learning to play, but also by founding a highly successful accordion school/band
of her own – The Tameside Junior Accordion Band. Taught by Cliff Wood in the
1980s, Betty persuaded her teacher to re-form his band, the Clifford Wood
Accordion Orchestra. After a few years playing in the CWAO, Betty left to form
the Tameside Juniors, a youth band which very quickly was 'up and running' in
the competition world. What Betty Pollard, a woman with the drive, leadership
and energy of Maggie Thatcher, has achieved with her juniors is little short of
miraculous. The district of Ashton and other parts of Tameside became an area
where it was 'cool' to play the accordion, and scores of youngsters wanted to be
taught by Betty and the teachers she co-opted into her organisation.

Her bands and soloists have reached high standards, winning many
contest titles and appearing in concerts. Much of her success is due to her ability to organise, to delegate tasks and to motivate. The TJAB field several bands,
and has become an established part of local and national festivals.

Qualifications Since 1935, accordionists in Britain have studied for the eight
grades in practical accordion playing and theory of music set by the British
College of Accordionists. The BCA also offers diplomas for teachers and
performers, and has a team of specialist examiners who regularly visit examination centres across the UK.

Since 1988, the Guildhall School of Music & Drama has set up its own
grade and diploma examinations. Many accordion teachers and performers
welcomed the Guildhall's examinations for accordion due to the fact that the
Guildhall has a status that is widely recognised throughout the world of music.

In 1989, following an approach from Professor Owen Murray and the
Royal Academy of Music, the Associated Board accepted the opportunity to
introduce a graded syllabus for the accordion.

The Royal Academy of Music, in conjunction with King's College,
University of London, now offers a Bachelor of Music (Performance) degree.
This is a four-year course with the accordion as the main subject, plus a wide
range of optional subsidiary musical courses. Information can be obtained by
contacting Owen Murray at The Royal Academy of Music, Marylebone Road,
London NW1 5HT; telephone 020 7873 7381 or e-mail: omurray@ram.ac.uk

Radio Cavell   North Manchester local radio station Radio Cavell broadcasts from Oldham on 1350 AM (medium wave), and its hour long programme KEYView, presented by professional organist Ian Wolstenholme, is meant to be for electronic organ enthusiasts, but frequently includes accordion music. Apart from playing recordings, there have been interviews with accordionists such as Gina Brannelli, Harry Hussey, Gordon Glenn and concertina maestro John Nixon. The programme also features news from the organ and accordion worlds, plus theatre and pipe organ music. The programme is transmitted live on the first Wednesday of each month at 6pm, and is repeated on the third Wednesday at the same time. For those unable to receive the broadcasts of Radio Cavell, there is a scheme whereby the programme can be sent on cassette via mail order. The broadcasts of Radio Cavell can also be heard at any time, anywhere in the world via the internet – simply type in www.organfax.co.uk   Radio Cavell can be contacted in various ways, including telephone 0161 628 4645.

Rea, Dominic   (1907-87) Manchester's so-called Italian Colony, based in Ancoats, was a tight-knit community that had its origins back in the 19th Century and openly maintained its national customs and traditions. Dominic Rea was one of the best-known musicians from the area, famous for his singing and outstanding prowess on the piano accordion. In his book, *Manchester's Little Italy*, Anthony Rea recalled the following: -

"On summer evenings the streets of Little Italy would come to life. The popular Mr Rizzi would play his accordion, people could be seen singing and dancing and men would dance the Tarantella outside the Green Dragon. One little boy, who watched all this and developed a love for the accordion, was to become a celebrity with the Italians and their English neighbours. This was Dominic Rea, dark and handsome, Ancoats' answer to Rudolph Valentino – as many of the ladies will, I am sure, remember!

Dominic was one of three brothers who were left in the care of their uncle, Marco Rea, after their parents died within three years of each other. The boys stayed under their uncle's wing until they were old enough to make their own way in life. 'Big Dominic', as he came to be known, was a character the like of whom these humble people had never seen before. His Valentino looks were not missed by the working girls from the factories around Jersey St, where he sang and played his accordion. He would make their young hearts flutter as he serenaded them with his gentle voice. He sang such songs as O Sole Mio and Roman Guitar, and he was a welcome sight at the local fairs and public houses, where he would delight everyone with his flair for music.

Dominic was often told that he was wasted in Ancoats and that he should seek his fame and fortune in the USA. However, he didn't heed this advice and continued to play his music around Manchester, much to the annoyance of the mill bosses, who had to order the girls back to their machines when Dominic's melodies filtered through the windows. They would all rush to catch a glimpse of Manchester's own Valentino!"

Reprinted with kind permission of Anthony Rea, Manchester's Little Italy, 1988

During the Second World War, all the men of the Italian Colony were deemed to be 'enemy aliens' and were interned on the Isle of Man. Dominic thus spent the war as a virtual prisoner-of-war, but used his music to keep his fellow internees entertained. Dominic was never really interested in a show business career, preferring to play part-time gigs whilst working full-time in the family ice cream business.

Recordings Edison's invention of the phonograph in 1897 has had a profound effect on the accordion movement worldwide by making the work of the great accordionists and composers available to future generations. Present and future generations of players and enthusiasts can listen to, and learn from, the compositions of Pietro Frosini, played by the man himself, or the classic recordings made by legendary names such as Toralf Tollefsen, Jimmy Shand, Charles Magnante, etc. The great worldwide accordion heritage built up over the last hundred years or so is preserved thanks to Edison's invention and subsequent technology.

The brothers Peter and Daniel Wyper, Scottish melodeon players in the late 19th/early 20th Century, are believed to be the first 'accordion family' musicians in the world to make recordings (in 1907 and 1910 respectively). In the USA, Guido Deiro was the first accordionist to record, starting in 1911 with *The Sharpshooter's March/Cirirribin.*

In the 1980s, Malcolm Gee's *Accordion Record Club* provided a mail order service, plus a trade stand presence at festivals, to make available, for the first time in this country, a comprehensive selection of accordion artistes' recordings representing many musical styles. The ARC did much to promote accordion artistes amongst enthusiasts.

At the present time, Trevani, Charlie Watkins and Loretta Rolston's *Accordion Times & News* are all very good sources of recordings featuring accordion artistes. Another really good source is the Internet. The website *Accordions Worldwide* includes a weekly Accordion CD Reviews feature, with reviews written by Tania Lukic-Marx, herself a world-class accordionist and teacher. The accordion magazines are also a regular source of reviews and information about recordings.

Caravelle Records has a varied selection of accordion records, cassettes and CDs - *see separate entry*. In Scotland the Smith/Mearns recording label has a catalogue listing CDs and videos featuring accordionists Mhairi Coutts, Jimmy Cassidy, Bill Black, Steven Carcary, Alex McIntyre, Wayne Robertson, Doug Milne, Davie Stewart and Peter Bruce. Smith/Mearns products are all available via their website or by telephone: 01738 552444. The Scottish *Deeay* label has recordings by Deirdre Adamson, Calum MacLean and Alastair Hunter & The Lorne Scottish Dance Band:– Deeay Recordings, 22 Westfield Drive, Forfar, Angus, Scotland DD8 1EQ.

Reeds An accordion's sound is determined by the quality of its reeds. These can be machine made and hand finished, or completely hand made – depending on the policy of the manufacturer. Usually, hand made reeds are the best: more responsive and requiring less bellows action, facilitating the player's ability to play louder or softer with less physical effort.

Relaxation The value of relaxation in performing music or any other form of activity cannot be overstated. With relaxation comes control, leading to good performances. On the other hand, too much anxiety can cause the performer to make mistakes, the effects of which may be compounded if the artist cannot recover composure quickly. This applies in all branches of music, theatre and sport. On stage, for example, an actor who is nervous fluffs a line on stage. The audience does not bother, but his anxiety increases. The result is, he fluffs another line. The audience then notice, and he senses the tension. It increases his. Next thing, the actor automatically compensates by speaking too loudly or gesturing too much. In short, he 'over-acts.' He spoils his performance by losing control. The great actors, however, take their time and are able to relax - to 'chill-out', as it were, on stage, even if things around them go wrong. A good actor, for example, is able to establish a presence on stage or screen by taking control and not being fazed by anything. David Jason on TV in *Only Fools & Horses* or *Frost* instantly assumes his roles through his very relaxed presence. In the theatre, watch an actor such as Tom Courtney and the same thing applies – a presence established straight away through relaxation, leading to control i.e. stage presence. In boxing, George Foreman resumed his career after a break of ten years and regained the heavyweight championship of the world at the advanced age of 45. How did Foreman manage to defy all the critics and fight successfully, way after his supposed 'sell-by date' as a sportsman? Was it his previous ring experience, his size, or his hard punch that made him a consistent winner, or was it all three factors? The answer is, none of them. Other retired boxers with similar qualifications have, in the past, tried to return only to fall on their faces – literally! The real secret of George Foreman's success was his state of relaxation. Foreman was a man at peace with himself, who knew what he wanted and how to achieve it, and with a total belief in himself – a man who genuinely believed he had nothing to worry about and was completely relaxed in mind and body. The result was that when George entered the ring to do battle, he felt no pressure and was in there not merely to win, but to enjoy himself! Foreman's complete state of relaxation, coupled with his preparation, experience and physical power, turned him into a very formidable opponent indeed. Similarly, the great stage performers of the accordion world are those who can quickly relax into the performance of their music, based on a lot of practice and preparation – a thorough knowledge of their subject matter.

In the article that follows, one of the accordion world's greatest ever players, the late Charles Magnante, from the USA, gives his thoughts on the subject of relaxation: -

198

Relaxation

If you should ask me which one phase of accordion playing is the most important to me, I would say, RELAXATION. The ability to relax mentally and physically is of great importance. True, you may not find many textbooks on the subject; nonetheless, it is a practice that should be taught even at the very earliest stages of the accordion student's career.

When every technical application fails, you can be sure relaxing every muscle in your body will unquestionably help. It works wonders for me!

This subject may or may not be a part of your curriculum. However, I do feel the following can be very helpful for the student, teacher and professional.

We all know that sleep is the greatest form of relaxation. Yet, in our sleep, we have no control, and that is why we have the strangest of dreams. To be in full control, we must be fully awake, mentally alert, and conscious of all our musical abilities. This requires a tremendous amount of discipline on our parts. We must apply all the willpower we possess to master this subject.

At every conceivable opportunity, you must say to yourself, "I am relaxed, I am relaxed." Saying it to yourself two hundred times a day is not nearly enough! The more you say it to yourself, the better. Remember, you are the one in complete control.

You can apply this concept with or without the accordion. Try closing your eyes for two minutes just before you start your study. Think only of the most beautiful thoughts you possess. Eventually, this mental relaxation will automatically bring on a complete physical relaxation, along with its inevitable feeling of well-being.

It is much easier for a pianist to relax both hands than for the accordionist. When the command is given to the pianist to relax both hands, they will undoubtedly naturally fall **down** into the piano keyboard, due to gravity. With the accordionist in the playing position, whether standing or sitting, the command to relax both hands will result in the right hand falling down from the keyboard and touching the thigh. The left hand, by virtue of the bass strap, prevents the left hand from falling and is automatically relaxed. Therefore, to bring the right hand up to the correct playing position, a few muscles in the arm and fingers are slightly tensed, just to hold the right hand in the proper playing position. I overcome this problem by relaxing every muscle in my right shoulder, arm and fingers, as well as in my wrist. The fingers can never be relaxed if your wrist is stiff or tense.

To induce relaxation, one must dismiss all unpleasant thoughts from one's mind. The sitting position is preferred to standing.

Without the accordion, try dropping both hands to your side, now, wriggle your wrist and fingers vigorously for about 10 seconds. This will stimulate the flow of blood to your fingers and, in turn, will help towards relaxation.

Now, wearing the accordion and with the bellows closed, let your right hand fall into the keyboard, without any concern of hitting correct notes. You may use your clenched fist, if you like. Just remember to keep your wrist supple at all times. Do this relaxed 'dead-weight' practice for one minute before starting your studies.

Being aware of finger relaxation at the earliest stages will surely pay off in extra dividends, as you progress.

All the foregoing has been developed and practised by me for decades. I believe it to be one of the most important basic elements of good technique.

Good technique provides one with the power to express oneself musically. It embraces all the physical and mental means through which our musical perceptions are expressed.

Charles Magnante, The Accordion Monthly News, 1984

Reilly, Tommy (1919-2000) Canadian-born Tommy Reilly played the harmonica as a boy, but was considered to be a prodigy as a violinist, with a great future predicted for him on the concert stage. In 1935, he moved to England and made a living playing the harmonica in the variety theatres of Britain and Europe in order to fund his intention to study the violin with a serious classical career in mind. In 1938 he gained admittance to the Leipzig Conservatory in Germany as a violin student, and was there when war broke out in September 1939. Soon afterwards, he was arrested by the Gestapo and finished up serving the next six years in prisoner of war camps in Germany and Poland. It was during his internment during the war years that Reilly began to seriously study and develop his technique on the harmonica, using his violin training and admiration of the virtuoso violinist, Jascha Heifitz, to develop a virtuoso classical style of his own.

Once the war was over, Tommy Reilly began to play and promote the harmonica in every way he could, and became an articulate voice for the instrument within the classical music world. Over the next few decades, Reilly worked with many of the best known people in show business, including such diverse talents as Vera Lynn, Peter Ustinov, Peggy Lee, Sammy Davis Jr, Peter Sellers, Bing Crosby, Julie Andrews and ex-Beatle George Harrison. In 1969, with sponsorship by M.Hohner Ltd, he produced the *Tommy Reilly Harmonica Course* – a double LP plus accompanying detailed tuition booklet. He also worked extensively in film, television and radio: his theme music for BBC television's *Dixon of Dock Green* and the BBC radio comedy *The Navy Lark* are two of his most memorable performances. He recorded several times with the Academy of St Martin-in-the-Fields, and also with the Indian-born Harpist, Skaila Kanga. These collaborations produced some of Tommy Reilly's finest recordings, showcasing his exquisite intonation and virtuosity to great effect. Tommy Reilly performed with many classical orchestras, and had a long-time partnership with the pianist James Moody.

During the 1930s, Reilly played harmonica in the variety theatres in Paris, and whilst there came into direct contact with the musette music of the era. Years later, in 1971, he recorded an LP *Harmonica Parisien*, featuring many of the famous French tunes and backed by a studio orchestra. Accordionist Mickey Binelli plays a musette instrument on a few of the tracks, adding to the French flavour. The beautiful sounds of the harmonica coupled with fine orchestral arrangements made this LP popular on its release. In 1999, the recording was re-released on CD, with several previously unheard bonus tracks in the same vein.

Tommy Reilly did a great deal to raise the status of the harmonica within the music world, and was also frequently heard by millions through countless radio broadcasts. In 1992 he was awarded the MBE for his services to music, the first harmonica player to be honoured in this way.

Selected discography: *Harmonica Parisien* (1971); *Music for Two Harmonicas Tommy Reilly & Sigmund Groven* (1976); *British Folk-Songs* – with harpist, Skaila Kanga (1987)

Ring, Donal A product of the Irish traditional scene, Donal Ring plays the Shand Morino three-row button accordion, leading the *Donal Ring Ceilidh Band* since the 1950s. Donal's band is something of a family affair, including nearly all of his family at one time or another. Featuring a mainstream acoustic Irish style, and always playing in a steady dance tempo, this band and its leader have been perennially popular at ceilidhs in Ireland for many years, with occasional visits to Scotland made.

Selected discography: In 1998, the band produced their own CD to celebrate forty years of playing and recording called *40 Years on Stage*. The line-up for this recording was as follows: Donal Ring (Shand Morino), Dermot Ring (5-row Morino), Donal Ring Junior (5-row Morino), Mary Ring (piano), Breda Ring (drums) and Pat O'Riordan (vocals).

Rolston, Robert Robert Rolston was an employee of Electronic Accordions Ltd, managing the company's Motherwell branch before starting out as proprietor of *Rolston Accordions*. His astute business acumen built up *Rolston Accordions*, agents for Borsini accordions, into a thriving business that frequented the various accordion festivals. In 1991 he became the owner of the *Accordion Times* in succession to Renaldo Capaldi, changing the magazine from a quarterly to a monthly publication. He also instituted an *Accordion Times Festival* in Paisley, and has occasionally arranged British tours for overseas accordion stars such as Marcosignori, Emil Johansen and Serge Duchesne. In 1997, he and his wife Loretta took over the running of the Caister festival following the untimely death of Malcolm Gee. The Rolstons organised Caister for a few years, then a new festival at Bridlington from 2001 onwards.

Romani, Graham (1917-1993) When Graham Romani passed away on the 6th July 1993, the accordion scene in this country lost one of its true 'founding fathers'. A Deputy President of the NAO, Graham had been a professional musician for 56 years, and had been at the forefront of the instrument's development all through the heady days of the 1930s right until the time he died.

Born in Oakwood, Surrey, he attended Reigate Grammar School and studied piano and organ before 'discovering' the piano accordion around 1930. He competed in the first All-Britain 'Accordion Day' Championships at the Central Hall, Westminster in 1935. This was the start of a lifelong 'love affair' Graham had with Accordion Day.

By 1937, Graham had changed his surname from Jupp to Romani, reflecting his involvement with a dance band he had formed called The Romani Rhythmic Players. In this year he began a serious study of the accordion at the BCA in London, under Conway Graves, Professor Eustace Pett and Matyas Seiber. 1937 also saw him become MD of the Redhill & District Piano Accordion Club.

During World War Two, Romani joined the RAF and became a pilot of transport class aircraft, and in 1943 he married his wife Dorothy (née Hall).

From 1946 to 1964, he taught at the London-based British College of Accordionists, and became conductor of the BCA Orchestra. The post-war years saw Romani also become an adjudicator at NAO festivals.

Romani's main interest was composing music for accordion, and in 1959 his *Ciacona Accademica* was used as the test piece for the CIA Coupe Mondiale World Championships in New York. It is believed that he wrote and transcribed over 500 pieces for accordion, plus many tutor books of various kinds for the instrument – a monumental achievement that may never be equalled or surpassed.

In 1971 Graham Romani was awarded an Honorary Fellowship of the BCA in recognition of his unrivalled service to the college. Later he became the Founder and Life President of the East Surrey Accordion Society.

Graham Romani was the most prolific writer the national and international accordion world has yet seen, and such was his work rate that nobody can put an accurate figure on his output of compositions and articles. He had an encyclopaedic knowledge of music, accordion history, instruments, people and events, and was always willing to share his vast knowledge with others – hence his incredible number of articles in accordion magazines, most notably the *Accordion Times*. A man of many talents, Romani regularly illustrated his articles with skilled line drawings of accordions, music and people. A few of Romani's articles are reprinted in this book as a tribute to his deep knowledge of matters accordionistic.

Roxton, Steve Although born in Preston, Steve Roxton is always associated with Jersey where he plays in hotels and also runs his accordion club, *Les Amis de L'Accordeon*. Although he plays up to six nights a week during the summer season on Jersey, Steve Roxton also has a full-time day job working as an electrician. How he fits in what are in effect two full-time careers within the limits of a 24-hour day is a mystery! He also admits that the money he earns does not even make him a rich man, such is the horrendously high cost of living on Jersey.

Steve plays the piano accordion and is also a singer with a fine tenor voice, and he entertains in many musical styles including French musette, bierkeller music, accordion classics, Country & Western, vocal standards, and the music of many other countries. Steve is certainly one of the most versatile and experienced accordion entertainers around today, and can adapt to most styles and situations.

Selected discography: *Bierkeller, British Style*; *Fields of Athenry* (1999); *Under Paris Skies* (2002)

Video: *The Entertainer*

Royal Academy of Music, The In 1986 The Royal Academy of Music in London became the first music college in this country to introduce the accordion, thanks to the dedicated work and idealism of Professor Owen Murray. A faculty of students has built up, including students from abroad.

Santilly, Bert At the time of writing, Cambridge-based Bert Santilly is a familiar figure in the accordion world as a teacher, festival workshop leader and performer. He is a member of a duo, with mandolin player Hugh Boyde, called *Café Mondiale*. In 2003, *Café Mondiale* released a CD featuring music from many parts of the world appropriately titled *World Tour*. Bert, who has an interest in playing jazz on the accordion, is also a member of a quintet called *Simply Jazz*; in this group, he sometimes doubles on vibraphone. Another outfit Bert plays in is the *Bungaloo Boogaloo Band**. As if that were not enough, Bert plays solo gigs, and has guested with *The Usual Suspects* on their recording *The Clock That Laughs*, and *Batanai Marimba*, a Zimbabwean group playing the music of Southern Africa. Bert is well known for running successful jazz workshops at accordion festivals, and for more generic music-making workshops around the country involving disabled and able-bodied musicians working together.

Discography: **Reeling Off The Tracks*; **Mosaic*; *World Tour* (2003)

Scala, Don (1919-1994) – real name, Don Scales. Don Scala played the accordion (and also sang) in variety theatres around the country from the 1930s until the 1960s, after which he continued playing in other venues and became a small-part supporting actor on television. He will, however, be best remembered by many as the man who, later in life, played every day in the streets of York – literally taking the music of the accordion out to meet the people.

Scala, Primo (1898-1957) London-born Harry Bidgood, the real name of Primo Scala, was a talented pianist, arranger and bandleader. The name itself was derived from Primo Carnera, Italy's World Heavyweight Boxing Champion in 1933/34, and top jockey Emilio Scala, winner of the 1933 Irish Sweepstake. In 1926, Harry Bidgood became recording manager for the Aeolian-Vocalion record company, and was directly responsible for promoting dance band music. To boost the record label's image, he employed a band of session musicians and issued their recordings under such fake names as *Bidgood's Broadcasters, The Riverside Dance Band, Manhattan Merrymakers, The Midnight Merry Makers*, to name but four aliases.

However, when Aeolian-Vocalion was bought out by the Crystolate Company in 1933, Bidgood found that he needed to change musical direction due to changes in the new company's policy. At that time, public interest in accordion music in general and accordion bands in particular was growing very rapidly. Bidgood himself was not an accordionist, but he was musician and businessman enough to know that the time was right in the early 1930s for an accordion band to successfully tour the variety theatres and make recordings. The best accordionists and rhythm players available were hired and the Primo Scala Accordion Band came into being in 1934, and was quickly in full operation touring the halls and making records. Also, the shrewd Mr. 'Scala' hired the best vocalists of the period, such as Sam Browne, Sam Costa, Dan Donovan and Cavan O'Connor, to give the band sure-fire appeal with the record-buying public.

Looking back at the Primo Scala era, the accordion bands of that time are erroneously viewed by many people as variety novelty acts, but this is quite untrue. The accordion bands of the 1930s, and Primo Scala in particular, were successful working bands on a par with the regular dance bands led by Lew Stone, Carrol Gibbons, etc.

Despite the great success of the Primo Scala band, Bidgood reverted to his old habit of using fake identities by using the Primo Scala members to produce recordings that were then issued under such names as *Rossini & His Accordion Band* and *Don Porto and his Novelty Accordions*, on other record labels. In doing so, Bidgood was virtually flooding and controlling a large market for accordion band music, dominating the genre whilst making lots of money for himself and his employees.

Harry Bidgood's shrewd management, in choosing and arranging music that had broad general appeal and presenting the band as popular entertainment, kept the Primo Scala Accordion Band in the public eye throughout the 1930s and 1940s. The line-up of the band varied quite a lot over the years, and often there were two line-ups – one for concert gigs and the other for recording studio engagements. The Primo Scala band recorded over four hundred tracks, many of which are still available, having been reissued on various LPs and CDs over the years.
Selected discography: *Primo Scala and His Accordeon Band* (1999)

Scotland's Accordion Heritage Scotland is such a great accordion country, with so many fine players, that it is difficult to do justice to the place in a single article: the Scottish accordion tradition should really be the subject of a book in its own right. Having said that, the purpose of this article is to give a brief outline

Douglas Muir

of the accordion's history in Scotland, and an overview of the present situation. Anyone who would like to know more about Scottish accordion music and dancing (the two are very closely linked) should read such excellent books as *Highland Balls and Village Balls*, by GW Lockhart (Luath Press Ltd, ISBN 0-946487-12-X) or *The Jimmy Shand Story*, by Ian Cameron (Scottish Cultural Press, ISBN 1-84017-019-0).

The accordion came to Scotland in the form of the melodeon (an entirely diatonic instrument) in the 19th Century, and became popular with the

Calum MacKinnon

working classes because the instruments were relatively cheap and easy to learn, and readily adaptable to all the well-known songs and tunes of the time. The fact that someone could become quite proficient on a melodeon in only a fraction of the time it took to master the fiddle made 'the box', as it was called, popular with the masses. Eventually, several outstanding players emerged in the late 19th Century from this developing tradition, including the Wyper brothers, Daniel (1882-1957) and Peter (1871-1950). They were inspired by George 'Pamby' Dick, Scottish Champion in 1887, 1888 and 1890. The Wyper brothers were the first British accordionists to make commercial recordings. Another contemporary was Peter Letham, from Edinburgh, who was acclaimed as a great player in the years before and after the First World War. These melodeon players were the 'kingpins' of the period that anticipated the rise of Jimmy Shand in the late 1920s and 1930s.

Jimmy Shand was an avid listener to the records and the styles of the Wyper brothers and others of their time, but pioneered a style and sound of his own plus a new kind of instrument – the British Chromatic, which had the treble of a melodeon and the Stradella bass of a piano accordion. Shand never aspired to be a soloist, and favoured the small dance band line-up of lead accordion, harmony accordion, fiddle, piano, string bass and drums that was to become standard practice. See the section **Shand, Jimmy**. As Jimmy Shand's playing and recording career took off in the middle 1930s, and the piano accordion simultaneously became overwhelmingly popular across the whole of Britain, the melodeon steadily became out of date, superseded by the more versatile British Chromatic and piano accordions.

The present day Scottish accordion scene's main impetus came in the post-war years with the rise to popularity of the dance bands of Jimmy Shand, Bobby MacLeod, Ian Powrie, Jimmy Blair and Jim Cameron in the 1950s, followed later by Jim Mcleod (celebrating forty years resident at Dunblane Hydro, and still going strong), Iain MacPhail, Ian Holmes, Bert Shorthouse, Bill Black, Jack Forsyth, Jim Johnstone, Jimmy Blue, and many others. The post-war rise of solo button player Will Starr similarly led to the development of interest in accordionists who were stage performers rather than dance musicians. Starr's colourful concert performances paved the way for the likes of Arthur Spink, Stuart Anderson, Jimmy Cassidy, Walter Perrie, Gordon Pattullo, Deirdre Adamson, the Donaldson Brothers, the Currie Brothers, and the Irishman, Paddy Neary.

The All-Scotland Championships founded in 1949 by Bill Wilkie, the doyen of organisers in Scotland and also the proprietor of Wilkie's Music House in Perth, has been an annual 'Mecca' for competitive accordionists plus those who want a great day out at an accordion festival. This festival was until recently a part of the NAO festival network in Scotland, but has now steered an independent line. The Scottish NAO area festivals date back to the NAO's formation in 1949, and have provided a focal point for those teachers and players who are competitively minded, for over half a century. The annual championships organised by the National Association of Accordion & Fiddle Clubs in Musselburgh since the 1970s have similarly provided a stimulus for accordion playing in Scotland.

Probably the greatest boost to the cause of the accordion in Scotland has been the growth of the accordion clubs – the Box & Fiddle clubs. This began in 1963 when accordionist Max Houliston started an accordion club at the pub he ran, *The Hole I' Th' Wall*, in Dumfries. The subsequent network of clubs all over Scotland has provided work and opportunities for generations of accordionists, naturally replacing the variety theatres of previous eras.

The popularity of Scottish country dancing in the 1950s coincided with the rising careers of singers Andy Stewart, Kenneth McKellar, Robert Wilson and Moira Anderson, followed soon afterwards by Robin Hall & Jimmy McGregor and The Corries – all purveyors of Scottish song and culture. These performers came separately to the attention of BBC radio and television, making them all well-known personalities in the space of a few years. A seminal moment was reached in 1958 when BBC screened *The White Heather Club*, bringing together all the leading and up-and-coming singers, dancers and musicians for a weekly showcase of Scottish entertainment. These shows also featured the dance bands of Jimmy Shand and Bobby MacLeod on alternate weeks; the other bands were featured as the show progressed. Thus it was that Scottish accordion sounds were a regular weekly part of this popular television feast of Caledonian culture. *The White Heather Club* caused many people to be attracted to the sound of accordions, though in later years the programme was criticised by those who thought that the *'White Heather'* image was somehow demeaning to Scotland's image, and just too corny for them. In the 1970s ITV produced its own version of *The White Heather Club*, called *Scotch Corner* – imitation being the sincerest form of flattery!

BBC radio for many years produced Scottish music shows, with Jimmy Shand having a long run in the 1950s and 60s. Eventually Shand was replaced with Jim McLeod, whose shows, usually from the Dunblane Hydro, were popular with listeners but eventually disappeared by the 1990s as the BBC chiefs of recent times became much less keen on live musical broadcasts. Sadly, *The White Heather Club* and *Scotch Corner* both disappeared from our television screens, ostensibly due to *"changing public tastes"* – strange considering that these programmes did not actually suffer from falling ratings, the usual reason for programmes being dropped. The steady disappearance of all music programmes from television (except for the BBC Henry Wood Proms) would seem to indicate that television planning has moved into the hands of people who apparently dislike all forms of live music.

The rise of accordion schools in Scotland in the late 1960s led to not only the development of accordion orchestras that competed in the NAO festivals, but also to the emergence of better trained accordionists. The pre-war and post-war accordionists on the Scottish dance band scene were frequently self-taught musicians, with a great 'feel' for the music and dancing. Since the 1980s, accordion players have acquired greater levels of technical accuracy due to more formalised training, though many people also believe that higher skill levels have correspondingly led to playing with generally less feeling than hitherto. This is a matter of ongoing controversy and debate in Scotland today.

The first of the Scottish accordion bands to make a substantial and enduring impact on the NAO competitive festival scene was that of Jimmy Blair, and by the 1970s the Blair orchestras were regularly 'cleaning up' the trophies at 'Accordion Day'. In the late 1980s, the G & B Laurie School fielded orchestras at every level from Preparatory to Advanced, and had dominance in the competitions over other Scottish schools such as JR Brown and Keith Dickson. Even when the Laurie brothers, Graham and Brian, split and went their separate ways, their new schools/orchestras continued to win at local and national NAO events.

A visit to the UK Championships at Scarborough will show how many very good solo, duet and orchestra/band entries come from Scotland, winning honours in all the various sections – not just the Scottish music sections. The Box & Fiddle club scene remains vibrant, and there are lots of Scottish accordion artistes performing and recording.

Scott-Wood, George (1903-78) Scottish-born George Scott-Wood has his place in history as Britain's first ever exponent of the piano accordion. He was very much an innovator, writing this country's first tutor book for the instrument, and was also

known for his accordion bands, compositions and prolific recording work.

Trained as a concert pianist, George Scott-Wood toured the USA in 1925 giving solo recitals, and while on tour began playing piano in the night-clubs of New York on his nights off, featuring jazz and popular standards.

During one of these sessions, Scott-Wood met the band leader Paul Whiteman, and was invited to play with the famous Paul Whiteman Orchestra. This meeting changed George Scott-Wood's life and musical direction forever.

On his return to Britain, Scott-Wood turned away from classical music and turned to entertaining in clubs, theatres and restaurants. He accepted a job as pianist with the Omega Collegians at the State Café, Liverpool, in 1927, and the band's repertoire included many tangos. Members of the Italian and Spanish consulates were regulars at the State Café, and some of them persuaded Scott-Wood that the tango would sound much better played on accordion. As a result, the Italian consulate arranged for George to import a Scandalli piano accordion from their country, and the talented musician set about teaching himself to learn tangos and other pieces. This, incidentally, was to be the start of a nationwide craze for the piano accordion that was to last until the 1939/45 war.

In 1927, there were no teachers of the piano accordion in this country, and George Scott-Wood decided not only to teach himself, but also to write a tutor for the instrument. In 1929, the *George Scott Wood Method for Piano Accordion* was published.

In 1930, the *George Scott-Wood Accordion Group* was formed, featuring Tommy Nicol, Vic Parker, Bill Bowness and the man himself. In the same year Scott-Wood became Director of Music for the Parlophone Record Company, and kept the post when Parlophone, Columbia, HMV and Regal-Zonophone amalgamated to form E.M.I.

1931 saw the formation of the London Piano Accordion Band, led by George Scott-Wood, a band that made recordings that are still obtainable today. This band included six accordions plus a varied rhythm section, which included guitars, Hawaiian guitar, marimba, bass and drums.

George Scott-Wood formed his *Six Swingers* in 1934, a jazz orientated outfit, and this group toured and recorded successfully.

Apart from his non-stop life of playing, touring and recording with his various groups/bands, George Scott-Wood also worked as an arranger, record producer and session musician. He was, for example, piano accompanist for Jimmy Shand on some of the legendary button player's early recordings in the 1930s. Scott-Wood also wrote music, and his compositions include *Blue Accordion, London Caprice, Flying Scotsman, Shy Serenade* and *Corn on the Cob*, his signature tune.

When war broke out in 1939, George Scott-Wood left E.M.I. and spent the next few years entertaining the troops and general public. After the war, he appeared in the country's variety theatres and made broadcasts on the BBC light Programme, playing accordion and piano on such programmes as *Accordion Club, Workers' Playtime* and *Music While You Work*. With the decline in the variety theatres in the 1950s, Scott-Wood gradually withdrew from public performances, concentrating thereafter on arranging and session work in recording studios.

George Scott-Wood's recordings continue to be reissued by the record companies, but his name is perpetuated forever by the accordion that bears his name – the Scandalli George Scott-Wood curved keyboard model, now considered to be a collectors' item.

<u>Selected discography</u>: *Hot Pie* (2003)

Scruton, Tommy (Born 1941) Manchester's Tommy Scruton has played the piano accordion for more years than he cares to remember, and is known in particular for his dedication to the music of the two great Pietros – Frosini and Deiro. Over the years, he has acquired a complete collection of the compositions of the two legendary Italian–American accordion pioneers, and is an authority on the lives and work of both men. Tom believes that Frosini and Deiro's works should be studied and performed by a larger number of young accordionists, and that the accordion world only gets to hear just a few of their compositions. Tom has sponsored two of the trophies in the annual Frosini Section at the UK Championships, and is always eager to discuss the two legends, or help and advise anyone who needs to know more. He can be contacted via Stockport Accordion Club on 0161 480 8858.

Seiber, Matyas (1905-60) Born in Budapest, Hungary, in 1905, Matyas Seiber studied the cello at the Royal Academy in his home city. He also studied composition with the famous Hungarian composer Zoltan Kodaly.

After graduation, Seiber became a Professor at Frankurt Conservatory in Germany, teaching harmony and composition. However, after a couple of years, he gave up his position in favour of travelling around Europe, then taking a job as a musician in an ocean liner's resident orchestra. In seeing the world, Seiber developed a keen interest in international folk music, jazz and blues – key features in his later compositions.

In 1929, Seiber returned to the Franfurt Conservatory where he set up a School of Jazz, one of the first attempts anywhere to teach/study jazz as a serious musical subject. The rise of Hitler to power in 1933 put a premature end to jazz in Germany, the Nazi Party frowning upon a form of music emanating from an alleged inferior race i.e. the Negro. By 1936, to escape Nazism, Seiber relocated to England where he became a part of the classical musical establishment. He also met up with some of this country's jazz and dance band musicians, and also became very interested in the possibilities of the accordion as an instrument for playing classical works. Seiber joined the staff of the newly founded British College of Accordionists, and soon was writing music for the instrument – usually under the pen name G.S.Mathis.

Matyas Seiber was an erudite composer whose classical compositions were held in high regard by his peers in the classical world. His many works for the accordion included the tangos *Gipsy Serenade* and *La Morenita*, the waltz *Sunlight and Shadow*, the orchestral pieces *Spring* and *Prelude and Fugue in the style of Buxtehude*. He also composed the Advanced Solo test piece *Galop Chromatique* for the NAO *'Accordion Day'* of 1949, and *Magyar Rhapsody* - the 1950 Advanced Band test piece. In 1938, as G.S.Mathis, he wrote the monumental ten-volume *Mathis Method for Accordion* – an accordion tutor that was in print until the 1970s.

Matyas Seiber was one of the few musicians connected with the accordion who also won equal, if not greater acclaim, in other forms of music. He was, for example, frequently employed by the British film industry as a composer of theme and incidental music, and similarly by the BBC for radio plays. He was known, too, in the jazz world, and collaborated with Johnny Dankworth in 1959 to produce *Improvisation for Jazz Band and Symphony Orchestra*.

Married with one daughter, Matyas Seiber was killed in a car crash during a visit to South Africa in 1960. The following year, M. Hohner published *Irish Suite*, his last work, for accordion orchestra. To this day, *Irish Suite* is a popular choice for accordion orchestras at the national UK Championships.

Sexton, James (Born 1933) James Sexton studied piano accordion at the London-based British College Of Accordionists in the 1950s under Graham Romani and Eddie Harris, and won many titles in NAO festivals. He was runner-up to Chiz Bishop for the Virtuoso title in the 1952 All-Britain Championships, and the pair were selected together to represent this country in the World Championships in Holland that year. At the time Sexton was doing his National Service in the RAF, and was posted in Egypt. The RAF agreed to release him for the competition, but would not give a free air passage home. This caused such a stir that his case was publicly aired in the House of Commons by Fenner Brockway, Sexton's MP, at Question Time, and the RAF were denounced for their *"mean and unpatriotic attitude."* The MP organised a public fund, and one of the contributors was HM Queen Elizabeth, who had previously heard James Sexton in concert. Eventually, the RAF relented, after much anger in the national press was expressed against the Air Ministry.

James Sexton was one of the first of a new breed of accordionists, who were keen to experiment with new music for the instrument in concerts and in contests, even if this displeased those who were suspicious and even hostile to new musical forms. Undeterred by criticism, Sexton switched to the 5-row button accordion and pioneered modernistic music. He was also a regular contributor to the pages of the *Accordion Times*, writing many erudite articles about his often-controversial views on music and the direction the accordion ought to be taking.

Shand, Sir Jimmy (1908–2001) Sir Jimmy Shand, the accordion scene's first ever Knight of the Realm, was born in Fife and took up the melodeon at eight years of age. Jimmy worked as a miner as a young man, but became unemployed during the Depression years in the early 1930s. As a recreation he had played the melodeon, becoming highly skilled at Scottish traditional music and playing at local dances, concerts and competitions. In 1933 Shand met Charles Forbes and became an employee at Forbes' Music Shop, initially attracted by the opportunity to learn to drive the firm's van. Forbes also arranged for Shand to travel to London to make some recordings, issued on the Regal Zonophone label. These 1933 records were the beginning of one of the recording industry's longest ever recordings careers, as Jimmy Shand went on making records – with Beltona (a Decca subsidiary), in the late 30s/early 40s, and EMI after the Second World War ended in 1945 – right up until the 1990s. EMI recognised that Jimmy Shand's recordings have no 'sell-by' date, and have been easily obtainable in the shops from the war years right up to the present.

Jimmy Shand played the two-row melodeon as a boy, changing to a two-row *L'Organola* diatonic accordion (push-pull action but with a three row Stradella bass left hand keyboard) by the time he made his first records. Shand's early records made such an impression that in 1936 the German based company M. Hohner Ltd designed a three row diatonic, with 102 Stradella system bass buttons – the proto-type British Chromatic accordion – especially for him. The negotiations for this new kind of accordion were thanks to Charles Forbes, an astute businessman who visualised a potentially large market in Scotland for the British Chromatic. This instrument was eventually refined and marketed in 1946 as the *Shand Morino*, renowned as the leading instrument of its kind. Jimmy's lifelong friend and fellow button accordionist, Dr Sandy Tulloch, had this to say in the 1976 biography *Jimmy Shand*, written by David Phillips, about the original British Chromatic designed for the maestro:-

"I'll never forget that accordion. It was way in front of its time in design, range and tone. I've never played an instrument that handled as easily as this one. The reeds were hand made, especially long in the tongue, and answered instantly to the slightest pressure or change of bellows movement. It was a four-voice accordion with a coupler to bring in the lower octave reeds. The bass side was superb and had full chording. The button action was unique – three rows of buttons linked to two rows of palettes in some miraculous fashion. The keyboard was real mother of pearl, the buttons were nearly flush, and so firm and positive in action that staccato triplets were a joy to play, something at that time distinctive to button box playing. Since then, piano accordions have improved beyond all recognition, but at the time, for staccato playing nothing could touch the button box, especially when played by Jimmy Shand."

Jimmy Shand's real fame originated in his dance band work, and this began in earnest in 1945 once the Second World War was over. The band that Shand formed and fronted played gigs not only all over Scotland, but England and Ireland as well. Travelling to 'gigs' is an experience most musicians find tiring and irksome, but according to Jim Johnstone who at one time played in the band on second box: *"Jimmy Shand was the exception. He thrived on it. Jimmy is a big, strong man and he had tremendous stamina."* 'Jimmy Shand & His Band' became a household name through his countless radio and television appearances, dances, touring, visits to America, Canada, Australia and New Zealand, plus his consistently high worldwide record sales. Jimmy's recording of *The Bluebell Polka* went to Number One in the singles chart in 1952, earning a gold record, and is still the only accordion instrumental to achieve this feat. Another first for Shand is that he became the first accordionist to be the subject of BBC television's *This Is Your Life* in 1977, when Eamonn Andrews, the original 'man with the red book', surprised the so-called '*Laird of Auchtermuchty*.' He was also a prolific composer, with over two hundred jigs, reels, hornpipes, polkas, strathspeys, two-steps and waltzes in print – a vast collection of music in the Scottish genre to perpetuate the great man's musical style. Shand was awarded the MBE in 1962 for services to Scottish music, and a knighthood in 2000. His name was and is synonymous with Scottish music and culture.

Biographies: *Jimmy Shand* (1976), David Phillips; *The Jimmy Shand Story* (1998), Ian Cameron, Scottish Cultural Press.

Website: www.jimmyshand.com

Video: *Dancing with the Shands* – filmed at a dance in Letham Village Hall in 1990, this one-hour video features the Jimmy Shand Junior Band plus Jimmy Shand Senior. A highlight is Shand Senior's performance of *The Bluebell Polka*. The video inexplicably took five years to be released but when it finally did reach the shops in 1995, sales were such that it reached number 7 in the national best-selling video charts! (1995).

Selected discography - the following list represents only a tiny fraction of Jimmy Shand's sixty years in the recording studios of Regal Zonophone, Decca and EMI: *The Legendary Jimmy Shand* (1989); *King of the Melodeon Men; Jimmy Shand Plays Jimmy Shand* (1995); *The Golden Years* (1999); *Dancing with the Shands* – CD version of the video (2001).

New releases:

Book of 44 Original Compositions by Sir Jimmy Shand MBE

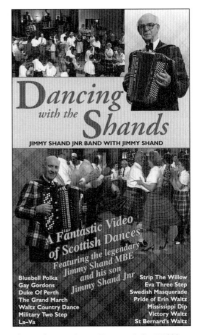

- CD – *Jimmy Shand and His Music* – to accompany above music book
- CD – *Vintage Classics Volume 1* – Jimmy Shand 1930s selections
- CD – *Waltzing Through the Years with Jimmy Shand & His Band*
- CD – *Old Tyme Classics Volume 1* (includes the Lancers + set dances)
- CD – *Jimmy Shand plays his Favourite Hymns*

All CDs are £13.00 each plus £1 postage & packing in the UK (overseas £2.50 p&p). The *Book of Original Compositions* is £12.00 each plus £1.25 p&p in the UK (overseas £3.25 p&p). Payment by cheque or postal order only, in Pounds Sterling (made payable to Jimmy Shand Junior). Send orders with full payment to Jimmy Shand Junior, Braeside Villa, Auchtermuchty, Fife KY14 7HP, Scotland; telephone 01337 828452.

Shand Junior, Jimmy (Born 1937) Son of the famous father, and a fine musician in his own right, Jimmy Shand Junior has endeavoured to develop his own style and front his own country-dance band. Jimmy Junior preferred the 5-row Continental Chromatic accordion to the 3-row British Chromatic used by Jimmy senior, and he grew up steeped in Scottish music but also with a background of formal music training that his father never had. Originally trained as a motor mechanic, Jimmy Junior studied the accordion and piano, and played in his father's band before branching out on his own in the 1950s. He made records, played on the radio and even appeared on television's *Opportunity Knocks*, introduced by Hughie Green in the early 1970s. In the mid-1970s, however, Jimmy Junior was afflicted with a mysterious condition that affected his fingers and ultimately put an end to his playing career for several years. Jimmy devoted his time to running a music shop and repairing accordions, and fortunately, in recent years has been able to resume playing for dances, and has since made more recordings.

Selected discography: *The Sound of Shand* (1971); *Three Generations of Shand* – also featuring daughter Diane as vocalist on 3 tracks and Jimmy Shand Senior on 3 tracks (1980); *The Best Of Jimmy Shand Junior* (1997); *Dancing with the Shands* (2001).

Video: *Dancing with the Shands* (1995) – also features Jimmy Shand Senior

Shand Morino   A three-row British Chromatic button accordion, with the treble buttons tuned in the keys of B/C/C# and the left hand buttons using the standard Stradella bass system, the Shand Morino was first designed/produced in 1946 to the specifications of Jimmy Shand. Shand popularised the sound of this accordion in the 1950s and 60s, and the model was used by many other leading Scottish players such as Will Starr, Jimmy Blue, Bill Black, Jimmy Lindsay, Fraser McGlynn, and Ireland's Donal Ring and Seamus Shannon. Many diatonic enthusiasts regard the Shand Morino as the *Rolls*

Andy Banks

Royce of button accordions, and they have become collectors' items since production stopped in the early 1990s. Club Accord member, player and avid enthusiast Andy Banks relates the full story of the Shand Morino below: -

The *'Shand Morino'* evolved in the following way:

Sir Jimmy Shand, while living in Dundee, was persuaded to enter Forbes Music Shop, and try some instruments, instead of *"window shopping"*. The result was the immediate offer of a job as salesman demonstrator.

The instruments at that time were 2 row melodeons in B/C or C/C#. Jimmy had been thinking of the advantages of effectively combining the two systems. His employer, Charles Forbes, used his connections with Hohner, to commission an instrument.

This had 3 treble rows, in B/C/C#, with 36 bass in Stradella format, which Jimmy had been attracted to, having seen the system on piano accordions. This was much more versatile than melodeon basses.

This instrument, marketed under the *'l'organola'* brand, was used by Jimmy for his first recordings in November 1933, at Abbey Road!

The main problem with the instrument was that 3 rows of buttons resulted in 3 rows of pallets, looked at end-on the instrument was almost square.

Jimmy and Charles then began working on a means of condensing 3 rows into 2. The result was an instrument that was the forerunner of the *'Morino'*. This was delivered in 1936. Further improvements came to a halt, due to the activities of a certain Austrian with attitude!

In 1946 the final batch of 4 *'Shand Morinos'* were delivered. This instrument was 4 voice Treble with 5 couplers. A feature of the reed layout had the 16" reeds in a separate reed block, tucked under the keyboard, with round pallets such as would be found in a concertina. The coupler system moved the linkage away from these levers when the reed bank was not required, the 8" reeds being controlled by the round slider system. Full Stradella bass was fitted, with a minor modification. The buttons were squared off, top and bottom (see photo) resulting in 117 basses. Two of the 5 bass reeds were in Cassotto. A mechanical bellows lock was fitted, separated by a lever recessed in the back of the keyboard. The treble end was attached to the bellows by the clamp system, which was usual on the *"Morino"* piano accordions.

Two versions were available. The standard size was 46 treble, 117 bass, and the smaller version was 40 treble, 105 bass. This was a limited edition. According to whom one listens to, they either made 13 or they made 36 – take your pick.

My own instrument, which dates from the early 1970s, has been 'standardised'. Reed layout is a standard 4-voice system, and the bass is standard 120 layout. Bellow clips replace the mechanical bellows lock. The last incarnation, before they stopped production, had the oval couplers, as fitted to most of the current Hohner range.

Andy Banks, Club Accord (Birmingham), 2003

Shannon, Seamus A three-row button accordionist from Elphin, Roscommon in the Irish Republic, Seamus Shannon inherited a rich tradition of Irish music that flourishes in the western counties of Roscommon-Sligo-Leitrim. A musician who specialises in Irish traditional music, Seamus Shannon has played a *Shand Morino* for most of his career. Seamus Shannon, also a vocalist, has worked and recorded as a soloist and in duet with his singer/guitarist brother Terry as the Shannon Brothers; he also often works with singer/guitarist PJ Murrihy, with whom he has also recorded. After years of working exclusively within the Irish traditional music circuit in Ireland and England, Seamus began to appear in accordion clubs in this country, where his fresh approach to music and great skill on the British Chromatic was readily appreciated. He has also appeared at accordion festivals in Blackpool and Chartres, and in Ireland presents his own weekly Sunday afternoon programme on Mid-West Radio.

Discography: *Seamus Shannon – Accordion* (1979); *The Traditional Way* – made with brother Terry (1988); *Irish Music & Song* (1994); *The Magic of Seamus Shannon* (1996); *PJ Murrihy & Seamus Shannon – My Old Native Sod* (1999). Video: *Music From The Elbow, Moate* (1997) – a live show recorded in an Irish pub.

Shannon, Sharon (Born 1968) Sharon Shannon is a superb musician who plays the two-row diatonic system, and uses no less than three accordions – a French-made Saltarelle, an Italian Castagnari and an Irish-made Cairdin model (manufactured at Rathkeale, County Limerick). Originating from County Clare and with her musical origins firmly in the Irish traditional scene (as a member of the band Arcady), Sharon Shannon has branched out into the folk scene and also into pop music as a member of The Waterboys. Her modernistic and somewhat jazzed  up version of Irish music may not please the purists, but she has won the approval of the record buying public and the popular music world, and her eponymously named debut CD was both a critical and commercial success. Shannon's music has taken her to many countries, including tours of the USA and Europe, including an appearance with Van Morrison at the Montreaux Jazz Festival. She appeared on The Waterboys' CD *Room to Roam*, and accompanied singer Christie Moore on his *Smoke and Strong Whisky* recording. Her version of *The Blackbird* is used as the theme music of Mike Harding's Folk On Two programme on BBC Radio 2. Sharon Shannon's recordings are easily available in mainstream retail record shops and she has done much to introduce the accordion to the general public, especially the younger generations.

Discography: *Sharon Shannon* (1992); *Out The Gap* (1994); *The Mighty Sparrow* (1995); *Each Little Thing* (1996); *The Best of Sharon Shannon* (1998). Video: *Bringing It All Back Home* (1989); *Tribute to Sharon Shannon* – from the *Late, Late Show*, an Irish TV show on Radio Telefis Eireann (1992).

Sharov, Oleg Born Leningrad, USSR, 1945. Oleg Sharov, a Professor of Music at the Conservatoire in St Petersburg, has been a frequent visitor to Britain and other countries in Western Europe since the advent of Perestroika in the late 1980s thawed international relations. Sharov, a virtuoso of the 5-row Bayan type accordion, is a master of the classics and his electrifying performances have made him a crowd puller and great favourite at festivals in Britain and in the English accordion clubs. His repertoire includes works by all the major composers, including JS Bach, Vivaldi, Johann Strauss, and Liszt, to Frosini.

Sharov's British debut was at Caister Accordion Festival in 1990, and he has since guested at festivals in Chartres, Scarborough and Perth. In 1995, he performed a new concert for accordion and orchestra composed by Ivor Hodgson (son of Ron Hodgson), together with the Manchester Camerata, at The Royal Northern College of Music in Manchester, receiving both great critical acclaim and a standing ovation.

Selected Discography: *Oleg Sharov – Bayan Collage* (1995)

Video: *Oleg Sharov – Accordion Miniatures* (1999); published by Lumic International.

Sharp, Bill (1934-2000) Bill Sharp played the piano from the age of eight, and took up the accordion when around 17 years old. He was taught by Charles 'Chick' Kelly, and joined the Coatbridge Accordion Band. In the early 1950s, he served an apprenticeship as an engineer, and in 1955/57 did his National Service in the army.

Bill's wife, Bunty, was a professional dancer, and his son, Jim, plays electronic accordion and runs his own dance band.

Bill Sharp's accordion school and orchestra were renowned for their high standards, for many competition successes and for raising many thousands of pounds for charities – most notable events in support of Children In Need. The Bill Sharp Accordion Orchestra performed on Radio Clyde and Radio Forth, and on ITV's Michael Barrymore Show – to name just three of many media appearances. They also toured France (playing a concert at the Eiffel Tower) and the USA.

Selected discography: *"Once More, For the Last Time…"* – a compilation CD that includes a very demanding arrangement of Frosini's *Pietro's Return*. The CD costs £10 including p & p (UK) or £11 (outside UK), and is available from Graeme Donald, 1 Upper Loan Park, Lauder DT2 6TR, Scotland.

Shine, Brendan *"A farmer by day, and an entertainer by night"* is one critic's description of Ireland's Brendan Shine. Known mainly for singing catchy and humorous songs such as *Catch Me If You Can, Do You Want Your Old Lobby Washed Down, Con Shine?* and *Pub Crawl*, Brendan Shine also plays a 5-row button accordion which he uses to accompany himself. On stage, Shine is a slick and very polished performer whose repertoire includes humorous songs, romantic songs, standards, ballads, Country & Western, and instrumental sets of Irish traditional tunes on his accordion.

Originally a product of the Irish ceili scene where he played accordion in his father's band, Brendan joined the Ciaran Kelly Ceili Band as vocalist/accordion player in the 1960s, after which he went professional as a solo singer with backing band. In the 1970s he began recording, and he is proud of the fact that, after Elvis Presley and Cliff Richard, he has the most hit singles in the Irish pop charts with over 30 entries, with The Beatles in fourth place with 27! His stage act, although popular with Irish people and C & W fans, has – in common with Foster & Allen – a broad base that is enjoyed by a wider range of audience. A few years ago, Terry Wogan frequently played Brendan Shine's recordings on his BBC Radio 2 programme, and this did much to introduce Shine to the general public and thus boost his general appeal. On St Patrick's Day a few years back, Brendan Shine made an appearance on the TVAM break-fast television show. Also on the show was Richard Clayderman, the popular French pianist, and the two were persuaded to perform an impromptu duet of Irish dance music for the occasion. The unlikely pairing fitted together well, despite their different styles.

Selected discography: *Ceili House* – an instrumental LP (1982); *The Brendan Shine* Collection (1983); *I'll Settle For Old Ireland* (2002)

Videos: *Live at Blazers* (1988); *Live at the Circus Tavern* (1990)

Shuldham-Shaw, Pat (1917-77) Pat Shaw, as he was generally known, was a many talented individual and the greatest composer the world of English folk dance music has yet produced – an English equivalent of Ireland's Turlough O'Carolan or Scotland's James Scott Skinner or Niel Gow.

Pat Shaw was born in Stratford-on-Avon, but brought up in London where he was introduced to folk dancing at six years of age. He was educated at Harrow Public School and Queen's College, Cambridge. Pat was interested in all aspects of folk music, and became a player of several instruments, an arranger and composer of tunes and songs, and a skilled performer of Morris, Sword and English country dancing. At Cambridge, he was a cast member of the 1938 University *'Footlights Revue'*.

After leaving Cambridge, Pat Shaw became Midlands Area Organiser for the English Folk Dance & Song Society, and then joined the National Fire Service during World War Two.

Once the war was over, Pat became a professional folk singer, playing guitar and specialising in singing songs of all nations in their original languages. He visited the Shetland Isles where he began collecting tunes and songs, and began playing the piano accordion. He played the accordion for country dancing and also for song accompaniment, becoming a highly skilled player in the process.

In 1949, he and fiddle player Nan Fleming-Williams formed the *Countryside Players*, initially to raise money for the Lerwick lifeboat, and this band played throughout the 1950s. During the 50s he was frequently heard on the BBC West of England radio programme *Country Dancing*, both as a singer and a caller.

Pat Shaw wrote many dances and dance tunes, many of which are to be found in the EFDSS manuals still in use today. His tunes are catchy and

217

melodic, and their popularity has endured with accordionists, fiddlers and other instrumentalists. Some of Pat's better-known compositions today include *Margaret's Waltz, Farewell to Devon, Walpole Cottage, Heswall & West Kirby Jubilee* and the tricky *Levi Jackson's Rag.*

In the 1950s, Shaw instituted the seasonal Christmas Carol concerts at Cecil Sharp House in London, the HQ of the EFDSS. He wrote all the orchestral arrangements, and these concerts are continued today in the same format.

In 1971, the EFDSS awarded Pat Shaw their highest honour, the Gold Badge, in recognition of his great service to the society in all aspects of its work.

When Pat passed away suddenly in 1977 at the age of sixty, the English folk dance world was deprived of its greatest and most creative talent. He was a multi-talented individual who excelled at everything he attempted. However, his many compositions, dances and collections of music are in general use, and survive as his legacy to present and future generations.

<u>Sight-Reading for Accordionists</u>
Trevani wrote the following article in the early 1980s, giving an accordion teacher's insight into the topic of sight-reading. During the 1980s, Trevani ran several highly successful and popular teaching studios for accordion in the London area.

Sight Reading

At each practice session do some sight-reading. You will only learn to read music if you try to read music. The pieces that you play will not necessarily be read after you have played them a few times. You will find that you are memorising a tremendous amount of the music and using it only as an 'aide de memoire'. You will remember whole chunks of bass vamp, you will remember the tune, and you will play mainly by ear.

So you must read something <u>new</u> each day. This means having access to a vast amount of music, and there are ways of obtaining this.

You can get books especially written for sight-reading, where the music is difficult to remember, but these are generally quite expensive, and again once you have read the music there is always some memory coming into function. These books are generally a little too advanced for your technique; they are written so that it is difficult to memorise and to play.

Try the local second hand bookshops. Some of them sell old music at a very low price and you can quickly accumulate a vast heap of dreadful old tunes that nobody would want to listen to but that are absolutely ideal for sight-reading.

Try the library, where you can get orchestral scores, and music for all instruments. Don't look for accordion music. Clarinet or violin music is excellent for sight-reading on the treble keyboard. Then just cover up the clef and try it on the bass – that's a good exercise.

The music should be proper music, not chord symbols or single bass notation. Piano music is good for accordion, and if the left hand is not suitable, busk it. That is good aural training. When sight-reading do not stop or hesitate, even when you know you are playing all the wrong notes. Try to keep the rhythm going and get back in as soon as you can. If you have to play with other musicians you will find that they don't wait for you when you go wrong. Keep the beat in your mind and busk when necessary, but always start on the right note and finish on the right note, at the right moment.

When sight-reading you should also practise transpositions. Take a simple tune and raise it to the next sharp or flat. For instance, if the melody starts on G then practise reading everything two lines higher up and adding a sharp to the key signature. Or play the tune starting in the space below and alter the key signature to one flat.

The accordion bass is relatively easy to transpose, as you will use the same finger patterns in all but the most difficult keys. If you get to the very top of your bass keyboard in the 6-7 sharp major keys, try dropping to the lower end and playing them enharmonically changed to their flat counterpart. Then, for a change, try reading the music upside down. You think I'm joking? Just try it; it is good practice. Some musicians I have heard sound as if they always play that way!

Aural practice is anything to do with the ear. That is a wide statement so let's be more specific. I have mentioned earlier in this article that a good reader is really playing by ear, because he is reading ahead and hearing what the notes will sound like before he plays them. This takes training and must be practised.

First of all learn to hear single notes. Start on middle C and then play the next degree higher in the scale, D. Listen to the pitches of C and D and then sing them out loud. A teacher can check if your pitch is correct. The quality of your singing does not matter. You may hum or whistle or make any sort of sound so long as it is of the correct pitch. Pitch the note in your mind before you give voice to it. When you sing it you must hit the correct pitch immediately and not slide around until it sounds like the note you are supposed to be singing.

When you have pitched, out loud, C and D, try C, D and E, then C, D, E and F, then C, D, E, F, and G. These were probably the first five notes you learned on the treble keyboard and formed a little five-finger scale, which you can remember to sing, even without listening to the notes being played. You may not get the right pitch for C, but so long as the other notes are relative – i.e., tone, tone, semitone, and tone – you will be learning fast.

When you have had your pitch checked against one note you should be able to _hear_ the relative intervals. Try 2nds, 3rds, 4ths and 5ths first of all. Play middle C on the treble keyboard, and then sing your chosen interval. After singing it, play the note on your keyboard to see if you were correct.

Some people tell me that they are 'tone deaf'. I do not believe this, as there are few medical reasons for this 'disease'. Their tone deafness is caused by lack of practice or training, or merely laziness. I have never yet had a pupil whom I could not get to sing the approximate pitch of notes or intervals after training and practice.

I have had pupils who have said that they only want to learn to play the accordion, not learn to sing, yet it is only by hearing you imitate vocally the pitch of notes that a teacher can tell if you are in fact hearing the notes. If the pupil will not sing, it is generally because of shyness or lack of confidence in the teacher, and both of these should be overcome.

Don't fight against aural: join in and get greater understanding from your music. If you have difficulty in hearing the correct intervals, try to think of a tune that has two very strong notes at the beginning that correspond to the interval you want. For instance, a 2nd is the opening interval of '*Put another nickel in, in the Nickelodeon*'. In fact, the whole melody is made up of 2nds. The 3rd and 5th are contained in the opening of *The Blue Danube* waltz – i.e., C-E-G, 1-3-5. The 4th is maybe more difficult for the beginner, but there are only one or two tunes with strong 1-4 openings. Try *Away in a Manger* or, if you know it, the *Grand March* from '*Tannhauser*'.

Now try to pick your own tunes which have these strong opening intervals, right through the chromatic scale, so that at any time, even when other music is playing, you can be sure to pitch all intervals, major, minor, perfect, augmented, and diminished, with relative ease. This is a good game to play with other musicians. To make it more difficult try to group tunes – e.g., all intervals must be the starts of carols, or of one composer. Then it really gets tough.

So for practice strike a note, sing the required intervals, and then check you are correct by playing the note on the treble keyboard. Then combine notes into groups of three, four or six, and go through the same process until you can 'pitch' whole melodies.

Trevani, The Home Organist, 1982

Smith, Heather Heather Smith began accordion lessons at the age of nine under the late Horace Crossland in Barnsley, travelling from her home in Middleton on the Wolds, East Yorkshire (quite a distance!!). Taking to the instrument 'like a duck to water' she won the under 10, 12, 14, & 16 years and then the Open British Championship, in contests organised by the British Association of Accordionists. At 17 years she gained second place in the CMA Junior World Championship, held in Hamburg, Germany. Heather has broadcast several times and appeared on television. A professional player and teacher (at 15 years she gained honours in the BAA Diploma examination) of piano accordion, organ and keyboard, Heather Smith joined with Tom Duncan in 1997 to become co-editor of *Accordion Profile*, a new monthly magazine. Later, Heather organised an accordion festival at Pakefield, East Anglia, to replace the void in that area left by the festivals organised by the late Malcolm Gee at nearby Caister.
Discography: *Heatherset* (1992) – a cassette including *Bel Fiore; La Valse à Pierrot; Nola; Corinne; Carioca; Tarantella Avolesa; Magic Fingers; Style Musette; Bel Viso; She's Funny That Way; Amantes; Accordion Polka.*

Spink, Arthur Scottish accordionist from Dundee whose imaginative arrangements and performances of Scottish and other music made him a popular stage performer and recording artiste in the late 1960s and 1970s. In the 1950s, Arthur Spink took part in NAO accordion festivals, and in the 60s he toured

Canada and the USA. Spink sometimes worked with tenor Dennis Clancy, and the two were also members of the Royal Clansmen, a Scottish concert party troupe alongside fellow accordionist, Will Starr. Arthur Spink emigrated to Australia in the early 1980s and left the music business, but he is remembered for a very fine series of LPs that were very popular in Britain.

Discography: *Dancing Fingers* (1970); *Arthur Spink's Hogmanay* (1971); *Hoot's Mon* (1971); *The Scottish World of Arthur Spink* (1972) *The Flying Scotsman* (1972); *The Continental Accordion of Arthur Spink* (1973); *Arthur Spink's Accordion Dance Party* (1973); *Arthur Spink's Country Box* (1979).

Stanley, Fintan (Born 1941) Ireland's Fintan Stanley, from Clougherhead, County Louth, began his musical life as a young boy playing traditional music on the BC two-row accordion, switching to the five-row Continental chromatic whilst still in his teens. In 1955, he won the All-Ireland Button Accordion championship, a prelude to a successful professional solo career. Resident in Boston, USA since 1976, Fintan Stanley was not seen in Britain for about twenty years until his successful short tour in 1998. In 2001, he again made a short tour of Britain, a highlight of which was a duet performance at Bolton Irish centre alongside his compatriot, Dermot O'Brien. Fintan Stanley, who claims not to read a note of music, has amazing keyboard dexterity plus a natural, in-built musicality that impresses audiences wherever he appears. Unlike most accordionists who come from the Irish traditional music scene, Fintan Stanley regularly plays a very wide range of international music including French musette, Italian (including Frosini pieces), Russian, Latin American, Scottish, light classical (Strauss, Lehar, Brahms, etc) and even some jazz, and his records and concerts thus have a very broad appeal. He also occasionally sings, and has a pleasant and humorous stage personality.

Discography: *On Tour* - Volume 1 (1973); *On Tour* – Volume 2 (1976)

Starr, Will (1922-1976) Scottish musician who has attained a legendary status since his untimely death in 1976, and who has been often cited by later and contemporary accordionists as an influence. Starr played the Shand Morino, playing Scottish traditional music plus some French musette pieces, generally in a bright and lively style, and was a concert performer rather than a dance musician. On stage, Starr would wear the kilt and move about, sometimes kicking his leg into the air like the showman he was. Starr's recordings were popular with enthusiasts, and his true legacy is that he inspired a lot of Scottish and Irish players, who came after him, especially solo musicians who aspired to be stage performers rather than members of dance bands. In his last years, Will Starr used a customised Shand Morino with four rows of buttons – the fourth row being dummy keys. This accordion is heard on Will Starr's last recordings, made in the early 70s, and is now in the collection owned by Ken Hopkins, of Northern Ireland (see picture of <u>Andy Banks</u>).

<u>Selected discography</u>: *In Starr Thyme* (1975); *Memories of Will Starr* (1980); *Accordion Hits* (1992); *The Early Years* – volumes 1 & 2 (2002)

<u>Stars of Today and Tomorrow</u> *A few of the accordion scene's current brightest talents!*

Roman Jbanov and
Demi Emorine

Lindsay Garvin

Gary Blair Jnr.

Bethany Johnson

l to r: Paul Chamberlain,
Oleg Sharov and David Nisbet

Lisa-Lee Leslie

Johnny-Lee Leslie

Stefan Bodell

Lucy Jackson

222

Stradella   Originally designed and introduced in Italy in 1876 by Mariano Dallapé, the Stradella bass system is easily the most universally employed left hand system for piano and chromatic accordions; it is also found on all British Chromatic accordions. The Stradella bass arrangement features two rows of single bass notes and up to four rows of pre-set major, minor, dominant seventh and diminished seventh chords. Although the Stradella bass has been popular with accordionists in most countries, it has been alleged by some musicians in the classical world that the pre-set chords are in effect mechanical and therefore uncreative and even unmusical. The development of the free-bass accordion has tended to counter these arguments, though the popularity of the Stradella system with the average player seems set to continue indefinitely.

Strange, but True...
The Flying Accordionist

Stockport Accordion Club member John Higham is a man of many interests, including skiing and hang-gliding. He often visits Switzerland, where he has a home, in pursuit of his hobbies, and on one occasion there he was photographed actually in mid-air on a hang-glider, playing an accordion! He flew several hundred yards, and went past a series of restaurants playing away merrily for the diners, who must have been astonished to be entertained by an accordionist in this way – from the air. This is prob-ably the first time an accordion player has played whilst hang-gliding, or restaurant-diners have been entertained by a flying accordionist!

The only bad publicity is no publicity

Anyone who has ever been involved with promoting an accordion festi-val or concert will know just how hard it can be getting the public interested in your events, and that the occasional publicity stunt can be worth its weight in ticket sales.

In October 1988, just prior to the first NAO North West Area Accordion Festival at Stockport Town Hall, Rob Howard (from the organising committee) and festival concert compère Eamonn O'Neal, an accordionist and presenter with BBC Greater Manchester Radio, together contrived a stunt to publicise the festi-val in the Manchester Evening News. Rob telephoned the journalist who wrote the nightly society gossip column known as *The Diary*, telling him that Eamonn O'Neal was *"absolutely furious"* that someone had told the media about his *"big secret"* i.e. that Eamonn played the accordion, and that this would not go down well with the BBC chiefs, and that his whole future as a broadcaster was now in jeopardy. Furthermore, Eamonn was now *"turning the town upside down"* inter-rogating all his so-called friends trying to find the source of the leak. The reporter lapped up all this nonsense, and the story in the following edition portrayed a *"distraught and vengeful"* Eamonn *"angrily"* trying to find the person who had blackened his reputation by revealing him to be an accordionist!

The newspaper write-up certainly did no harm at all to the festival's publicity, and large numbers from far and wide supported the first Stockport NAO Championships throughout the day, and the evening concert (which featured Eamonn O'Neal as both compère and a performer) sold out the 720-seat Town Hall.

Accordion Hit Squad

In early 1990 an accordion band called *Those Darn Accordions!*, from California, USA, that included some eccentric extroverts in its ranks, decided to raise public awareness of the accordion in San Francisco. They toured the city, in the evenings, in a large, un-marked van scouring the darkness for 'victims' i.e. looking for restaurants. Once a restaurant was located the van would quietly slide as close to the front door as possible, and pull up. The doors would open, and out would jump up to a dozen accordionists – like a riot squad – and gatecrash the unsuspecting restaurant, staff and diners alike. The accordionists would rush in, all playing *Lady of Spain, Valencia* and *El Relicario* in succession. The initial reaction of the involuntary 'audience' was usually one of shock, generally followed by wild applause and even participation as people, especially waiting and kitchen staff, joined in by dancing and banging utensils in time to the music.

Not Impressed!

In February 1941, the legendary Jimmy Shand needed a drummer for a booking, and was told about a local man by name of Owen McCabe. Shand went to see McCabe, who was at his place of work, and offered him a gig that evening, which Owen, known as 'Owney', readily accepted.

Owen spent all day in a state of high excitement, and turned up at the dance hall full of adrenalin, ready to give the performance of his life. What Owen did not realise, however, was that Jimmy Shand often looked rather dour and severe on stage, and had the habit of turning away from the crowd, as if in distaste at the sound of his playing. This had the effect of causing Owen to believe, incorrectly as it turned out, that Shand was unhappy with the drummer's performance.

When Owen's wife asked him later how the gig went, he replied despondently that although he did his best, Shand *"kept turning round and giving me dirty looks"*!

As things turned out, Owen McCabe became Jimmy Shand's drummer for the next twenty years.

Accordion Marathon

In 1982, Tom Luxton from the West Midlands set a new accordion-playing record of 84 hours non-stop on his 5-row instrument. Tom's 'Accordion Marathon' was a sponsored event in aid of the Wolverhampton Heart Monitoring Machine Appeal Fund. Fellow Club Accord member John Gould, whose support was no doubt very welcome and helpful, joined in with Tom for some of the time. The new record (beating the previous record set in the 1970s by Norman English from Somerset) was reached just after midnight on Saturday August 7th, at a pub called The Robin Hood. The marathon raised £1,600, and newspapers, radio and television reported Tom's efforts. The new record of 84 hours entered the Guinness Book of Records.

You Can't Win Them All!

Macclesfield's John Jones, well known for his fund raising for charity, recalls that not every audience has appreciated his accordion playing. In the late 1980s, he was staying on a campsite near Worksop, Nottinghamshire, and early one morning he awoke to find about thirty ducks standing outside his tent. Out of curiosity as to the ducks' reaction to music, John donned his accordion, went outside and began playing. After a few seconds, all the ducks – as one – turned around, and walked solemnly away in single file – as if a hidden signal had been given. In less than half a minute, the entire 'audience' had gone!

Many years later, John was photographed, wearing his accordion, at a Christmas fair standing next to a Shire horse (this picture appeared on the front cover of the December 2002 issue of *Accordion Profile*). As soon as the photo had been taken, someone asked John to play a tune. As soon as John began to play, the giant horse turned his head in the opposite direction, and promptly walked off. As the great comedian WC Fields once famously said: *"Never perform with children or animals"*.

Man's Best Friend

Accordionist Eric Reed, from Congleton in Cheshire, plays regularly on his midi instrument for ballroom dancing, and his dog accompanies him on all his gigs. While Eric performs a programme of quicksteps, waltzes, foxtrots, etc, the dog lies down close to where his master is playing. Eric always finishes with *The Last Waltz*, and as soon as he gets past the introduction and into the melody, his dog gets up and walks out through the nearest exit – as regular as clockwork!

Accordion to him….

Stockport accordionist Rob Howard, a teacher at St Pius RC High School in inner city Manchester during the 1980s, ran an accordion band at the school as an extra-curricular activity. This was very successful for a few years, with about 25 players at one point, such was the interest. He remembers that the very first time he took his accordion into school (before the band existed), he went into the music room for a play during break. Outside the room and unknown to him, a fight broke out between two boys, watched by a small crowd. However, the sound of the accordion from inside the room proved to be more interesting than the fisticuffs, and the crowd abandoned the fight and went instead to watch the accordionist. Finally, even the two combatants abandoned their altercation and joined the onlookers!

Later, when the St Pius school band was up and running, two of its members – John O'Grady and Gerard Mannion – had an argument that became a fight. Mr Howard, the teacher, intervened, broke up the fight and tried to calm the situation by asking what the trouble was about. He listened to conflicting versions of the boys' disagreement, then turned to one and said: *"Accordion to him it's this…"* and to the other *"Accordion to you it's about that..., but accordion to me....".* Soon, the three dissolved into laughter, and it was all back to normal.

Dancing Accordionists

Sylvia Bennett – in the years before she became Mrs Chiz Bishop – never intended to take up the accordion, and was a dedicated dancer. Her dance teacher was the famous Madame Courtney, who was also a renowned accordion teacher. One day, Madame Courtney announced to her dance class that they were going to be involved in a pantomime she had written. However, the panto script called for the dancers to become an accordion band at one stage of the show, and all fifteen members of the dance class had to learn to play. After their initial consternation, the dancers set to work under Madame's tuition, and the transformation – painful though it was at times – became a reality, and the pantomime proceeded as planned. Sylvia went on to compete in the All-Britain Championships, and eventually marry the great Chiz Bishop, the greatest national accordion champion of them all.

Will an accordion on fire curb Rolf's burning desire to perform?

In early August 2002 Rolf Harris was all set to go on stage to perform for an audience numbering 300 at the Maidenhead & Bray Cricket Club, when

his accordion suddenly burst into flames. The instrument had been placed too close to powerful stage lights, sparking off a blaze. Pianist Laurie Holloway grabbed the accordion, and guests, including TV chat show host Michael Parkinson, threw glasses of water over it until the flames were extinguished. Rolf, as professional as they come, gave the accordion a brief inspection, played a few smoky test chords, and carried on with the show. The accordion apparently looked a mess, but miraculously sounded fine. *"It was a case of spontaneous combustion – imagine the insurance claim!"* Rolf commented afterwards.

Anglo-Austrian Relations

Manchester accordionist Johnny Coleclough and his wife Phyllis went on holiday to Austria, and the evening entertainment included a pair of accordionists who played lots of their national music. When the interval came, Johnny engaged the two Austrians in conversation, and when he told them that he was the resident at the *Bierkeller* in Manchester, the next thing that happened was that he borrowed an accordion and went on stage to play some tunes and sing a few songs. Afterwards, the hotel entertainers asked John if he had made any recordings as they would like to learn some of his repertoire. Johnny promised to send them a tape, and as soon as he arrived home he found a tape and mailed it off to Austria.

However, almost as soon as he had left the Post Office, John had misgivings about the cassette he had just sent. At the Bierkeller, in addition to performing, another of Johnny's duties was to keep order on the dance floor, and he remembered too late that the tape had been unedited, and would include songs occasionally punctuated by loud calls such as *"Get that ....pint pot off the dance floor, you ...."* and *"Stop doing that you ...., and .... off out of the way"*!! He then had visions of the two Austrians playing merrily away to the holidaymakers and inadvertently shocking them with some new numbers containing various fruity ad-libs!

Offensive Weapon

Glasgow's Gary Blair tells a true story concerning an American female accordionist who lives in Seattle, USA, but took a flight to Vancouver for her lessons with teacher Joe Morelli. On one occasion, there was no flight available and the lady decided to make the long drive into Canada. When she arrived at the border, the Canadian customs men decided to check the inside of her car, and when one of them spotted her accordion on the back seat, she was asked (in all seriousness) *"Do you have any more weapons?"*!!!

Brotherly Love

Although it is generally accepted today by most people that Guido Deiro was the first person to play the piano accordion professionally on stage in the USA, for many years his younger and ultimately more illustrious brother, Pietro, disputed Guido's claim. In the 1930s, the brothers allegedly fell out about which one was the true original piano accordion pioneer, and a famous court case ensued that ended inconclusively. The brothers apparently settled out of court, and Guido was thereafter credited with the right to claim to be the first. However, if one reads the newspapers of the time, there is the distinct impression given that the whole episode was a choreographed sham designed purely as a publicity stunt. The so–called 'dispute' certainly did no harm to either of the brothers' careers.

Street, Karen   Karen Street, originally from Burton-on-Trent, was All-Britain Virtuoso Champion in 1982 and 1983, and a competitor at the 1984 Coupe Mondiale, held in Folkestone (won by the American, Peter Soave). Karen began playing the accordion by having lessons with the late Marion Schofield in Burton. Later, during her time as a student at Bath University and at the Welsh College of Music and Drama, she studied the accordion  with Mario Conway. By the time Karen competed at Folkstone in the Coupe Mondiale, she was studying with Ivor Beynon. After a long spell away from the accordion spent playing saxophone in the all-female and much publicised Fairer Sax, and getting married and raising a family, Karen returned to the accordion in the late 1990s. She has appeared in accordion clubs, and in 2001 has made a CD featuring her own compositions. Also in 2001, Karen won the Composers' Competition at the London Accordion Festival with *In the Ballroom with the Rope*.

Discography: *Finally...A Beginning* (2001)

Sundequist, Jorgen (Born 1962) Sweden's Jorgen Sundequist, somewhat unusually for someone from a Scandinavian country, plays the piano accordion and has stayed with this instrument throughout his career. He met and studied with Anthony Galla-Rini in the USA in the 1980s, and the great American maestro influences his playing style. In the early 1990s, Sundequist came to Britain to play at the Caister Festival, and has since become very popular in this country through his many club and festival appearances. He has a wide repertoire of accordion classics, classical music and Swedish traditional music, and he has both a strong playing technique and a commanding stage presence.

Swingler, Harry Harry Swingler, from Wolverhampton, played a Guillietti piano accordion without ever having a music lesson or being able to read music, yet possessed an amazing facility for performing almost any kind of music, and with great style. During his service in the Royal Navy, he entertained frequently on board HMS Birmingham, and later found his true 'home' as a founder member of Club Accord where he became well-known for his impromptu duets with the late George Karklins, a notable jazz accordionist. Harry and George contributed tracks to the Malcolm Gee-produced Club Accord LP *It's All Accordion To What You Like*. Harry died from cancer in 1990.

Syrett, George (Born 1937) Yorkshire-born and based musician and personality, well known for playing, compèring and leading workshops at accordion festivals. Also a singer and composer, George Syrett is an entertainer who has worked extensively inside and outside the accordion world, presenting his own individual brand of music, song and humour. Often in the company of his equally madcap drummer, Rodney McNamara, a concert performance is likely to feature George Syrett's lively version of Frank Sinatra's *New York, New York*, gloriously climaxing with high kicks resembling Basil Fawlty's famous goose-stepping sequence in the Fawlty Towers episode, *The Germans*.

George Syrett's musical background has been rich and varied, to say the least. During National Service, he played the piano and accordion in the army dance band, and so frequently that he claims to have never done a guard duty! He has played the piano in pubs, the electronic organ in clubs and the cinema organ in his home city of Leeds. He has played 'dep' gigs as pianist with such great bands as Joe Loss, Ted Heath and Harry Gold & his Pieces of Eight, and even played the famous Wurlitzer organ at Blackpool Tower. As an accordionist, he plays an Elkavox and makes appearances in accordion clubs and at the Bridlington Festival, plus occasional playing trips to Seattle, USA, where he has been popular for many years.

In 2003 George was fittingly dubbed *'The King of Stand Up Accordion'* by compère Ron Bennett following a concert performance in West Sussex.

Technique *The article that follows was written by Charles Magnante, an all-time great of the accordion world: -*

The Mastery of Technique

Technique is a matter of hard work. With a little talent and a lot of technique a musician can go far.

The art of interpreting music should consist ideally of 50 per cent native gifts, such as those of a good ear and a good sense of time and rhythm for phrasing, and 50 per cent technique. With really hard work, however, the ratio can be something nearer to 25 and 75 per cent.

Muscles

Technique can only be acquired by constant practice involving the development of the individual muscles of the fingers. If you roll up your sleeve and watch the muscles of your arm, you will find that the action of the fingers involves a great many arm muscles. These muscles have to be developed for the special purpose of playing just as those of a boxer or a wrestler have to be developed for their very different techniques.

Fingers

I have evolved my own method of finger exercises, practised for ten minutes daily without the accordion. The exercises I used on the accordion were also my own invention, especially those for the left hand. As a student I read a great deal of piano music and went through many albums of technical piano exercises.

In the early stages of accordion study I believe in training the student in the mechanical and technical exercises intended for the piano. Such, at least, was my own personal experience. A grounding in piano technique helps immeasurably in training the muscles, the eye and the brain in smooth coordination.

The position of the right and left hand is most important in the earliest stage of training in accordion playing. The fingers should always be held parallel to the keys and well rounded. This is an invariable rule.

In the right hand, the finger position parallel to the keys must be maintained as far as possible in all registers. This is often difficult when actually playing, not just practising with this position definitely in view. My way of dealing with the difficulty is to lower my shoulders when playing in the high register.

One by one

In the left hand, the fingers should be even more rounded than in the right. I make a point of keeping the second joint of the thumb on the edge of the box near the diminished chords. This thumb position ensures the correct placing of the left hand throughout, whatever you are playing.

For purely mechanical exercises I recommend closing the bellows so that no tone is produced. Then hold five white keys down; raise one finger at a time and strike the same key about twenty times without moving the other four fingers. This should be practised with each finger in turn. When you begin to get an aching feeling throughout the entire arm, you have done the exercise well and earned a rest.

Slow beats

You rest one arm at a time by relaxing the muscles. To do this let it drop like a dead thing, hanging from your shoulder. While the right arm is thus resting, put the left hand and arm through the silent finger exercises. The only difference in the case of the left hand will be that the thumb, of course, cannot be used.

For both hands the aim should be to lift the fingers as high as possible. It does not matter if you cannot combine altitude with speed. Slow beats will do.

Manicure

Here I must put in a word of advice about manicure, which may not be popular with lady accordionists who regard their instrument as an opportunity for the display of slender, tapering fingers, finished off with a quarter-inch or more of pointed nail. I feel it is extremely important, particularly on the right hand, to have the nails trimmed to a medium length, level with the finger tips either straight across or rounded; never pointed. On the left hand, I personally prefer to wear my nails a little shorter.

The reason

There is a reason, of course, for all this attention to detail. The fingers of the human hand are all of different lengths and weights. It would be better from the point of view of playing key board musical instruments – and, no doubt, performing many other actions – were the fingers all equal. The object of practise is to overcome these anatomical disadvantages as far as possible.

Pressure

Well-curved fingers, lined up evenly as if all the fingers were of the same length, are conducive to even playing. In the left hand the only natural playing position is with well-rounded fingers. The construction of the small buttons on the instrument make this essential.

Each finger should likewise register the same pressure in terms of weight per pound; but the tendency is for the thumb, being of larger and heavier construction, to carry more weight than the fourth and fifth fingers.

Self-observation

This tendency can be overcome by repeated conscientious practice and the use of a little "science" with self-observation. For example, play the C major scale from C to G and back again with five fingers, and try to work out the right, equal pressure on each key.

Feel it

To get the "feel" of it, I advise doing this exercise *legato* at first. It is not necessary to raise the fingers more than half an inch or so off the keys. To be able to feel the sensation of equal pressure on all keys and recognise the perfect *legato* (which we are all striving for but seldom achieve) complete relaxation of hand and arm is essential.

The test

The feeling under each finger in action must be as if it were holding up the weight of the whole hand. To test your finger pressure, lay the left hand and forearm flat, palm downwards on a table. With the right hand do the five-finger exercises on your forearm, observing the pressure of the individual fingers. The forearm register immediately becomes a mental register, a highly-sensitive, individual mechanism which each player tries to create for himself. Your teacher can help you, but cannot do it for you.

Without this personal criterion of finger pressure, it is impossible to attain a flawless technique. It is the foundation; it is fundamental and cannot be side-stepped.

Charles Magnante, Accordion World Review (1956)
Reproduced with the kind permission of Adrian Dante

Tex-Mex Tex-Mex, Tejano or Norteno are three of the names by which the accordion-driven folk music of the Americans of Mexican origin living in Texas is known. This music is usually performed on diatonic button accordion accompanied by bajo (a type of 12 string guitar) plus rhythm, and conjures up mental images of giant cacti landscapes, old adobe haciendas, and John Wayne & The Alamo! This music goes back into the 19th Century when Texas was being colonised by Mexicans arriving from over the border, and by European immigrants. Many of the latter were Germans who worked on the railways, in mines and in the construction industry, some of whom were responsible for introducing the Hohner button accordion to their adopted homeland. The Mexican settlers took readily to the accordion and introduced it (and many of the German and other European polkas and waltzes) into their own indigenous music, known as Ranchera. The Tex-Mex style thus evolved from Latin and European roots into a music identified with the State of Texas. Like other folk traditions, Tex-Mex music has an emotional vein running through it. The songs tend to be about love, passion, work, dreams and drinking – aspects of everyday life. The songs and tunes come in many tempos, but the polka is the favourite – complete with lots of staccato notes and phrases that typify the style.

Leading accordion players of the Tex-Mex tradition are Flaco Jimenez and his father and brother, both called Santiago, Ruben Valdez and Leon Garcia. Flaco Jimenez has performed in England several times with great success, though the Tex-Mex genre has never really caught on in Britain – unlike its neighbouring Cajun and Zydeco styles, which are now played by people born and brought up in this country.

Thatcher, Amy A product of the famous Banks Lane Junior School in Stockport, where the energetic and charismatic Liza Austin-Strange MBE taught her music, Amy Thatcher plays both Stradella and free bass Pigini piano accordion. She has worked with top folk musicians such as Northumbrian piper Kathryn Tickell, accordionist Karen Tweed, and as a member of The Chase. To

date she has recorded 4 albums, including as a duo with fellow accordionist Murray Grainger (see **Grainger, Murray**). Amy has, to date, appeared at such prestigious venues as Manchester's Bridgewater Hall and Royal Northern College of Music, and the Royal Albert Hall in London.
Selected discography: *Paper Bird* – made with Murray Grainger (2003)

Theory of Music for Accordionists, by Eddie Harris, is a unique book in that an accordionist writes authoritatively about all aspects of the topic. Originally published in 1960 by Hohner Concessionaires Ltd, and revised in 1987 by Graham Romani, this invaluable aid to musical theory is out of print at the time of writing (2003), but it is worth looking out for a second-hand copy. Perhaps there will be another reprint?

Thomas, Stewart Manchester-born Stewart Thomas was a member of the original Clifford Wood Accordion Orchestra, and was taught the accordion by Cliff Wood. In the 1950s and 60s he competed several times in the All-Britain Championships, both as a soloist and as a member of the CWAO. Stewart had a brilliant technique, especially on French musette music, at which he excelled, and his playing was much admired by casual listeners. Stewart was an engraver by trade, and very artistic by nature; some of his work involved producing exquisite artwork designs on accordions. He was also a brilliant artist, and some of his paintings were exhibited in Salford Art Gallery. Stewart was something of a maverick by nature, forever acting on impulse and turning up unexpectedly in places e.g. acting on the spur of the moment, he went to Paris during an accordion trades exhibition week, and then spent every night sleeping on a bench in a park. Stewart was very well known around accordion clubs and festivals, but had an introverted personality, and he made very few appearances anywhere on stage. He was, however, frequently to be seen and heard at accordion festival trade stands playing his fabulous music and surrounded by groups of curious and envious onlookers. Stewart died in tragic circumstances in June 2000 at the age of 56, and was widely mourned by all who had known him.
Discography: Stewart's brother Steve Thomas issued *Accordion Solos* - an eleven-track music CD, made from a homemade tape recording, shortly after Stewart died. The cover and the disc included two of Stewart's excellent landscape paintings.

Thoumire, Simon (Born 1965) Edinburgh-born Simon Thoumire plays the English concertina and he sprang to national prominence by winning the 1989

BBC Young Tradition Award, a competition for young and outstanding folk musicians. Very few concertina players perform jazz, and still fewer play Scottish traditional music on the English concertina – but Thoumire does both, and with an innovative style and high degree of technical proficiency. His unique mix of instrument and genres has made people sit up and take notice at folk festivals and folk clubs at home and abroad, and he has performed across Europe, Canada and the USA. When the Scottish Parliament opened in 1999, Simon Thoumire was commissioned to compose and perform music for the official ceremony. More recently, he was a guest artiste at the 2003 national accordion championships in Helsinki, Finland, appearing in a live television broadcast.

Selected discography: *Hootz* (1990); *Waltzes for Playboys* (1993); *March, Strathspey and Surreal* (1996); *Celtic Connections Suite* (1998); *Music for a New Scottish Parliament* (1999); *The Big day In* (2000).

Timoney, Mike (Born 1944, Manchester) Mike Timoney won several regional titles in NAO competitions before turning professional in the early 1960s, pioneering the Cordovox electronic accordion. On his eighteenth birthday, Timoney became resident entertainer on the Queen Mary, fronting his own quartet. After a few years on liners, he became an entertainer in night clubs in and around Manchester, presenting electronic accordion sounds playing his own arrangements of the popular music of the day to the general public. Eventually, Timoney became resident at the Warren Club in Stockport, during which time he recorded an LP (in 1971) titled *The Astounding Sound Of The Cordovox*. The tracks on this outstanding LP were: *Love Is Blue, Cast Your Fate To The Wind, A Whiter Shade Of Pale, Wheels, The Good the Bad & the Ugly, Je T'Aime, Stranger On The Shore, Time Is Tight, Afrikaan Beat* and *Elizabethan Serenade*. In recent years, Mike Timoney has become a session musician mainly using keyboards, though he has occasionally worked as an accompanist for well-known touring vocalists, most notably Luciano Pavarotti.

Tollefsen, Toralf (Born 26th August 1914, Glemmen, Norway; died 27th November 1994.) Without doubt, Toralf Tollefsen (known as 'Tolly' or just Tollefsen) was for more than half a century one of the most popular accordionists worldwide, revered by audiences and fellow accordionists alike – an all-time great of the accordion world. Toralf Tollefsen was born into a musical family and began to play first the harmonica, then the two-row diatonic button accordion at five years of age. At seven, the family moved to Oslo where young Toralf studied the violin at the Oslo School of Music. By his eleventh birthday, Tollefsen had switched to the 5 row chromatic accordion and was soon playing for dances in his locality.

As a teenager, Tollefsen was taught by Ottar E. Akre, then a prominent accordionist in Norway. By the age of fifteen, Tollefsen was regularly entertaining in a restaurant together with a saxophonist. The pair would play and sometimes also sing in harmony, and they were soon to be heard on radio broadcasts. As a soloist, in 1934 Tollefsen made a tour of Norway and made his first records.

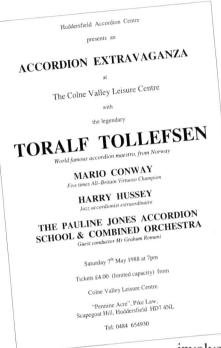

The following year, during the summer of 1935, Tollefsen was heard playing in a seaside restaurant by a conductor from a British liner, as a result of which Tollefsen was engaged by the Moss Empire for a series of variety theatre appearances in England. It was not long before Tolly came to the attention of the BBC, and he was featured in 1936 both on radio and television, the latter then in its infancy in this country, and also in Pathé news films. In 1938, Tolly married British-born Nona, and they had a working honeymoon in Australia, playing in variety shows and making radio appearances.

By the outbreak of war in September 1939, Tollefsen's British work permit had expired and he and Nona were living in Norway, and during the German occupation Tollefsen was actively involved with the resistance movement. By this time, they had a daughter and Nona was known to hide guns in the bottom of the pram, with young Sonja Marie sitting on top of them. During the war period, Tollefsen spent a lot of time delving into classical music, developing and perfecting a repertoire of the works of Bach, Handel, Chopin and other great composers.

Once the war was over in 1945, Tollefsen and family returned to England. In the post war years Tollefsen continued to play the variety theatres, but also established a new career in concert halls as a classical accordionist. Apart from Pietro Frosini and the brothers Guido and Pietro Deiro in the USA a generation before, it was very unusual for an accordionist to openly pursue a career performing classical music, and Tollefsen was now breaking new ground – certainly in Europe. A recital at London's Wigmore Hall led to a notable concert at the Royal Albert Hall on March 14th 1947, where he performed the Pietro Deiro *Concerto in E* accompanied by the London Symphony Orchestra. Solo classical recitals followed in many venues in Britain, including the Royal Festival Hall, leading to extensive tours of the USA, South Africa and Rhodesia. It was during the 1950s that Tollefsen began to explore the possibilities of the free bass accordion, then something of a novelty in the accordion movement. Tollefsen, a pioneer of the free bass system, had this to say:

"It was my greatest wish during all those years, especially when I started in the concert field, to have a more flexible bass with which I could play

all sorts of music. It was always difficult to find suitable music from the old masters that would lend itself to the accordion, and it was these old masters that I had to play mostly in the kind of concerts I was giving. Now, of course, that the free bass has established itself through the efficiency of the young accordion generation, much music has been written for the accordion, both good and bad, but more and more I am convinced that the accordion will win more ground and earn due respect as time goes on.

"*I feel that the young generation are doing a fine job. In a small way I did give some assistance by writing a free bass tutor book, which followed the tutor books on C, B and piano systems, but I feel I am not the exponent of the free bass that I would wish for. But so it is in all things, real progress needs young people, and the new ideas with which the Lord blesses us.*"

In 1955, Tollefsen and Swedish accordionist Nils Nielsen opened *Accordion Central*, a retail accordion business, at 3 Wood Lane, Shepherd's Bush, London. The business traded on Tollefsen's fame and Nielsen's reputation as an accordion tuner.

In 1961 Tollefsen returned to Norway, becoming an accordion teacher at a music school in Oslo. He scaled down his annual schedule of concert appearances, concentrating instead on teaching, arranging and composing. Tollefsen continued making records and his 1977 LP *Norske Folktoner Og Danser* (Norwegian Folksongs & Dances) won him an award from his country's record industry. In 1978, Toralf Tollefsen announced that he had retired from the concert platform, and by 1981, Tollefsen retired from teaching and all other performing, devoting most of his time to family life.

In November 1986 Tollefsen made a brief comeback to the concert stage as chief guest artiste at the Caister Autumn Accordion Festival, organised by Malcolm Gee. At this event, Tollefsen was treated with an incredible amount of reverence by the festival-goers, holding a large and very attentive audience in the palm of his hand during the Friday evening main concert as he performed a programme of nostalgic favourites, and afterwards he spent about two hours autographing records and chatting with admirers. Two years later, Tollefsen made a final stage appearance in Britain, headlining an accordion showcase concert in Huddersfield (organised by the late Joe Kulvietis) that also featured Mario Conway, Harry Hussey and the Barnsley Accordion Sinfonia.

Selected discography: *Spotlight Accordion* (1958); *Dancing Accordion* (1960); *Classical Favourites* (1961); *Accordion Evergreens* – an LP/cassette featuring the music of Pietro Frosini and Pietro Deiro (1986); *Reflections from a Summer Holiday* – an LP/cassette featuring a melodic suite of Tollefsen's own compositions (1988); *Verdensartisten* – a compilation featuring many of Tollefsen's classic recordings (1994)

Tune book: the music Tollefsen composed for the recording *Reflections from a Summer Holiday* was published by Kestrel Publications in the 1990s.

Tremolo As far as accordions are concerned, the word tremolo refers to two sets of reeds at the same octave, with one set tuned at normal pitch, and the other tuned sharp. Sometimes tremolo tuning is mistakenly referred to as musette tuning, and this is incorrect as proper musette tuning requires three sets of reeds – not two sets.

Trevani The man known to one and all simply as Trevani is one of the most shrewd and enterprising individuals to be found in the accordion world. His Croydon-based business retails a colossal amount of music books, sheet music, CDs, cassettes, videos, accessories and accordions – much of which cannot be obtained elsewhere in Great Britain. Trevani's catalogues are constantly updated, and his material from France is a godsend for musette enthusiasts. If you want to acquire French musette recordings on CD or cassette, plus the sheet music of that genre, then Trevani has enough to satisfy most tastes. He can be contacted on 020 8656 1450 or e-mail: music@trevani.co.uk

Trevani himself was a professional accordionist with a commercial act specialising in Russian song and dance music. The 1980 Soviet invasion of Afghanistan, however, led to a worldwide boycott of anything Russian, including the Moscow Olympics. Trevani was a victim of the international anti-Soviet feeling, and his act was suddenly not wanted anywhere anymore. As a result, Trevani opened a studio in Croydon teaching the accordion, and his method was so successful that eventually he had several *'Trevani Studios'* operating across London. In the early 1980s, Trevani wrote several magazine articles about learning music and the accordion, and an excerpt from one is reproduced in this book, with kind permission from its author. From this, Trevani also became an NAO area festival organiser and a promoter of concerts featuring guests plus his own pupils. In the 1990s, Trevani gradually scaled down his teaching studios whilst building up a retail accordion accessories business. His shrewd business acumen, with a sharp eye on the retail market, has made the Trevani retail outlet – often to be seen at Accordion festivals – as successful as his former teaching studios.

Tutor Books *The following tutor books are all available in this country, at the time of writing, from retailers such as The Music Room, Trevani, Allodi Accordions, Gina's Music World (UK), Hobgoblin, Bill Wilkie's New Music Store, Geoff Holter and Charlie Watkins – see* **Accordion Retailers in the United Kingdom**. *In addition, there is also the section* **Video tuition for accordion, concertina melodeon & harmonica**.

Piano accordion
The Complete Piano Accordion Tutor by Ivor Beynon This tutor book is written by one of the accordion world's greatest ever teachers and is suitable for

beginners and players up to intermediate standard. Contains musical theory and guidance for developing playing techniques.

Sedlon Accordion Method This ten volume American series has stood the test of time, having been on sale in this country for around half a century. Basic to advanced levels.

You Can Teach Yourself Accordion – Mel Blay Written by Neil Griffin, this book has 96 pages and gives simple and clear guidelines in the basics of playing, including how to use the bellows to best effect. There is also a CD version of this book, divided into 63 segments. The book and CD can be used separately or together.

Mel Blay's Deluxe Accordion Method An accordion tutor written by American accordionist Frank Zucco, which includes music theory and playing techniques.

Buttons & Keys – Scottish Piano Accordion Tutor, by DJ McKenzie Vol. 1 The student is taught the essentials of playing the accordion, from basic tunes to such favourites as *Mrs McLeod* and *The Rowan Tree*.

Buttons & Keys – Scottish Piano Accordion Tutor, by DJ McKenzie Vol. 2 A follow-on from Vol. 1, or can be used as a general tune book. Includes lots of tunes used at ceilidhs, such as *Margaret's Waltz* and *The Athol Highlanders*, arranged in accordion settings.

Chromatic accordion

The Anzaghi Method This long-established tutor book teaches how to play using five digits on the right hand, and contains a lot of material for developing playing technique.

The Art of Bayan Playing, by Friedrich Lips The world's leading expert on the topic of playing the Russian Bayan system gives an easy-to-understand presentation dealing with the concept of tone creation, keystrokes, bellows control, vibrato and articulation.

Melodeon tuition

Mally's Absolute Beginners, by Dave Mallinson The classic tutor book for the D/G melodeon takes the reader from absolute beginners stage through to playing simple tunes with bass accompaniment. Easy to understand and very informative for beginners.

Handbook for Melodeon Roger Watson gives an easy-to-follow guide through the basics of melodeon playing, using well-known folk songs and dance tunes for learning.

B/C two-row button accordion

The Box, by David C. Hanrahan A beginner's guide to the Irish traditional button accordion, including playing techniques, the basics of music and a graded selection of typical dance tunes. Fully illustrated with photographs and diagrams; 96 pages. A cassette is also available to accompany the lessons.

The BC Button Accordion, by Derek Hickey This is a CD Rom tutor (not a book) that is organised in two sections – beginners and advanced – and deals comprehensively with a wide range of playing techniques common in Irish music such as playing cuts, rolls, triplets and sliding. The tutor also includes 17 tunes to learn and play.

Concertina

Handbook for the English Concertina A clearly written method for learning the English concertina, with the aid of diagrams and an easy-to-follow text. Fingering charts are included, and there are photographs to accompany the text. The book contains a section of tunes with fingering for each note. Concertina care and maintenance is also included.

Handbook for the Anglo Concertina A complete tutor for the Anglo concertina, and no previous knowledge of music is presumed. An easy to follow text with diagrams takes the reader from first steps to playing well-known folk melodies.

The Anglo Concertina Demystified, by Bertram Levy A series of eleven lessons for playing the 30-button G/C Anglo concertina. The book comes with two cassettes.

The Irish Concertina, by Mick Bramich A systematic approach to learning the Anglo concertina through Irish traditional music. Lots of different types of tunes are included.

Tweed, Karen An excellent and dedicated piano accordion player from Northampton who specialises in Irish traditional music, and is very well known throughout the folk scene in this country. She plays a Guerrini, regularly tuned by Nils Nielsen, and prefers a single reed sound to musette or tremolo, which is unusual for players in the Irish style. Karen has played with the Kathryn Tickell Band and the all-female band, The Poozies; she also works with guitarist Ian Carr. Although rooted in Irish music, Karen has travelled Europe extensively and has become proficient in other forms of music, especially the traditional music of Scandinavia.

In 1994, Karen arranged 93 tunes, which appeared in the book *Irish Choice*. Two CDs were simultaneously issued – *Drops of Springwater* and *The Silver Spire*. The recordings feature Karen on accordion, backed by Seamus O'Sullivan (piano), Gordan Tyrall (guitar) and Peter Houlahan (bodhran). Dave Mallinson Publications published the book and both CDs.

Selected discography: *Drops of Springwater* (1994); *The Silver Spire* (1994)
Tune book: *Irish Choice* (1994)

Uniform Keyboard A New Zealander, John H. Reuther, who lived in the USA, invented the Uniform keyboard accordion system. The Uniform keyboard is a keyboard with small white and black keys arranged in a system, which standardises the playing of scales. The system was briefly popular in America in the 1940s, and in this country was used for some years by Scotland's Jimmy Blair. Other exponents of this system included Svend Tollefsen, brother of the legendary Toralf Tollefsen, and George Shearing – the blind jazz pianist and composer.

John Reuther

Irishman Ken Hopkins, famous collector of accordions, plays the Uniform accordion as part of his act. Although its exponents claimed that the Uniform system was logical and straightforward, its popularity was not sustained, and like other 'logical' ideas such as the everlasting match and Esperanto, the international language, the uniform keyboard accordion has virtually passed into history.

Unusual Accordion Systems *Pictured here are three of a number of accordion keyboards that somehow never caught on. Gary Blair, to whom the author is indebted, supplied two of the photographs.*

The picture on the left shows an instrument with two piano keyboards, from a collection of rare and historic accordions owned by Frenchman Francis Lepipec. Madame Franssen van San, the Dutch competitor in the 1967 Coupe Mondiale, caused a sensation by using a two-sided piano keyboard model. Francis Wright, UK adjudicator, noted that the dynamics of this kind of accordion were quite poor.

The large 9-row button accordion pictured in the centre carries the name Ditta Salas, circa 1932. This instrument was actually a giant sized BCC# diatonic (one of the earliest examples of what later became known as the British Chromatic system), with vast numbers of repeat treble notes, and no less than 280 bass buttons. Hohner later perfected this kind of accordion in an instrument designed for Jimmy Shand (see **Shand Morino**).

On the right is a Kravtsov accordion – an instrument from Eastern Europe. Gary Blair, owner of the model pictured, tells us *"The Kravtsov has all the characteristics of a traditional piano accordion. This system gives the piano keyboard player the advantages of the chromatic button accordionists, i.e. two octave stretch. It is easy to play chord passages legato, and the shape of the keys also allows you to play all types of glissando.".*

United States of America The accordion scene in the USA is truly vast, and even a brief survey is beyond the scope of this book. Anyone interested in knowing about the American accordion scene's rich history and great players such as Anthony Galla-Rini, Charles Magnante, John Molinari, Myron

Floren, Art Van Damme, etc, should obtain *The Golden Age of the Accordion*, written by Ronald Flynn, Edwin Davison and Edward Chavez. This excellent large size volume is available in Britain only by special order via accordion dealers.

Valerio, Peter (1925 – 1955) Peter Valerio, at only eleven years of age, won the very first All Britain solo title in 1935, and was considered to be a prodigy with a great future. He made records, and appeared on both radio and television before his twelfth birthday, and looked all set for a musical career by the time war broke out in 1939. During World War Two, he joined the RAF and was sent to Canada to train as a pilot. One of his great experiences at that time was that during a leave in Canada, Peter and a friend hitchhiked all the way to Hollywood to visit the great film studios. Once the war was over, he became a full-time professional accordionist, and was soon making radio broadcasts for the BBC. On one such broadcast, Peter played a debut radio performance of a Kramer/Wolmer composition called *Il Treno* (*The Train*), and he afterwards recalled feeling so nervous about playing this difficult piece that the bellows shakes were achieved without any effort whatsoever! In November 1955, whilst working in a band at Hastings on the south coast, Peter drowned in the sea while deep sea diving on a day off.

Verchuren, André The *'Bal Musette'* era of the 1930s in Paris produced many highly talented accordionists, but few have had either the longevity of career of André Verchuren or the flamboyant stage routine. He began to make his presence felt on the musette scene in Paris during the 1930s, but when World War Two came and the Germans occupied France in 1940, Verchuren was deemed to be subversive and was arrested, along with some of his friends, and incarcerated in Dachau concentration camp. Somehow he managed to stay alive and survive the war, and returned to France to pick up the pieces of his life. In the post-war years, Verchuren began playing again, and built up a highly successful playing and recording career. He has shrewd business acumen, and invested his savings in buying property in Paris and surrounding districts. He also invested in his own recording studio, made his own recordings, plus those of others, using the Poly Gram Company for national and international distribution.

As a performer, André Verchuren has a both a flamboyant personality and a high standard of musicianship on the 5-row chromatic button accordion.

He is also quite versatile, with a large repertoire that includes standard accordion classics, classical music and Latin American music in addition to the musette pieces he made his name playing several decades ago. For stage shows, Verchuren maintains and fronts a show band that includes his two sons, singers and dancers who together put on a choreographed spectacular – led, of course, by the main man with his Fratelli Crosio accordion. André Verchuren is one of the few accordionists whose career spans the period when the great 'names' were people such as Emile Vacher, Michel Peguri and Gus Viseur, right through to the present day musette scene when players of the calibre of Daniel Colin, Alain Musichini, Alexandra Paris, etc, are the stars. Verchuren has, of course, been a guest at Chartres Accordion Festival, where this evergreen octogenarian's music continues to weave its considerable charms on audiences young and not so young.

André Verchuren's son, André Junior but known professionally as Harry Williams, is also a talented accordionist, with many excellent recordings to his name.

Selected discography: *Les Plus Beaux Pasos du Monde* (1993); *Les Plus Celebres de Valses Vienne* (1995); *Double D'Or – 40 succes* (2001)

Video: *Les Grandes Bals de France* (1994)

Vernon, David Born in Dumfries but living in Edinburgh, David Vernon is a full-time professional accordionist known for his wide international repertoire and also his sense of humour. An extremely versatile accordionist, David Vernon performs at Scottish and Irish ceilidhs, French and Italian themed evenings, Jewish weddings, world music events, or anything else requiring his specialist skills and music. In October 2003, David was one of the chief guest artistes at Bridlington International Accordion Festival.

Contact - e-mail address: Dvernon100@aol.com

Discography: *The Flying Scotsman* – a selection of traditional Scottish favourites e.g. *The Flying Scotsman, Jacqueline Waltz, Para Handy*; *Playing With Fire* – a world music CD including tunes from Israel, Brazil, Italy, France, Poland.

Viazzini, Romano (Born 1966) London's Romano Viazzini has played the piano accordion for most of his life, and is highly proficient in a number of styles. His repertoire ranges from the Italian favourites of his parental heritage to classical music, with much else in-between. He is well known in the accordion clubs in London and the Home Counties, having appeared as a guest artiste a number of times.

As a teenager, Romano formed *L'Orchestra Rara* – a dance band, which later became *The High Society Dance Orchestra*. He played in both bands, and also did most of their arrangements. Romano has also composed music, including a concerto titled *Valceno: A concerto for Accordion and Orchestra,* and some of his other compositions have been used for television documentaries by the BBC and Channel 4.

In December 2001 Romano Viazzini organised the London Accordion Festival, a star-studded two-day event at Wembley Conference Centre (see **Festivals**). This ambitious event underlined Romano's great enthusiasm for the accordion, in all its forms.

Video Tuition for Accordion, Concertina, Melodeon and Harmonica *There have been videos offering tuition on musical instruments since the beginning of the 1980s, and it has taken the accordion movement quite a long time to catch up and make use of this medium. Unlike the guitar, for example, for which there is a bewildering number of video tapes available, there are only a few devoted to tuition on free reed instrument. See also the section called* **Tutor books**. *The videos that have been currently available are listed and described below: -*

Accordion Styles And Techniques is the title of an eighty minutes' length tuition video/DVD made by American accordionist Joey Miskulin in 1990. Aimed at players of at least intermediate standard rather than beginners, subjects covered include bellows shake, phrasing, arpeggios and chord inversions, rhythms, fills, leads, and different styles of playing. An interesting and educational presentation, though the musical content is set within an American context. This video was first made available in this country in 1997, and a lot of copies have since been sold. Published by Homespun Tapes Ltd, Box 694, Woodstock, NY 12498, USA.

Learn to Play Piano Accordion with Chris Parkinson. Aimed at absolute beginners, this video is a set of six steps in an easy to understand format, and designed to show the functions and relationship between the two keyboards. The viewer is carefully guided through simple tunes. No previous musical knowledge is required.

Learn Scottish Accordion. Sandy Brechin, who plays piano accordion, gives a step-by- step guide through the techniques and intricacies involved in playing Scottish country dance music. Aimed at players who already have an intermediate level playing standard.

Learn to Play the BC Button Accordion. One of Ireland's best players, P.J.Hernon, gives a step-by-step guide in a one and a half hour video. Ideal for the complete beginner. The techniques covered include playing triplets, rolls, cuts, vibrato, plus much more. Included are some stage performances.

Irish Button Accordion Techniques. Peter Browne demonstrates his various techniques on the BC and C#/D button accordions, including different kinds of triplets, cuts, rolls, syncopation, vibrato, scales and exercises, and more.

Learn to Play Irish Concertina. John Williams teaches the basics of the 20 and 30 key Anglo concertina, with reference to Irish traditional music. Includes how to hold the concertina, basic scales, using the bellows, playing some basic tunes note for note, cross fingering playing triplets, grace notes, etc.

How to Play the English Melodeon. This is a three volume series by John Kirkpatrick, teaching the basics of the one & two row melodeons, and set within the genre of English country-dance and Morris tunes. No previous musical knowledge is presumed, and the viewer is taken through lucid explanations of a large number of techniques for right and left hands, including lots of tunes. The teaching method is by ear and by sight.

Learn to play the Cajun Accordion Vol.1. A video tutor described as being for 'intermediate to advanced players' – with tuition by Dirk Powell.

How to Play the Cajun Accordion. Tuition by Marc Savoy & Tracey Schwartz.

Tex-Mex Accordion. All aspects of playing in the Tex-Mex style covered in great detail by Flaco Jiminez and Tim Alexander.

Mel Blay's Complete Chromatic Harmonica Method. Tuition by Phil Duncan. Includes melody and phrase production, hand and air vibrato, tongue blocking technique, use of the slide button, and playing in different keys.

Mel Blay's You Can Teach Yourself Harmonica. Phil Duncan provides instruction about playing the diatonic harmonica. No previous musical knowledge required.

Anyone Can Play Harmonica. Phil Duncan teaches how to play basic tunes on the ten hole diatonic harmonica; includes a tuition booklet.

Watkins, Charlie London-based Charlie Watkins has a key place in the story of the accordion in Great Britain for his innovative work in the field of accordion amplification: designing, manufacturing and retailing a range of internationally renowned WEM speakers. The clarity and purity of sound marks out WEM speakers from previous accordion amplification, and the fact that most professional accordionists in Great Britain use them is testimony to their quality. Charlie Watkins is also a pioneer in the development of midi equipment. The most commercially successful product both invented and marketed by Charlie Watkins, however, is the echo unit, a device that enhances the basic sound of accordions and other instruments. The Watkins '*Copicat*' echo unit has been sold in large numbers, and is widely used by accordionists and other instrumentalists around the world.

Charlie Watkins operated within the pop music scene for many years, and has worked as sound engineer for the Rolling Stones. The accordion scene is his first love, however, and he retails not only amplification but also accordions (some of which carry his own WATKINS brand name), and music books, CDs, videos and a wide variety of accessories. Charlie also occasionally publishes his own magazine called *Accordion Today*, carrying the sub-heading *Published in defiance of logic and sentiment*. As if all this were not enough activity, Charlie even makes occasional guest appearances at accordion clubs where his beloved Galanti Super Dominator can he heard on renditions of his renowned theme tune *Blaze Away,* and the well-known accordion classics.

Whiteley, Peter Manchester-born musician who plays and teaches piano, piano accordion, keyboard and electronic organ; he is also Musical Director of the *Stockport Accordion Club Band*, for whom he also does arrangements. A founder member of the *Clifford Wood Accordion Orchestra*, Peter Whiteley was taught by the late George Harris, and entered accordion festivals as a solo and duet competitor (with Adrienne Sharpe) on and off for many years. In 1989, he achieved second place (to winner Gordon Shand) in the Open Polka Section at the UK Championships, in an exceptionally strong section containing no less than 28 players. Apart from his musical expertise, Peter has advanced craft skills and is a qualified electrician, and he is undoubtedly the leading accordion repairs technician in the North West of England; he also maintains church organs. In recent years, Peter has acted as weekend MD at Blackpool and Pakefield festivals, where he has also given enlightening workshops on the topic of MIDI. Peter Whiteley has written the article on MIDI in this book.

Whitehead, Robert Northumbrian-born Robert Whitehead is a specialist at playing strict tempo Scottish dance music, and has played and recorded in this genre for more than thirty years. In 1968, he won an All-Scotland title in Perth, and is to date the only Englishman to achieve this feat. He has appeared in accordion clubs north and south of the border, both with his Danelaw Country Dance Band and as a solo artiste, and has taken his music abroad several times, most notably to the Chartres Accordion Festival in 1990 as the British representative.
Selected discography: *The Whitehead Brothers Vol.1* – made with brother Jon on drums & vocals (1979); *Strictly Scottish* (1997)

Wilkie, Bill Born in 1922, Bill Wilkie's contribution to the accordion world, especially in Scotland, has been pivotal due to his annual Accordion & Fiddle Festival (a.k.a. the All-Scotland Accordion Championships). This annual festival – large-scale one-day event held each October in Perth – has been a competitive springboard for the careers of many famous Scottish accordionists. Bill and his late wife, Ena, instigated the Perth festival in 1949, and until recently the event was also an NAO area festival.

Bill played the harmonica from five years of age, switching to the piano accordion when he was twelve. He had lessons initially from a Mr Moonie of Dundee, and then Dr Sarafin in Perth, and when he was sixteen he entered and won an accordion competition in Dundee, playing his Hohner Organola. During the 1930s Bill worked in dance bands, playing all kinds of music including ballroom dance music.

During World War Two, Bill served in the RAF, during which time he joined Squadron Leader Ralph Reader's *Gang Show*, performing alongside the likes of Norrie Paramor and Peter Sellers. The *Gang Show* entertained the forces in many places, including an extended tour of India and Ceylon (now Sri Lanka). Bill played in a small group called the *Jive Five*, featuring Peter Sellers on drums.

After the war ended, Bill – by now married to Ena – became a professional accordionist, but soon diversified into other lines of business, eventually founding Wilkie's New Music House in Perth. This business is today a large-scale operation, running in tandem with the ongoing annual All-Scotland Championships festival.

Wood, Clifford (1921-2002) Stockport-born Clifford Wood began accordion lessons with the late 'Pip' Walker in the 1930s and went on to become a player in dance bands and an accordion teacher. War service in RAF Bomber Command temporarily interrupted his progress as a musician, but by the 1950s he had become a very active teacher, player and instrument repairer. In 1956 he formed the *Clifford Wood Accordion Orchestra*, and subsequently led this band in annual regional NAO festivals and the All-Britain finals with much success until the CWAO disbanded in the early 1970s. Cliff carried on teaching and servicing instruments, but in 1987 formed a new CWAO, entered competitions again, and in 1988 became regional organiser for the NAO, setting up the first of a series of North West Area Festivals at Stockport Town Hall. Clifford Wood became the first President of Stockport Accordion Club in 1995, but left SAC a couple of years later and resumed teaching and repair work in a private capacity.

C.W.A.O. 1988. (Cliff Wood back row, centre)

World Accordion Championships There are different versions of the world solo accordion championship, the CIA (*Confédération Internationale des Accordéonistes*) Coupe **Mondiale** and the CMA (*Confédération Mondiale de l'Accordéon*) **Trophée Mondiale**. The British Association of Accordionists and National Accordion Organisation both joined the CIA upon its inception in 1949. Soon afterwards, however, the BAA and a number of representative bodies from other countries withdrew from the CIA on the issue of the alleged extent of the extent of the involvement of M.Hohner Ltd in the running of the

245

Coupe Mondiale. This led to the forming of the rival CMA. The schism was never resolved, and the different versions of the World Championship continue until the present day.

World War Two *The late Percy Holland, a well-known accordion teacher in the post-war decades, in 1949 wrote the following memoirs of his time as a prisoner of war.*

For three years eight months I was an unwilling guest of the Mikado of Japan. However, I had been an accordionist for many years previously and would like to tell you the story of how an accordion helped to bring new spirit into the notorious Changi, Singapore, POW Camp.

In the first instance, being one of the fortunate few who returned safely (and with only recurrent malaria as a reminder of the past), I would like to pay tribute to all my former comrades and acquaintances on their wonderful spirit throughout a precarious and sordid three & a half years, and to place on record their wonderful examples of British endurance and courage.

First, let me say that the accordion, although almost unknown as an accordion, always seemed to be adopted by the people in the Far East as a natural first choice. There are, in fact, oriental instruments very similar to the accordion in conception, consisting of a keyed treble with a hinged bellows behind, the left hand 'flapping' the bellows in and out. And throughout India and Burma I found the accordion extremely popular with the natives. In fact, due to vaguely similar bajaboxes (music boxes) being so prevalent, it was actually quite easy to get re-tuning, of a sort, done in Calcutta!

But the Japanese take a lot more understanding, as we who were under their ministrations were quick to find out. And it was left to the unpredictable quirks of their strange mentality as to whether we were allowed to run primitive concerts as some solace to our wearisome imprisonment. Sometimes they would allow us a 'ramsammy' (sing-song and show) and then, without any reason at all, these would be stopped, and all music of any sort, even singing on the march by the toil-worn working parties returning to camp, be declared prohibited.

To the best of my recollection (it is all beginning to become faded and distant, like a nightmare in which I could not have participated) I was in camp 'hospital' when the first concerts were allowed. I was discharged, after thirteen months' sickness, just before an old peacetime cinema was taken over for camp concerts, and it was in this ramshackle building, nicknamed the Palladium, that I made my debut – so I can always say that I've been on the bill at the Palladium!

Trust an accordion to find its way into an army crowd, even in a Jap POW camp! As a matter of fact, I believe colleagues Barry Dawson and Desmond Hart had accordions in the Arakan area of Burma, while with the 11th Army and 81st West African Division respectively. And so, thousands of miles from our dear homeland, and with a gap of three long years in my playing career, once again I found myself with an accordion to play. 'Wardrobes' were made from the most unlikely articles of our tattered clothing, and a motley collection of other musical instruments was assembled, ready to build up a show.

I was partnered by another Sergeant of Signals, J.V. Wray-Gibson, who was to do many concerts with me – he was an excellent player, and when time permitted, we used to rehearse under the magical moon and stars of the romantic East – an item we did not appreciate very much at the time!

However, we made up quite a fair act – and I shall never forget the ovation we received on our opening night. Captain McGarrity, whom I believe was in the Indian Army Medical Corps, was the organiser, and he was delighted with the whole effort.

On the second night, after the show, one of the Jap sentries came back stage, and in the usual crude manner, and very broken English, grunted: *"Next night I bring forty Nippon soldiers, hear accordion."* I didn't take too much notice at the time, but next night we heard the ominous tramp, tramp of Jap soldiers coming up the Changi Road, and obviously making for the Palladium, complete with full jungle gear, short rifles and bayonets, etc. Captain McGarrity remarked to me: *"I hope they're not coming in here."* But I knew that they were.

However, instead of the usual grim import of the advent of the Jap soldiers, this turned out to be quite a relief. They stamped down the hall, filed quietly enough into seats, and were the best-behaved Japs for the rest of that evening that I have ever seen. The sentry who had brought them looked me out before the show and grunted: *"You play tango La Cumparsita, I give you cigarette."*

So, after our usual act, Captain Bush, AIF, announced the encore as La Cumparsita, and added, *"This being more of an order than a request!"* After the show our bamboo 'dressing room' was invaded by the whole forty Nips, and I was not slow in thanking my lucky stars that I knew La Cumparsita, and taking advantage of the cigarettes they proffered. The cast at least had a decent smoke 'on' the accordion – real tailor-made cigarettes, vastly different from camp 'cheroots' made of dried tealeaves rolled in newspaper.

Shortly after this concert, the old accordion again stood me in good stead. I had been dismissed of Jap roll-call at six in the evening, and had strolled over to see my friend Cpl Frank Booth of the 2nd Battalion Gordon Highlanders.

When I reached their part of the camp, they had not been dismissed, so I 'froze' quietly, as still as a log, while the parade was on. Suddenly a Jap spotted me, and as they were always doing, started to shout and rave in Japanese. My blood turned to water, and I thought to myself: *"Here we go again – another session of Japanese 'treatment'."* Imagine my profound relief when I heard from among the chatter of words *"Englando one number Accordiano."* My shaking with suppressed fear turned to shaking with laughter, both with relief and with the dawning realisation that the long lines of statue-still POWs were Colonels, Brigadiers and other officers of high rank. Apparently the Jap thought more of recognising the accordion-player than of attending to his duty – I take it he was at the concert we had given – at any rate, even the 'brass hats' were highly amused at the standing in the camp that the accordion had brought me! It was to be a perpetual good luck charm from then on, and featured in many incidents, laughable now in retrospect.

One such incident occurred upon a sweltering Singapore afternoon when, during a break in our working party's task, up walked three Jap soldiers, one carrying an accordion he must have looted from somewhere. One of our lads, a real schemer for a smoke, immediately pointed me out, and in pidgin-English-cum-Japanese, called me everything from Kramer to Magnante in the accordion business. The Jap grunted at me (by the way, when they want any particular person they just grunt) and then: *"You play do,"* he growled. Fags for the boys was my first thought, so I said; *"You give cigarette, I play; no cigarette, no play, too tired."*

Sure enough, out came the cigarettes, and we skinned the Japs right out! I almost failed to get one for myself. All the boys crowded around, and I saw the cigarettes rapidly disappearing as the grimy eager hands made the most of this most unusual opportunity. *"Don't forget me"* I yelled, strapping on the dilapidated accordion. *"I'm only the bloke who's doing the playing."*

Perhaps you can imagine the scene – a clearing in the jungle, all the lads burnt black as the natives by the tropical sun, wearing only a pair of patched shorts, most bare-footed, the lucky ones sporting slippers or boots. They lay on their backs, grinning contentedly, smoking their 'tailor-made' cigarettes, while I burst into recurring bouts of perspiration in providing *España* and *La Cumparsita*, etc, for our would-be conquerors.

During one of the periods, in 1944, when the Japs stopped all concerts, I was visiting one of my friends in the 'hospital'. I saw all these long, tattered bamboo-made huts packed with men lying shoulder to shoulder, unable to move, and thought, as we all did, that it is your pal today, yourself tomorrow – and I realised that I could do something to cheer them a little. I approached my old friend and partner, Gibson, and he willingly consented to go the rounds with me. We played in each hut systematically for about three-quarters of an hour, doing two huts each evening after being out on the incessant working parties all day.

Then, with typical unpredictableness, concerts were suddenly permitted again, and with their recommencement came an order from the Japanese General Officer commanding the southern regions for a concert for his benefit, with insistence that he especially wanted to hear an accordion. We all thought that this would mean about ten cigarettes each but we actually received half a pint each of thin meal soup!

To digress – this reminds me of the Mikado's birthday in 1942. Each man received four small pineapple cubes and two spoonfuls of juice – you can imagine what sort of a birthday we wished him!

Another accordionist in the camp was Frank Quinton. I did not see him for long, as he went north on the building of the notorious Burma-Thailand Railway. I was lucky in so far as to escape being sent on this worst of working parties because of six months in 'hospital' with leg ulcers. Frank could doubt-less recount many amusing brushes with the men from the Land of the Rising Sun. Many other folk from the entertainment business did splendid work in the camps – Bill Williams, pianist and vocalist was a great favourite, and I was delighted to hear his Variety Bandbox broadcast. Others included a padre who sang brilliantly in Italian, and Signalman Rennison, who scored and played from memory one of the Schumann piano concertos. Both of these, alas, died on that terrible Burma-Thailand working party.

Another splendid morale raiser was violinist Dennis East, who I believe later joined the London Philharmonic Orchestra, whilst yet another was Leo Britt, who organised and appeared in many a camp concert.

Well, even the war ended (as must this story) and from a radio hidden in a boiler-room we heard of the capitulation. I was in Changi jail at the time, and we all broke out to welcome the airlift supplies of food and medical necessities dropped by parachute. I was due to start giving lessons to a Jap the next week, and what with him wanting to learn Japanese music, and knowing no English, and me knowing no Japanese, the end of the war arrived just in time!

An ENSA concert party was amongst the first arrivals by road, and Captain Bush introduced me with great ceremony. As this young lady was the first white woman I had seen for nearly four years, I could only stammer and shake with embarrassment, acutely conscious as I was of my beard, missing teeth, shrunken frame, and exiguous attire consisting of the usual tattered shorts. I asked her for her autograph!

(Article courtesy of Accordion Profile)

World War Two - another story *Joe Scott was a Canadian who volunteered to join the British army in 1940, but eventually found himself a prisoner of the Germans, together with his trusty accordion. His story is told below:-*

Well – in 1936 I purchased a Hohner *'Carmen 11'* 24 bass accordion in England. I played it (for my own amusement) regularly, until the outbreak of war in 1939. In April of 1940 I joined the British army and took along my accordion with me. On October 3rd 1940 I was drafted overseas, to the Middle East – still taking my accordion! Needless to say, it was played incessantly, especially aboard ship. In March 1941, I was drafted to Crete, off the coast of Greece, where I eventually got taken prisoner-of-war on the island's fall. The only means of musical entertainment during that time was my 'squeeze box', as it was called.

Immediately preceding the capitulation of Crete, the island was under intense bombardment from the air, and most of that time we spent in bunkers underground in the company of the Cretan inhabitants. My accordion was then kept mostly with us in the shelter, where I was asked to play tunes for the civilians – they made up song lyrics insulting the enemy! When we received orders to evacuate the island, we had to leave everything behind except our army equipment.

On going into the bunker to look at the accordion (with the intention of putting a knife through the bellows so that it could not be used by the enemy), I found a huge Cretan civilian sitting on the case. On taking it out of the case, I found all of the treble keys immovable – so I figured it to be broken and left it there.

After capture as prisoner-of-war, we were put into a cage only three miles away, about two weeks later. Food was unobtainable so the German Commandant gave orders for groups of P.o.Ws under guard to go on forage parties to get food. My Company Sergeant went out with a group of men and thought it would be a good idea to go back to the area where we were stationed before capture.

Imagine my intense surprise and joy to be given back my trusty old 'squeeze box' on their return! Apparently, on going to our old area, the local civilians, on seeing him and the others, gave him not only food, as that was the official reason for them going there, but also a lot of my comrades' old clothes, etc – also my accordion. I naturally expected that it would have been broken in some way, after the condition it was in the last time I saw it; but no, it played as well as ever.

A young Cretan, who used to sing with us at our billet and in our bunker, had taken it on our departure, and had fixed it up like new. The case was broken so, when I received it in the P.o.W cage, I had to carry it on my back by the straps from then on. All this was happening, you must understand, in a country where the temperature soared to over 100 degrees during the day, and dropped to maybe 45 degrees at night sometimes.

We were taken to the borders of Greece and Turkey by ship, that is, in the hold of a coal boat, where the coal dust was an inch thick, where we were kept for three weeks before transportation to Germany. In that time my little accordion was loaned to a variety of people, for which I received things in return. First, on the ship, one of the German guards took it for an hour and I then thought I had lost it. But no, he brought it back, and also he gave me three cigarettes. You can imagine what those cigarettes meant to us, there being about twenty men in my particular group.

Then, during the one-hour-a day exercise, when they let a group come on deck, the men asked me to play. I had to shout down into the hold for the instrument, and on getting it on deck, played for a few minutes. Just then, the Italian Captain on the bridge sent a message down asking would I play *Stormy Weather*. In return, the Captain sent down two black bread rolls and about a handful of fried potatoes (cold). Then, in Solinka, where we stayed for three weeks, some Serbian P.o.Ws who worked in the kitchens borrowed the accordion for one night. For this they managed to get an extra bowl of soup for me each day (with meat).

For four years, I was a P.o.W, most of the time in Germany, and all during that time I carried the accordion on my back from place to place, in all weather – winter and summer, and it played as well in 1944 as well as it did in 1936. It had many adventures, and eventually I sold it to a New Zealander in 1944 for 1,500 cigarettes. I guess the real reason for parting with it was that it was getting heavier and I was getting weaker!

To my mind it was a remarkable thing that such a complicated instrument as a piano accordion should stand up to so much misuse and still play as well as ever. I thought you might find this story interesting, and wish to say again that it was all perfectly true.

Joseph G. Scott, Ontario, Canada, Accordion Times (1955)

Wright, Francis (1918–1997) Francis Wright was one of the great names of the accordion movement in this country, and a contemporary of Graham Romani, Eddie Harris, Ivor Beynon, Albert Delroy – people whose lifelong contribution was pivotal in the instrument's growth in the middle and late 20th Century.

From being a teenager, Francis Wright was a career soldier who learned the accordion in the pre-World War Two years, but did not make music a career until the early 1950s. In 1943 and serving in Italy, his regiment pushed the Germans out of Castelfidardo, and set up an occupying base in the town. As a wireless operator, Francis was based in the Settimo Soprani factory building, and he spent all his off-duty time working on instruments and learning a great deal about the internal details of accordions, including the art of reed making. To crown it all, Francis had an instrument specially made for him by Daniele Cintiole, one of Settimo Soprani's master craftsmen.

From 1954 onwards, Francis Wright set about building up a music shop and also the highly successful Leicester School of Music, supported in this venture by Arthur Bell (of Bell Musical Instruments of Surbiton, Surrey, fame). This, in turn, led to the establishment of an accordion band in 1956, prestige concerts, and ultimately the staging of the CIA version of the World Championships, the Coupe Mondiale, in 1968.

In the 1960s, Francis Wright became Chairman of the NAO and Vice President of the CIA, and this led to the staging of the All-Britain Championships ('*Accordion Day*') in Leicester, at the De Montfort Hall. Amongst his closest friends, Charles Camilleri and Jimmy Shand are notable for their appearances at events organised by the maestro- turned- impresario.

In 1965, Francis took over the British College of Accordionists, relocating the BCA to Leicester from London, and guaranteeing its perpetuity by establishing permanent Governing Council. He already owned Charnwood Music Ltd, and then ran the two organisations side by side. Charnwood was, and is, a specialist publisher of sheet music for the accordion, presenting works by many leading names – including Francis Wright himself.

Also during the 1960s, Francis Wright wrote *A Comprehensive Instructor for the Piano Accordion* – a tutor book, published by Dallas Publications of London, and part of the *Dallas Master Methods* series. Charnwood later published several tutor books and teaching cassettes for the accordion, these being another of Mr Wright's long-term contributions to the accordion movement.

Another major contribution made by Francis Wright was the revival of the *Accordion Times* in 1982. In 1974, after a lean period for the accordion in general and the *Accordion Times* in particular, the magazine ceased publication. Eight years later, various friends persuaded Francis Wright that the accordion needed its own press, and that he should revive the *Accordion Times*. This he did, and the historic magazine was revived in January 1982, to great acclaim around the country. The re-emergence of the accordion's own press helped a revival of interest and activity during the early 1980s.

In 1997, Francis Wright was honoured at the UK Accordion Championships in Scarborough with the NAO Merit Award, in recognition of his lifetime services to the accordion. It was a fitting finale for one of the accordion movement's great pioneers of the 20th Century.

Wright, Rosemary Born in 1952, Rosemary Wright began learning the piano accordion at the age of three. Her father, Francis Wright, ensured that Rosemary read music and also developed a thorough grounding in music theory. By the age of fourteen, she had passed through all the British College of Accordionists grades and gained the LBCA Diploma. During these years Rosemary also competed successfully in many NAO area and national festival, and in 1966 won the All-Britain Junior Championship. In 1968, she was runner-up to Janusz Zukowski in the Virtuoso Championship.

Rosemary Wright has some notable achievements to her credit: for example, when she won the Junior Championship in 1967, she was the first competitor to win using a Free Bass accordion. She was also the first accordionist to play on a local radio station, performing on the newly instituted BBC Radio Leicester in November 1967. Another 'first' was gaining the newly introduced LBCA (Teachers' Diploma) in 1973.

As a solo concert performer, Rosemary has appeared in numerous venues in England, Scotland and Malta since making her stage debut at five years of age.

In 1963, she joined the BCA Orchestra, became its Leader in 1973, and held this position until 1982.

From 1975 until 2000, Rosemary was an Examiner for the BCA, officiating at examination centres all over the UK and also in Malta. Between 1983 and 1999 she was also the Principal of the BCA, during which time she tutored at various College courses and seminars. These years also saw Rosemary acting as an adjudicator at numerous NAO festivals around the country.

Rosemary has composed and arranged several works for accordion, notably the *Music Box Polka*, and for sixteen years also worked for the Charnwood Music Publishing Company.

During the period in which her father, Francis Wright, was the editor and publisher of the *Accordion Times*, Rosemary wrote a series of excellent articles aimed at helping others to become better players and performers. With Rosemary's kind co-operation, these articles have been reproduced in this book for the benefit of readers.

Rosemary began teaching the accordion in 1968 at the Leicester School of Music, of which she eventually became Principal. Over the years she has also studied the piano, guitar, violin, plus each of the woodwind instruments. At the present time, she offers tuition in no less than ten instruments, and is now concentrating exclusively on private teaching.

Xmas Presents Choosing presents for someone interested in the accordion should not be a problem. Buying a new accordion to give as a present may not be realistic, but there are lots of accessories, music books, CDs, cassettes and videos on the market that will fill any Christmas stocking (or birthday) problem. The first step is to contact Trevani, Charlie Watkins' W.E.M Music, Caravelle Records, Gina's Accordion Exchange & Music World (UK), The Music Room (Cleckheaton), or other dealer, and you are on your way…

Yetties, The Vocal/instrumental trio from Dorset – Bonny Sartin (lead vocals, percussion), Mac McCullough (vocals, guitar, banjo), Pete Shutler (vocals, accordion, English concertina, keyboard, bowed psaltery). Originally a quartet, The Yetties turned full-time professional in 1967 and have appeared at folk clubs and festivals throughout Britain and also abroad. Featuring Pete Shutler on a Guerrini piano accordion, the group have appeared at Caister Festival, and have a very large number of recordings and videos to their name. They have also had their own series on BBC Radio 2, and have made many appearances on television. Although best  known as a vocal/instrumental outfit with a large repertoire of mainly popular folk music material, The Yetties also operate as a ceilidh band, in which their lead singer, Bonny Sartin, changes role to become dance caller. Another feature of The Yetties' activities are their specialist Thomas Hardy shows, featuring selected readings of poetry and prose plus music associated with this great 19th Century novelist and poet (and country dance fiddle player and tune collector) from Dorset. The Yetties occasional newsletter provides details of their activities, gigs, CDs, cassettes, videos and song books, and can be obtained by sending a SAE to PO Box 3, Sherborne, Dorset DT9 3AL. The Yetties' e-mail address is info@theyetties.co.uk

Website: http://www.theyetties.co.uk

Selected discography: Since 1968, The Yetties have made around 50 LP/cassette/CD recordings, plus some videos. A selection from their prolific output of recordings includes: *Fifty Stones of Loveliness* (1969); *Keep A' Runnin'* (1970); *The World of Irish Dancing* (disguised as O'Dalaigh's Ceili Band, 1971); *Dorset is Beautiful* (1972); *All at Sea* (1973); *Up in Arms* (1974); *The World of the Yetties* (1975); *The Yetties of Yetminster* (1975); *Up Market* (1977); *A Proper Job* (1981); *Cider & Song* (1983); *The Musical Heritage of Thomas Hardy* (1988); *Come to The Yetties Barn Dance* (1992); *Wild Mountain Thyme* (1999); *Rolling Home to England* (2001); Christmas Album *Rejoice & Be Merry* (2002); *Messing About on the River* (2003).

Videos: *It's A Fine Thing To Sing; Journey Thro' the Purbecks; The Yetties at Yetminster Fair; All Over Dorset; Along the River Frome* (two tapes).

Young, Gerald (1931-95) Gerald Young's professional playing career got off to a flying start when he appeared on *Opportunity Knocks* on Radio Luxembourg, this leading to appearances on other popular radio shows on the BBC such as Vic Oliver's *Playhouse*, *Variety Bandbox* and Henry Hall's *Guest Night*. During the 1950s he appeared on television and made records, but in 1958 was forced to give up what had become a very successful show business career through ill-health. In the 1960s, Gerald Young made a comeback playing the electronic organ, and in the 1980s reverted to playing the accordion. He also taught music, and became a member of a Roman Catholic religious order at Quarr Abbey on the Isle of Wight.

Zhang, Guoping (Born 1960) A product of the Beijing Conservatory, Zhang Guoping (in China, the surname precedes the first name) plays the free-bass piano accordion (a top-of-the-range Parrot), and is a virtuoso of world-class. In the early 1990s, he made his European debut and performed with distinction at such places as the Klingienthal Competition in Germany and the International Accordion Seminar in Poland, followed by performances at the Chartres Accordion Festival in France, where he also made a strong impression. He proved himself to be a very sensitive interpreter of the works of Frosini, Deiro, and classical composers such as List, Chopin and Johan Strauss II.

Mr Zhang made his British debut in May 1994, with concerts at the Royal Academy in London, Harlow Accordion Club, Club Accord (Birmingham), Stockport AC, Corby AC, Gwent AC and Guildford AC.

Stockport Accordion Club's Rob Howard recalls: *"When we booked Zhang Guoping for a Club Night concert on May 17th, I thought it would be a good idea to notify the Chinese Consulate in Manchester on the off chance someone there might be interested. At the time, I worked next door to the Consulate – a large old house surrounded by high security fencing – and knew their telephone number. Not expecting a positive response, I was surprised to receive a telephone call at home at 5.30 on the day of the concert, informing me that there would be Consulate representation that evening. Sure enough, three limousines with sinister-looking darkened windows turned up at the club HQ, and a number of dark suited Chinese men and women paid to see their compatriot perform. They were very appreciative, and at least one of them bought a CD at the end. However, Mr Zhang himself was disinclined to socialise with the diplomats, preferring the company of another Chinese man (a university employee) whose son played the accordion during the evening. Still, at least the Consulate guys made an effort to support their man.*

In the concert itself, I was under the impression that Guoping spoke little or no English and consequently did all his talking for him. After the show was over, I was taken aback, though also amused, when I heard him conversing in perfect English with one of our members! Still, we had a great concert from a brilliant musician."

Zukowski, Janusz (Born 1954, Bury, Lancashire.) Taught piano accordion by the late George Harris, from Bolton. Later, Jan was self-taught but received general music guidance from a priest who was the music teacher at Thornleigh College, a Jesuit institution. He later reflected that being coached by a non-accordionist musician did much to develop a sense of musicality that he might otherwise have lacked. Jan was an outstanding competitor in NAO regional/national festivals in the middle and late 1960s, winning many titles including the All Britain Junior in 1963, the All-Britain Senior in 1966, and the Virtuoso Championship in 1967 and 1968. He competed in the 1969 Coupe Mondiale world championships in New York, but was unplaced against very strong competition. Many years later, reflecting on his Coupe Mondiale experience, Jan commented that the players from the USSR and other communist bloc countries, because of their state sponsorship, were in reality full-time musicians, and competing against them was virtually a match between professionals and amateurs. After the Coupe Mondiale, Jan's attention turned to developing a career, and he dropped out of the competitive accordion world. Jan Zukowski studied dentistry at Manchester University, after which he went into practice in Bury, his hometown. He retired due to ill health in the mid-1990s, then, after many years of playing inactivity, reappeared on the accordion scene in the late 1990s with highly acclaimed concert appearances at accordion clubs, the Stockport NAO North West Festival, and the Blackpool International Accordion Festival. A specialist in classical music, at which he excels, Janusz Zukowski plays a large Hohner Morino free bass instrument, with a 45 note treble keyboard. He is also a pianist and a church organist.

Zydeco Zydeco is a style of music, generally favoured by black musicians and audiences, which developed in the 1940s from Cajun, a genre indigenous to the people of French ancestry in the American state of Louisiana. Zydeco is strongly influenced by Rhythm & Blues and also by soul, jazz and the music of the Caribbean islands, and its rhythms are also considerably more syncopated than its longer established Cajun cousin. Zydeco song lyrics may be in French, occasionally in English, and sometimes even bilingual, with verses alternately in French and English.

Unlike Cajun music, where the one row accordion is standard choice lead instrument, Zydeco accordion players are inclined to use either piano accordions or three row diatonics. A typical Zydeco band sound is usually accordion driven, with rub-board percussion plus electric guitar, keyboard and bass guitar. The use of electronic instruments and the absence of fiddles are two of the most noticeable differences between Zydeco and Cajun. Zydeco is related to Rhythm & Blues, whilst its Cajun cousin is stylistically closer to the 'white' music of the Country & Western scene.

The most commercially successful Zydeco accordionist to date is the late Clifton Chenier, whose recordings are still available. Clifton Chenier, a piano accordion player is really the 'Jimmy Shand' of Zydeco – an innovative musician who personally evolved and spearheaded the Zydeco tradition in the 1940s, and went on to become the genre's dominant figure until his death in 1987. Clifton's son, CJ Chenier, has carried on from where his father left off, and has brought his lively music overseas to Britain and Europe several times in recent years. Queen Ida & the Bontemps Zydeco Band, its leader being a three-row player and another popular Zydeco artiste, have also performed in Britain several times over the last few years. The band, Buckwheat Zydeco, whose video and recordings have been widely distributed in the UK since the 1980s, have had commercial success in recent years.

Stockport Accordion Club Pakefield 2003

Left to right: Beryl Pritchard, Derek Pritchard, Johnny Coleclough, Brian Jenkins, Marilyn Chapman, Heather Smith, Chris Green, Marj Howard, Dick Thomas, Anne Kearney, Rob Howard, Adrienne Sharpe, Derek Hulme, Rocky Howard, Peter Whiteley, Margery Nixon, John Nixon.